TERRORIST ATTACKS AND NUCLEAR PROLIFERATION
Strategies for Overlapping Dangers

Edited by

DEMETRIOS JAMES CARALEY
LOREN MORALES KANDO

THE ACADEMY OF POLITICAL SCIENCE
NEW YORK

Published by
The Academy of Political Science
475 Riverside Drive, Suite 1274
New York, NY 10115

Cover design: Loren Morales Kando

Cover credits: U.S. Air Force and U.S. Army photos

Library of Congress Cataloging-in-Publication Data

Terrorist attacks and nuclear proliferation strategies for overlapping dangers / edited by Demetrios James Caraley, Loren Morales Kando.
    p. cm.
  "Examines strategies to combat terrorism and counter nuclear proliferation, and discusses related moral, ethical, and constitutional consequences"—Provided by the publisher.
  ISBN 978-1-884853-06-7 (pbk.)
  1. Terrorism—Prevention. 2. Nuclear nonproliferation. I. Caraley, Demetrios. II. Kando, Loren Morales, 1975-

HV6431.T526 2007
363.325'17–dc22

2007006415

Printed in the United States of America
p 5 4 3 2 1

Contents

Foreword

DEMETRIOS JAMES CARALEY

This book is a sequel to two volumes previously published by the Academy of Political Science: *September 11, Terrorist Attacks, and U.S. Foreign Policy* and *American Hegemony: Preventive War, Iraq, and Imposing Democracy.* The purpose of this latest book is to bring within one volume essays that examine the continued threat of terrorist attacks, the proliferation of nuclear capacity, and, worst of all, the possibility of a nuclear weapon coming into the hands of and being used by these terrorists. In this kind of scenario, terrorists could kill not just 3,000 but 30,000, or even 300,000 Americans in a matter of hours. There are also chapters that look at the ethical, moral, and constitutional repercussions that have come from fighting these threats.

The so-called war on terrorism started after 11 September 2001, when terrorists hijacked airliners and crashed them into the World Trade Center towers in New York City and the Pentagon in Washington DC. Within a short time of the attacks, security agencies identified the chief terrorists as working for Osama bin Laden, the head of al Qaeda, who was at his headquarters in Afghanistan, protected by the Taliban government. On 20 September, President George W. Bush sent a message to the Taliban leaders who were in control of Afghanistan that they must either give up bin Laden and all of the leaders of al Qaeda hiding within Afghanistan or face attack by the United States. The Taliban did not reply. The United States then launched an air attack on 7 October and infiltrated Special Forces who, with a coalition of anti-Taliban Afghan tribes called the Northern Alliance, quickly captured the capital of Kabul and brought the Taliban down. But this attack was not successful in actually capturing or killing bin Laden. With his top lieutenants and high Taliban operatives, bin Laden went into hiding in the mountains of Tora Bora on Afghanistan's eastern border with Pakistan. Five and one-half years later, bin Laden is still there, releasing anti-American videos from time to time that are aired over Arab and Western television networks. Furthermore, many more al Qaeda terrorists became well trained in Iraq to kill both Americans and Iraqis with suicide attacks and truck bombings, despite efforts to stop them.

DEMETRIOS JAMES CARALEY is President of the Academy of Political Science and Editor of the *Political Science Quarterly.*

In his January 2002 State of the Union message, President Bush introduced the concept of the "Axis of Evil," which he defined as Iraq, Iran, and North Korea, even though none of these nations had had any connection with September 11, bin Laden, or other al Qaeda leaders. Hidden from public view, the President and the Pentagon Special Forces were already being diverted from tracking down bin Laden and the displaced Taliban leaders in order to prepare for an invasion of Iraq. In his graduation address at West Point in June 2002, President Bush first made public his preventive war doctrine that said essentially that the United States has the right to launch preventive wars against any nation in order to end a military or terrorist threat that might materialize in the future and, in addition, assumed responsibility for converting non-democratic nations to democracies by force.

The attack and invasion of Iraq in March 2003 and the chaos that followed diverted the United States from the war on terrorism, cost many American, coalition, and innocent Iraqi lives, and inflamed Muslim public opinion. It also meant that the United States became fully occupied and militarily involved with the Iraq war and could not stop the development of nuclear capacity by other members of the "axis of evil"—Iran and North Korea. It also taught all other nations that considered themselves in danger from attack by the United States, Israel, or a geographic neighbor, like India or Pakistan, to develop even a few nuclear bombs to serve as a deterrent.

Developing strategies for finding terrorist cells based all over the globe, including within the United States, is a difficult and elusive task and one that renders U.S. military superiority less important than strengthened homeland security forces. Unlike in conflicts of the past, the United States and its allies cannot force a series of major battles against terrorists and, when successful, have the defeated terrorist leaders sign surrender documents that will totally end further attacks. There is little question that the American homeland will be attacked again. It is only a question of when and how. But it is not more military power that the United States needs; rather, strengthened intelligence and security forces, as well as better diplomacy toward other anti-terrorist nations, will count most in reducing and possibly stopping new terrorist attacks on Americans.

Americans live in the most open society in the world. Given the vulnerabilities of such an open society and a world in which information and material flow freely across national boundaries, Americans should expect that terrorist groups will use existing technology such as blockbuster truck bombs and car bombs, as well as individual suicide bombers, and that they will eventually develop, steal, or purchase biological, chemical, and nuclear weapons to use against the American homeland. Since the United States, like other governments, lacks effective means to shield all important potential targets, including its civilian population, it must harden the most lucrative targets and greatly strengthen intelligence efforts with the help of allies. Other nations must be aware that while the United States became the prime target for large-scale terrorist attacks in the last decade, other nations will come to be in the cross-hairs and will suffer attacks, as Spain, Britain, Indonesia, Egypt, and Turkey already have. All governments must be persuaded to see a common interest in destroying both indigenous terrorist groups and those that can move across national borders. If pooled intelligence forces can find and infiltrate terrorist groups, either at home or overseas, then police, intelligence forces, and military power can be used to destroy them and abort attacks already planned, whether with precision bombing and Special Forces or with more conventional military and police techniques.

A constitutionally healthier label for the fighting of international terrorism would be not "war" but a word that would describe the kind of police and intelligence actions that are used to combat domestic crimes. City mayors and police commissioners have never talked in terms of a continuous war on violent crime that allows them to abridge constitutional due process protections until the commission of crimes ends. The more realistic objective has been, while acting within the constitutional system, to prevent the level of those crimes from increasing and as much as possible to decrease it. When the campaign against terrorists is referred to as a "war" and a "war without end," presidents are tempted to assert unilateral "war powers" at home and abroad, as done temporarily by Abraham Lincoln in fighting the Civil War and Franklin Roosevelt, fighting World War II.

One possible silver lining is that the United States—including both the president and, independently, the Congress—might learn not to embark on war so rapidly when the threat to the United States is remote in time and place, the intelligence reports are murky and inconclusive, the cost of the war is substantial, and the international community fails to see the threat and thus refuses to provide support. Another good lesson to be learned is that the human and monetary costs of a war may turn out to be many times greater than originally projected, especially if, as is inevitable, the war takes costly turns that were not originally foreseen. As Winston Churchill wrote after the Boer War: "Let us learn our lessons. Never, never, never believe any war will be smooth and easy, or that anyone who embarks on the voyage can measure the tides and hurricanes he will encounter."[1]

ACKNOWLEDGEMENTS

I thank the authors of the essays in this collection. It is a pleasure for me, in my capacity as Editor of *Political Science Quarterly*, that over half the essays published in the volume were unsolicited submissions to *PSQ*. The rest were written at my request to appear in this book under a tight deadline. As is normal, the views expressed in the essays are those of the authors and not of the institutions with which they are affiliated. I am especially grateful to Robert Jervis and Walter LaFeber, two long-term members of *PSQ*'s editorial board, not only for helping me organize and for writing chapters for this book, but also for having over the years provided all

---

[1] Winston Churchill, *My Early Life* (New York: Scribner, 1996), 232.

kinds of valued assistance and advice. Others on our small staff at the Academy who warrant my warm thanks are Marylena Mantas, *PSQ*'s managing editor, and Amy Pivak, my research assistant. Loren Morales Kando, Vice President and Business Manager of the Academy, has with this project expanded the reach of her excellent talents by getting deeply involved in the organization, editing, and production of this volume, for which she is appropriately listed as co-editor. Ms. Kando also designed the book's cover.

Part I:
INTRODUCTION

Overview

WALTER LaFEBER

In late 2006, nearly four years after President George W. Bush ordered the invasion of Iraq, the Iraq Study Group, which had been commissioned by members of Congress to investigate the results of the invasion, issued its much anticipated *Report*. The distinguished panel, co-chaired by Texas Republican and former U.S. Secretary of State James A. Baker III, and a former Chair of the House of Representatives Foreign Affairs Committee, Lee H. Hamilton, began their report to the President and the American people ominously: "The situation in Iraq is grave and deteriorating. There is no path that can guarantee success. But the prospects can be improved."[1]

As debate about the document's assessment and seventy-nine recommendations erupted, the question for Americans quickly began to revolve around whether they wanted to pay the price for accepting the *Report*'s belief that a "short-term redeployment or surge of American combat forces to stabilize Baghdad, or to speed up the training and equipping mission" could require tens of thousands more U.S. troops. These troops would particularly be needed to train the Iraqi military, which had been singularly ineffective in providing stability. "The United States," the Baker-Hamilton analysis stressed, "should not make an open-ended commitment to keep large numbers of American troops deployed in Iraq." On the other hand, the panel "also rejected the immediate withdrawal of our troops, because we believe that so much is at stake."[2] Indeed, during the invasion itself, in 2003, it became clear that the United States was not planning to leave the strategically located and oil-rich country after overthrowing the dictatorial regime of Saddam Hussein. Authoritative reports concluded that Washington planners intended to keep a series of permanent bases patterned on the new base structure already implemented in Afghanistan, which

---

[1] James A. Baker III and Lee H. Hamilton, Co-Chairs, *The Iraq Study Group Report*, manuscript copy, 6.
[2] Ibid., 50, 51.

WALTER LaFEBER is the Andrew and James Tisch University Professor Emeritus at Cornell University, where he is also a Weiss Presidential Teaching Fellow. His recent books include *The Clash: U.S.-Japan Relations Throughout History* (1997), which received the Bancroft Prize and Hawley Prize, and *America, Russia, and the Cold War, 1945-2006*, 10th ed. (2007).

the United States and its allies had invaded in October, 2001.[3] The Iraqi and Afghan bases could be developed to deal with neighboring Iran, an American enemy since 1979, and to protect and guide the development of the fields of liquid gold.

At the end of 2006, as the *Report* was being intensely debated, the number of American military men and women who had died in Iraq since March 2003 reached 3,000. This number surpassed the total of those killed in the 11 September 2001 terrorist attacks on New York City and Washington DC and in the plane that crashed that day in Pennsylvania after al Qaeda terrorists tried to commandeer it but were stopped by courageous passengers. The number of Iraqis who had died between 2003 and 2006 was difficult to establish. From the start of the war, the U.S. government was most reluctant to specify how many Iraqis, either civilian or military, had been killed during the American occupation. Washington officials recalled how so-called body counts of the enemy had been published during the Vietnam conflict; such reports had seemed only to fuel both American anti-war movements at home and the Vietnamese communists' determination to drive out the United States. The best U.S. estimates were that the number of Iraqi civilian dead reached 47,000 to 52,000 in the three and a half years after the invasion (although public health officials at Johns Hopkins University put it at 650,000). The Iraqi health minister estimated the number to reach as high as 150,000.[4]

The death toll, at times the specific targeting, of civilians over the past century is unique in world history; the numbers of civilians dying in wars have ratcheted upward, especially since World War I. Michael Gross's essay in this volume is important because it provides a context for this historic upturn. He notes, moreover, how the killing of civilians has become more common with the growth of insurgency warfare; carried to its conclusion, it means "retaliating evil with evil," or "you kill our civilians and we will kill yours," which is how both sides in the terrorist struggle define the tactics necessary to gain victory. Iraq becomes a case study for Gross's thesis.

Among the Iraqi dead, the most notable was former ruler Saddam Hussein, overthrown by the U.S. invasion after nearly a quarter century in power. Tried and convicted by an Iraqi court for killing Iraqis who had threatened to oppose his rule, Saddam was hanged on 30 December 2006. As the Baker-Hamilton *Report* had implied several weeks earlier, however, Saddam's execution merits little more than a footnote in the unfolding story. The central narrative was now about a devastating civil war developing between Islamic sects. Within the country itself, terrorist bombings claimed dozens and sometimes hundreds of noncombatant lives each day. More ominously, the intensifying civil war threatened to spill over

---

[3] Thom Shanker and Eric Schmitt, "Pentagon Expects Long-Term Access to Four Key Bases in Iraq," *The New York Times*, 19 April 2004.

[4] Larry McShane, "U.S. Iraq War Toll Passes that of 9/11," *ABC News*, 27 December 2006, accessed at http://abcnews.go.com/US/print?id=2751554, December 2006; Congressional Research Service, "Iraqi Civilian Deaths Estimated," *CRS Report for Congress*, 22 November, 2006, 1–5.

into the broader Middle East to endanger such pivotal U.S. allies as Israel, Saudi Arabia, and Jordan, while also threatening the world's major source of oil.[5]

Placing this post-2003 turn in a broader framework reveals how stunningly U.S. power, both military and economic, had diminished since the attacks of September 11. The unchallenged global superpower after the Soviet Union's collapse in 1991, the United States dominated the political-diplomatic-cultural arenas over the next dozen years. One commentator lauded the superiority as marking a "unipolar era" in which U.S. dominance was unchallenged and apparently unchallengeable. Americans began to accept such praise as immutable and an indefinite fact of life. U.S. officials beefed up defense expenditures until the Pentagon's budgets surpassed those of the next fourteen countries combined.[6] The target of such U.S. spending was not any contemporary challenge, for no military-economic-cultural rival approached the American level. The expenditures were to help ensure that potential adversaries could not emerge to challenge U.S. superiority—or the resulting freedom of action that Americans had viewed for more than 220 years as the foreign policy side of their revered individualism at home. They had placed that freedom of action at the center of their foreign policy since Thomas Jefferson had instructed them in 1801 to avoid "entangling alliances." Jefferson especially warned Americans about the different-minded European powers, or, as the Bush administration updated Jefferson's views in 2001–2003, "old Europe." The update began to appear questionable in the world of 2004–2005, when U.S. officials pleaded with Europe to help them contain the growing insurgent movements in Iraq and Afghanistan.[7]

Five years after the attacks of September 11, therefore, U.S. power turned from being supposedly unchallengeable to being directly challenged. The number of American, Iraqi, and Afghanistan war dead spiraled upward, while intensifying civil war wracked both Afghanistan and Iraq. The half-century-old U.S.–European alliance so essential to winning the Cold War in the 1980s was badly divided. In 2006, Republicans, after winning the national elections in 2002 and 2004 largely because of their perceived ability to conduct effective security and foreign affairs policies, lost control of Congress to the Democrats. Americans, who

---

[5] A series of stories on some of these events, centered around the Saddam execution, can be found in *The New York Times*, 31 December 2006.

[6] For the "unipolar era" quote and the context of the defense budgets, see John Micklethwait and Adrian Wooldridge, *The Right Nation: Conservative Power in America* (New York: The Penguin Press, 2004), 210–212. Charles Krauthammer's "unipolar era" essay was printed in 1993 and can be found in Andrew J. Bacevich, ed., *The Imperial Tense: Prospects and Problems of American Empire* (Chicago, IL: Ivan R. Dee, 2003), 47–65.

[7] The best analysis of Secretary of Defense Donald Rumsfeld, his use of the "old Europe" phrase, and the context, both historical and contemporary, is Lloyd C. Gardner, "Mr. Rumsfeld's War?" in Lloyd C. Gardner and Marilyn Young, eds., *Iraq and the Lessons of Vietnam* (New York: New Press, 2007); James Mann, *Rise of the Vulcans* (New York: Viking, 2004), 21–36, 56–73, 209–214, is especially helpful in analyzing Bush administration officials—notably Paul Wolfowitz and Richard Cheney—and the Defense Department documents in 1992 and 2002 that warned about the need to deal with potential competitors before they became equal competitors.

had given President Bush a remarkably high 90 percent approval rating for his early responses to the attacks of September 11, gave him an equally remarkably low approval rating, in the 30 percent range, by late 2006.[8]

This volume explores and helps explain these turns in the history of what some observers have called the "American empire." Americans usually do not consciously think of themselves as an "empire" (at least not since the 1780s, when George Washington and his colleagues used the term to define their new nation[9]) and have been particularly reluctant to do so, because the word has been too easily associated with the Nazi, Soviet, and Japanese military empires, and the British, French, and Belgian colonial empires, of the nineteenth and twentieth centuries. This reluctance notably began to change in 2001–2002, when U.S. global power was dominant. Some influential authors, including several British authorities, urged Americans to confront their own supposedly beneficent imperial history and their responsibility to remove dangerous rulers (such as Iraq's Saddam Hussein), and to institute democratic-style stability in their place.[10]

This collection of essays particularly traces these turns in U.S. policy (and how Americans think about that policy) by approaching the causes and effects of post-September 11 U.S. foreign relations from two perspectives: the Bush administration's changing worldviews, which led to the invasion of Iraq in March 2003, and the unlooked-for results of that supposedly anti-terrorist campaign during and after 2003. The essays examine crucial issues arising out of the war itself, such as the charges of torture brought against U.S. military and civilian officials. They also analyze more indirect but quite related results of the wars in Afghanistan and Iraq, including the surge in U.S. presidential power and the ability (or inability) of Washington and its allies to stop the growing dangers of nuclear proliferation in North Korea and Iran, or to roll back the growing Islamic jihadism (holy war, understood by Muslims to be a sacred duty), which Westerners largely viewed as terrorism.

This terrorism had developed in the 1980s and after. It posed a new challenge to the United States, because it differed fundamentally from earlier terrorist campaigns. Previous terrorism had been tied to nations that directly supported and

---

[8] Notably useful in tracing the several turns in U.S.–European relations after September 11 is Matthew Evangelista and Vittorio Emanuele Parsi, eds., *Partners or Rivals? European-American Relations after Iraq* (Milan: V&P, 2005), especially the Parsi, Hopf, Dembinski, and Gheciu essays; and Congressional Research Service, "European Views and Policies Toward the Middle East," *CRS Report for Congress*, 9 March 2005, 1–27. For polling on Bush's performance, note the useful series of polls available at PollingReport.com, "CNN Poll, Conducted by Opinion Research Corporation, Dec. 15-17, 2006," accessed at http://www.pollingreport.com/iraq.htm, December 2006, which provide some perspective.

[9] Richard Van Alstyne, *The Rising American Empire* (London: Routledge and Paul, 1960), 1–20.

[10] Note especially Tony Judt's overview and discussion of new books on the subject, "Dreams of Empire," *New York Review of Books*, 4 November 2004, 38–39; Niall Ferguson, *Colossus: The Price of America's Empire* (New York: The Penguin Press, 2004); for a collection of essays, pro and con, on the idea of an American "empire," see Bacevich, ed., *The Imperial Tense*.

guided the terrorists. Al Qaeda, however, which evolved in the 1980s and 1990s, had no national base, moved across many borders to mobilize and carry out campaigns, and drew on multinational sources of financial and logistical support. It cared less about dominating a nation than ultimately establishing a group of Islamic countries under a caliphate, or Muslim regime. Analysts examining the new terrorists' primary motives have often disagreed. Quintan Wiktorowicz and Karl Kaltenthaler's well-constructed essay in this volume begins by exploring various explanations of Islamic terrorism and jihadism. The authors then advance an argument that, they emphasize, involves both religion and rational choice. Radical Islamic groups persuade potential recruits that participation in terrorism "produces salvation on judgment day and entrance to Paradise in the hereafter." Thus, an interesting paradox appears: "seemingly irrational behavior [terrorism] becomes understandable as a rational choice."[11]

In his essay, David P. Auerswald quotes Osama bin Laden's declaration that al Qaeda must obtain weapons of mass destruction (WMD) because "the defense of Muslims is a religious duty." Auerswald notably discusses how bin Laden's "rational choice" could turn out. Classic deterrence policies, which, during the 1945–1991 Cold War, helped prevent the Soviet Union's use of nuclear weapons, have little deterrent effect on terrorists, Auerswald argues. For one thing, the new terrorists are not sitting in states but are ever-moving, decentralized organizations. For another, persons seeking to become martyrs in suicide terrorist operations are unlikely to be deterred by a threat of force. Auerswald develops the argument that terrorists hoping to use WMD against the United States can be deterred only when they are denied such weapons, and he suggests how to move toward that goal.

Thinking through the global policy implication of such dangers posed a complex challenge to President Bush and his allies, who had only known the nation-based international system that had been shaped over the previous 350 years. To think outside that venerable system in order to deal with the complexities and dangers noted by Wiktorowicz, Kaltenthaler, and Auerswald was a challenge of historic proportions.

After the attacks of September 11, President Bush, as Robert Jervis explains in his essay, developed a set of policies to deal with this historic test. Labeled the Bush doctrine, it warned that while the United States intended to capture and bring to justice the new terrorist groups, the President also intended to target nations supporting the terrorists. When he demanded that the Taliban-controlled government of Afghanistan surrender the head of the al Qaeda network, Osama bin Laden, the Taliban refused. In October 2001, U.S. forces working closely with and depending heavily on anti-Taliban Afghan forces deposed the Taliban government. They also isolated Osama bin Laden and other al Qaeda leaders in the mountainous eastern area shared with neighboring Pakistan, now a U.S. ally. Bush

---

[11] For an influential analysis that complements and also, at points, dissents from this view, see Richard A. Pape, *Dying to Win: The Strategic Logic of Suicide Terrorism* (New York: Random House, 2005), 8–23, 79–101.

swore to capture or kill bin Laden, but the al Qaeda leader has never been found. By early 2002, U.S. Arabic specialists and the military's Special Forces were removed from Afghanistan to prepare for what turned out to be an invasion of Iraq in early 2003. Secretary of Defense Donald Rumsfeld was determined to use smaller forces for a lightning strike against the Taliban and then to pull out, thus avoiding a Vietnam war–type trap. He believed that other nations should assume the responsibilities of helping to repair and rebuild one of the poorest countries in the world. Thus, bin Laden was not pursued. But conditions by no means improved. By late 2006, the Taliban, reorganized and reinforced, regained important sections of Afghanistan as they moved out from their firmly controlled bases in neighboring Pakistan. This anti-U.S. campaign was helpfully funded by the largest crop of poppies (used for heroin sold mostly in the United States and Europe) that poppy-rich Afghanistan had ever produced.[12]

As Jervis indicates, by 2002, the Bush doctrine had moved well beyond targeting al Qaeda. The President turned to the idea of undercutting terrorism by creating a more peaceful Middle East, if not world, through the spread of democratic systems, "including by war" if necessary, as Jervis phrases it. Pursuing those who attacked New York City and Washington was one policy, but threatening stable authoritarian (and often pro-U.S.) governments in the Middle East with democratic reform was something else. Between this ill-thought-out policy of spreading democracy and trying to create his first major democratic success in Iraq, which instead quickly turned into a bloody, anti-U.S. insurgency and then civil war, Bush became, in Jervis's words, "more disliked than bin Laden" in crucial parts of the Middle East and elsewhere in the Islamic world.

Traditional American allies, especially in Europe, responded to help in Afghanistan. The North Atlantic Treaty Organization (the U.S.-led military alliance, which after 1949 had protected Europe and anchored Allied diplomacy during the Cold War) undertook its first mission beyond the European continent when its forces tried to stabilize Afghanistan after 2001. With the notable exception of the British, however, the Europeans refused to play a similar role in Iraq after the 2003 U.S.-led invasion.

The reason for this refusal was the European belief that Bush had determined to go into Iraq for his own purposes and without paying adequate attention to their concerns. As Jervis underlines, the Bush administration, drawing from several centuries of American history and especially the heady "unipolar" power belief of 1990 to 2003, determined that it had the right and the necessary force to invade Iraq if it believed Saddam Hussein had to be overthrown. And it so believed.

---

[12] Richard Clarke, *Against All Enemies: Inside America's War on Terror* (New York: Free Press, 2004), 245; note also the discussion in Thomas E. Ricks, *Fiasco: The American Military Adventure in Iraq* (New York: The Penguin Press, 2006), 71, 127; for the Taliban resurgence, see Carlotta Gall and Ismail Khan, "Taliban and Allies Tighten Grip in Northern Pakistan," *The New York Times*, 11 December 2006; Karen DeYoung, "Afghanistan Opium Crop Sets Record," *The Washington Post*, 2 December 2006, especially A1, A10.

When Bush entered the White House in January, 2001, anti-terrorism and Iraq were not top priorities. Top officials who anticipated future foreign policy threats ranked China at the top of their list at that time and, consequently, stressed anti–ballistic missile (ABM) defenses against future Chinese nuclear capability. On 11 September 2001, National Security Council adviser Condoleezza Rice was scheduled to give a speech in which she would identify ABMs as a top diplomatic priority. No analysis was to be made in the speech, which was never given, of the terrorist threat.[13] As was to be exemplified in Afghanistan, the Bush administration, particularly Secretary of Defense Rumsfeld, was also determined not to become involved in the costly, long-term efforts of nation building. They knew that American efforts at such nation building in the Caribbean (notably Haiti), Central America, and, during the 1990s, the Balkans had hardly been quick successes; most were not successes at all. The attacks of September 11 did not immediately turn the President and Rice away from problems with China and Russia. However, relations with both countries remarkably improved in 2002–2003 because the United States, Russia, and China shared the common goal of destroying Islamic terrorism, which had threatened each of them over the previous decade. The Beijing and Moscow governments went so far as to tolerate, even encourage, the U.S. invasion of Afghanistan, despite the long Chinese and especially Russian view that the country was part of their own backyards.

The United States also enjoyed considerable support from allies, particularly those in Europe and the Middle East, in cutting off funding for the new terrorists. As Anne L. Clunan argues in this collection of essays, the effort was difficult for Americans because it meant rethinking the modern U.S. assumption about the "public good of open financial systems." Responsible capitalism operates best in such open systems, but so do terrorist networks. The Republican administration had to institute increasing amounts of governmental oversight and interference to stop monetary support that moved too easily across national boundaries to support terrorists. This effort meant, moreover, cooperating closely with allies, which did not come easily to President Bush and many Americans, who, in their zeal to advance the nation's interests, sometimes sought less the give and take of cooperation than simple acquiescence from their partners. Isolationism has never meant American withdrawal from the world, but rather, Americans' desire to enjoy maximum freedom of action to expand and protect their global interests. Two-hundred-year-old habits are not easily dropped.[14]

---

[13] *The Washington Post*, 1 April 2004, A1, has a useful look back at the pre–September 11 Bush policies; Clarke, *Against All Enemies*, 24; Thomas H. Kean, Chair, and Lee H. Hamilton, Vice Chair, *The 9/11 Report: The National Commission on Terrorist Attacks Upon the United States* (New York: St. Martin's Paperbacks, 2004), 373–381 provides context for the Bush administration's views of terrorism between early summer and 11 September 2001.

[14] A discussion of many of these points in the context of a post-1980 American conservative movement and the post–September 11 attacks is also found in Micklethwait and Wooldridge, *The Right Nation*, 8, 295–298, 348.

Certainly, President Bush was determined to maintain maximum freedom of action as he pursued those who had supported the attacks of September 11. He could finally depend on cooperation from leading countries (such as Saudi Arabia, which had previously provided massive funding for its native son, Osama bin Laden) and international organizations to reduce the terrorists' financial support. Except for Great Britain, however, he did not receive similar support from any top-ranking military ally in his invasion of Iraq, or, more importantly, in his attempt afterward to stabilize the country.

That the President was, by mid-2002, targeting Iraq for invasion surprised many of these friends and allies. Iraqi dictator Saddam Hussein's links to Osama bin Laden and al Qaeda were vague, if not actually hostile. Indeed, secret U.S. intelligence analyses provided during the year before the invasion repeatedly disputed that Iraq had been linked to al Qaeda terrorism, but such conclusions seemed to have little or no effect on top Bush administration officials. Immediately after the U.S. invasion succeeded in the spring of 2003, President Bush claimed that Iraq had been "an ally of al Qaeda," but four months later, he admitted, "We've no evidence that Saddam Hussein was involved with September 11." Nor did any other authoritative investigation discover significant Saddam–al Qaeda connections. Such conclusions were not surprising, given that Saddam, heading a secular regime, feared an al Qaeda fused with religious fanaticism as a dangerous competitor.[15]

The debate over whether to invade Iraq raged within the United States as well as between U.S. officials and the United Nations and especially European leaders throughout 2002 into early 2003. Evidence has since emerged, however, that Bush had decided on the operation by mid-2002. The President constantly indicated that he would go to war in Iraq only as "a last resort," but as early as July 2002, the head of British intelligence conferred with top officials in Washington, then reported to his government that the Americans had decided on war. They were only waiting to ensure that "the intelligence and facts" would be "fixed around the policy." The phrase "intelligence and facts" referred to the need to confirm that Saddam Hussein had WMD, chemical and/or biological in nature, while he was supposedly trying to develop nuclear weapons. British military officials publicly expressed deep unease about such invasion plans and worried that the results could be disastrous. Richard Perle, a noted Pentagon adviser, dismissed such fears as irrelevant, then charged that invading Iraq was "a political judgment that these guys [the British military officials] aren't competent to make." Perle turned out to be wrong, the British military officials correct.[16]

---

[15] For the declassified report on pre-war U.S. intelligence, which the Bush administration did not follow, see Jonathan Weisman, "Iraq's Alleged Al-Qaeda Ties Were Disputed Before War," *The Washington Post*, 9 September 2006, A1; *The New York Times*, 7 June 2004, has the quotes and contexts; note also Ivo H. Daalder and James M. Lindsay, *America Unbound: The Bush Revolution in Foreign Policy* (Washington DC: Brookings Institution Press, 2004), 147.

[16] The quotes are found in many places, including Frank Rich, "The Secret Way to War," *The New York Review of Books*, 6 April 2006, 53, which provides the quotes and a succinct context;

Perle was part of a so-called neoconservative group that held influential governmental positions. They were led by Deputy Secretary of Defense Paul Wolfowitz, Undersecretary of Defense Douglas Feith, and Perle. Since the early 1990s (and, in Wolfowitz's case, the late 1970s), the neoconservatives had been deeply concerned about the Iraqi threat to the region, especially to Israel, the major U.S. ally. They urged flexing the unparalleled American force to remove Saddam and his threat of WMD. The neoconservatives hoped then to use Iraq as a base for replacing the monarchical-authoritarian regimes in the Middle East with democratic governments and thus, the Americans too easily concluded, pacifying and stabilizing the region—even though such policies could pose grave danger to nondemocratic regimes, as in Egypt and Saudi Arabia, that were longtime friends of the United States.[17]

As Daniel Byman's essay in this collection argues, U.S. officials and many Americans believe that fighting terrorism and fighting nuclear proliferation are simply two sides of the same coin; indeed, so much so that these Americans conclude they have the right to act "alone if international consensus cannot be achieved" in order to destroy this dual threat. In reality, Byman emphasizes, few links have existed between the two in U.S. policies. President Bush had to deal on a crisis basis with the Iranian and Pakistani programs for developing nuclear weapons, while both nations were "problematic" in dealing with terrorism, Byman notes. But the President has focused on the nuclear threat from Iran, not terrorism, while focusing on Pakistan's murky relationship with Islamic terrorists, not its growing nuclear weapons stores. And when President Bush dealt with the developing Iranian and North Korean nuclear programs, he did so not unilaterally (as he usually has acted in fighting terrorism in Afghanistan and Iraq), but through multilateral negotiations led, interestingly, by China and leading European nations. In other words, Byman argues, Americans must stop assuming that there are easily grasped, direct links between terrorism and nuclear weapons proliferation. Dealing with one does not automatically help solve the other critical problem.

This was precisely what President Bush and his advisers discovered as they prepared Americans for the invasion of Iraq. As noted, the President initially claimed that Saddam Hussein supported al Qaeda terrorism. In the months before U.S. troops became bogged down trying to pacify Baghdad, however, U.S. officials did not make major claims of a Saddam–al Qaeda connection. Instead, Washington charged that Saddam was developing a WMD program that would threaten not only the Middle East but, ultimately, the United States.[18]

Richard Norton-Taylor and Julian Borger, "Iraq Attack Plans Alarm Top Military," *The Guardian* (London), 30 July, 2002, 1, 4.

[17] The best overall accounts of the neoconservatives, especially Wolfowitz, and their rise and worldview are Mann, *Rise of the Vulcans*, 21–36; Daalder and Lindsay, *America Unbound*, 15; and, notably, Micklethwait and Wooldridge, *The Right Nation*, 172–224.

[18] Ricks, *Fiasco*, 49–61.

A most unfortunate example of that pivotal argument occurred with the so-called Curveball episode.

Curveball was the code name of an Iraqi exile who told German intelligence that he had personally seen Saddam's mobile laboratories designed to develop mass destruction biological weapons. The mobility allowed them to be moved and kept out of UN inspectors' sight. U.S. officials never met or talked with Curveball because the Germans who held him would not allow the Americans to get close. A top German intelligence official did warn the Americans that Curveball was "crazy" and not to be trusted. The Central Intelligence Agency's (CIA's) head of operations in Europe refused to believe Curveball. But CIA Director George Tenet and top Bush administration officials did believe him. They seemed to do so in part because of their unproven assumption that Saddam was indeed continuing to develop WMD, because more than a decade earlier, he had actually used chemical weapons (although not of mass destruction) against his own people when he feared they were planning to overthrow him, and because Curveball's claims neatly fit in with the Americans' developing argument about the need to invade Iraq to remove Saddam and his WMD.[19]

In February 2003, approximately one month before the invasion of Iraq, Secretary of State Colin Powell gave a three-hour speech at the UN Security Council that incorporated Curveball's supposed evidence. Powell argued that Saddam was defying UN resolutions and world opinion by developing WMD. His charge ran directly counter to reports of UN weapons inspectors in Iraq indicating that they had found no evidence of WMD. But Powell was a distinguished and trusted official. His speech had an enormous effect in building up pro-war sentiment in the United States and elsewhere, particularly as leading media believed in the Secretary of State's integrity and consequently accepted his Curveball-shaped argument. In 2004, nearly a year after the invasion, the CIA admitted that Curveball's information had been totally false. Saddam apparently feared that rebuilding his WMD programs after they had been discovered and destroyed by the UN in 1991 would trigger another U.S.-led invasion. He was also afraid, however, that if he revealed the truth (that he had no WMD), it would embolden his enemies, including the United States and neighboring Iran. UN inspection teams continued in early 2003 to find no WMD programs in Iraq. When they asked for help from Vice President Richard Cheney and Defense Secretary Rumsfeld, who had charged that Saddam definitely had such weapons, the U.S. officials gave no help. It turned out that they had no hard evidence that such weapons even existed, let alone where the arms might be specifically located in Iraq.[20]

---

[19] James Risen, *State of War: The Secret History of the CIA and the Bush Administration* (New York: Simon & Schuster, 2006), 109–115; Ricks, *Fiasco*, 91.

[20] Risen, *State of War*, 115–116; Karen DeYoung, *Soldier: The Life of Colin Powell* (New York: Alfred A. Knopf, 2006), 440–452, 491–492.

By invading Iraq in order to destroy Saddam's WMD, President Bush, with significant support from Democrats in Congress, leading media, and American public opinion, went to war on behalf of an illusion. Within days of the invasion, U.S. troops and those from some three dozen other mostly small states now faced not the job of dismantling Saddam's WMD, but the infinitely more difficult task of stabilizing and rebuilding Iraq. Secretary of Defense Rumsfeld outmaneuvered the State Department to maintain control of Iraqi affairs even though he had no apparent plans to rebuild the invaded nation and little personal interest in doing so. Such a job, he believed, should be left to the new Iraqi officials who, in reality, had few immediate resources, large parts of the nation to rebuild, and a growing anti-U.S. insurgency on their hands. The insurgency was in part fueled by small al Qaeda groups who tried to take advantage of the growing chaos, but these did not represent more than between 5 to 20 percent of the early opposition. U.S. officials had, unfortunately, quickly disbanded Saddam's Baathist (Sunni) army, and tens of thousands of these soldiers, complete with their weapons and unable to find jobs, joined the insurgency. Iraqi oil revenues, which Wolfowitz and others confidently believed would pay for the rebuilding, never fully materialized. Wracked by inefficiencies and sabotage, the revenues that were to be drawn from 3 to 3.5 million barrels of oil produced each day instead had to be drawn from half that amount. Once one of the world's leading oil exporters, by late 2003, Iraq had to import fuel from neighboring states.[21]

As the killing and destruction spread, the head of the twenty-two-member Arab League declared in 2004 that "the gates of hell are open in Iraq." The Arab League adamantly opposed terrorism, and its top official did not believe those "gates" could close until Iraqis regained their sovereignty. There had to be an "end" to "the American occupation."[22] At this point, the United States showed no intention of leaving, however. The American hold grew even more tenuous as the majority Shiia sect (60 percent of Iraq's population) supplanted Saddam's Sunnis (20–25 percent) as the dominant force in the government. Saddam had forced many Shiia leaders into exile. They had gone for refuge to Iran, an Islamic Shiia state. When they returned after the U.S. invasion, many brought Iranian influence and interests with them. Despite these multiplying difficulties, Rumsfeld refused to inject larger numbers of troops to contain the spreading violence and outside influence.[23]

---

[21] Michael R. Gordon and Bernard E. Trainor, *Cobra II: The Inside Story of the Invasion and Occupation of Iraq* (New York: Pantheon Books, 2006), 475–484; Thomas Powers, "Bringing Them On," *The New York Times Book Review*, 25 December 2005, 13; for the views of the top U.S. official in Iraq on the questions of dissolving the Baathist military and evaluating the oil problem, see Paul Bremer III, *My Year in Iraq: The Struggle to Build a Future of Hope* (New York: Simon & Schuster, 2006), 53–58, 108–112.

[22] "'Gates of Hell' are open for Iraq, Warns Arab League Chief," *Agence France Presse*, 14 September 2004; I am indebted to Cory Fraser of Pennsylvania State University for this press report.

[23] Peter J. Boyer, "The Political Downfall: How Donald Rumsfeld Reformed the Army and Lost Iraq," *The New Yorker*, 20 November 2006, 56–65; Congressional Research Service, "Iran's Influence in Iraq," *CRS Report for Congress*, 29 September 2006, 5–6.

The growing convergence between the Shiia in Iraq and Iran presented President Bush with a policy dilemma. In his 2002 State of the Union address, he had labeled Iraq, Iran, and North Korea as an "axis of evil." The United States and Iran had been enemies since the Iranians overthrew the pro-American Shah's regime in 1979. During the 1980s, President Ronald Reagan even helped Saddam Hussein fight an eight-year war against Iran. But now, following September 11, President Bush, while publicly defining Iran as "evil," had overthrown two of Iran's most dangerous (and neighboring) enemies by defeating the Taliban in Afghanistan, then destroying Saddam's Sunni regime in Iraq. The influence of "evil" Iran thus grew ominously, not only inside Iraq, but throughout the entire Middle East as a partial result, ironically, of Bush's invasion of Afghanistan and Iraq.[24]

That danger became a major global issue in 2004–2006 as the Iranians rushed to develop nuclear power. Indeed, one of the most notable consequences, as well as perhaps the most dangerous consequence of the U.S. invasion of an Iraq that had no WMD with which to defend itself was the apparent determination on the part of two leading enemies of the United States—Iran and North Korea—to push nuclear development so that they would not similarly be without WMD defense. In this sense, as Andrew Flibbert and James Walsh argue in this collection of essays, the invasion of Iraq might well have created a world more dangerous after 2003 than before. "The war launched by the United States," Flibbert believes, "could generate the greatest proliferation pressure of all."

The danger will not ebb. Walsh presents a superb overview of internal Iranian politics, in which the people are often seen by American media as having fundamental differences with their religious rulers; he believes that "the nuclear program may enjoy more political support today [2006] than it did six years ago," and he notably warns against any U.S. (or Israeli) strike on Iran's nuclear facilities. After demonstrating how this crisis evolved over the 1980s–1990s, Flibbert notes that President Bush hoped to counter the nuclear danger in part by spreading democracy throughout the Middle East. Flibbert deflates that hope, then argues that only a Middle East "regional order" can halt the headlong quest for nuclear weapons. The United States, he concludes, can play only a peripheral role in the establishment of such an "order."

Victor D. Cha and David C. Kang's essay dissects President Bush's approach to dealing with the ongoing North Korean nuclear weapons program. The two authors disagree on the questions of how serious the danger actually is and the exact role of Washington in the crisis. But they agree on the proper chronology of the North Korean program, and they focus on the central question: whether the Bush administration's choice of working multilaterally with others to stop

---

[24] Bob Woodward, *Plan of Attack* (New York: Simon & Schuster, 2004), 86–96; Bruce W. Jentleson, *With Friends Like These* (New York: W.W. Norton, 1994) provides a most helpful account of U.S.–Iraq relations in the 1980s.

the North Korean program can work, given the divisions among the partners. The same question has to be asked of the U.S. reliance on a multilateral response to the Iranian nuclear program—assuming, of course, that another effective alternative actually exists.

Another crisis, constitutional in nature, meanwhile appeared within the American system. To carry out its war against terrorism, the Bush administration developed what its advocates termed a *unitary presidency*: they viewed presidential powers not simply as equal to the powers of Congress and the Supreme Court, but—especially in matters of war—as superior to those of the other two branches. Michael C. Dorf believes presidential power has reached the highest levels since the "imperial Presidency" of the 1960s and 1970s, which climaxed with the U.S. involvement in Vietnam and the criminal wrongdoing that forced President Richard Nixon to resign. Dorf's essay in this collection examines three U.S. Supreme Court rulings that (since Congress failed to do so) threatened to control, indeed roll back, the powers of the unitary presidency. The Court did so particularly by questioning the constitutionality of President Bush's handling of captured "enemy combatants." In 2006, a Republican-controlled Congress gave the President new powers that it believed he could use to circumvent the Court's rulings. As Dorf infers, however, pivotal questions in Washington are never settled, especially on fundamental issues in which Americans' individual liberties have to be weighed against the collective security— as defined and carried out by the President—of the nation.[25]

One of President Bush's most controversial policies has arisen out of the revelation that U.S. military and intelligence agents tortured "unlawful enemy combatants"—a term carefully chosen by the Bush administration, as Dorf notes, to circumvent U.S. and international laws that make the torture of captured military opponents a crime. Jerome Slater's essay in this volume carefully examines the strong U.S. consensus that in "nearly every civilized society," torture is considered to be "an unmitigated evil." Slater provides textbook definitions of torture, notes three major positions that can be taken on the issue, then argues on behalf of one of those positions, which he believes is required in a post–September 11 world.

The Bush administration's anti-terrorism campaign has thus produced surprising, wide-ranging, and from the 2001 perspective, quite unpredictable results. Shortly after the tragedies of September 11, Vice President Cheney stated his belief that "for the first time in our history, we will probably suffer more casualties here at home in America [as a result of terrorism] than will our troops

---

[25] For the unitary presidential powers concept and its relationship to Bush's creation of new authority, especially to deal with prisoner issues, see Congressional Research Service, "Undisclosed U.S. Detention Sites Overseas: Background and Legal Issues," *CRS Report for Congress*, 12 September 2006, especially 1–3; Congressional Research Service "Presidential Signing Statements: Constitutional and Institutional Implications," *CRS Report for Congress*, 20 September 2006, 1–2, 15–18; David Cole, "What Bush Wants to Hear," *New York Review of Books*, 17 November 2005, 8–12; see Elizabeth Drew, "Bush's Power Grab," *New York Review of Books*, 22 June 2006, 15, for a useful overview of the unitary presidential question as it developed after September 11.

overseas."[26] In the five years after the tragedies of September 11, bloody and highly costly terrorist attacks struck London, Madrid, and parts of Southeast Asia, among other places, though not the United States. The invasions of Afghanistan and Iraq, along with unrelated intelligence operations, killed many al Qaeda members, but did not, after a half decade of effort, capture the top leadership. Instead, quite unpredictably, at the end of that half decade, Afghanistan was again under siege from Taliban–al Qaeda forces, and the chaos in Iraq became a recruitment and training ground for terrorists, who then fanned out to other parts of the world. A September 2006 declassified U.S. national intelligence estimate admitted that while "United States-led counterterrorism efforts have seriously damaged the leadership of al Qaeda and disrupted its operations," the grave threat continues: "We ... assess that the global jihadist movement, which includes al-Qaeda, affiliated and independent terrorist groups and emerging networks and cells, is spreading and adapting to counterterrorism efforts. ... If this trend continues, threats to U.S. interests at home and abroad will become more diverse, leading to increasing attacks worldwide."[27] Such words were not expected on 1 May 2003, when President Bush, aboard a U.S. aircraft carrier outside the port of San Diego, announced the successful invasion of Iraq while standing under a huge banner that announced "Mission Accomplished."[28]

Some observers have tried to measure the difficulties encountered by the American anti-terrorism campaign, especially in Iraq, by comparing it to the Vietnam tragedy of the 1960s and early 1970s. There are valid comparisons, among them the highly doubtful, if not untruthful, presidential claims aimed at convincing Americans to support the efforts. In both instances, moreover, there were fundamental arguments over whether U.S. military troop strength, no matter how high it is escalated, could deal with the complex, revolutionary forces let loose in both Vietnam and Iraq. But the differences are more instructive.

For one, since September 11, the United States has been involved in a new type of campaign to destroy stateless enemies who move across boundaries, not a war to contain a state, such as North Vietnam, along a commonly recognized boundary. The invasion of Iraq and its consequences will finally be judged within the context of that anti-terrorist campaign and on whether the high cost paid by the United States, while attempting to pacify Iraq (and contain the "axis of evil" Iranian government) in the framework of a post–September 11 world, effectively reduced—or enlarged—the new terrorist dangers. For another, withdrawal

---

[26] See *The New York Times*, 4 November 2001 and 11 November 2001, for a story that, among other points, notes al Qaeda's attempts to build chemical weapons. Such WMD could be more easily and immediately used against the United States than could nuclear weapons.

[27] "Full Text: US Intelligence Findings," transcript of U.S. National Intelligence Estimate, 27 September 2006, posted 28 September 2006, accessed at http://english.aljazeera.net/english/DialogBox/PrintPreview.aspx?F, December 2006.

[28] *The Washington Post*, 21 March 2006, A14 has a useful retrospective of quotes from Bush, Cheney, Rumsfeld, and others about the apparent successes of the anti-terrorist campaign.

from Vietnam meant little or nothing in terms of the region's (and the world's) balance of power. U.S. officials had, in part, justified that war by arguing that they were containing China. By the late 1970s, however, China and Communist Vietnam were actually at war, not cooperating to dominate Asia. In the Middle East, however, a U.S. withdrawal, or even drawdown of troops, could mean that Shiia Iran, beset by political and economic troubles though it is, could merge with a cooperative Shiia-governed Iraq to become a regional hegemon. In a third difference, leaving Vietnam did not mean leaving access to important economic resources. President Bush himself has noted, however, that retreating from Iraq could result in giving up all-important leverage over one of the world's greatest oil reserves. As noted at the beginning of this essay, the Baker-Hamilton Commission began its *Report* by emphasizing, "We believe that so much is at stake [in Iraq]."[29]

As this volume's essays demonstrate, the ongoing debate over the post–September 11 course of U.S. foreign policy involves historic questions: whether Americans can adjust their policies to deal with new types of terrorism, whether they can at the same time control and make presidential power openly responsible, and whether they can revive the badly wounded system of alliances that helped win the Cold War and is essential for dealing with transnational terrorism. It also involves the question of whether Americans can accomplish these objectives while creating a more equitable, democratic system at home. As Alexis de Tocqueville prophesied in his classic study of the United States 175 years ago, it has always been difficult for Americans to maintain their freedoms at home while fighting wars abroad.[30] And the war on terror is likely to be of long duration. The essays in this volume offer needed background and perspectives on de Tocqueville's unfortunately timeless warning.

[29] Peter Baker, "Bush Cites Oil as Reason to Stay in Iraq," *The Washington Post*, 5 November 2006, A1, accessed at http://www.truthout.org/docs_2006/110506Z.shtml, December 2006, as well as the *Post*.

[30] At several points, de Tocqueville warns that the U.S. domestic democratic system could be incompatible with a foreign policy that has to concentrate on areas well beyond the nation's borders; note especially Alexis de Tocqueville, *Democracy in America*, vol. I (New York: Alfred A. Knopf, 1948), 234–236.

Why the Doctrine of American Hegemony Cannot Be Sustained

ROBERT JERVIS

With the reelection of George W. Bush, the apparent progress of democracy in Iraq and other countries in the Middle East, and the agreement of allies that Iran and North Korea should not be permitted to gain nuclear weapons, the prospects for what can be called the Bush Doctrine seem bright. I believe this impression is misleading, however, and politics within the United States and abroad is more likely to conspire against the course that Bush has set.

The Bush Doctrine, set out in numerous speeches by the President and other high-level officials and summarized in the September 2002 "National Security Strategy of the United States," consists of four elements.[1] First and perhaps most importantly, democracies are inherently peaceful and have common interests in building a benign international environment that is congenial to American interests and ideals. This means that the current era is one of great opportunity because there is almost universal agreement on the virtues of democracy. Second, this is also a time of great threat from terrorists, especially when linked to tyrannical regimes and weapons of mass destruction (WMD). A third major element of the Bush Doctrine is that deterrence and even defense are not fully adequate to deal with these dangers and so the United States must be prepared to take preventive actions, including war, if need be. In part because it is difficult to get consensus on such actions, and in part because the United States is so much stronger than its allies, the United States must be prepared to act unilaterally. Thus the fourth element of the Doctrine is that although the widest possible support should be sought, others cannot have a veto on American action.

---

[1] For a more detailed discussion, see Robert Jervis, "Understanding the Bush Doctrine," *Political Science Quarterly* 118 (Fall 2003): 365–388.

ROBERT JERVIS is Adlai E. Stevenson Professor of International Politics at Columbia University and former president of the American Political Science Association. He is author, most recently, of *System Effects: Complexity in Political and Social Life* and *American Foreign Policy in a New Era,* from which this essay is adapted.

Taken together, these elements imply an extraordinarily ambitious foreign policy agenda, involving not only the transformation of international politics, but also the re-making of many states and societies along democratic lines. As Bush has so often and so eloquently said, most clearly in his second inaugural address, evil regimes can no longer be tolerated. "The survival of liberty in our land increasingly depends on the success of liberty in other lands. The best hope for peace in our world is the expansion of freedom in the world." Some may wonder at such far-reaching goals and sense of the virtue of the American cause, but John Adams was correct in explaining to Thomas Jefferson that "Power always sincerely, conscientiously, de tres bon Foi, believes itself Right. Power always thinks it has a great Soul, and vast Views, beyond the Comprehension of the Weak; and that it is doing God's Service, when it is violating all his Laws."[2] The unprecedented extent of American power has allowed the United States to embark on its course, but does not mean that it can endure. In fact, I think it will collapse because of the Bush Doctrine's internal contradictions and tensions, the nature of America's domestic political system, and the impossibly heavy burden placed on America's ability to understand the actors that are seen as potentially deadly menaces to it.

Internal Tensions

The Bush Doctrine combines a war on terrorism with the strong assertion of American hegemony. Although elements arguably reinforced each other in the overthrow of the Taliban, it is far from clear that this will be the case in the future. Rooting out terrorist cells throughout the world calls for excellent information, and this requires the cooperation of intelligence services in many countries. American power allows it to deploy major incentives to induce cooperation, but there may come a point at which opposition to U.S. dominance will hamper joint efforts. The basic unilateralism of the U.S. behavior that goes with assertive hegemony as exemplified by the war in Iraq has strained the alliance bonds in a way that can make fighting terrorism more difficult.[3]

Iraq highlights a related tension in the Bush Doctrine. The administration argued that overthrowing Saddam Hussein was a part of the war on terrorism because of the danger that he would give WMD to terrorists. Bush calls Iraq "the central front" in the counterterrorist effort, and he rhetorically asks, "If America were not fighting terrorists in Iraq, . . . what would these thousands of killers do, suddenly begin leading productive lives of service and charity?"[4]

---

[2] Adams to Jefferson, February 2, 1816, in Lester Cappon, ed., *The Adams-Jefferson Letters*, vol. 2 (Chapel Hill: University of North Carolina Press, 1959), 463.

[3] For an example, see Douglas Jehl and Thom Shanker, "Syria Stops Cooperating with U.S. Forces and C.I.A.," *New York Times*, 24 May 2005.

[4] Bush's speech to the Army War College in May 2004: "President Outlines Steps to Help Iraq Achieve Democracy and Freedom," White House press release, 24 May 2004; "Remarks by the President at the United States Air Force Academy Graduation," White House press release, 2 June 2004.

I join many observers in finding this line of argument implausible and in believing that the war was, at best, a distraction from the struggle against al Qaeda. To start with, diplomatic, military, and intelligence resources that could have been used to seek out terrorists, especially in Afghanistan, were redeployed against Iraq. In perhaps an extreme case, in June of 2002, the White House vetoed a plan to attack a leading terrorist and his poison laboratory in northern Iraq because it might have disturbed the efforts to build a domestic and international coalition to change the regime,[5] and Abu Musab al-Zarqawi later emerged as the most important insurgent in Iraq and second only to Osama bin Laden on the overall most-wanted list. More generally, thanks to the war, the United States is now seen as a major threat to peace, and in many countries, George Bush is more disliked than bin Laden.[6] Of course, foreign policy is not a popularity contest, but these views eventually will be reflected in reduced support for and cooperation with the United States. Finally and most importantly, if the United States is fighting terrorists in Iraq, the main reason is not that they have flocked to that country to try to kill Americans but that the occupation has recruited large numbers of people to the terrorist cause. Although evidence, let alone proof, is of course elusive, it is hard to avoid the inference that the war has created more terrorists than it has killed, has weakened the resolve of others to combat them, and has increased the chance of major attacks against the West.[7]

Even without the stimulus of the American occupation of Iraq, the highly assertive American policy around the world may increase the probability that it will be the target of terrorist attacks, inasmuch as others attribute most of the world's ills to America. Whether terrorists seek vengeance, publicity, or specific changes in policy, the dominant state is likely to be the one they seek to attack. American power, then, produces American vulnerability.[8] If the United States wanted to place priority on reducing its attractiveness as a target for terrorism, it could seek a reduced role in world politics. The real limits to what could be done here should not disguise the tension between protection from terror and hegemony.

[5] NBC News, 2 March 2004, Jim Miklaszewski, "Avoiding Attacking Suspected Terrorist Mastermind," accessed at http://www.msnbc.msn.com/id/4431601/, 5 March 2004. Scot Paltrow, "Questions Mount Over Failure to Hit Zarqawi's Camp," *Wall Street Journal,* 25 October 2004.

[6] Susan Sachs, "Poll Finds Hostility Hardening Toward U.S. Policies," *New York Times,* 17 March 2004; no author, "Bush vs. bin Laden (And Other Popularity Contests)," *New York Times,* 21 March 2004; Alan Cowell, "Bush Visit Spurs Protests Against U.S. In Europe," *New York Times,* 16 November 2003.

[7] This view is held by a wide range of observers, including France's leading anti-terrorism investigator and Pakistan's President Pervez Musharraf, as well as (more predictably) France's Chirac: Douglas Frantz, Josh Meyer, Sebastian Rotella, and Megan Stack, "The New Face of Al Qaeda," *Los Angeles Times,* 26 September 2004; cnn.com, "Musharraf 'Reasonably Sure' bin Laden is Alive," 25 September 2004, accessed at http://www.cnn.com/2004/WORLD/asiapcf/09/25/musharraf/, 26 September 2004; Craig Smith, "Chirac Says War in Iraq Spreads Terrorism," *New York Times,* 18 November 2004. It was even endorsed by the head of the CIA in early 2005: Dana Priest and Josh White, "War Helps Recruit Terrorists, Hill Told," *Washington Post,* 17 February 2005.

[8] For a related argument, see Richard Betts, "The Soft Underbelly of American Primacy: Tactical Advantages of Terror," *Political Science Quarterly* 117 (Spring 2002): 19–36.

The Bush Doctrine argues that combatting terrorism and limiting proliferation go hand in hand. They obviously do in some cases. The danger that a rogue state could provide terrorists with WMD, although implausible in the case of Iraq, is not fictitious, and controlling the spread of nuclear weapons and nuclear material contributes to American security. But this does not mean that there are no trade-offs between nonproliferation and rooting out terrorism. Most obviously, Iraq's drain on American military resources, time and energy, and on the support from the international community means that the ability to deal with Iran and North Korea has been reduced. These two countries figured prominently in administration fears before September 11 and are more dangerous and perhaps more likely to provide weapons to terrorists than was Iraq. But the way the Bush administration interpreted the war on terror has hindered its ability to deal with these threats, and, in an added irony, if Iran gets nuclear weapons, the United States may be forced to provide a security guarantee for Iraq or permit that country to develop its own arsenal. Furthermore, even if better conceived, combating terrorism can call for alliances with regimes that seek or even spread nuclear weapons. The obvious example is Pakistan, a vital American ally that has been the greatest facilitator of proliferation. The United States eventually uncovered A. Q. Kahn's network and forced President Pervez Musharraf to cooperate in rolling it up, but it might have moved more quickly and strongly had it not needed Pakistan's support against al Qaeda. This compromise is not likely to be the last, and the need to choose between these goals will continue to erode the Bush Doctrine's coherence.

Despite its *realpolitik* stress on the importance of force, the Bush Doctrine also rests on idealistic foundations—the claim for the centrality of universal values represented by America, the expected power of positive example, the belief in the possibility of progress. What is important is that these have power through their acceptance by others, not through their imposition by American might. They require that others change not only their behavior but their outlook, if not their values, as well. For this to happen, the United States has to be seen as well-motivated and exemplifying shared ideals. America's success in the Cold War derived in part from its openness to allied voices, its articulation of a common vision, and a sense of common interest. Although we should not idealize this past or underestimate the degree to which allies, let alone neutrals, distrusted U.S. power and motives, neither should we neglect the ways that enabled influence to be exercised relatively cheaply and allowed the West to gain a much greater degree of unity and cooperation than many contemporary observers had believed possible.

Then, as now, the United States needed not only joint understandings but also multilateral institutions to provide for cooperation on a wide range of issues, especially economic ones. Perhaps the United States can ignore or diminish them in the security area without affecting those such as the World Trade Organization (WTO) on which it wants to continue to rely, but the possibility of undesired spillovers is not to be dismissed. If others do not expect the United States to respect limits that rules might place on it, they are less apt to see it as a trustworthy partner.

Just as the means employed by the Bush Doctrine contradict its ends, so also the latter, by being so ambitious, invite failure. Not only is it extremely unlikely that terror can ever be eradicated, let alone the world be rid of evil, but the fact that Saddam lost the war in Iraq does not mean that the United States won it. Ousting his regime was less important in itself than as a means to other objectives: reducing terrorism, bringing democracy to Iraq, transforming the Middle East, and establishing the correctness and the legitimacy of the Bush Doctrine. Although the effects of the invasion have not yet fully played out, it is hard to see it as a success in these terms. Indeed, despite the fact that the January 2005 elections in Iraq were relatively successful, the political outlook for the country is not good. Ironically, the dramatic and disabling insurgency has distracted American if not Iraqi attention from what is probably the even less-tractable problem of establishing a political settlement among those who have not (yet) resorted to arms. Overly ambitious goals invite not only defeat, but disillusion; if the experiment in Iraq does not yield satisfactory results, it will be hard to sustain support for the Doctrine in the future.

Finally, the Bush Doctrine is vulnerable because although it rests on the ability to deploy massive force, its army, despite being capable of great military feats, is not large enough to simultaneously garrison a major country and attack another adversary, and may not even be sufficient for the former task over a prolonged period. Thanks to the occupation of Iraq, the United States could not now use ground force against Iran or North Korea, and, indeed, the occupation appears to be gravely damaging the system of a volunteer army, reserves, and national guard that has proven so successful since the draft was abolished more than a quarter-century ago.

IMPERIAL OVERSTRETCH?

To succeed, the Bush Doctrine will need prolonged support from the American economic and political system. Before turning to the latter, I want to discuss the more familiar claim that the United States, like so many great powers before it, is falling victim to "imperial overstretch" as the country takes on ever more extensive and expensive commitments.[9]

This has been a common trajectory throughout history, but does not tell us much about the likely fate of the United States and the Bush Doctrine. The U.S. defense budget consumes only a small portion of gross domestic product (less than 4 percent); the proportion devoted to the war on terrorism, although impossible to determine with any precision, obviously is even smaller. The U.S. economy can afford this war, even for the indefinite future. Granted, there are economic impediments to continuing on the current path. Deficits in the

---

[9] The term is taken from Paul Kennedy, *The Rise and Fall of the Great Powers: Economic Change and Military Conflict from 1500 to 2000* (New York: Random House, 1987). A parallel argument was made earlier by Robert Gilpin, *War and Change in World Politics* (New York: Cambridge University Press, 1981).

federal budget and balance of payments are enormous and make the United States vulnerable to external pressures because they cannot be sustained without heavy inflows from abroad.

But, as many commentators have noted, increased defense spending is not the major cause of the problem: the American policy is not doomed to fail because of lack of resources. The United States could easily balance its budget if it were willing to increase taxes. Bush has done the opposite, making this the first war in American history during which taxes have gone down, not up. The problem of an army too small for multiple commitments is probably a better case of "imperial overstretch," but here, too, it is willpower rather than manpower that is in short supply. Higher pay or the reinstitution of a modest draft could provide what is needed.

A more political argument is that these resources cannot be tapped because of resistance from Bush supporters; that is, those in the highest income brackets, who have benefitted so much from the tax cuts, would not support the expansive foreign policy if they were not being rewarded in this way, and their backing is necessary to sustaining this policy. This argument is not without its appeal, but I do not think it is correct. The rich are very happy with Bush's tax cuts, but there is no evidence that they would have opposed him and his foreign policy without them. Some targeted favors and spending programs, especially increases in agricultural subsidies, may have been necessary to maintain domestic support for the administration, but the tax cuts were not.

DOMESTIC REGIME AND POLITICS

This general line of argument points in the right direction, however. Public opinion, the structure of the U.S. government, and domestic politics make it difficult to sustain the Bush Doctrine or any other clear policy. "It seems that the United States was a very difficult country to govern," Charles de Gaulle is said to have told British Prime Minister Harold Macmillan when explaining why it was hard to count on the United States.[10] The General was correct: democracies, and especially the United States, do not find it easy to sustain a clear line of policy when the external environment is not compelling. Domestic priorities ordinarily loom large, and few Americans think of their country as having an imperial mission. Wilsonianism may provide a temporary substitute for the older European ideologies of a *mission civilisatrice* and "the white man's burden," but because it rests on the assumption that its role will be not only noble but also popular, I am skeptical that it will endure if it meets much opposition from those who are supposed to benefit from it.

---

[10] Quoted in Marc Trachtenberg, *A Constructed Peace: The Making of the European Settlement, 1945–1963* (Princeton, NJ: Princeton University Press, 1999), 244. More consistency is seen by Stephen Sestanovich, "American Maximalism," *National Interest* 79 (Spring 2005): 13–23; and Richard Betts, "The Political Support System for American Primacy," *International Affairs* 81 (January 2005): 1–14.

Under most circumstances, the American state is not strong enough to impose coherent and consistent policy guidance, which means that courses of action are shaped less by a grand design than by the pulling and hauling of varied interests, ideas, and political calculations. This is the model of pluralism that is believed by most scholars to capture a great deal of American politics. During the Cold War, realists argued that the national interest abroad, unlike the public interest at home, was sufficiently compelling to override domestic differences and enable even a relatively weak state to follow a policy of some coherence. But the prevalence of realist calls for countries and their leaders to pursue the national interest in the face of conflicting domestic claims indicates that the latter are so powerful that they are likely to prevail under ordinary circumstances.

One might think that domestic support could be arranged with adequate public education: if the experts agree, the public can be brought around. In the late 1940s, the architects of containment were able to work with opinion leaders to develop strong foundations for the policy, but by the end of the century, trust in government and other organizations was low and the sort of civic leaders that were powerful earlier had disappeared. Only conspiracy theorists see the Council on Foreign Relations as much more than a social and status group. "Captains of industry" are absent, with the possible exception of a handful of leaders in the communications and information sectors who lack the breadth of experience of earlier elites. Union leaders have disappeared even faster than unions. University presidents, who were national figures at mid-century, have become money raisers. Those newspapers that have survived are much less relied upon than was true in the past, and television anchors do not have the expertise and reputation that would allow them to be influential, even if the large corporations that own the networks would permit them to try. Known to the public now are "celebrities," largely from the sports and entertainment industries, who lack the interest and knowledge necessary to undertake the public educational campaigns we saw in the past. Thus, it is not surprising that despite Bush's convincing a majority of the American people that they would be safer with him as president than with John Kerry, he has not been able to generate strong support for his general foreign policy.

Separation of powers means that the president cannot control Congress, which can undermine the president's policies. In a minor but telling example, the need to garner crucial Congressional votes for a broad package of trade legislation made Bush promise representatives from textile-producing districts that he would maintain strict limits on clothing made in Pakistan, creating resentment in that country.[11] The judiciary also is independent, giving citizens the ability to bring suits that run contrary to the policies of the executive branch, as shown by several human rights cases brought under the Alien Tort Claims Act, a 1789 law resurrected and put to new purposes, and by the families of September 11 victims, who are suing leading figures in Saudi Arabia for having financed Islamic extremism.

[11] Keith Bradshear, "Pakistanis Fume As Clothing Sales to U.S. Tumble," *New York Times,* 23 June 2002.

At first glance, it would seem that much as the experts criticize the Bush Doctrine for its unilateralism, on this score, at least, it rests on secure domestic foundations. The line that drew the most applause in the President's 2004 State of the Union address was: "America will never seek a permission slip to defend the security of our country." In fact, the public is, sensibly, ambivalent. Although few would argue that the lack of international support should stop the United States from acting when a failure to do so would endanger the country, polls taken in the run-up to the war in Iraq indicated that international endorsement would have added as much as 20 percentage points to support for attacking.[12] Even in a country with a strong tradition of unilateralism, people realize that international support translates into a reduced burden on the United States and increased legitimacy that can both aid the specific endeavor at hand and strengthen the patterns of cooperation that serve American interests. Furthermore, many people take endorsement by allies as an indication that the American policy is sensible. This is a great deal of the reason why Tony Blair's support for Bush was so important domestically, and this means that the Bush Doctrine is particularly vulnerable to British defection.

In summary, although the combination of Bush's preferences and the attack of September 11 have produced a coherent doctrine, domestic support is likely to erode. Congress will become increasingly assertive as the war continues, especially if it does not go well; the Democrats, although lacking a consistent policy of their own, have not accepted the validity of Bush's strategy; and although the public is united in its desire to oppose terrorism, the way to do so is disputed. The United States remains a very difficult country to govern.

Requirements for Intelligence

It is particularly difficult for the Bush Doctrine to maintain public support, because preventive wars require more-accurate assessment of the international environment than intelligence can provide. The basic idea of nipping threats in the bud, of acting when there is still time, implies a willingness to accept false positives in order to avoid more-costly false negatives. That is, the United States must act on the basis of far from complete information, because if it hesitates

---

[12] Richard Benedetto, "Poll: Support for War is Steady, But Many Minds Not Made Up," *USA Today*, 28 February 2003; an even larger effect was reported in Michael Tackett, "Polls Find Support for War Follows Party Lines," *Chicago Tribune*, 7 March 2003. Some findings indicate that what was seen as crucial was support from allies, not necessarily the UN: Gary Younge, "Threat of War: Americans Want UN Backing Before War," *The Guardian* (Manchester), 26 February 2003; for data and analysis that shows continued American support for multilateralism, see the Chicago Council on Foreign Relations 2004 public opinion survey, accessed at http://www.ccfr.org/globalviews2004/main.html, 22 November 2004; and Ole Holsti, *Public Opinion and American Foreign Policy*, rev. ed. (Ann Arbor: University of Michigan Press, 2004), especially ch. 6.

until the threat is entirely clear, it will be too late: it cannot afford to wait until the smoking gun is a mushroom cloud, to use the phrase the administration favored before the Iraq war. In principle, this is quite reasonable. The costs of a WMD attack are so high that a preventive war could be rational even if retrospect were to reveal that it was not actually necessary.

Even if this approach is intellectually defensible, however, it is not likely to succeed politically. The very nature of a preventive war means that the evidence is ambiguous and the supporting arguments are subject to rebuttal. If Britain and France had gone to war with Germany before 1939, large segments of the public would have believed that the war was not necessary. If the war had gone well, public opinion might still have questioned its wisdom; had it gone badly, the public would have been inclined to sue for peace. At least as much today, the cost of a war that is believed to be unnecessary will be high in terms of both international and domestic opinion and will sap the support for the policy. (Indeed, in the case of Iraq, the administration chose not to admit that the war was not forced on it despite the clear evidence that the central claims used to justify it were incorrect.[13]) Even if the public does not judge that the administration should be turned out of power for its mistake, it is not likely to want the adventure to be repeated.

Preventive war, then, asks a great deal of intelligence. It does not bode well for the Bush Doctrine that not only did the war in Iraq involve a massive intelligence failure concerning WMD (which is different from saying that it was caused by this failure), but also the United States started the war two days ahead of schedule because agents incorrectly claimed to know the whereabouts of Saddam Hussein and his sons. The amazing accuracy of the munitions that destroyed the location only underlined the falsity of the information.

The case for preventive war against Iraq turned on the claim that it had active WMD programs, and so, in retrospect, the question is often posed as to whether the intelligence was faulty or whether the Bush administration distorted it.[14] I think the former was dominant but the latter should not be ignored.

---

[13] Supporters of President Bush believe that such weapons were found, however: see the survey by the Program on International Policy Attitudes, University of Maryland, "The Separate Realities of Bush and Kerry Supporters," 21 October 2004, accessed at http://www.pipa.org/OnlineReports/Pres_Election_04/Report10_21_04.pdf, 29 October 2004.

[14] The official American and British post-mortems not only provide a good deal of information, but exemplify, and indeed parody, the conventional wisdom about the two countries' political cultures. The Senate Select Committee on Intelligence (SSCI) report, *US Intelligence Community's Prewar Intelligence Assessments on Iraq* (7 July 2004) is more than just critical of the CIA, it is both a brief for the prosecution and quite partisan. It is also extremely long and detailed. It exemplifies the American penchant for as much information as possible and an adversarial approach to public policy questions. The WMD Commission Report to the President of 31 March 2005 is better. The British report of a committee of Privy Counselors chaired by the Rt Hon The Lord Butler of Brockwell KG GCB CVO, *Review of Intelligence on Weapons of Mass Destruction* (14 July 2004), is shorter, displays a good understanding of the problems of intelligence, is embarrassingly exculpatory, but makes some good points in a subtle manner.

The possibility of intelligence being "politicized" (that is, being a product of policy more than an input to it) comes in multiple forms, of which two are the most obvious.[15] One is decision makers' giving inaccurate accounts of intelligence reports, and the other is their putting pressure on intelligence so that they get back the message they want to hear. I believe that both forms were present but that the latter was a relatively small part of the story. Top administration officials made claims that went significantly beyond what was in intelligence estimates, and, indeed, contradicted them. When they did not say that their statements were grounded in agreed-upon intelligence, this was implied. Most famously, the President said that the British reported that Saddam had sought uranium from Africa (true, but a reasonable listener would infer that American intelligence agreed, which was not true), the Vice President and the Secretary of Defense said that there was solid evidence for connections between Iraq and al Qaeda, and many policy makers insisted that the WMD threat was "imminent." The intelligence community disagreed, and, indeed, CIA Director George Tenet testified that he privately corrected officials for claims like these.[16]

Many people have argued that intelligence was politicized in the sense that there was great pressure on intelligence to tell the policy makers what they wanted to hear. It became obvious that the intelligence community had stretched to support policy when it released a declassified report that painted a more vivid and certain picture of WMD capabilities than it had presented in the classified counterparts, dropping fifteen "probablies" and several dissents.[17] But I believe that few of the major misjudgments can be attributed to political

[15] A devastating analysis of the way in which the administration distorted and misstated intelligence is Senator Carl Levin, "Report of an Inquiry into the Alternative Analysis of the Issue of an Iraq–al Qaeda Relationship," 21 October 2004, accessed at www. Levin.senate.gov, 28 October 2004. On politicization in general, see H. Bradford Westerfield, "Inside Ivory Bunkers: CIA Analysts Resist Managers' 'Pandering', Part I," *International Journal of Intelligence and Counterintelligence,* 9 (Winter 1996/97): 407–424; H. Bradford Westerfield, "Inside Ivory Bunkers: CIA Analysts Resist Managers' 'Pandering', Part II," *International Journal of Intelligence and Counterintelligence,* 10 (Spring 1997): 19–56; Jack Davis, "Analytic Professionalism and the Policymaking Process," Sherman Kent for Intelligence Analysis Occasional Papers, vol. 2, October 2003 (Washington DC: CIA); and Richard Betts, "Politicization of Intelligence: Costs and Benefits" in Richard Betts and Thomas Mahnken, eds., *Paradoxes of Intelligence: Essays in Honor of Michael Handel* (London: Cass, 2003), 59–79. My analysis assumes that the administration believed that Saddam had WMD. Although no evidence has been produced to the contrary, one significant bit of behavior raises doubts: the failure of U.S. forces to launch a careful search for WMD as they moved through Iraq. Had there been stockpiles of WMD materials, there would have been a grave danger that these would have fallen into the hands of America's enemies, perhaps including terrorists. I cannot explain the U.S. failure, but the conduct of much of the U.S. occupation points to incompetence.

[16] Douglas Jehl, "C.I.A. Chief Says He's Corrected Cheney Privately," *New York Times,* 10 March 2004.

[17] Jessica Mathews and Jeff Miller, "A Tale of Two Intelligence Estimates," Carnegie Endowment for International Peace, 31 March 2004; Donald Kennedy, "Intelligence Science: Reverse Peer Review?" *Science* 303 (March 2004): 194; Center for American Progress, "Neglecting Intelligence, Ignoring Warnings," 28 January 2004, accessed at http://www.americanprogress.org/site/pp.asp?c=biJRJ8OVF&b=24889, 28 January 2004.

pressure. The report of the Senate Select Committee on Intelligence and that of the WMD commission found little politicization, and while the former is itself a political document, intelligence officers truly believed that Saddam was actively pursuing WMD programs and few of them have complained, even anonymously, that they acted under duress.

Three kinds of comparisons raise further doubts about the role of political pressure. First and most obviously, in other areas, the CIA came to conclusions that were unpalatable to the administration. Three months before the war, the National Intelligence Council warned that the aftermath of the invasion was not likely to be easy and that attacking might increase support for terrorists in the Islamic world.[18] Even more strikingly, intelligence consistently denied that there was significant evidence for Saddam's role in September 11 or that he might turn over WMD to al Qaeda, holding to this position in the face of administration statements to the contrary, endlessly repeated inquiries and challenges that can only be interpreted as pressure, and the formation of a unit in the Defense Department dedicated to finding evidence for such connections. The administration's pressure was illegitimate, but the lack of success not only speaks to the integrity of the intelligence officials, but also cuts against, although cannot disprove, the claim that the reports on WMD were biased by the desire to please.

The other two comparisons also point in the same direction. Although we do not know the details of the estimates of German and French intelligence, it appears that their views paralleled those of the CIA despite the fact that their governments opposed the war. This indicates that the American judgment could be reached without political pressure (and perhaps in the face of pressure to conclude the contrary). A comparison with the Clinton-era estimates also is informative. Under Bush, intelligence reported a more robust program, including the claim that Iraq had restarted its nuclear program and had a stockpile of biological agents.[19] But quite a bit of new information, only later revealed as misleading, supported these changes and, even more importantly, the gap between the Bush and Clinton estimates was less than that which separated the latter from what we now believe was true.

Although the intense political atmosphere cannot explain the fundamental conclusion that Saddam had active WMD programs, it was not conducive to critical analysis and encouraged judgments of excessive certainty. Analysts and intelligence managers knew that any suggestion that Saddam's capabilities were limited would immediately draw hostile fire from their superiors. Indeed, in this political climate, it would have been hard for anyone to even ask if the conventional wisdom about Saddam's WMD programs should be reexamined.

---

[18] Douglas Jehl and David Sanger, "Prewar Assessment on Iraq Saw Chance of Strong Divisions," *New York Times,* 28 September 2004.

[19] The best analysis is Joseph Cirincione, Jessica Mathews, George Perkovitch, and Alexis Orton, *WMD in Iraq: Evidence and Implications* (Washington DC: Carnegie Endowment, January 2004); also see David Isenberg and Ian Davis, "Unravelling the Known Unknowns: Why No Weapons of Mass Destruction Have Been Found in Iraq," British American Security Information Council Special Report 2004.1, January 2004; David Cortright, Alistair Millar, George Lopez, and Linda Gerber, "The

Political pressures represent the tribute that vice plays to virtue and may be a modern phenomenon. That is, leaders, at least in the United States and the U.K., now need to justify their foreign policies by saying that they are based on the findings of intelligence professionals, as is illustrated by the fact that Secretary of State Colin Powell demanded that Director of Central Intelligence Tenet sit behind him when he gave his speech to the UN outlining the case against Iraq. This is a touching faith in the concept of professionalism and in how much can be known about other states. It is not the only way things could be. A leader could say, "I think Saddam is a terrible menace. This is a political judgment and I have been elected to make difficult calls like this. Information rarely can be definitive and, although I have listened to our intelligence services and other experts, this is my decision, not theirs." Perhaps unfortunately, this is politically very difficult to do, however, and a policy maker who wants to proceed in the face of ambiguous or discrepant information will be hard pressed to avoid at least some politicization of intelligence.[20]

This returns us to the fundamental question of why the intelligence was so wrong. First and most fundamentally, intelligence is hard and there is no *a priori* reason to expect success. Intelligence services are engaged in a competitive game, with hiders and deceivers usually having the advantage. Failure may not call for any special explanation, but it may be what we should expect in the absence of particularly favorable circumstances. This is not a new insight; the only fault with what Carl Von Clausewitz has to say is that he implies that the difficulties are less in peacetime: "Many intelligence reports in war are contradictory; even more are false, and most are uncertain."[21]

Second and relatedly, the United States had little reliable information about Iraq. It lacked well-placed agents and, in their absence, could not readily see that most of the reports it did receive were unreliable or deceptive. Some of these reports may have been inadvertently misleading if they accurately reported what Saddam's officials believed, because it turns out that Saddam was misleading them.[22] Ironically, the problem was magnified by the fact that the Iraqi WMD program became a top priority for American intelligence. Because everyone in the intelligence chain knew that the government was extraordi-

Flawed Case for the War in Iraq," Fourth Freedom Forum and Kroc Institute for International Peace Studies, University of Notre Dame, Policy Brief F12, June 2003; "Opening Statement of Senator Carl Levin at Senate Armed Services Committee Hearing with DCI Tenet and DIA Director Jacoby," 9 March 2004, accessed at http://www.fas.org/irp/congress/2004_hr/levin030904.html, 10 March 2004.

[20] It now appears that some of the friction between Undersecretary of State John Bolton and intelligence officials over how to characterize Cuban biological programs concerned whether his speech represented a political judgment or a report on the intelligence consensus: Douglas Jehl, "Released E-Mail Exchanges Reveal More Bolton Battles," *New York Times,* 24 April 2005; Douglas Jehl, "Bolton Asserts Independence On Intelligence," *New York Times,* 12 May 2005.

[21] Michael Howard and Peter Paret, eds., *On War* (Princeton, NJ: Princeton University Press, 1976), 117. Anyone who sees intelligence errors in terms of the failure to "connect the dots" does not understand the problem.

[22] SSCI, *U.S. Intelligence,* 65.

narily interested in what Iraq was doing in this area, all sorts of reports were generated and passed on, thereby producing the incorrect impression that with this much smoke, there had to be fire. The problem was compounded by the failure to tell the analysts that photographic coverage had increased in 2002, leading them to incorrectly infer that the increased activity they saw at chemical sites represented increased activity rather than increased surveillance.[23]

Third, intelligence agencies learned—and overlearned—from the past. After the 1991 Gulf War, intelligence was shocked to learn how much it had underestimated Iraq's WMD programs, especially in the nuclear area, and it was not going to make this error again. Relatedly, intelligence had learned how effective Saddam's programs of deception and denial were, and this meant that any failure to find specific evidence could be attributed to Iraq's success at hiding it. All this was compounded by the Rumsfeld Commission of 1998 that berated the CIA for basing its missile estimates on the assumption that adversaries would adopt the same methodical path to acquiring these weapons that the United States had followed.

Fourth, once a view of the other side becomes established, it will remain unquestioned in the absence of powerful information to the contrary. Intelligence analysts, like everyone else, assimilate incoming information into their pre-existing beliefs. In the early 1990s, almost everyone came to believe that Saddam had active WMD programs. Without complete and thorough inspections to show that this was not the case, it was natural that people would interpret ambiguous information as not only consistent with but also as confirming this "fact."

The driving role of preexisting beliefs and images is shown by the fact that people who were predisposed to believe that Saddam might ally with Osama bin Laden gave great credit to the scattered and ambiguous reports of such ties, while those whose general views of the Iraqi regime made them skeptical that it would do this found the evidence unconvincing. Similarly, the differences in evaluations of the reports that Saddam was trying to acquire uranium from Niger and that his unmanned aircraft might be intended to strike the United States are explained not by the evidence, which was held in common by all involved, or by better or worse reasoning power, but rather by the analysts' differing general beliefs about whether such policies did or did not make sense.

The final explanation is probably most important: given Saddam's behavior, his protestations that he had disarmed were implausible. That is why most opponents of the war did not dispute the basic claim that Saddam had active WMD programs. If he did not, why did he not welcome the inspectors and actively show that he had complied? Doing so under Clinton could have led to the sanctions being lifted; doing so in 2002–2003 was the only way he could have saved his regime. Iraq could have provided a complete and honest account-

---

[23] WMD Commission, "Report to the President," 92–93.

ing of its weapons programs as called for by the UN resolution, and although the Bush administration would not have been convinced, other countries might have been and domestic opposition might have been emboldened. Similarly, Iraq could have mounted an effective rebuttal to Powell's UN speech. The regime's failure to do these things left even opponents of the war with little doubt that Saddam had active and serious WMD programs.

Even in retrospect, Saddam's behavior is puzzling. The post-war Duelfer Report, although speculative and based on only scattered information because Saddam and his top lieutenants did not speak freely, gives us the best available evidence. This evidence reveals that Saddam felt the need to maintain the appearance of WMD in order to deter Iran, that he feared that unlimited inspections would allow the United States to pinpoint his location and assassinate him, that private meetings between the inspectors and scientists were resisted because "any such meeting with foreigners was seen as a threat to the security of the Regime," and that "Iraq did not want to declare anything that documented use of chemical weapons [in the war with Iran] for fear the documentation could be used against Iraq in lawsuits."[24] Saddam's general policy seems to have been to first end sanctions and inspections and then to reconstitute his programs, all the while keeping his real and perceived adversaries at bay. "This led to a difficult balancing act between the need to disarm to achieve sanctions relief while at the same time retaining a strategic deterrent. The Regime never resolved the contradiction inherent in this approach."[25] This is putting it mildly. Full compliance with the inspectors was the only way that sanctions were going to be lifted, especially after September 11. It is true that revealing that he had no WMD would have reduced his deterrence, but the fear of such weapons could not and did not prevent an American attack, and Iran was hardly spoiling for a fight and could not have assumed that the West would stand aside while it greatly increased its influence by moving against Iraq. Saddam's policy was, then, foolish and self-defeating and goes a long way to explaining the Western intelligence failure. When the truth is as bizarre as this, it is not likely to be believed.

Although this last factor made the Iraq case particularly difficult, future cases are not likely to be easy, and intelligence will continue to be faulty. The National Security Strategy document says that in order to support preventive options, the United States "will build better, more integrated intelligence capa-

---

[24] "Comprehensive Report of the Special Advisor to the DCI on Iraq's WMD," 30 September 2004 (Duelfer Report), 29, 55, 62, 64. John Mueller had earlier speculated that Saddam's limitations on the inspectors were motivated by his fear of assassination: "Letters to the Editor: Understanding Saddam," *Foreign Affairs* 83 (July/August 2004): 151.

[25] Duelfer Report, 34, 57. Ending economic sanctions and ending inspections would not necessarily have coincided and it is not clear which of them was viewed as most troublesome, or why. The UN resolutions provided for the latter to continue even after the former ended, and Saddam had terminated inspections in 1998. This presents a puzzle, because if inspections had been the main barrier, Saddam should have resumed his programs at that point, as most observers expected he would. But it is hard to see how the sanctions were inhibiting him, because after the institution of the Oil for Food program, the regime had access to sufficient cash to procure much of what it needed.

bilities to provide timely, accurate information on threats, wherever they emerge," but this is not likely to be possible.[26] Of course the CIA will get some important cases right, but I suspect that success will be less the rule than the exception. It appears that the United States knows even less about the nuclear programs of Iran and North Korea than it did about Iraq's, and the latter failure's main contribution to improving intelligence about the former has been to reduce the confidence with which judgments are expressed. This is useful, but hardly solves the problem. The establishment of a Director of National Intelligence and the accompanying reorganization is not likely to improve things much either, and the demoralization and dislocation is almost certain to decrease the quality of intelligence in the short run. A policy that can only work if the assessments of other actors are quite accurate is likely to fail. Thus, the Bush Doctrine places a heavier burden on intelligence than it can bear.

Rebuttal

Proponents of the Bush Doctrine can argue that this line of argument is irrelevant. As noted earlier, the dominant view in the administration is that a state's foreign policy follows from its domestic political system. This is a very American approach, extending back to Woodrow Wilson if not earlier, and having significant appeal to liberal elites and the public. It also fits with a cursory look at the last century's history, with Joseph Stalin and Adolf Hitler being two leaders who tyrannized over their own subjects before turning their venom on the wider world. In this view, evil regimes follow evil foreign policies. This means that consequential assessment errors will be quite rare. Even when intelligence has difficulty estimating the other's capabilities, it is very easy to tell when its regime is repressive. Thus, knowing that North Korea, Iran, and Syria are brutal autocracies tells us that they will seek to dominate their neighbors, sponsor terrorism, and threaten the United States.

Indeed, in the wake of the failure to find WMD after the war in Iraq, this has become the main line of the Bush administration's defense of its actions. Perhaps the United States had a few more years to respond than was believed, but because removing Saddam was the only way to remove the danger, this error was minor. As Bush told Tim Russert, "Saddam was dangerous with the ability to make weapons."[27] This approach turns on its head the normal mantra

---

[26] White House, "The National Security Strategy of the United States," (Washington DC: September 2002), 16. Similarly, in defending the idea of preventive war, Condoleezza Rice said that it "has to be used carefully. One would want to have very good intelligence": *Online NewsHour,* "Rice on Iraq, War and Politics," 25 September 2002, accessed at www.pbs.org/newshour/bb/international/july-dec02/rice_9-25.html, 15 September 2003.

[27] NBC, *Meet the Press,* interview with Tim Russert, 8 February 2004, accessed at http://www.msnbc.msn.com/id/4179618/, 2 November 2004; also, see Bush interview with Diane Sawyer, "Ultimate Penalty," 16 December 2003, accessed at http://abcnews.go.com/sections/primetime/US/bush_sawyer_excerpts_1_031216.html, 20 December 2003. Colin Powell said something similar in "Remarks on the Occasion of George Kennan's Centenary Birthday," 20 February 2004, accessed at http://www.state.gov/secretary/rm/29683pf.htm, 21 February 2004, despite having taken a somewhat different position

of conservative intelligence analysis that one should concentrate on capabilities, not intentions. For a regime like this, Bush and his colleagues claim, what is crucial is that it was evil and had the intention to get WMD.

This approach has two difficulties, however. First, taken to its logical conclusion, it implies a very much reduced need for intelligence. It does not take spies or expensive satellites to determine that a country is repressive, and if that is all that we need to know, we can save a great deal of money. Second, even if it is true that the countries that abuse their neighbors are those that have abused their own people, many of the latter follow a quiescent foreign policy. Mao's China, for example, was second to none in internal oppression but followed a cautious if not benign foreign policy. Thus, although knowing that only repressive regimes are threats to the United States would indeed be useful, it does not solve the basic conundrum facing the doctrine of preventive war: deciding which countries pose threats grave enough to merit taking the offensive.

Understanding Adversaries

My previous discussion, like most treatments of the subject, has concentrated on specific intelligence problems of the mis-estimates of Iraq's WMD programs. But the war also revealed a broader kind of failure, one that is quite common and that also makes it difficult to sustain the Bush Doctrine: the inability to understand the way Saddam viewed the world and the strategy that he was following, and the related failure of the United States to adequately convey its intentions and capabilities to him. As subsequent events demonstrated, the United States had the ability to rapidly overthrow Saddam, if not to rapidly pacify the country, and to capture him. It also seemed clear to most of the world that the United States would carry out its threat if need be. Saddam then seemed willfully blind, and as a result, the United States could not coerce him despite its great capability and credibility. This is puzzling. During the Cold War, we became accustomed to the disturbing fact that although the United States could not protect itself, it could deter the Soviet Union from attacking or undertaking major adventures. Elaborate, controversial, and, I believe, basically correct theories were developed to explain how deterrence was possible in the absence of defense. But we now have the reverse situation, and this represents the failure of both policy and theory. Because the United States had the ability to defeat Saddam and the incentives to do so if necessary, Saddam should have backed down, and invasion should not have been necessary.

Four possible explanations are compatible with general theories of coercion but cast doubt on the effectiveness of many American strategies that could be used to support the Bush Doctrine. First, despite the fact that most observers

---

the week before: Glenn Kessler, "Powell: Arms Doubts Might Have Affected View of War," *Washington Post*, 3 February 2004.

believed the American threats, Saddam may not have. Dictatorships are notoriously impervious to unpleasant information; dictators are usually closed-minded and often kill those who bring bad news. Saddam could have believed that even if his troops could not defeat the invading army, they could delay them long enough to force mediation by France and Russia. Perhaps he also thought that the United States would be deterred by the recognition that it could not consolidate its military victory in the face of insurgency, nationalism, and political divisions among the anti-Baathist groups.[28] Although this chain of reasoning now has some appeal, it is far from clear that it was Saddam's and, on balance, it remains hard to see how he could have expected to keep the United States at bay. Second, Saddam could have preferred martyrdom to compliance. Political and perhaps physical death could have given him personal honor and great stature in the Arab world; both honor and stature could have been gratifying and the latter might have furthered his political dreams. Although we cannot rule this out, these values and preferences do not seem to accord with his previous behavior.

Third, Saddam may have underestimated the incentives that Bush had to overthrow him. As hard as this is to believe, Duelfer reports that high-level interrogations indicate that "by late 2002 Saddam had persuaded himself that the United States would not attack Iraq because it already had achieved its objectives of establishing a military presence in the region."[29] Finally, Saddam may have believed that he did not have an alternative that would leave him in power. As Thomas Schelling stressed long ago, making threats credible will do no good unless the actor simultaneously conveys a credible promise not to carry out the undesired action if the other side complies.[30] During most of the run-up to the invasion, the Bush administration made clear that its goal was regime change. Only for a few months in late 2002 when the administration sought support from Congress and the UN did it argue that it would be satisfied by Saddam's compliance with UN resolutions. It would have been easy, and indeed rational, for Saddam to have believed that this American position was a sham, that submitting would give him at best a brief lease on life, and that the only possible route to survival was to bluff and exaggerate his WMD capability in the hope that the United States would back down rather than risk the high casualties that WMD could inflict.[31]

---

[28] For evidence for reasoning along these lines, see the Duelfer Report, 11, 66–67.

[29] Ibid., 32. It is also possible that Saddam believed that the United States actually knew he did not have WMD and this, too, would have reduced the pressures on the United States to invade: Bob Drogin, "Through Hussein's Looking Glass," *Los Angeles Times,* 12 October 2004. For another attempt to recreate Saddam's views, see David Kay, "Iraq's Weapons of Mass Destruction: Lessons Learned and Unlearned," *Miller Center Report* 20 (Spring/Summer 2004): 7–14. Also see Hans Blix, *Disarming Iraq* (New York: Pantheon, 2004), 265–266.

[30] Thomas Schelling, *Strategy of Conflict* (Cambridge, MA: Harvard University Press, 1960).

[31] Indeed, shortly before the war, the Bush administration returned to the position that to avoid invasion, Saddam would not only have to disarm, but also would have to step down: Felicity Barringer and David Sanger, "U.S. Says Hussein Must Cede Power To Head Off War," *New York Times,* 1 March 2003.

This argument is certainly plausible and probably is part of the answer. But doubts are raised about the adequacy of this or any particularistic account by the fact that the phenomenon is quite general.[32] The United States failed to understand the beliefs and calculations that led Stalin to authorize the North Korean invasion of the South in June of 1950 or the People's Republic of China intervention several months later, for example. Other countries can be similarly blind: despite its intensive study of its adversary, Israel was unable to grasp the strategy that led Anwar Sadat to launch his attack across the Suez Canal in October of 1973, or to go to Jerusalem four years later, for that matter.

What is most striking and relevant to the Bush Doctrine is that since the end of the Cold War, there have been five instances in which the United States has had to use force because the threat to do so was not perceived as credible despite being supported by adequate capability and willpower. The first case was Panama in 1989. Here it can be argued that Manuel Noriega had little reason to believe the threat, because the United States had not carried out operations like this before, public support was unclear, and memories of Vietnam lingered. Furthermore, as in Iraq, the adversary's leader might not have been able to change his behavior in a way that would have allowed him to remain in power.

The second case was the Gulf War. Because the United States made no attempt to deter an attack on Kuwait, the puzzle here is not why Saddam invaded,[33] but his refusal to withdraw despite the presence of 500,000 coalition troops poised against him. In fact, he may have been convinced at the last minute, with the war attributable to the difficulties in making arrangements with so little time remaining and the American preference to destroy the Iraqi forces rather than allowing them to withdraw and be available for future adventures. Other factors may also have been at work, such as Saddam's residual belief that he could deter the United States by inflicting large numbers of casualties, or his calculation that a bloodless withdrawal would cost him more in the eyes of his own people and his Arab neighbors than would a limited military defeat. Nevertheless, this incident is a disturbing failure of coercion despite massive military superiority and a display that convinced most observers that the United States would use it.

---

[32] For excellent studies of when coercion does and does not succeed in changing behavior, see Alexander George, David Hall, and William Simons, *The Limits of Coercive Diplomacy* (Boston, MA: Little, Brown, and Co., 1971); Alexander George and William Simons, eds., *The Limits of Coercive Diplomacy,* 2nd ed. (Boulder, CO: Westview, 1994); Robert Art and Patrick Cronin, eds., *The United States and Coercive Diplomacy* (Washington DC: U.S. Institute of Peace, 2003). For a discussion of failures of coercion that cannot be explained by standard theories, see Richard Ned Lebow and Janis Gross Stein, "Deterrence: The Elusive Dependent Variable," *World Politics* 42 (April 1990): 336–369; Richard Ned Lebow and Janis Gross Stein, "Beyond Deterrence," *Journal of Social Issues* 43 (No. 4 1987): 5–72.

[33] For good if conflicting accounts, see Gregory Gause III, "Iraq's Decisions to Go to War, 1980 and 1990," *Middle East Journal* 56 (Winter 2002): 47–70; and Fred Lawson, "Rethinking the Iraqi Invasion of Kuwait," *Review of International Affairs* 1 (Autumn 2001): 1–20.

The third case is Haiti in 1996. Although Bill Clinton did not have to fight to oust the junta, he did have to put the invasion force into the air before General Raoul Cedras and his colleagues believed that they had no choice but to abdicate.[34] This was, then, a close thing, and although the previous American hesitations may have given Haitian leaders reason to doubt that the United States would use force, as the American position hardened, most observers understood that Clinton would act if he needed to. Of course, here, as in Panama, the resistance was greatly heightened by the fact that the American demand entailed removing the adversary from power. It remains striking, however, that this coercion proved so difficult.

The next case of failed coercion was the operation in Kosovo. Clinton and his colleagues believed that if Slobodan Milosevic did not back down in the face of the American/NATO threat to use force, he would do so after a day or two of bombing. In the event, it took much more than that; although an actual invasion was not needed, the amount of force required was quite large. Again, the reason is, in part, that the United States was requiring a great deal from Milosevic. He viewed Kosovo as part of Serbia, had gained power by arousing public opinion on this issue, and had reason to fear that he would be overthrown if he withdrew, as, in fact, proved to be the case. Indeed, the puzzle of why he did not back down initially is complemented by the questions surrounding his eventual concessions. What happened during the air campaign to lead him to change his mind? Many individual authors are sure of the answer, but each gives a different one and we cannot yet determine the relative importance of the bombing of Serbian army units, the damage to Belgrade, the targeting of assets that belonged to Milosevic's circle of supporters, the lack of backing and eventual pressure from Russia, and the fear of a ground invasion. What is clear and crucial is that the United States did not understand Milosevic's perceptions and strategy, just as he almost surely did not understand the American preferences and options.

These thumbnail sketches lead to four conclusions. First, intelligence failures are often bilateral, if not multilateral.[35] That is, the American surprise at finding that its adversaries could not be coerced was mirrored by the adversaries' misreading of what the United States would do. Second, whatever policy the United States adopts, it is important for it to do a better job of understanding its adversaries and conveying its promises and threats to them. Although the task is difficult, it is striking how little the U.S. government has sought to learn from these troublesome cases, despite the fact that it now has access to many of the decision makers on the other side. The American propensity to treat past events as mere history is nowhere more evident and costly than here.

---

[34] For the argument that this extreme military pressure made a political settlement more difficult to reach, see Robert Pastor, "The Delicate Balance Between Coercion and Diplomacy: The Case of Haiti, 1994" in Art and Cronin, eds., *The United States and Coercive Diplomacy*, 119–156.

[35] For further discussion, see Robert Jervis, *System Effects: Complexity in Political and Social Life* (Princeton, NJ: Princeton University Press, 1997), 44–45.

Third, it is unlikely that even excellent studies will provide a base of knowledge sufficient to prevent all such errors in the future. The ways in which adversaries can perceive and calculate are too numerous and surprising to permit confident projections. The past decade's meetings of Cold War veterans reveal mutual amazement that the other side could have believed what it did, and the current task is more difficult still because the United States is no longer dealing with one fairly stable adversary over a prolonged period.

Finally, the Bush Doctrine places heavy demands on judging adversaries. If the United States is to block proliferation and engage in preventive wars when rogues get close to WMD, it will need a far better understanding of others than it has been able to muster so far. Conversely, if the United States is not able to gain more discriminating intelligence about the capabilities and intentions of potential rogues, the Doctrine will require the use of force to change any number of regimes. But it is unlikely that American domestic politics would support such a policy.

DEMOCRACY AS THE ANSWER?

Here, as in the earlier problem of intelligence failure, the Bush administration's faith in democracy provides a rebuttal: these threats will disappear as more and more countries become democratic. I am doubtful, however, that the United States will, in fact, vigorously support the establishment of democracies abroad, that such efforts will succeed, and that democratic regimes will always further American interests.

The question of whether to press for democracies abroad arose during the Cold War, and the basic problem was summarized in John F. Kennedy's oft-quoted reaction when the dictator of the Dominican Republic, Rafael Trujillo, was assassinated in May of 1961: "There are three possibilities, in descending order of preference: a decent democratic regime, a continuation of the Trujillo regime, or a Castro regime. We ought to aim at the first, but we really can't renounce the second until we are sure that we can avoid the third."[36] Despite the fact that the United States has more room to maneuver now that it does not have to worry about a new regime allying with a major enemy state, there appears to be a great deal of continuity between the U.S. policy during the Cold War, what it did in the first decade after it, and Bush's actions. While the United States hopes to replace hostile dictatorships with democracies, only rarely does it push for democracy when doing so could destabilize friendly regimes. It would be tiresome to recount the sorry but perhaps sensible history of U.S. policies toward Egypt, Pakistan, and Saudi Arabia, and I will just note that when the latter arrested reformers who had called for a constitutional monar-

---

[36] Quoted in Arthur Schlesinger, Jr., *A Thousand Days: John F. Kennedy in the White House* (Boston, MA: Houghton Mifflin, 1965), 769.

chy and independent human rights monitoring, Colin Powell said that "each nation has to find its own path and follow that path at its own speed."[37] Over the past year, Bush and his colleagues have taken a somewhat stronger position, but the depth of the American commitment still remains unclear.[38]

Ironically, the war on terrorism, although accompanied by greater stress on the value of democracy, has increased the costs of acting accordingly by increasing the American need for allies throughout the globe. Without the war, the United States might have put more pressure on the nondemocratic states of the former Soviet Union, or at least not supported them. But the need for bases in Central Asia has led the United States to embrace a particularly unsavory set of regimes. The pressure to democratize Pakistan is similarly minimal, in part because of the fear that greater responsiveness to public opinion would lead to an unacceptable Islamic regime. This danger, and that of any kind of instability, is magnified because of Pakistan's nuclear arsenal. Although Egypt lacks nuclear weapons, instability in such a powerful and centrally placed country is also greatly to be feared. In other parts of the Middle East and areas such as the Caspian basin, it is the need for a secure flow of oil that leads the United States to support nondemocratic regimes. As events in Uzbekistan in the spring of 2005 show, it seems that there are few places that are unimportant enough to run the experiment of vigorously supporting democracies where they do not now exist when the existing repressive regime has good control. Bush can increase the (verbal) pressure on Vladimir Putin to democratize, in part because his government has such a secure grip.

Furthermore, the Bush administration appears to be driven more by the politics of the regimes it is dealing with than by an abstract commitment to democracy, as is shown by its stance toward if not its role in the opposition (constitutional or otherwise) to, Hugo Chavez in Venezuela and Jean-Bertrand Aristide in Haiti. In a continuation of the Cold War pattern, leftist governments are seen as dangerous and authoritarian regimes of the right are acceptable. On other occasions, it is the specific policies of a leader that make him unacceptable despite his popular approval. The American refusal to treat Yasser Arafat as the Palestinians' leader was rooted in the belief that he was unwilling to stop terrorism, not in his inability to win an election, and the United States withdrew its recognition of President Rauf Denktash in Turkish Cyprus when he opposed proposals for reunifying the island.[39]

---

[37] Quoted in Barbara Slavin, "U.S. Softens Stance on Mideast Democratic Reforms," *USA Today*, 12 April 2004; for later developments, see Barbara Slavin, "U.S. Toning Down Goals for Mideast," *USA Today*, 27 May 2004. For a general discussion of the prospects for liberalization in the Middle East and the American efforts, see Tamara Cofman Wittes, "The Promise of American Liberalism," *Policy Review* 125 (June/July 2004): 61–76.

[38] For some of the tensions and contradictions, see Elisabeth Bumiller, "The First Lady's Mideast Sandstorm," *New York Times*, 6 June 2005.

[39] No author, "U.S. Recognizes New Leader for Turkish Cypriots," *New York Times*, 27 May 2004; The refusal to deal with Arafat has been extended to Hamas, despite its electoral success: Steven Weisman, "U.S. to Shun Hamas Members, Even if Electorally Elected," *New York Times*, 7 June 2005.

But even vigorous support for democracy might not produce that outcome. The fate of Iraq may not yet be determined, and, at this writing, anything appears to be possible, from a partially democratic regime to a civil war to the return of a national strongman to the loss of national unity. But it is hard to believe that the foreseeable future will see a full-fledged democracy, with extensive rule of law, open competition, a free press, and checks and balances.[40] The best that can be hoped for would be a sort of semi-democracy, such as we see in Russia or Nigeria, to take two quite different countries.

The Bush administration's position is much more optimistic, however, arguing that for democracy to flourish, all that is needed is for repression to be struck down. With a bit of support, all countries can become democratic; far from being the product of unusually propitious circumstances, a free and pluralist system is the "natural order" that will prevail unless something special intervenes.[41] President Bush devoted a full speech to this subject, saying: "Time after time, observers have questioned whether this country, or that people, or this group, are 'ready' for democracy—as if freedom were a prize you win for meeting our own Western standards of progress. In fact, the daily work of democracy is itself the path of progress."[42] This means that for him, the prospects for Iraq are bright. In his view, although it is true that you cannot force people to be democratic, this is not necessary. All that is needed is to allow people to be democratic.

We would all like this vision to be true, but it probably is not. Even if there are no conditions that are literally necessary for the establishment of democracy, this form of government is not equally likely to flourish under all conditions. Poverty, deep divisions, the fusion of secular and religious authority, militaristic traditions and institutions, and a paucity of attractive careers for defeated politicians all inhibit democracy.[43] Although Bush is at least partly right

[40] A cautionary tale is provided by the memoirs of the British commander in the newly created Iraq after World War I: Sir Arnold Wilson, *Mesopotamia 1917–1920: A Clash of Loyalties* (London: Oxford University Press, 1931), 259, 268–272, 311–312.

[41] For the concept of natural order, see Stephen Toulmin, *Foresight and Understanding: An Enquiry into the Aims of Science* (Bloomington: Indiana University Press, 1961). For an intriguing argument that democracy will indeed flourish in the absence of imposed obstacles, see John Mueller, *Capitalism, Democracy, and Ralph's Pretty Good Grocery* (Princeton, NJ: Princeton University Press, 1999); for an excellent analysis that is skeptical of the ease of democratic transitions, see Thomas Carothers, "The End of the Transition Paradigm," *Journal of Democracy* 13 (January 2002): 5–21.

[42] "President Bush Discusses Freedom in Iraq and Middle East," White House press release, 6 November 2003, 3; also see "President Discusses the Future of Iraq," speech to the American Enterprise Institute, White House press release, 26 February 2003; "President Attends International Republican Institute Dinner," White House press release, 18 May 2005.

[43] See Ian Shapiro, "The State of Democratic Theory" in Ira Katznelson, ed., *Political Science: The State of the Discipline* (New York: Norton, 2002), 235–265; Barbara Geddes, "The Great Transformation in the Study of Politics in Developing Countries" in Ira Katznelson, ed., *Political Science: The State of the Discipline* (New York: Norton, 2002), 342–370; Adam Przeworski, Michael Alvaraz, Jose Antonio Cheibub, and Fernando Limongi, *Democracy and Development: Political Institutions and Well-Being in the World, 1950–1990* (Cambridge: Cambridge University Press, 2000); for a critique, see Carles Boix and Susan Stokes, "Endogenous Democratization," *World Politics* 55 (July 2003): 517–549.

in arguing that some of these conditions arise out of authoritarian regimes, they are causes as well and there is no reason to expect the United States to be able to make most countries democratic even if it were to bend all its efforts to this end. Indeed, movements for reform and democracy may suffer if they are seen as excessively beholden to the United States. As Colin Powell noted after one American attempt of this type had to be abandoned in the face of cries of U.S. bullying, "I think we are now getting a better understanding with the Arab nations that it has to be something that comes from them. If you don't want us to help, you don't want us to help."[44]

Is it even true that the world would be safer and the United States better off if many more countries were democratic? The best-established claim that democracies rarely, if ever, fight each other is not entirely secure, and the more sophisticated versions of this theory stress that joint democracy will not necessarily produce peace unless other factors, especially economic interdependence and a commitment to human rights, are present as well. This makes sense, because democracy is compatible with irreconcilable conflicts of interest. Furthermore, even if well-established democracies do not fight each other, states that are undergoing transitions to democracy do not appear to be similarly pacifistic.[45] Putting these problems aside, there is no reason to expect democracies to be able to get along well with nondemocracies, which means that establishing democracy in Iraq or in any other country will not make the world more peaceful unless its neighbors are similarly transformed.

The Bush administration has also argued that other countries are much more likely to support American foreign policy objectives if they are democratic. The basic point that democracies limit the power of rulers has much to be said for it, but it is far from clear how far this will translate into shared foreign policy goals. After all, at bottom, democracy means that a state's policy will at least roughly reflect the objectives and values of the population, and there is no reason to believe that these should be compatible between one country and another. Why would a democratic Iraq share American views on the Arab–Israeli dispute, for example? Would a democratic Iran be a closer ally than the Shah's regime was? If Pakistan were truly democratic, would it oppose Islamic terrorism? In many cases, if other countries become more responsive to public opinion, they will become more anti-American. In the key Arab states of Jordan, Egypt, and Saudi Arabia, cooperation with the United States could not be sustained if the public had greater influence; the elections in Pakistan in September of 2002 reduced the regime's stability and complicated the efforts to combat al Qaeda, results that would have been magnified had the elections been truly free; in Europe, the public is even more critical of the United States than are the leaders. In the spring of 2004, Paul Bremer declared that "basically

[44] Quoted in Steven Weisman, "U.S. Muffles Sweeping Call To Democracy In Mideast," *New York Times,* 12 March 2004.

[45] Jack Snyder and Edward Mansfield, *Electing to Fight: Why Emerging Democracies Go to War* (Cambridge, MA: MIT Press, 2005).

Iraq is on track to realize the kind of Iraq that Iraqis want and that Americans want, which is a democratic Iraq."[46] Leaving aside the unwarranted optimism, the assumption that Iraqis and Americans want the same thing reveals a touching but misplaced faith in universal values and harmony of interests among peoples and therefore among democratic regimes. Indeed, the only possible way for Iraq to be pro-American may be for it to be nondemocratic (although it is likely to end up being both authoritarian and anti-American).[47]

THE SHAPE OF THINGS TO COME?

Over eighty years ago, Walter Lippmann famously argued that the public could not act responsibly in politics, and especially in foreign policy, because it was driven by stereotypes and images of the external world that were crude and rigid.[48] There is much to this, but ironically it now applies to large segments of the Republican foreign policy elite more than to the general public. Lippmann's description of how stereotypes do more than conserve our intellectual effort is particularly appropriate and disturbing: "The system of stereotypes may be the core of our personal tradition, the defenses of our position in society. . . . They may not be a complete picture of the world, but they are a picture of a possible world to which we are adapted. In that world people and things have their well-known places, and do certain expected things."[49] Ideologies can provide a comforting way of understanding a complex world and a guide to swift action. But even under the best of circumstances, they are likely to distort, to miss a great deal, and to inhibit adjustment to changing circumstances. When the world is new and confusing, the temptation to rely on stereotypes and ideologies is greatest. But these are exactly the circumstances under which this pattern is most dangerous.

The Bush Doctrine is extraordinarily ambitious and relies heavily on the premise that a state's foreign policy is largely determined by its domestic system. By rejecting the standard international politics argument that the behavior of states is most strongly influenced by their external environment, the Bush

---

[46] Quoted in Douglas Jehl, "U.S. Says It Will Move Gingerly Against Sadr," *New York Times,* 7 April 2004. Similarly, in the run-up to the war in Kosovo, General Wesley Clark endorsed the view that the problem was caused by the fact that the Belgrade regime was not a democratic one. Wesley K. Clark, *Waging Modern War: Bosnia, Kosovo, and the Future of Conflict* (New York: Public Affairs Press, 2002), 128.

[47] Public opinion data in the spring of 2004 was ambivalent but not encouraging: while most Iraqis were glad that Saddam was ousted, said their own lives were better off because of the invasion, and thought that their country would be less safe if Coalition forces left, they viewed those forces as occupiers rather than liberators, thought they should leave immediately, and viewed George Bush unfavorably; accessed at http://www.cnn.com/2004/world/meast/04/28/iraq.poll/iraq/poll.4.28.pdf, 5 May 2004.

[48] Walter Lippmann, *Public Opinion* (New York: Macmillan, 1922).

[49] Ibid., 95, 381–382. It is also worth noting that Lippmann's chapter on intelligence argues: "It is no accident that the best diplomatic service in the world is the one in which the divorce between the assembling of knowledge and the control of policy is most perfect."

administration is led to conclude that tyrannies are uniquely dangerous, especially because of the dangers posed by WMD. As the President said in his second inaugural address, "The urgent requirement of our nation's security ... [is the] ending of tyranny in the world." This means that American vital interest requires not the maintenance of the status quo, but the transformation of world politics, and indeed, of the domestic systems of many countries. This project is more far-reaching than traditional empires that sought only to conquer. Although difficult to achieve, this could be accomplished by superior military power. For the transformation Bush has in mind, superior force is necessary but not sufficient; it can succeed only through the efforts of others. Furthermore, not only must the populations and elites in currently dictatorial regimes undergo democratic transformations, but America's allies must work with it in a wide variety of projects to sustain the political and economic infrastructure of the new world. The unilateralist impulses in American policy are likely to inhibit such cooperation, however.

If the Bush administration overestimates the extent to which it can and needs to make the world democratic, it incorrectly assumes that the American domestic system will provide the steady support that the Doctrine requires. The very American preponderance that makes the Doctrine possible also gives the United States great freedom of action. Although states with great power often find projects that require its exercise,[50] this particular project is not compelled or likely to be supported over the long run by America's inward-looking public opinion and fragmented domestic political system.

Although it is unlikely that the Bush Doctrine can be sustained, future events will, of course, affect its prospects. Most obviously, a great deal depends on developments in Iraq. Although a full analysis is beyond the scope of this essay (and beyond my knowledge), as I noted earlier, putting down the insurgency will not automatically solve the political problems that, over the long run, pose a greater challenge to Iraq and to American hopes for it and the region. Even when the violent opposition of the Sunnis comes to an end, the difficulties in creating a stable and tolerant Iraq will remain.

A second uncertainty concerns the war on terror in general and the prospects of another major attack on the United States in particular. It is almost certain that the coming decade will see large terrorist attacks on the West, perhaps with WMD, especially if we put radiological weapons ("dirty bombs") in this category. What is much less predictable is the reaction to this. It is possible that the American public would see an attack as showing the failure of the Bush Doctrine and would call for more attention to homeland defense and less to taxing foreign policy goals. It is also possible that the response would be more preventive strikes and perhaps redoubled efforts to encourage democratic regimes. In either event, we are likely to see heightened restrictions against immigrants as well as restrictions on civil liberties. Although these will not directly affect the fate of the Bush Doctrine, they are likely to reduce America's appeal abroad.

[50] For further discussion, see Jervis, "Understanding the Bush Doctrine," 379–383.

Turning to what is already clear from events since September 11, the Bush Doctrine and the war in Iraq have weakened Western unity and called into question the potency of deterrence by claiming that the United States could not have contained a nuclear-armed Saddam. I think this belief was incorrect,[51] but because deterrence rests on potential challengers' understanding that the defender is confident of its deterrent threats, the American demonstration of its lack of faith in this instrument will diminish its utility. Even if future administrations adopt a different stance and affirm the role of deterrence, some damage may be permanent.

The largely unilateral overthrow of Saddam has set in motion even more important irreversible changes in relations with allies. Before Bush came to power, the emerging consensus was that the United States was committed to multilateralism.[52] This is not to say that it would never act without the consent of its leading allies, but that on major issues, it would consult fully, listen carefully, and give significant weight to allied views. International institutions, deeply ingrained habits, the sense of shared values and interests, close connections at the bureaucratic levels, public support for this way of proceeding, and the understanding that long-run cooperation was possible only if the allies had faith that the United States would not exploit its superior power position all led to a structure that inhibited American unilateralism. This partial world order, it was argued, served American interests as well as those of its partners, because it induced the latter to cooperate with each other and with the United States, reduced needless frictions, and laid the foundations for prosperity and joint measures to solve common problems. This way of doing business had such deep roots that it could absorb exogenous shocks and the election of new leaders.

Recent events have shown that although the argument may have been correct normatively, it was not correct empirically. It is quite possibly true that it would have been wise for the United States to have continued on the multilateral path, to have maintained a broad coalition, and to have given its allies more influence over the way it fought terrorism. But we can now see that it was wrong to conclude that the international system and U.S. policy had evolved to a point that compelled this approach.

---

[51] See Robert Jervis, *American Foreign Policy in a New Era* (New York: Routledge, 2005), ch. 3.

[52] See, for example, G. John Ikenberry, *After Victory: Institutions, Strategic Restraint, and the Rebuilding of Order After Major War* (Princeton, NJ: Princeton University Press, 2001); John Gerard Ruggie, *Winning the Peace: America and the New World Order* (New York: Columbia University Press, 1996); John Steinbrunner, *Principles of Global Security* (Washington DC: Brookings Institution, 2000). See Joseph Nye, *The Paradox of American Power: Why the World's Only Superpower Can't Go It Alone* (New York: Oxford University Press, 2002), 154–163, for a good discussion of the different circumstances under which unilateralism and multilateralism are appropriate; also see John Van Oudenaren, "What Is 'Multilateral'?" *Policy Review* 117 (February–March 2003): 33–47; and John Van Oudenaren, "Unipolar Versus Unilateral, *Policy Review* 124 (April–May 2004): 63–74. For the argument that even in the Cold War, the United States was unilateralist, see Sestanovich, "American Maximalism," and Betts, "Political Support System for American Primacy."

This does not mean that the United States is now firmly set on a new course. Indeed, I do not think that the Bush Doctrine can be sustained. Bush's domestic support rests on the belief that he is making the United States safer, not on an endorsement of a wider transformationist agenda. Especially in the absence of a clear political victory in Iraq, support for assertive hegemony is limited at best. But if Bush is forced to retract, he will not revert to the sort of coalition-building that Clinton favored. Of course there will be a new president elected in 2008, but even if he or she wanted to pick up where Clinton left off, this will not be possible. Although allies would meet the United States more than half-way in their relief that policy had changed, they would realize that the permanence of the new American policy could not be guaranteed. The familiar role of anarchy in limiting the ability of states to bind themselves has been highlighted by Bush's behavior and will not be forgotten.

The United States and others, then, face a difficult task. The collapse of the Bush foreign policy will not leave clear ground on which to build: new policies and forms of cooperation will have to be jury-rigged above the rubble of the recent past. The Bush administration having asserted the right (and the duty) to maintain order and provide what it believes to be collective goods, an American retraction will be greeted with initial relief by many, but it is also likely to produce disorder, unpredictability, and opportunities for others.

Machiavelli famously asked whether it is better to be feared or to be loved. The problem for the United States is that it is likely to be neither. Bush's unilateralism and perceived bellicosity have weakened ties to allies, dissipated much of the sympathy that the United States had garnered after September 11, and convinced many people that America was seeking an empire with little room for their interests or values. It will be very hard for any future administration to regain the territory that has been lost. At best, the policy is a gigantic gamble that a stable and decent regime can be established in Iraq and that this can produce reform in the other countries and a settlement between Israel and the Palestinians. In this case, the United States might gain much more support and approval, if not love. But anything less will leave the United States looking neither strong nor benign, and we may find that the only thing worse than a successful hegemon is a failed one. We are headed for a difficult world, one that is not likely to fit any of our ideologies or simple theories.*

* I would like to thank Robert Art, Richard Betts, Demetrios James Caraley, Marc Trachtenberg, and Kenneth Waltz for comments, discussion, and encouragement. An earlier version of this essay appeared in *American Foreign Policy in a New Era* (New York: Routledge, 2005), chapter 5.

Part II:
TERRORIST ATTACKS

The Rationality of Radical Islam

QUINTAN WIKTOROWICZ
KARL KALTENTHALER

Why do Islamist radicals engage in high-cost/risk activism that exposes them to arrest, repression, and even death? At a group level, it appears perfectly rational: zealous contention places enormous pressures on adversaries and increases the likelihood that the group will achieve its objective. Robert Pape's study of suicide terrorism provides some empirical evidence that extreme forms of activism do indeed produce concessions from opponents.[1] Yet, although extreme tactics may be deployed as part of a logical, coherent, and rational strategy to maximize group goals, is it "rational" for the *individual* perpetrators? Why not free-ride off the efforts of others rather than jeopardize personal self-interest?

We argue that radical Islamic groups offer spiritual selective incentives to individuals who are concerned with the hereafter. Although some radical Islamists are compelled by economic incentives or personal psychological needs that may have nothing to do with religious conviction (the need for revenge against perceived oppressors, a need for a sense of empowerment, or a desire for prestige), religion matters for many. In cases where individuals take spirituality seriously, movement ideologies offer strategies for fulfilling divine duties and maximizing the prospects of salvation on judgment day. In essence, these ideologies serve as heuristic devices or templates that outline the path to salvation. Where individuals believe that the spiritual payoffs outweigh the

---

[1] Robert Pape, "The Strategic Logic of Suicide Terrorism," *American Political Science Review* 97 (August 2003): 343–362.

QUINTAN WIKTOROWICZ is the author of *The Management of Islamic Activism* (2001); *Global Jihad* (2002); *Radical Islam Rising: Muslim Extremism in the West* (2005); and numerous articles and book chapters on Islamic movements in the Middle East and Europe. He is also the editor of *Islamic Activism: A Social Movement Theory Approach* (2004). KARL KALTENTHALER teaches political science at the University of Akron. His research focuses on political economy, mass behavior, and public attitudes toward terrorism. He is author of *Germany and the Politics of Europe's Money* and has written journal articles on the political economy of European integration, central bank decision making, the political sources of economic outcomes, and public attitudes toward a range of economic policies.

negative consequences of strategies in the here and now, high-cost/risk activism is intelligible as a rational choice.

This essay uses al-Muhajiroun as a case study to demonstrate the rationality of radical Islam. Based in the UK, with branches throughout the Muslim world, this movement supported al Qaeda; jihad against the United States in Afghanistan, Iraq, and Saudi Arabia; terrorism against Israel; attacks against the United Nations; military coups against governments throughout the Muslim world; and the establishment of an Islamic state in Britain. After September 11, it garnered extraordinary media attention in the UK and raised serious concerns among governments combating Islamic terrorism. Although it was less radical than groups such as al Qaeda, al-Muhajiroun openly promoted an assortment of extremist causes and is a good example of high-cost/risk activism. The movement was formally disbanded in October 2004, but its activists continue to operate through two successor organizations: al-Ghurabaa' (the Strangers) and the Saviour Sect. Al-Muhajiroun's leader and founder, Omar Bakri Mohammed, left the UK for Lebanon in August 2005 and was barred from returning as a result of the British government's crackdown on Islamic extremism after the terrorist attacks on the tube system earlier in July.[2]

The focus of this essay is on how spiritual incentives inspire Islamic radicalism. As a result, it does not directly address why individuals initially chose al-Muhajiroun over more moderate Islamic organizations that require less sacrifice. Nor does it focus on the process of preference reordering. These are important issues and are addressed extensively by the first author in a separate publication, which points to the importance of social networks, low levels of prior religious knowledge, identity crises, negative experiences with moderate Islamic figures and organizations, the public outreach activities of al-Muhajiroun, and perceptions about the credibility of the movement's leader as compared with moderate alternatives and radical rivals.[3] All of these drew individuals into study circles, where they were socialized into the movement ideology.

For those who eventually accepted the ideology as "true Islam" (and this was heavily influenced by perceptions about the credibility of the movement leader as an interpreter of Islam rather than the superiority of al-Muhajiroun's spiritual incentives relative to other groups),[4] why did they engage in high-cost/risk activism? Why not simply continue taking lessons without graduating to riskier behaviors? In other words, why not free-ride off the sacrifice of others?

We argue that the choice to move to high-cost/risk activism can be understood as a rational decision if we take the content of the movement's ideology seriously. Al-Muhajiroun's ideology outlines an *exclusive* strategy to salvation, which entails a number of costly and risky behaviors. Any deviations

---

[2] For details on the dissolution, see Quintan Wiktorowicz, *Radical Islam Rising: Muslim Extremism in the West* (Lanham, MD: Rowman & Littlefield, 2005), 213–217.

[3] Wiktorowicz, *Radical Islam Rising*.

[4] See Wiktorowicz, *Radical Islam Rising*.

from this strategy mean that an individual will not enter Paradise, thus eroding tendencies toward free-riding. For those who accepted the movement ideology and sought salvation, a refusal to engage in high-cost/risk activism was tantamount to violating self-interest, because it meant that they would go to Hell.

Before proceeding, it is important to note limitations in conducting fieldwork on radical Islamic groups. The primary obstacle is access. Although surveys and large samples are preferable, they are rarely possible, given the secretive nature of these movements. As a result, one is left with small samples of respondents and ethnographic methods, if access is granted. In this study, the first author conducted thirty interviews (many tape-recorded) with movement leaders and activists and interacted with about one hundred other activists and movement "supporters." In addition, he attended movement-only lessons, public study circles, demonstrations, and community events, and collected movement documents and audio/written materials, including leaflets, protest announcements, training books, taped lessons/talks, and press releases. Although this hardly represents a probability sample of individuals, publications, and activities, the fieldwork results offer rare empirical evidence that addresses individual rationality.

RATIONAL RADICALISM?

Most studies of the causes of Islamism offer a grievance-based explanation implicitly rooted in functionalist social psychology accounts of mass behavior, which view collective action as derived from exogenous structural strains, system disequilibrium, and concomitant pathologies (alienation, anomie, atomization, normative ambiguity, etc.) that create individual frustration and motivation for "deviant" social behavior.[5] The model posits a linear causal relationship in which structural strains, such as modernization, industrialization, or an economic crisis, cause psychological discomfort, which, in turn, produces collective action. The implication is that participation is the result of "irrationality."

The preponderance of research argues that the underlying impetus for Islamic activism derives from the crises produced by failed secular modernization projects in the Middle East.[6] Rapid socioeconomic transformations and manipulated economic policies concentrated wealth among the Westernized

---

[5] See, for example, Ralph H. Turner and Lewis Killian, *Collective Behavior* (Englewood Cliffs, NJ: Prentice-Hall, 1957); William Kornhauser, *The Politics of Mass Society* (Glencoe, IL: The Free Press, 1959); Neil J. Smelser, *Theory of Collective Behavior* (New York: Free Press, 1962).

[6] Susan Waltz, "Islamist Appeal in Tunisia," *Middle East Journal* 40 (Autumn 1986): 651–670; R. Hrair Dekmejian, *Islam in Revolution: Fundamentalism in the Arab World*, 2nd ed. rev. (Syracuse, NY: Syracuse University Press, 1995); Valerie J. Hoffman, "Muslim Fundamentalists: Psychosocial Profiles" in Martin E. Marty and R. Scott Appleby, eds., *Fundamentalisms Comprehended* (Chicago, IL: University of Chicago Press, 1995); Mahmud A. Faksh, *The Future of Islam in the Middle East* (Westport, CT: Praeger, 1997).

elites, state bourgeoisie, and corrupt government officials. Large swathes of the population, in contrast, faced housing shortages, insufficient municipal services and infrastructure, rising prices, declining real wages, and unemployment. The professional classes and lumpen intelligentsia, in particular, faced blocked social mobility and relative deprivation as a result of economic malaise and widespread employment preferences that emphasized *wasta* (connections) above merit.[7] The crises were compounded by the bitter Arab defeat in the 1967 war with Israel, the legacy of colonialism and cultural imperialism, and political repression.[8] According to this perspective, individuals responded by seeking to re-anchor themselves through a religious idiom.

Rather than viewing Islamists as grievance-stricken reactionaries, recent research has reconceptualized Islamic activists as strategic thinkers engaged in cost–benefit calculations. Lisa Anderson, for example, observes that "the closer the movements were to the prospects of sharing power, the more pragmatic they appeared to be."[9] Empirical studies of the Muslim Brotherhood in Jordan illustrate this point: the Brotherhood has demonstrated its willingness to sacrifice ideological ideals for political gains.[10] And movement activists make strategic decisions about organizational resources and relationships,[11]

---

[7] Saad Eddin Ibrahim, "Anatomy of Egypt's Militant Islamic Groups: Methodological Notes and Preliminary Findings," *International Journal of Middle East Studies* 12 (December 1980): 423–453; Hamied N. Ansari, "The Islamic Militants in Egyptian Politics," *International Journal of Middle East Studies* 16 (March 1984): 123–144; Henry Munson, Jr., "The Social Base of Islamic Militancy in Morocco," *Middle East Journal* 40 (Spring 1986): 267–284; Waltz, "Islamist Appeal in Tunisia," 651–670; Hoffman, "Muslim Fundamentalists"; Carrie Rosefsky Wickham, *Mobilizing Islam: Religion, Activism, and Political Change in Egypt* (New York: Columbia University Press, 2002), chapter three.

[8] Yvonne Y. Haddad, "Islamists and the 'Problem of Israel': The 1967 Awakening," *Middle East Journal* 46 (Spring 1992): 266–285; Franois Burgat and William Dowell, *The Islamic Movement in North Africa* (Austin: Center for Middle Eastern Studies at The University of Texas at Austin, 1993); Nikki R. Keddie, "The Revolt of Islam, 1700 to 1993: Comparative Considerations and Relations to Imperialism," *Comparative Studies in Society and History* 36 (July 1994): 463–487; John L. Esposito, *Islam and Politics*, 4th ed. (Syracuse, NY: Syracuse University Press, 1998).

[9] Lisa Anderson, "Fulfilling Prophecies: State Policy and Islamist Radicalism" in John L. Esposito, ed., *Political Islam: Revolution, Radicalism, or Reform?* (Boulder, CO: Lynne Rienner, 1997), 26.

[10] Sabah El-Said, *Between Pragmatism and Ideology: The Muslim Brotherhood in Jordan*, policy paper no. 3 (Washington DC: The Washington Institute for Near East Policy, 1995); Glenn Robinson, "Can Islamists Be Democrats? The Case of Jordan," *Middle East Journal* 51 (Summer 1997): 373–388; Malik Mufti, "Elite Bargains and the Onset of Political Liberalization in Jordan," *Comparative Political Studies* 32 (February 1999): 100–129; Quintan Wiktorowicz, *The Management of Islamic Activism: Salafis, the Muslim Brotherhood and State Power in Jordan* (Albany: The State University of New York Press, 2001).

[11] Christopher Alexander, "Opportunities, Organizations, and Ideas: Islamists and Workers in Tunisia and Algeria," *International Journal of Middle East Studies* 32 (November 2000): 465–490; Wiktorowicz, *The Management of Islamic Activism*; Ziad Munson, "Islamic Mobilization: Social Movement Theory and the Egyptian Muslim Brotherhood," *The Sociological Quarterly* 42 (Fall 2001): 487–510; Diane Singerman, "The Networked World of Islamist Social Movements" in Quintan Wiktorowicz, ed., *Islamic Activism: A Social Movement Theory Approach* (Bloomington: Indiana University Press, 2004), 143–163.

participation in political alliances,[12] responses to economic liberalization,[13] and intra-movement competition.[14]

Even radical movements previously described as unflappable, ideological zealots trapped by rigid adherence to dogma are now analyzed as strategic thinkers. Shaul Mishal and Avraham Sela, for example, argue that Hamas strategically responds to changes in the political context.[15] Prior to the al-Aqsa intifada in 2000, the growing popularity of the Palestinian–Israeli peace process challenged the viability of Hamas. Strict intransigence toward peace was likely to erode support from a population that sought an end to the economic and social hardships of occupation, thereby threatening the organizational survival of Hamas. In response, Hamas tactically adjusted its doctrine to accommodate the possibility of peace by framing it as a temporary pause in the jihad. Mohammed M. Hafez uses an implicit rational-actor model to explain Muslim rebellions in Algeria and Egypt during the 1990s. He contends that violence erupted as a response to "an ill-fated combination of institutional exclusion, on the one hand, and on the other, reactive and indiscriminate repression that threaten[ed] the organizational resources and personal lives of Islamists."[16] To defend themselves against regime repression, the Islamists went underground and formed exclusive organizations, leading to a process of encapsulation and radicalization. Stathis N. Kalyvas views the Islamist-led massacres that plagued Algeria in the 1990s as strategic assaults intended to deter civilian defections "in the context of a particular strategic conjuncture characterized by (a) fragmented and unstable rule over the civilian population, (b) mass civilian defections toward incumbents and (c) escalation of violence."[17] Several scholars have argued that the tactic of suicide bombing is rational in that it helps Islamic (and other) terrorist groups achieve their group goals.[18] And Michael Doran conceptualizes al Qaeda as a rational actor, arguing that "when it comes to matters related to politics and war, al Qaeda maneuvers around its dogmas

---

[12] Benjamin Smith, "Collective Action with and without Islam: Mobilizing the Bazaar in Iran" in Wiktorowicz, ed., *Islamic Activism*, 185–204; Jillian Schwedler, "The Islah Party in Yemen: Political Opportunities and Coalition Building in a Transitional Polity" in Wiktorowicz, ed., *Islamic Activism*, 205–228.

[13] M. Hakan Yavuz, "Opportunity Spaces, Identity, and Islamic Meaning in Turkey" in Wiktorowicz, ed., *Islamic Activism*, 270–288.

[14] Janine Astrid Clark and Jillian Schwedler, "Who Opened the Window? Women's Activism in Islamist Parties," *Comparative Politics* 35 (April 2003): 293–312.

[15] Shaul Mishal and Avraham Sela, *The Palestinian Hamas: Vision, Violence, and Coexistence* (New York: Columbia University Press, 2000).

[16] Mohammed M. Hafez, *Why Muslims Rebel: Repression and Resistance in the Islamic World* (Boulder, CO: Lynne Rienner, 2003), 21–22.

[17] Stathis N. Kalyvas, "Wanton and Senseless? The Logic of Massacres in Algeria," *Rationality and Society* 11 (August 1999): 245.

[18] Ehud Sprinzak, "Rational Fanatics," *Foreign Policy* 120 (September/October): 66–73; Assaf Moghadam, "Palestinian Suicide Terrorism in the Second Intifada: Motivations and Organizational Aspects," *Studies in Conflict and Terrorism* 26 (March/April 2003): 65–92; Pape, "The Strategic Logic of Suicide Terrorism," 343–362.

with alacrity."[19] In this understanding, "al Qaeda's long-term goals are set by its fervent devotion to a radical religious ideology, but in its short-term behavior, it is a rational political actor operating according to the dictates of realpolitik."[20]

Although these studies represent a clear departure from caricatures of zealots narrowly driven by grievances, they tend to focus on the group as the unit of analysis. In other words, tactics and activism are viewed as rational in the sense that they are effective means for promoting group goals. But what about the individuals who actually engage in activism on behalf of the group? Why do individuals within these groups voluntarily agree to engage in personally risky actions? In research on Islamic extremism, there has been surprisingly little research at the *individual* level of analysis from a rational-actor perspective.

In addressing this lacuna, our starting point is the rational-choice emphasis on individual strategies designed to produce personal payoffs. The strategy (or action) is the *best means* for the actor to achieve her most desired outcome or preference, given available information. Rational choice theory does not provide an explanation of preference formation, but rather offers a framework for explaining strategy choices under a given set of stable, ordered preferences. Rationality is evaluated in terms of whether the strategy is intended to obtain an individual's primary preference, not according to whether the preference itself seems reasonable to the outside observer. In other words, we cannot judge an action as irrational simply because we do not agree with the studied actor's preference ordering. As long as the actor committing the action believes that she is seeking to optimize her top preference, the individual is acting in a rational manner.[21]

So how does a rational-choice perspective help us understand the high-cost/risk activism of the activists in al-Muhajiroun and other radical Islamic groups? On the face of it, participation seems to defy the logic of collective action. Islamic radicals are, in essence, offering to produce collective goods that will benefit all Muslims: establishment of the Islamic state, expulsion of the United States from Muslim lands, divine justice, etc. This presents a classic collective action problem: why would individuals choose to contribute to the production of the collective good when they can free-ride off the efforts of others? This question is especially pertinent given the risks and costs associated with radical Islamic activism.

Rational-choice theory points to the use of selective incentives or side payments as means of inducing participation and overcoming the free-rider dilemma. These are benefits that individuals only accrue if they contribute to

[19] Michael Doran, "The Pragmatic Fanaticism of al Qaeda: An Anatomy of Extremism in Middle Eastern Politics," *Political Science Quarterly* 117 (Summer 2002): 178.

[20] Ibid., 182.

[21] Jon Elster, "Introduction," in Jon Elster, ed., *Rational Choice* (New York: New York University Press, 1986), 4.

the collective good.[22] Although early models of rational choice assumed that individuals were primarily interested in maximizing some wealth function,[23] scholars have since expanded their view of human preferences. For example, rational-choice studies of voting behavior have focused on nontangible incentives to explain why an individual chooses to vote regardless of whether her vote is really likely to maximize the probability of producing a particular public policy outcome vis-a-vis the election. Voting is seen as providing nontangible psychological gratification for those who feel as though they are fulfilling their civic duty.[24]

Most radical Islamic groups offer a nontangible *spiritual* incentive to attract participants: participation produces salvation on judgment day and entrance to Paradise in the hereafter. The difference among Islamic groups is over *how the spiritual payoff should be pursued* (that is, strategy). Each proffers its ideology as an "efficient" (and often exclusive) path to salvation, which serves as a heuristic device for indoctrinated activists to weigh the costs and benefits of certain actions and behaviors. A cornerstone of these ideological templates is that individuals must face high risks and costs because God demands this as a condition for the spiritual payoff. In other words, radical Islamists choose to face great personal risks and costs because otherwise they are not pursuing their self-interest. Just as importantly, because individuals are judged as *individuals* on judgment day according to whether they personally followed the commands of God, free-riding jeopardizes salvation.

In this sense, even seemingly altruistic behavior can be understood as rational self-interest. A study of Mother Teresa, for example, argues that:

> While empathetic and self-sacrificial, Mother Teresa's charity ... was not altruistic, that is, motivated strictly by the desire to benefit the recipient without expectation of external reward. "Works of love," she laid down, "are always a means of becoming closer to God" (Mother Teresa 1985: 25).... Closeness to God, not the alleviation of human pain itself, was the preferred religious product. Indeed in Mother Teresa's assessment, poverty, suffering, and death were positive occasions of divine contact and imitation.[25]

This is not to argue that tangible selective incentives are irrelevant. Islamic groups in Egypt, for example, provide material incentives to attract supporters,

---

[22] Mancur Olson, *The Logic of Collective Action* (Cambridge, MA: Harvard University Press, 1965), 133–134.

[23] Gary Becker, "The Economic Approach to Human Behavior" in Jon Elster, ed., *Rational Choice*, 109.

[24] Brian Barry, *Sociologists, Economists, and Democracy* (New York: Macmillan, 1978); William Riker and Peter Ordeshook, "A Theory of the Calculus of Voting," *American Political Science Review* 62 (March 1968): 25–42; William Riker and Peter Ordeshook, *Introduction to Positive Political Theory* (Englewood Cliffs, NJ: Prentice Hall, 1973).

[25] Susan Kwilecki and Loretta S. Wilson, "Was Mother Teresa Maximizing Her Utility? An Idiographic Application of Rational Choice Theory," *Journal for the Scientific Study of Religion* 37 (June 1998): 211.

including jobs, health services, education, day care, and financial support.[26] In Jordan, the Muslim Brotherhood's charity network provides patronage employment and selective access to goods and services.[27] Both Hamas and Hezbollah provide social services and basic goods and services to communities and supporters. And there is evidence that at least some (although most likely a small minority) of those who joined the Armed Islamic Group in Algeria did so to obtain the economic benefits of insurgency, such as smuggling.[28] The point is not to dismiss these material payoffs, but rather to highlight the importance of nontangible incentives as well. This is particularly important when considering radical Islamic groups that offer few tangible rewards but demand risky activities.

We argue that in the case of al-Muhajiroun, the perceived spiritual payoffs outweighed the risks and costs associated with activism for those who chose to participate. Indoctrinated individuals viewed activism and even risk itself as means to achieve salvation and entrance into Paradise. Guided by the movement ideology, participants viewed suffering and effort as a testament to the certitude of belief (assurance that they would achieve the spiritual payoffs). From this perspective, the strategy of high cost/risk is strategically rational.

A Case Study: Al-Muhajiroun

Omar Bakri Mohammed (known as OBM) launched al-Muhajiroun (AM) in the UK in 1996 after leaving Hizb uh-Tahrir.[29] It subsequently became the most visible radical Islamic movement in the country and spread throughout the UK in a number of different cities and neighborhoods. AM also established branches in a variety of other countries, including Lebanon, Ireland, the United States, and Pakistan (this branch eventually claimed independence from the overall al-Muhajiroun movement), which were connected through cyberspace meetings, lectures, lessons, and public events.

After September 11, AM became a central focus in debates about political expression and national security in the UK because of its support for the use of violence. A core tenet of the movement was the use of military coups to establish Islamic states wherever there are Muslims, including Britain. It also condoned the use of violence against Western militaries operating in Muslim countries. AM activists encouraged Britons to fight for the Taliban against American-led forces in Afghanistan,[30] and AM issued a statement supporting

---

[26] Denis J. Sullivan, *Private Voluntary Organizations in Egypt: Islamic Development, Private Initiative, and State Control* (Gainesville: University of Florida Press, 1994); Wickham, *Mobilizing Islam*.

[27] Wiktorowicz, *The Management of Islamic Activism*, 83–110.

[28] Luis Martinez, *The Algerian Civil War* (New York: Columbia University Press, 2000).

[29] AM was originally formed in Saudi Arabia as a "cover" for Hizb uh-Tahrir activities during the 1980s, but OBM was forced to flee the country and settled in the UK.

[30] *The Observer*, 28 October 2001; *The Associated Press*, 7 January 2002; *Agence France Presse*, 4 December 2002.

jihad against coalition forces in Iraq in 2003.[31] OBM and leaders in AM issued other controversial statements as well, including *fatwas* (jurisprudential opinions) condoning attacks against John Major and Tony Blair if they set foot in a Muslim country and a statement supporting the 1998 U.S. embassy bombings in Africa.[32]

Perhaps the most contentious action came a year after September 11 when AM sponsored a conference titled "A Towering Day in History" at the Finsbury Park Mosque, reflecting upon the consequences of the attacks and the aftermath for Muslims. The advertising for the conference was framed in such a way that it implied a "celebratory tone," and the press billed it as an event commemorating the triumph of September 11, which did not sit well with the public.[33] Eight months later, reports indicated a possible connection between al-Muhajiroun and the British suicide bombers who killed three Israelis during an attack on Mike's Place, a bar in Tel Aviv.[34] This was followed by advertisement for a second September 11 event titled "The Magnificent 19" (referring to the nineteen hijackers), which was prevented from being held.

In the UK, there were 160 "formal members" known as *hizbis* (partisans). The small number reflects a selective induction process: individuals only became members after the leadership was convinced that they had fully internalized the movement ideology. As OBM explained, a member of the movement "is an identical copy of the way I think, and he has my adopted culture [ideology], and he teaches it to the people."[35] These activists were qualified to develop and teach others: they were authorized to give lessons and to speak to the public on behalf of the movement. As "life cells," formal members were often sent to other countries to establish branches, indicating OBM's confidence in their ideological internalization.

There were also 700 "students," who took weekly lessons taught by OBM and the formal members. Although these students were not formal members, the vast majority participated in the array of movement activities and took on risk and cost on behalf of the cause. Some even held leadership positions. In the U.S. branch of the movement in the 1990s, for example, the al-Muhajiroun's spokesperson was not actually a formal member. He did not attend the formation meeting that established the branch in 1996, and lived in Springfield,

---

[31] Al-Muhajiroun, "Fight the Invaders vs. Stop the War," 20 March 2003.

[32] These statements were widely covered in the press and confirmed in the first author's interviews with Omar Bakri in 2002.

[33] See, for example, "Radical Muslim Clerics to Meet on Sept. 11 to Celebrate Anniversary of Attacks," *The Associated Press*, 7 September 2002; "London Rally to 'Celebrate' Terror Attacks," *Sunday Times*, 8 September 2002; "Fanatics to Meet to 'Celebrate' Twin Towers Terror Attacks," *Sunday Mirror*, 8 September 2002.

[34] "British Urged to Curb Anti-Semitic Incitement," *The Times*, 14 May 2003. Al-Muhajiroun responded to the reports by denying the connection ("Blatant Lies from the Sunday Times," al-Muhajiroun Press Release, 4 May 2003).

[35] First author's interview with Omar Bakri Mohammed, London, December 2002.

Missouri, far away from the New York City branch headquarters and the movement leadership.[36] To confuse matters further, many of the students referred to themselves as "members," something the formal members encouraged to make students feel important.[37] To make some distinctions, in this essay we use the term "activist" to refer to both formal members as well as committed students who participated in risky activism. "Member" refers only to those committed activists who actually went through the formal membership process (the *hizbis*).

At the periphery of the movement, there were thousands of "contacts," potential participants who attended a handful of lessons and events.[38] These contacts were, in effect, sampling al-Muhajiroun's activities to see whether they wanted to become more deeply involved. Although newspapers erroneously reported an estimated 7,000 al-Muhajiroun "members," this number probably accurately represented the number of contacts. Alone, however, the number tells us very little, inasmuch as it is impossible to determine the level of commitment within this aggregate. Some contacts may have come to a single public event. Others may have indulged in deeper religious sampling and may have progressed toward becoming actual students.

Participation in the high-profile and contentious activism of the movement carried a number of costs and risks for activists, particularly in the post-September 11 period. There were enormous commitments of time and energy, including religious training, outreach projects, and public demonstrations. Activists sacrificed relationships with former friends, family, and the mainstream Muslim community. And they were subject to an assortment of laws related to terrorism, treason, public order, and inciting religious and racial hatred. Arrests were common, and activists were conscious that their participation risked legal consequences. At first glance, it appears that they were engaged in irrational behavior that threatened self-interest.

Costs for the Commited Activist

Gregory L. Wiltfang and Doug McAdam argue that in deciding whether to participate in activism, individuals are influenced by a subjective assessment of costs and risks.[39] *Risks* are threats to an individual's well-being, such as threats to employment or physical safety. *Costs* are factors associated with the demands of participation that require the sacrifice of other commitments or interests. According to rational-actor models, we expect that individuals are unlikely to participate in high-risk, high-cost activism unless there is an off-

---

[36] First author's interview with this activist by phone, April 2003.

[37] First author's interviews with various activists, UK, March, June, and December 2002.

[38] First author's interview with Omar Bakri Mohammed, December 2002.

[39] Gregory L. Wiltfang and Doug McAdam, "The Costs and Risks of Social Activism: A Study of Sanctuary Movement Activism," *Social Forces* 69 (June 1991): 987–1010.

setting payoff. From this perspective, the behavior of AM activists appears irrational at first glance, given the dangers and sacrifices derived from belonging to the movement.

Perhaps one of the most important indicators of high *cost* is the time commitment, as demonstrated by the dizzying array of weekly activities. Although these activities were only required for formal members, committed students participated in them as well, thus incurring the general time costs. So although the activities detailed below are outlined in terms of formal-member requirements, they were attended by activists in general.

Members were required to attend a two-hour study session held by the local *halaqah* (circle) every week, unless they were excused because of traveling needs, sickness of a family member, an emergency, or permission of the leader.[40] These circles were intensive, member-only religious lessons that revolved around the movement ideology, and students had to spend time preparing. Given the intensity of these sessions, a lack of preparation incurred the ire of OBM and social pressure from other participants, thereby discouraging consistent indolence.[41] The overall tone at these lessons was captured in the movement bylaws: "Each member must understand that the Halaqah is a serious discussion and not a chat."[42] Although the *halaqah* sessions were only scheduled for two hours, many ran much longer. The first author attended a Thursday session at the movement's headquarters that lasted from 9:00 p.m. until 1:30 a.m. Interviews with participants indicated that this particular lesson typically ran until 5:00 a.m.

Members were required to host at least one public study circle, which was advertised at the local mosque and in the movement newsletter; and there were numerous AM-sponsored public talks, *tafsirs* (explanations of Qur'anic verses), and community events, which were intended to draw interest from potential recruits.[43] Although some of these activities were not "required," all those interviewed stated that they tried to go to as many as possible, in some instances traveling with OBM throughout the country (usually during the evenings). The first author's own participation at public talks and community events in London, Slough, and Luton indicated that this was indeed the case.

Every Saturday, members were required to set up a *da'wa* (propagation) stall in their local community from 12:00 p.m. until 5:00 p.m. In reality, these tended to start a bit later (usually a half hour or an hour late) but generally lasted at least four hours. They were held outside local tube stops, public libraries, municipal buildings, and other public locales. The stalls reflected an activist *da'wa*, which centered on raising public awareness about the plight of Muslims and responsibilities in defending the global *umma* (Muslim com-

---

[40] Al-Muhajiroun, *The Administration of al-Muhajiroun*, no date.
[41] This pressure was observed by the first author at a movement-only lesson in June 2002.
[42] Al-Muhajiroun, *Administration*.
[43] Ibid.

munity). Activists put up posters, chanted slogans, shouted through loud-speakers, and interacted with observers and passing pedestrians. In effect, these were small protest rallies, usually attended by about ten to twenty local activists.

Members also participated in weekly demonstrations that lasted approximately two hours. The particular topic of the protests varied from week to week, depending upon the "pressing issue" of the day, and they could be volatile events. At a rally outside the Pakistani embassy, protesters screamed "Musharaf, we are coming to kill you!" and chanted slogans, such as "Musharaf watch your back, Bin Laden coming back."[44] Other examples include demonstrations against the governments of Egypt, India, and Qatar. There were also a number of other required functions, including a monthly meeting of all members and special events (such as during Ramadan). In addition, the movement encouraged members to commit themselves to independent activities and community outreach (for example, following politics and news, studying the ideas of other movements, and promoting the movement ideology through interactions at work, school, and the mosque). This was based on movement principles about the necessity of action and outreach;[45] and interviews indicated that movement members were dedicated to more than the bare minimum and voluntarily promoted the movement ideology in every aspect of their lives. One must also take into account routine Muslim rituals (prayer, fasting during Ramadan, etc.) and social interactions with other members, which often involved religious discussion, movement planning, and solidarity building. Considering that most members had jobs or were in school, this was an enormous sacrifice of time.

There was a set of disciplinary measures that provided sanctions for members who did not attend the required activities.[46] For example, if on three separate occasions within a single year a member failed to attend the *halaqah* or monthly gatherings or refused to distribute movement materials or attend movement activities (without a good excuse), the disciplinary proceedings called for the "complete expulsion from all Halaqah and closed monthlies and exclusion from all Administrative procedures of Al-Muhajiroun (including informing him/her about Al-Muhajiroun activities) for a period specified by the Mu'tamad [the leader responsible for the country branch of the movement]."[47] In some cases, an individual might have legitimately believed he or she had a valid excuse. If the leadership did not agree, however, the individual was temporarily excluded from all *halaqahs* and closed monthlies for a minimum period of one month. In this case, the leader could also levy a modest fine before readmitting the offender.[48]

[44] This event was tape-recorded by the first author.
[45] Al-Muhajiroun, *Administration*.
[46] Ibid.; first author's interviews with leaders and other members, 2002.
[47] Al-Muhajiroun, *Administration*.
[48] Ibid.

These sanctions were for *formal* members alone; and although this implies the importance of sanctions in motivating action, as Mancur Olson argues for small group dynamics, the fact that activists who were *not* formal members participated in many of the risky and costly activities indicates that there must have been some other incentive.

To maintain the flexibility necessary for the frenetic schedule of movement activities, some activists chose less-lucrative employment opportunities (part-time jobs, for example), thus incurring a material cost. Members were also required to pay dues and donate a portion of their salary to the movement, because AM was self-funded.[49] The donation was according to the individual's ability to pay (it generally seemed to follow the calculations used for Islamic charity).

Time commitments and the ideological views of the movement frequently produced social costs, the most important of which was related to family pressures. Almost uniformly, respondents in this study noted their parents' opposition to activism. Parents did not object to religious education per se, but they believed in a personal, apolitical Islam and set different goals, such as getting *halal* (religiously permitted) food in schools.[50] Some concerned parents contacted Zaki Badawi, founder of the Muslim Council of Britain, and asked him to intervene after discovering their children's involvement.[51] This kind of family opposition created social pressure not to participate.

Nonetheless, activists defied their parents and participated. As one respondent put it, "They warn you and say don't go with these people, but then they see you are firm and what can they do?"[52] A Somali member reiterated this sentiment: "If the boys are convinced, the parents can't do much. They can tell them not to go, but they can't stop it."[53]

One rather common way that activists attempted to avoid familial friction was by hiding their involvement.[54] This, however, did not necessarily eliminate the social cost, because the ideology required propagation, leading to heated debates with family members. There is little evidence that traumatic altercations shattered families or created irreconcilable differences, but they certainly

---

[49] In an effort to maintain its independence, **AM** relies solely on its membership for funding and has, at least according to one member, turned down some sizable donations, including one from the Iranian government.

[50] For the typical concerns of Muslims in the UK, see Tariq Modood, "The Place of Muslims in British Secular Multiculturalism" in Nezar Al Sayyad and Manuel Castells, eds., *Muslim Europe or Euro-Islam: Politics, Culture, and Citizenship in the Age of Globalization* (Lanham, MD: Lexington Books, 2002).

[51] First author's conversation with Zaki Badawi, London, June 2002.

[52] First author's interview with Hassan, London, June 2002. Note: for rank-and-file members, pseudonyms or other anonymous indicators are used to protect the privacy of respondents.

[53] First author's interview with Somali member, London, June 2002.

[54] First author's interviews with Somali member, Kamal, and Mohammed (movement leader), London, June 2002.

produced tensions. One joiner recalled that because his father "stands with Union Jack," they used to have rather heated discussions.[55] Another recounted a story in which he shocked his extended family as they discussed the stand-off between Pakistan and India in 2002 by boldly declaring his support for nuclear war. This, he argued, was a religious obligation and for the sake of Islam. His father was a staunch supporter of Britain, and this created a great deal of consternation.[56] These types of interactions indicate that although parental ignorance about participation may have softened family pressure, it was unlikely to eliminate the cost altogether.

RISKY ACTIVISM

All public displays of activism entail some risk, whether it is the possibility (even if remote) that a rally will degenerate into chaos or (in more extreme cases) result in death. One common measure of risk in studies of protest is the perceived possibility of arrest.[57] By this measure, the personal risk for those involved in AM was high. Large numbers of movement activists were arrested, and each public event was seen as a risky venture in which police intervention and arrest (or at least threats of arrest) were possible. The risks became accentuated in the post-September 11 period because al-Muhajiroun was often accused of supporting terrorism.

Arrests (or threats of arrest) frequently occurred at the *da'wa* stalls. It was not the act of protesting itself that raised risk but rather the presentation of grievances. Activists used "moral shock"[58] to evoke emotional responses and elicit sympathy for the cause, whether it was the plight of Iraqis, the Israeli occupation of Palestinian territories, or Indian repression in Kashmir. Pictures are more effective in generating visceral responses from observers, so AM activists used shocking pictures of mutilated and decapitated bodies. Pictures of malnourished or mutilated children were common because they evoked the most consistent emotional response, regardless of whether observers were Muslim. These pictures, more than anything else, drew the ire of police, who were frequently in attendance at the stall or were called in by local business owners and concerned citizens. Altercations with police over whether the pictures were "free speech" often led to arrests.

This was confirmed by observations at a *da'wa* stall outside a public library in London. About ten activists gathered around a display table and an easel adorned with grotesque pictures of the "oppressed": mutilated bodies

---

[55] First author's interview with Rajib, Slough, June 2002.

[56] First author's interview with Khalid, London, June 2002.

[57] See, for example, Wilftang and McAdam, "The Costs and Risks of Social Activism," 987–1010.

[58] James M. Jasper and Jane Poulsen, "Recruiting Strangers and Friends: Moral Shocks and Social Networks in Animal Rights and Anti-Nuclear Protests," *Social Problems* 42 (November 1995): 493–512; James M. Jasper, *The Art of Moral Protest: Culture, Biography, and Creativity in Social Movements* (Chicago, IL: University of Chicago Press, 1997).

from the alleged Israeli "Jenin massacres" (the UN did not find any evidence to support the accusations).[59] The pictures, to say the least, were shocking images—an old man with half his face missing, children with massive injuries, and bodies with organs exposed through the skin. The graphic nature of the pictures prompted a flood of calls to the police,[60] and six officers responded and arrived at the stall about an hour after it opened. The protesters were told that they could continue their message verbally and use pictures of bombed buildings, but that they had to remove the pictures of the mutilations. A heated argument ensued. The demonstrators argued that they were merely showing "the truth" (facts that the Western media refused to publish) so that people would understand what was happening to Muslims worldwide. The police retorted that the pictures were offensive and that because they were being displayed in a public place, bystanders (including children) had no choice about exposure. The argument was impassioned, and the police threatened arrest. In this particular case, the pictures were taken down. AM activists cited the confrontation as another example of Western repression against Muslims. Interviews with various members of AM, a police officer at the scene, and eight participants at the stall indicated that this kind of altercation was common. Demonstrators were most frequently arrested under the Public Order Act, which provided wide latitude for police officers at the scene to determine whether it represented a public disturbance warranting arrest.[61]

There are other instances in which activists faced risk because of the content of the message. In one example, two members were arrested under the Public Order Act at a protest against homosexuals, because of a leaflet entitled "Gay Today, Pedophile Tomorrow?" They were both convicted and fined £160.[62] Another activist was arrested during a verbal tirade against Israel.[63] In a famous case, Iftikhar Ali, a movement leader, was arrested after distributing leaflets quoting passages from the Qur'an in a context that authorities interpreted as a threat against the Jewish community. He was found guilty of inciting racial hatred (Jews are considered an ethnic group under UK law) and sentenced to a £3,000 fine, a £1,500 reimbursement cost, and 200 hours of community service.[64] Several members lost employment as a result of their activism (religious discrimination is not currently covered by British law). And there was the ever-present risk of arrest under the new terrorism laws.

[59] For more on the Israeli incursion into Jenin, see Human Rights Watch Report, "Jenin: IDF Military Operations," May 2002, accessed at http://www.hrw.org/reports/2002/israel3/, 18 April 2006.

[60] First author's interview with the lead police officer at the scene, London, June 2002.

[61] Ibid.; first author's interviews with AM members, London, 2002.

[62] First author's interview with one of the arrested activists, London, June 2002.

[63] First author's interview with this activist, London, June 2002.

[64] See http://news.bbc.co.uk/2/hi/uk_news/england/1966839.stm, accessed 18 April 2006.

Anjem Choudary, the leader of the UK branch of AM, aptly summarized the risks and costs of participation:

> Being part of al-Muhajiroun is not really the most prestigious thing. People don't become a part and say "mashallah" [what God has willed, indicating a good omen] and go around saying I am a member of al-Muhajiroun because obviously we get attacked by the government and our members are arrested regularly at demonstrations and at stalls because they speak out openly and publicly about what they believe. They might get arrested because they talk about homosexuality or they might think he is a homophobe or think he is racist and anti-Semitic because he is talking about Palestine. We have had a number of prosecutions. You met Iftikhar Ali. He is the first person in this country to be arrested for incitement to religious hatred for quoting a verse from the text [Qur'an] which was considered to be racist. This has never happened before. It is a landmark decision and he is a member of our organization. If they join and stay that is because they believe in the cause, they believe in the struggle. We ask our members to interact with the culture and to go out regularly on talks and demonstrations, and they will attend weekly and monthly gatherings, and a fair amount of their time will be taken up. And obviously they will be asked to contribute financially as well, because we don't receive any finances from the government. We contribute ourselves.[65]

In addition to the costs and risks of activism, there is an important question as to whether there would be a payoff in which the movement achieved its goals. Although AM may have affected the political views of some Muslims, its prospects for success in the UK were minimal, given that a primary stated goal was the establishment of an Islamic state in Britain. Even OBM recognized the futility: "Practically, it is not going to happen except in a Muslim country."[66]

The sense that activism was against individual self-interest is deepened by the availability of other fundamentalist groups whose activities entailed fewer risks (and lower costs, in some cases), including Hizb uh-Tahrir, Jama'a Tabligh, and various reformist Salafi groups, such as those at the Brixton Mosque and Jam'iat Ihyaa' Minhaaj al-Sunnah. In fact, AM offered very few unique selective incentives. For example, solidary incentives derived from group identity, social interactions, and religious activities were offered by other fundamentalist groups, including moderate movements. There were no material incentives, in the sense of magazines or concrete outputs available only to formal members. And other movements and groups offered similar purposive incentives because of their fervent religious missions. According to AM members themselves, all of the fundamentalist movements (moderate and radical, including AM) shared about 95 percent of the same religious precepts. So why take on the costs and risks? Without making a tautological argument (and implying that somehow radicals are deviants and psychologically disturbed

---

[65] First author's interview with Anjem Choudary, by phone, June 2002.
[66] First author's interview with OBM, London, June 2002.

because they get a psychological payoff from engaging in risky behavior), the observer is left with the initial impression that this behavior violated the principle of self-interest and thus reflects the irrationality of zealotry.

SPIRITUAL INCENTIVES AND HIGH-COST/RISK ACTIVISM

To make sense of why individuals would still participate in such activism, regardless of high costs/risks and the prospects for free-riding, one must address activist views of incentives and strategic assessments of utility. These were rooted in the movement ideology, which offered guidelines about what activists must do to achieve salvation. Deviations from the ideological proscriptions were interpreted as threats to an individual's utility maximization and desire to be saved on judgment day.

The cornerstone of AM's ideology was its particular understanding of *tawhid*—the oneness of God. *Tawhid* begins with the *shahada*, or testimony of faith that signals a conversion to Islam: "I testify that there is no God except Allah and that Mohammed is His messenger." It defines God as the only true lord and sovereign of the universe worthy of worship. The Qur'an and *hadiths* (recorded traditions of the Prophet) are filled with dire warnings about the consequences for those who violate *tawhid* by ascribing partners to God (*shirk*) (in other words, polytheism):

> Lo! Whoso ascribeth partners unto Him, for him Allah has forbidden Paradise. His abode is in the Fire. For evil-doers there will be no helpers (Qur'an 5:72).
> Lo! Allah forgiveth not that a partner be ascribed Unto Him. He forgiveth (all) save that to who He will. Whoso ascribeth partners to Allah, he hath indeed invented a tremendous sin (Qur'an 4:48).

Although all Muslims accept the general principle of *tawhid*, there are differences over its precise meaning and application. Many Islamic fundamentalists, for example, reject traditional Sufi practices, such as praying at the tombs of saints, as examples of *shirk*. Even within the Islamic fundamentalist community there are differences. Some Islamic activists, for example, accept the possibility of working through democratic institutions, whereas others view adherence to man-made law as egregious *shirk*. What constitutes *shirk* is a matter of contention among Muslims.

For al-Muhajiroun activists, every action, decision, and behavior was seen as an act of worship if it was in accordance with divine law. Any deviation from the straight path of Islam, in contrast, represented a violation of *tawhid*. Those who adhered to *tawhid* gained entrance to Paradise; those who engaged in *shirk* would suffer the hellfires:

> Tawheed prevents man from eternally remaining in the Hellfire. The Prophet Mohammed (SAW) stated in an authentic report: Whoever dies and has so much as a mustard seed of faith in his heart shall enter al-Jannah [the garden of Paradise]. Faith here signifies a correct belief in Allah and His Messenger

Mohammed (SAW) and all that they instructed, commanded and prohibited for mankind."[67]

The calculus for individuals is clear: follow the divine rules and receive a spiritual payoff; remain deviant and suffer eternal consequences. But what are the divine rules and how does an individual Muslim identify proper adherence? Islamic movements offer religious interpretations represented in ideologies as guidelines to answer this question. These ideologies are, in essence, outlines of strategies for obtaining the spiritual payoff—what individuals must do to ensure salvation.

All Islamic fundamentalist groups base their proffered strategies on the model of the Prophet Mohammed—the Muslim exemplar whose path (*Sunna*) is considered the perfection of Islam in practice. There are divergences, however, over the specifics of the prophetic paradigm and its application in the contemporary context. Each group believes it is following the proper model and interpretation, and these differences matter in terms of the potential for salvation. The Prophet predicted that the Muslim community would fracture into sects after his death and warned his followers to remain focused on his example and the Qur'an for guidance: "I am leaving you two things and you will never go astray as long as you cling to them. They are the Book of Allah and my Sunnah."[68] Many fundamentalist groups believe that there is one correct understanding of the straight path of Islam; ipso facto, all others are deviations and will not receive divine reward. This thinking is based upon authentic *hadiths*, such as "And this Ummah will divide into seventy-three sects all of which except one will go to Hell and they are those who are upon what I and my Companions are upon."[69] Many groups consider themselves to be this "saved sect" (*firqa al-najiyya*) and therefore argue that their adherents will be saved on judgment day.

Al-Muhajiroun's particular interpretation of the model and its relevance for salvation was aptly captured by Omar Bakri Mohammed:

> The [prophetic] methodology is the only way. If I follow it, I remove the sin from my neck. The only way of accepting His command [God] is by following the methodology of the messenger of the Prophet Mohammed. So the Prophet he cultured society; he exposed man made law in society (commanding good and forbidding evil); and he sought support from those sincere [Muslims in the army] who accept Islam from him and give him power from the army. This is the only way we can remove the sin from our neck.[70]

OBM and other AM activists concluded that the only way for individuals to ensure personal salvation was to engage in these activities so as to "remove the

---

[67] Omar Bakri Mohammed, *Kitab ul-Imaan*, movement training manual, n.d., 17.

[68] As quoted in Jam'iat Ihyaa' Minhaaj Al-Sunnah, *A Brief Introduction to the Salafi Da'wah* (Ipswich, UK: Jam'iat Minhaaj Al-Sunnah, 1993), 5.

[69] Ibid., 3.

[70] First author's interview with Omar Bakri Mohammed, December 2002.

sin" from their necks. Thus, regardless of the risks and costs, individuals had to promote a proper understanding of Islam (a radical interpretation that included support for *jihad* against the United States, Russia, Israel, and others); publicly denounce un-Islamic behavior (including democracy) through overt activism; and work to establish the Caliphate (Islamic state) by means of a military coup (even in the UK).

Al-Muhajiroun argued that because the Prophet accomplished these duties by working with a group, individual Muslims must do likewise to "remove the sin" from their necks and receive a payoff in the hereafter. The AM ideology distinguished between divine duties that can be fulfilled as an individual and those that can only be fulfilled by working with other Muslims. The central argument is that the Prophet and his companions worked as individuals when they addressed *individuals*, but formed collectivities when addressing society. The various divine duties of activism, in particular, were fulfilled by working as groups. For AM, this was reflected in Qur'an 3:104: "Let there rise from among you group(s) calling society to Islam, commanding society to do what Allah orders and to refrain from what He forbids and these (group(s)) are the ones who are successful" (AM translation).

The emergence of a group, however, is not enough to remove sin. Those who fail to participate remain sinful and thus are not part of the saved sect. More importantly for a rational-choice perspective, group membership or belonging alone does not produce the desired spiritual payoff. The group is merely a vehicle for fulfilling individual obligations, so individuals still must engage in the methodology and fulfill duties to remove the sin from their necks. As Omar Bakri explained:

> If any one of them or some of them did a duty or engaged in any duty e.g. political struggle in any part of the world, it does not mean that all of them are rewarded for it, nor does it mean that all the members are fulfilling their duties, rather those who did it alone will be rewarded and will remove the sin from their necks whereas the others remain sinful if they did not fulfill their duties.[71]

This is because, as Omar Bakri argued, "Allah (swt) will account as individuals [on Judgment Day], not as an entity."[72] Where salvation on judgment day is a concern, this ideological precept essentially undermined the potential for free-riding within the group. Each individual had to engage in activism within the group, because he or she would not benefit from the work of others. Only active participants received the payoff. Anjem Choudary, the UK leader of al-Muhajiroun, nicely summarized the spiritual incentive for joining the movement: "The only benefit that they [the activists] have, which is a great benefit unto itself, is that they fulfill a duty and ultimately will be rewarded in the hereafter. We don't pretend they are going to get anything apart from that."[73]

[71] Omar Bakri Mohammed, Questions and Answers, "Is the group an entity?" n.d.
[72] Ibid.
[73] First author's interview with Anjem Choudary.

A refusal to replicate the model in terms of the method (working with a group) or the specific duties jeopardized an individual's status in the hereafter. In effect, such a refusal was a rejection of *tawhid* and thus evidence of apostasy.[74]

Within the mechanism of the group, individuals had to fulfill three primary divine duties: educate Muslims about proper Islam (i.e., the movement ideology), including exhortations to *jihad*; actively command good and prevent evil through overt (and controversial) activism; and struggle to establish an Islamic state through a military coup. First, individuals had to engage in *tarbiya* (culturing society in proper Islamic belief and behavior) and *da'wa* (propagation). For al-Muhajiroun, this necessitated lessons and activities to teach people about their divine duties and responsibilities as Muslims, according to movement precepts. An important component of this was promoting support for *jihad* against infidels in Muslim lands as an individual Muslim obligation: "Any aggression against any Muslim property or land by any Kuffar [unbelievers] or non-Muslim forces whether American, British or Jews of Israel makes Jihad (i.e. fighting) against them an obligation upon all Muslims."[75] This mandated armed struggles against the Russians in Chechnya; the United States in Afghanistan, Iraq, and Saudi Arabia; India in Kashmir; Israel (both in the occupied territories and the state of Israel, which AM considered Muslim territory); and the United Nations (specifically in Iraq).[76]

Because *tawhid* demands the full application of divine law, al-Muhajiroun argued that all Muslims are obligated to fulfill the responsibility of *jihad* or risk jeopardizing salvation. Omar Bakri was explicit about this utility calculation at a conference titled "Terrorism and Osama Bin Laden" held in East London in 2000: "You all have an obligation to support the jihad. Or you will be punished on the Day of Judgment! You will get a reward for fighting. You must send your children to jihad."[77] Obviously, calling for such action amounted to support for terrorism and, in certain instances, even implied sedition when the call to *jihad* involved British interests, but the risks were acceptable for those who calculated costs and benefits in terms of the hereafter.

To save themselves and fulfill their duties toward *jihad*, AM activists practiced what they preached by providing not only verbal support but financial and physical assistance as well. AM openly raised money for *jihads* throughout the Muslim world, especially for Chechen rebels, *jihadis* in Kashmir, and *Hamas* in the Palestinian territories. Changes in anti-terrorism laws, however, made this fundraising illegal. Interviews with Omar Bakri indicate that financial sup-

---

[74] Under many understandings of Islamic law, the ultimate sanction for an individual convicted of apostasy is death, although this is rarely enforced in practice.

[75] Shari'ah Court of the UK (an al-Muhajiroun organization headed by Omar Bakri), "Fatwa against the Illegitimate State of Israel," n.d.

[76] See, for example, Shari'ah Court of the UK, Case No. Russia / F41, Fatwa Concerning the Russian Aggression, n.d.; Shari'ah Court of the UK, Fatwa on Jihad against the Illegitimate State of Israel; al-Muhajiroun Press Release, "The United Nations—A Legitimate Target?" 25 August 2003.

[77] Aaron Klein, "My Weekend with the Enemy," *The Jerusalem Post*, 30 May 2000.

port for the struggles might still have occurred through charity front organizations, which raised money for general "charitable" purposes. A number of activists actually went to fight in the *jihads*, not as representatives of al-Muhajiroun as an organization but as individuals fulfilling their personal duty to God "to support their Muslim brothers and sisters."[78]

The second divine duty fulfilled through the group was the command to promote virtue and prevent vice (*al-amr bi'l-ma-ruf wa'l-nahy 'an al-munkar*). Activism to fulfill this obligation was a required duty that must be fulfilled to follow *tawhid* and remain a Muslim. The movement cited the following *hadith*: "There is no prophet that Allah sent before me but he had supporters and companions who did what he said and obeyed his commands. After them there are many successors and they will say what they don't do and do what Allah forbids. Whoever fights them with his hand is a believer, whoever fights them with his tongue is a believer, whoever fights them with his heart is a believer and if you do nothing you can't claim you are a Muslim."[79] The punishment for those who failed to rise is the hellfires. The true believers and activists would receive eternal reward.

The third divine duty was to work for the reestablishment of the Caliphate (Islamic state). Once again, this duty was posited in terms of individual interest in removing sin to ensure personal salvation. Al-Muhajiroun argued that initially, after the collapse of the Caliphate in 1924, its reestablishment was a collective duty (*fard kifaya*), meaning an obligation that can be fulfilled by some on behalf of the *umma*. However, after a period of time without an Islamic state, "working to establish the Khilafah [Caliphate] [becomes] Fard [a divine duty] upon all Muslims (i.e., Fard Kifayah Muhattam) or a sufficient duty binding immediately without a time limit upon all Muslims and those who engage in it remove the sin and the burden on their necks until they accomplish the task. Whereas those who do not engage in working to establish the Khilafah nowadays are sinful [except for those exempted in sharia]."[80]

For AM, the proper method for establishing the Islamic state was a military coup. As a result, activists contacted members of the military in an attempt to foment a military rebellion that would seize power and establish the Caliphate. Because the religious sources did not specify a particular locale for the Islamic state, Muslims were obligated to work to establish it wherever they lived, including the UK.

In terms of individual calculations, it is irrelevant whether the prospects were likely to succeed. Omar Bakri readily admitted that the establishment of an Islamic state in the UK was highly unlikely. But success did not matter, because individuals are judged on the basis of whether they *worked* to establish

---

[78] Al-Muhajiroun press release, November 5, 2001.

[79] Omar Bakri Mohammed, *Jihad: The Method for the Khilafah?* (London: MNA Publications, n.d.), 19.

[80] Omar Bakri Mohammed, Questions and Answers, "Are we obligated to work for the Khilafah?" n.d.

the Caliphate. In other words, salvation does not hinge upon whether activists actually succeeded in reaching stated movement goals; they are judged according to whether they worked toward these objectives. The duty is the effort and not the outcome of collective action. The Qur'an emphasizes that divine reward and punishment are meted out according to whether individuals "go forth in the cause of Islam" (that is, exert effort):

> O ye who believe! What is the matter with you, that, when ye are asked to go forth in the cause of Allah, ye cling heavily to the earth? Do ye prefer the life of this world to the Hereafter? But little is the comfort of this life, as compared with the Hereafter. Unless ye go forth, He will punish you with a grievous penalty, and put others in your place; but Him ye would not harm in the least. For Allah hath power over all things (Qur'an 9:38–39).

When asked about whether a demonstration in front of the Indian embassy attracted much attention and support, Anjem Choudary could thus dismiss the importance of a large showing and media coverage as relatively irrelevant, because he "had fulfilled [his] duty to command good and forbid evil."[81]

Rational-choice studies of rebellion have argued that individuals assess the prospects for success when deciding whether to participate;[82] but in the case of radical Islam, this outcome may be less important. At the individual level, the primary objective is not the establishment of an Islamic state or the success of a demonstration. These are only ways of fulfilling obligations to God, which, in turn, is the only way to achieve salvation. In terms of personal calculations, the very act of participation in itself produces the payoff in the hereafter.

Not only is high-cost/risk activism necessary to produce the desired outcome, but the act of suffering itself is viewed as a divine signal that the activist is on the right path and will achieve salvation as part of the saved sect. The Prophet initially suffered at the hands of the Quraysh (the dominant tribe in Mecca), yet continued to fulfill his obligations to God. AM activists emphasized that regardless of the difficulties, true believers speak out:

> The Prophet [Mohammed] and all the Anbiyya [Prophets], all the Sahabas [Companions], they got tortured, they struggled, they went through pain. For what? Was it because they testified? It was because they implemented in action. The Lord said "Why do you say something that you do not do, you do not act upon?" When we see the Prophet Mohammed, and the Anbiyya, and the Sahabas, they struggled, they did da'wa, they commanded good and forbid evil, they exposed

---

[81] First author's interview with Anjem Choudary.

[82] Susanne Lohmann "A Signaling Model of Informative and Manipulative Political Action," *American Political Science Review* 88 (June 1993): 319–333; Susanne Lohmann, "Dynamics of Informational Cascades: The Monday Demonstrations in Leipzig, East Germany, 1989-1991," *World Politics* 47 (June 1994): 42–101; Karl-Dieter Opp, *The Rationality of Political Protest: A Comparative Analysis of Rational Choice Theory* (Boulder, CO: Westview Press, 1989); Karl-Dieter Opp, Peter Voss, and Christiane Gern, *Origins of a Spontaneous Revolution: East Germany, 1989* (Ann Arbor: University of Michigan Press, 1993).

the idolatry of the society, and they introduced the shahada. But no one is doing that today. This is an obligation that is upon every single Muslim when they see *munkar* [evil]. When they see evil and corruption, it becomes an obligation.[83]

This historical precedent was used for *qiyas* (reasoning by analogy), whereby hardships were interpreted as evidence that they were on the right path. In other words, what rational-actor models typically view as risks and costs associated with activism were in fact benefits to the AM participant who viewed them as confirmation of the correctness of belief:

> Al-Muhajiroun says, "Look at the Prophet Mohammed, he went to Taif, and he got stones thrown at him." I think why did he get stones thrown at him and we aren't getting stones thrown at us? So when I see the police and they come to us and speak to us, I say "*alhamdulillah* [praise be to God], we are on the right path." If they didn't come to us and said we are very nice people, we are wrong, because Allah said in the Qur'an: the Jews and Christians will never be happy with you until you follow their way of life.[84]

Activists believed that if the authorities treated them well, it was a sign that they were on the wrong path. The Prophet was attacked by the authorities of his day. Obviously, he was on the straight path as the messenger of God, and the authorities were unbelievers. Drawing an analogy to the present, activists believed that if the police or government accommodated a movement, it was a sign of incorrect beliefs. This was reflected in AM's disdain for the Muslim Council of Britain and scholars and movements throughout the Muslim world that cooperate with regimes. The ideology framed overtures and friendly gestures by the authorities as signs of an insidious plot to destroy the truth of Islam, based upon Qur'an 9:8: "Verily if the unbelievers have authority over you, they will not respect you any trust, agreement, or covenant. With their mouths they will have fair words in front of you but their hearts are averse from you and most of them are rebellious, betrayers, and wicked" (AM translation). As one respondent put it:

> I feel good because I feel that [our way] is the only way, because the only way to be a good Muslim is like this—as long as someone is struggling and finds everything against him, then that person is on the right path. The only way to know that someone is really on the right path is, for example, that all the leaders are against him, all the government people are against him. And they don't compromise. So as long as someone is trying and struggling then hopefully he is on the right path. The Prophet he was like that as well. Everyone was against him. He got kicked out of his home land, Mecca, and he had to go to Medina. So that is the way we look at it.[85]

In addition, respondents also maintained that suffering was part of a more general test of certitude and commitment. One activist argued that "it is a test

---

[83] First author's interview with Somali member.
[84] Ibid.
[85] First author's interview with sixteen-year-old member, London, June 2002.

for everyone. And Allah even said that there will be a time when the majority of people will leave Islam or will neglect Islam, and that He will replace people with those who fulfill his command."[86] Others referred to an oft-quoted *hadith* as evidence of the test of will: "Hold all of you fast to the rope of Allah and do not separate yourselves."

As a result, activists reveled in their tales of confrontation with the police as proof of their own beliefs and eventual salvation.[87] Suffering was affirmation, and movement participants saw themselves as following in the Prophet's shoes, in a way living his experience in modern times. The fact that the activists were condemned by the mainstream Muslim community furthered their conviction and certitude, because the Prophet and his companions were a minority in a sea of *jahiliyya* (disbelief). This produced quite a heady sense of purpose and certitude in a mission that was seen as providing activists with strategies for producing the spiritual payoff.

Comprehending radical Islam necessitates rendering individual decisions about participation and behaviors intelligible. Although recent work has shown that extremism is strategically rational at the group level, there is far less theorizing and data about the individual level of analysis. To address this, we have offered a rational-choice explanation that focuses on spiritual incentives. Radical Islamic movements offer an important spiritual incentive: join the group and engage in risky and costly activism and receive eternal salvation as part of the saved group.

This challenges perspectives that dismiss the possible usefulness of a rational-actor approach to Islamic activism. Roxanne Eueben, for example, argues that "even the most austere version of rational actor theory has very little to say about fundamentalism because, given its basic assumptions, it concludes only that fundamentalists have a revealed preference for fundamentalism."[88] But this kind of argument confuses religious methods with goals or interests. The preference is not for fundamentalism. Fundamentalism is a strategy or method for obtaining the preference of salvation as an end. It is a way of approaching religious interpretation that emphasizes literalism and strict adherence to *tawhid*. Activists follow this interpretive approach because they view it as an exclusive strategy for the pursuit of Paradise. If we recognize that value and instrumental rationalities are frequently related, radical Islamic activism becomes intelligible within a rational-actor framework.

We fully recognize that not everyone who participates in radical Islamic groups is driven by spiritual desires. It is folly to assume uniformity. In addition, there are almost certainly important differences between the utility calculations of leaders and those of followers and affiliates. This, of course, is open

---

[86] First author's interview with Islam (local leader), London, June 2002.

[87] This was observed by the first author in several instances, including a large gathering of members prior to a lesson, where they swapped stories about confrontations with police.

[88] Roxanne L. Euben, *Enemy in the Mirror: Islamic Fundamentalism and the Limits of Modern Rationalism* (Princeton, NJ: Princeton University Press, 1999), 33.

to empirical investigation. Our point is to initiate a broader understanding of rational action in the study of radical Islam by emphasizing the role of beliefs and relationships among ideology, individual utility calculations, and behavior. If we accept that religion does matter, seemingly irrational behavior becomes understandable as a rational choice.

Deterring Nonstate WMD Attacks

DAVID P. AUERSWALD

A terrorist group armed with a weapon of mass destruction (WMD) is arguably the greatest threat to the United States and its allies in the current era.[1] Porter Goss, former Director of Central Intelligence, starkly made this point in 2005 testimony before Congress. "Al Qaeda is intent on finding ways to circumvent U.S. security enhancements to strike Americans and the Homeland. It may be only a matter of time before Al Qaeda or another group attempts to use chemical, biological, radiological, and nuclear weapons."[2] The U.S. government has reason to be afraid. Recent terrorist attacks in London, Madrid, and Bali were horrific, but were carried out with conventional explosives. The physical, economic, and psychological damage from a terrorist WMD attack could easily equal or exceed that of the 11 September 2001 attacks, to say nothing of its effects on the pace of globalization, which may explain why al Qaeda leader Osama bin Laden has voiced an interest in acquiring WMD.[3]

> Acquiring [WMD] weapons for the defense of Muslims is a religious duty. If I have indeed acquired these weapons, then I thank God for enabling me to do so. And if I seek to acquire these weapons, I am carrying out a duty. It would be a sin for

---

[1] For the purposes of this essay, WMD include nuclear, radiological, chemical, and biological weapons.

[2] *Current and Projected National Security Threats to the U.S.: Hearings before the Senate Select Committee on Intelligence*, 109th Cong., 1st Sess (testimony of Porter Goss, 16 February 2005, 2). Also see National Intelligence Council, *Mapping the Global Future* (Washington DC: Government Printing Office, 2004), 93–95. For similar comments in 2003, see *The International Terrorist Threat: Hearings before the House International Relations Committee, Subcommittee on International Terrorism*, 108th Cong., 1st Sess. (testimony of Cofer Black, 26 March 2003). As Audrey Cronin notes, religious terrorists show little restraint in the conduct of war (*jus in bello*) once they have justified going to war (*jus ad bellum*). Audrey Cronin, "Rethinking Sovereignty," *Survival* 44 (Summer 2002): 119–139.

[3] Thomas Friedman, *The World is Flat* (New York: Farrar, Straus and Giroux, 2005), 391–413.

DAVID P. AUERSWALD is a professor of strategy and policy at the National War College in Washington DC. He has published articles and books on coercive diplomacy, the politics of military interventions, and Congress and foreign policy.

Muslims not to try to possess the weapons that would prevent the infidels from inflicting harm on Muslims.[4]

Of equal and related concern, there have been repeated attempts to smuggle chemical and nuclear WMD materials from former Soviet territory over the last several years.[5] More recently have come revelations that one or more Pakistani scientists provided uranium enrichment technology, expertise, and nuclear warhead designs to Libya, Iran, North Korea, and possibly, even to Syria and Iraq.[6] Allegations have circulated that these same officials may have passed information to al Qaeda on how to construct a radiological "dirty bomb."[7] Other allegations exist that arms traffickers from the former Soviet Union have been approached by al Qaeda for nuclear materials.[8]

Two things are surprising, given the seriousness of a potential terrorist WMD attack. First, the idea that religiously oriented terrorists cannot be deterred from attacking Western interests or from using WMD if the terrorists acquire such weapons is a relatively unexplored assumption, based on anecdotal evidence.[9] Nonetheless, this assumption is consistently made by most academicians and the U.S. government. Consider that the heart of the George W. Bush administration's preemption doctrine is the idea that terrorist groups

[4] John Parachini, "Comparing Motives and Outcomes of Mass Casualty Terrorism Involving Conventional and Unconventional Weapons," *Studies in Conflict and Terrorism* 24 (September 2001): 389–406.

[5] William Potter, "Nuclear Smuggling from the Former Soviet Union" in David Marples and Marilyn Young, eds., *Nuclear Energy and Security in the Soviet Union* (Boulder, CO: Westview Press, 1997): 139–159; John Berryman, "Russia and the Illicit Arms Trade," *Crime, Law and Social Change* 33 (March 2000): 85–104; Joby Warrick, "Smugglers Enticed by Dirty Bomb Components," *The Washington Post*, 30 November 2003; and Tom Parfitt, "The Nuclear Nightmare," *The Times* (UK), 3 March 2004.

[6] Peter Slevin, John Lancaster, and Kamran Khan, "At Least Seven Nations Tied to Pakistani Nuclear Ring," *The Washington Post*, 8 February 2004; William Broad, "Libya's A-Bomb Blueprints Reveal New Tie to Pakistani," *The New York Times*, 9 February 2004.

[7] Owais Tohid, "Pakistan and its Proliferator," *The Christian Science Monitor*, 6 February 2004, 1.

[8] Lyudmila Zaitseva and Kevin Hand, "Nuclear Smuggling Chains," *American Behavioral Scientist* 46 (February 2003): 822–844.

[9] Joseph Lepgold, "Hypotheses on Vulnerability: Are Terrorists and Drug Traffickers Coerceable?" in Lawrence Freedman, ed., *Strategic Coercion: Concepts and Cases* (Oxford: Oxford University Press, 1998), 131–150; Gerald Post, "Psychological and Motivational Factors in Terrorist Decisionmaking: Implications for CBW Terrorism" in Jonathan Tucker, ed., *Toxic Terror: Assessing the Terrorist Use of Chemical and Biological Weapons* (Cambridge, MA: Harvard University Press, 2000), 271–290; Daniel Byman, "Scoring the War on Terrorism," *National Interest* 72 (Summer 2003): 75–84; Paul Davis and Brian Jenkins, *Deterrence and Influence in Counterterrorism* (Santa Monica, CA: RAND, 2002), 12–14; Adam Dolnik, "Die and Let Die: Exploring Links between Suicide Terrorism and Terrorist Use of Chemical, Biological, Radiological, and Nuclear Weapons," *Studies in Conflict and Terrorism* 26 (January–February 2003): 17–35; and Thomas Friedman, "War of Ideas, Part 1," *The New York Times*, 8 January 2004. For somewhat opposing views, see Gerald Steinberg, "Rediscovering Deterrence After September 11, 2001," *Jerusalem Letters/Review*, no. 467, 2 December 2001; John Parachini, "Putting WMD Terrorism into Perspective," *The Washington Quarterly* 26 (Autumn 2003): 37–50; Lawrence Freedman, *Deterrence* (Malden, MA: Polity Press, 2004), 124.

cannot be deterred from launching attacks on the United States. Second, there is little discussion in academic or policy circles as to how terrorists might acquire WMD, other than to assert that state sponsors of terrorists should be deterred or coerced to withhold such material, or that weapons stockpiles should be consolidated and better guarded and that weapons scientists should be paid a living wage.[10]

This essay rectifies both points. I first explore the general problem of how one might deter WMD attacks by terrorist actors. In essence, this is a demand-side question, in that Western deterrence would be aimed at decreasing terrorist demand for WMD. Key to understanding the problem of deterring terrorist groups is reexamining the fundamental tenets of deterrence theory and assessing whether the past inability to deter terrorists was due to some intrinsic characteristics of those groups or instead to the incomplete application of deterrence theory by nation-states. I argue that both are true and to a large extent unavoidable. Deterring terrorists by threatening punishment is extremely difficult, given terrorist motivations and liberal democratic values, and may even be self-defeating. A deterrence strategy that would deny terrorists any gains from mass casualty WMD strikes is also difficult for nation-states to sustain, even for states as powerful as the United States.

Given the difficulties associated with deterring a terrorist WMD attack, I then discuss how to deny terrorists the *means* to launch devastating attacks. This is a supply-side question. I focus attention on transnational organized crime as a likely source of WMD and WMD materials and argue that deterrence threats can work when aimed at such groups. A wide literature on organized crime groups, and on the deterrence relationship between threatened punishment and criminal behavior, supports the idea that transnational organized crime groups should be susceptible to deterrence threats, given particular, achievable circumstances. In short, I advocate a strategy of preventing WMD terrorist attacks by deterring potential nonstate WMD suppliers via a deterrence strategy. I conclude by reviewing the policy implications of my argument.

The Calculus of Deterrence

The supposed track record of deterring terrorists is not good, even for powerful states or states willing to retaliate after an attack. For instance, unrivaled hegemonic power has not kept the United States safe from terrorist attack; nor has often-brutal retaliation deterred suicide attacks in Russia or Israel. The

---

[10] For examples of the former perspective, see Derek Smith, "Deterrence and Counter-proliferation in an Age of WMD," *Security Studies* 12 (Summer 2003): 152–197; Andrew Newman, "Arms Control, Proliferation and Terrorism," *Strategic Studies* 27 (March 2004): 59–88. The Cooperative Threat Reduction initiative is a cornerstone of the latter perspective. Our ability to deter state proliferation to terrorists is at the heart of the President's statements that "You are either with us or against us." See Jasen Castillo, "Nuclear Terrorism: Why Deterrence Still Matters," *Current History* (December 2003): 426–431.

problem is that in the former case, it is unclear that the United States has actually signaled a broad deterrence threat against terrorists. Instead, we have vowed to kill or capture any terrorists we find, regardless of whether they have attacked us. A similar dynamic is at work in the Russian and Israeli cases, compounded by the fact that neither country has offered an alternative inducement to the Chechens or the Palestinians, respectively, to provide them an incentive to stop fighting. Given these and other more general problems associated with attributing deterrence success and failure, this paper explores the dynamics involved in deterring a terrorist WMD attack in the abstract. I find that terrorist groups should indeed be hard to deter, due to both terrorist motivations and the inherent (and proper) constraints that liberal democracies place on their own behavior. But before applying any deterrence model, it is important to define terms.

Deterrence is a dynamic, interactive process between at least two entities. Deterrence policies are predicated on threatening an adversary with pain if that adversary changes its behavior in ways that you find detrimental to your interests. The threatened pain can take any number of forms, from military violence to financial penalties to diplomatic ostracism. You do not actually have to inflict the pain to be successful at deterrence. In fact, resorting to retaliation means that your deterrence policy has failed. Instead, successful deterrence relies on influencing an adversary's perceptions and expectations of pain. You must make them believe that you will inflict pain if they change their behavior in ways that you do not like, regardless of whether you actually plan on causing pain should deterrence fail. You also may need to promise to withhold your threat should the adversary not change their behavior, and have that promise believed (or there is no reason for the adversary to comply with your demands). For all of these reasons, deterrence success is heavily dependent both on signaling the adversary of your intentions and on that adversary interpreting your signals correctly. Communication, through words and deeds, is thus central to a deterrence relationship.

For deterrence to work against an individual, a terrorist or crime group, or a nation-state, you must either increase the costs that the entity has to pay, or decrease the benefits they get, should they change their behavior. In the parlance of deterrence, threatening to increase the adversary's costs is often referred to as deterrence by punishment.[11] American threats of massive nuclear retaliation against Soviet cities, had the Soviets invaded western Europe, is an example of deterrence by punishment. Threatening to decrease or nullify the benefits reaped by an adversary should it change its behavior is often referred to as deterrence by denial. Targeting Soviet weapons and troops in the field was a Cold War example of deterrence by denial, in that their destruction would deny the Soviets the ability to control western Europe.

---

[11] Glen Snyder, *Deterrence and Defense: Toward a Theory of National Security* (Princeton, NJ: Princeton University Press, 1961).

A deterrence-by-denial strategy is often equated with defensive measures in standard treatments of deterrence. But whereas defense is the use of brute force to repel or defeat an attack, deterrence by denial uses the *threat* of defeat to prevent the attack before it occurs. To use a concrete example, homeland security capabilities are pure defenses to the extent that they can defeat a terrorist attack. They are a deterrent only if their existence changes a terrorist's perceptions of likely success, leading to an abandonment of the terrorist attack.

Distinguishing deterrence from defense yields two related points. First, deterrence by denial is usually discussed in the context of potentially violent conflicts in which what is being denied is a military objective. The concept of denial could just as easily be applied to nonmilitary objectives, however, such as the broader political or religious goals of a terrorist movement. The deterrent policy attempts to create the perception that a terrorist's goals cannot be achieved, which should decrease the rationale for violent terrorist attacks. Second, deterrence by denial has often been applied to confrontations between opposing military forces, yet a deterrence-by-denial strategy could employ nonmilitary means. For example, an opposition party's threat to boycott an election should the government party prohibit international observers is an example of a nonmilitary deterrence-by-denial strategy, at least if opposition participation is crucial to the election's legitimacy and the government values such legitimacy. The opposition's threats are not defensive; they do not prohibit votes for the government party. Instead they threaten to conditionally deny the government any benefit from the election, thus qualifying as deterrence by denial.

Deterrence by punishment is a difficult but possible strategy against nonstate actors. It requires convincing signals that we could identify *whom* to retaliate against. In other words, do our potential adversaries believe that we can link those responsible for an attack to the events themselves? Second, we have to convincingly signal that we can identify *what* to retaliate against to inflict pain. That is, we must be able to identify what an adversary values. As I discuss below, terrorist and crime groups have numerous component parts, including leaders, foot soldiers, financiers, logisticians, etc. A crucial facet of a deterrence-by-punishment strategy is signaling that we know what is valued by each component of a nonstate organization and where it is located. Third, we have to signal that we have the *will* and *capabilities* to inflict pain against those things valued by each actor's component parts. That is, we must demonstrate that our threats are credible. Doing so may require everything from publicly maintaining appropriate capabilities, to overcoming the legal and organizational impediments for their use, to the public release of successful instances of retaliation. Most importantly, our deterrence threats stand a better chance of appearing credible if we demonstrate that we have no choice but to implement our threats should that be necessary.[12]

---

[12] Thomas Schelling, *The Strategy of Conflict* (Cambridge, MA: Harvard University Press, 1960); Thomas Schelling, *Arms and Influence* (New Haven, CT: Yale University Press, 1966).

Deterrence by denial, as defined here, has different requirements. To deny an opponent any benefit from an attack on us requires that we identify the opponent's *goals* with some specificity. This requires excellent intelligence capabilities regarding the adversary's priorities and decision-making apparatus. It also requires that we understand the consequences of the steps we take to deny the adversary their goals. For instance, threatening military retaliation for terrorist attacks on us may be counterproductive, in that military retaliation could enhance the adversary's goals of martyrdom or appearing as victims of Western imperialism.

We must also convincingly signal that we have the ability to *prevent* an opponent from achieving its goals (preferably whether or not we retaliate for an attack). If the power to hurt is bargaining power, then denying that power to opponents diminishes their power.[13] For instance, if a terrorist's goals would be advanced via the destruction of a specific class of targets (that is, embassies, ships, aircraft, etc.) or through the use of particular forms of attack (that is, computer attacks, car bombs, WMD, etc.) deterrence could be enhanced if the opponent believed that we were aware of its plans and/or had the ability to defend against them, rendering those plans relatively harmless. If a terrorist group wants the United States out of the Middle East, maintaining a robust U.S. presence in the region, regardless of the cost, threatens that terrorist goal.

There are a number of potential problems associated with each type of deterrence. Deterrence by punishment requires excellent intelligence, particularly when applied to terrorists. Without good intelligence, we cannot identify the perpetrators of attacks or appropriate retaliatory measures. Punishing terrorists also may require relaxing the laws of war to allow for the targeting of noncombatants, with all the serious repercussions that this would entail. On the other hand, a deterrence-by-denial strategy could require public signals that we know an enemy's targets or goals, which could lead to alternative targets being selected or create domestic panic. In addition, we must publicly disseminate at least some information regarding our defensive measures, if defenses are to act as a deterrent, or our political intent, if denying broad terrorist goals is our intent. The result of doing either could be that those very defenses or that political intent would be undermined, or that terrorists would choose a softer target or shift goals. Finally, defenses and demonstrating political staying power are both potentially expensive.

This short conceptual discussion points to serious dilemmas associated with deterring WMD attacks using either threats of punishment or denial. Moreover, any solution will of necessity have limited applicability if attempted across the spectrum of nonstate organizations and possible scenarios of attack. Indeed, deterrence requires a case-by-case approach, because nonstate actors vary tremendously in terms of their goals, organization, and support. The following

---

[13] Branislav Slantchev, "The Power to Hurt: Costly Conflict with Completely Informed States," *American Political Science Review* 97 (February 2003): 123–135.

section discusses the difficulty of deterring WMD attacks from extreme religious terrorist groups.

Deterring Terrorist WMD Attacks

The United States is currently most concerned about preventing attacks from religious fundamentalist groups such as al Qaeda, particularly those attacks that might produce mass casualties and/or involve WMD. Indeed, this section will demonstrate that it is almost impossible to devise an effective deterrent threat against terrorist WMD attacks by religious fundamentalist groups, for multiple, reinforcing reasons.[14] First, such terrorists are highly motivated, and deterrence tends to fail against such opponents. Our notion of retaliatory punishment may in fact benefit (and even encourage) such terrorists. Second and related, we may undermine our own effort. The response of religious terrorists to our threatened implementation may be exactly the opposite of what we intended, because we do not understand the impact of our retaliation on a terrorist group's standing in their own communities. Moreover, our overriding need to defend against terrorist attacks may in some instances undercut our deterrence threats. Third and finally, terrorist actors may be difficult to locate, because they are transnational in nature and blend in with civilian populations, and we cannot credibly threaten pain against those we cannot find.

Deterrence by Punishment

Terrorist motivations and their consequences. Deterrence by punishment is one possible but extremely daunting means of preventing such attacks. Deterring an al Qaeda WMD attack via threats of U.S. punishment requires understanding what to retaliate against and how to do so for the greatest effect. As Thomas Schelling noted in the 1960s, knowing what an opponent values is a necessary condition for deterrence success. The motivations of al Qaeda operatives, therefore, are crucially important to this facet of the deterrence equation. To summarize a voluminous literature, al Qaeda is a group that feels threatened by the secular modern world and oppressed by corrupt Middle East regimes. As a result, al Qaeda aims to drive the United States out of the Middle East and overthrow those regimes friendly to the West. In their place would be created a Muslim caliphate, governed by strict adherence to Islamic law. But that said, al Qaeda is an evolving entity. The group increasingly has taken on the status of a movement or an ideology rather than a formal organization.[15] In that sense, al Qaeda and its affiliated groups are like a cancer growing in the modern world and seeking to destroy that world from within.

[14] Cronin, "Rethinking Sovereignty," 130; Davis and Jenkins, *Deterrence and Influence*, 3–7.

[15] Raymond Bonner and Don Van Natta, "Regional Terrorist Groups Pose Growing Threat, Experts Warn," *The New York Times*, 8 February 2004; Jamie Glazov, "Symposium: Diagnosing Al Qaeda," *Front Page Magazine*, 12 August 2003; Byman, "Scoring the War on Terrorism."

But knowing what motivates this movement as a whole is not enough for determining an appropriate form of threatened punishment. Members of al Qaeda are not all alike or interchangeable, and al Qaeda is not the only group of concern when it comes to potential WMD attacks. The movement comprises different types of people with different levels of training and expertise. Most importantly, each component part may respond differently to retaliatory deterrence threats—responses that may seem counterintuitive at first glance.

Paul Davis and Brian Jenkins disaggregate al Qaeda into senior leaders, lieutenants, foot soldiers, recruiters, and supporters among the populace and among religious leaders. Bruce Hoffman groups the organization into leaders, professional cadres, trained amateurs, local walk-ins, and affiliated groups. Regardless of what specific categories one uses, al Qaeda seems to have relatively few senior leaders, a greater number of highly trained lieutenants, anywhere from 50,000 to 70,000 trained foot soldiers from its camps in Sudan and Afghanistan, and an indeterminate (but increasing) number of relatively untrained volunteers like Richard Reed, Jose Padillo, and an unknown number of recruits in Iraq.[16] Add to that, the movement actively recruits new volunteers through appeals in mosques, on the Internet, and in Arab language media. The movement receives financial support from a host of sources, ranging from direct donations from individuals and front organizations, to profits from drug smuggling, to indirect donations siphoned from legitimate charities.

Any deterrence strategy must incorporate the fact that each component of a terrorist organization may have different specific motivations and values. For instance, senior al Qaeda leaders have not led suicide missions in the United States or Iraq, or fought to the death in the mountains of Afghanistan, even though they claim not to fear death. Instead, they have been deeply involved in the planning, logistics, and financing of such attacks, leaving implementation to their lieutenants. If senior leaders are averse to dying, then threatening their lives could be a useful deterrent to the mass-casualty, "spectacular" attacks that senior al Qaeda leaders are alleged to plan and direct.[17] Were such a strategy to work, it would obviate the need to worry about WMD attacks by lower level members.

Two possible consequences could undermine such a deterrence strategy, however. First, assassination is morally repugnant to many, and advocating it absent an attack and a clear evidentiary trail to the correct perpetrators might create a public backlash, particularly given current skepticism regarding intelligence claims.[18] Second, we would have to credibly commit to spare terrorist

---

[16] Davis and Jenkins, *Deterrence and Influence*.

[17] Bruce Hoffman, "The Leadership Secrets of Osama Bin Laden," *The Atlantic Monthly* 291 (April 2003): 26–27.

[18] Brian Jenkins, *Should our Arsenal against Terrorism Include Assassination?* (Santa Monica, CA: RAND, 1987); and Catherine Lotrionte, "When to Target Leaders," *Washington Quarterly* 26 (Summer 2003): 73–86.

leaders that withheld WMD attacks if threatened assassination were to work as a deterrent. Terrorists have no incentive to restrain themselves absent our credible commitment on that score. The implications are profound. Withholding U.S. action in the name of deterrence, absent attack, contravenes the stated U.S. policy of degrading terrorist capabilities whenever possible. One cannot do both. But it is unclear whether an elected official can survive politically by arguing that the country should engage in a risky and by no means certain attempt to deter a terrorist attack at the expense of leaving a terrorist group's capabilities intact.

If we cannot deter terrorist leaders, perhaps we can deter lower level operatives. Unfortunately, threats of lethal punishment are unlikely to deter lieutenants and foot soldiers either. These lower level operatives seem to embrace martyrdom to a much greater extent than do their leaders. Death in combat with the infidel is seen as a benefit, not a punishment, which makes deterrence threats self-defeating; they simply increase the enemy's motivation to attack. Extreme threats such as threatening to bomb Islamic holy sites or to bury so-called martyrs in pig fat to deny them entry to heaven would only reinforce accusations that the West was engaged in a clash of civilizations against the Muslim world and could increase terrorist recruitment, much as rumors of rifle cartridges lubricated with pig grease hastened the nineteenth-century Indian mutiny against the British.

Deterrence may not work even against those terrorists who choose martyrdom as a means of providing material and psychological benefits to their families—as has been the case with some suicide bombers in Israel—rather than for promised rewards in the afterlife.[19] In those cases, threatening the lives or livelihood of (presumably) innocent family members of known or suspected terrorists might work as a deterrent, but is morally reprehensible to many. Moreover, the record of Israeli reprisals when family members of suspected terrorists have been killed (intentionally or not) does not hold out much promise for this tactic.

Deterrence is complicated by one final, potentially unintended consequence. To deter a terrorist group requires signaling our abilities and intent. Given that we have no private, direct communication link with terrorist groups, we must communicate indirectly, with the significant possibility of that becoming public knowledge, or communicate publicly for the world to hear. Yet we face a dilemma if a terrorist group does not take responsibility for an attack. Intentional or inadvertent public linkage of an attack to a terrorist group may build our reputation for good intelligence, but doing so also may bolster that group's image or drive them into hiding, to say nothing of possibly compromising intelligence sources and methods.[20] The result is that the communication necessary for deterrence by punishment may strengthen the very groups we want to stop.

[19] Dolnik, "Die and Let Die," 29.
[20] Davis and Jenkins, *Deterrence and Influence,* xii.

This does not mean that deterrence is doomed to fail, but it does mean that over time, we may have to deter an increasingly popular opponent.

Operational difficulties. There are a number of practical difficulties that make deterrence by punishment unattractive. We have to find the terrorists to punish them, and liberal democracies have so far shown little ability to locate even the most senior leaders of terrorist organizations, to say nothing of the vast numbers of terrorist underlings. Remember that successful deterrence by punishment requires that we demonstrate that we can identify who is behind an attack. This is hard to do on our own soil, as we saw with the stymied investigations into the anthrax- and ricin-laden letters sent to the U.S. Senate. Finding the perpetrators of an attack overseas arguably is more difficult. Intelligence failures associated with the September 11 attacks, with Operation Iraqi Freedom, and in the continuing hunt for bin Laden signal the world community that our intelligence assets may not be capable of correctly identifying the perpetrators of a terrorist attack.

Changing international perceptions on this score is a difficult although not insurmountable task. What we cannot do is jump to unsubstantiated conclusions in a rush to lay blame for a future attack. Being wrong will only reinforce the impression of faulty or politicized intelligence that the U.S. government already suffers from. If we can avoid that temptation, social psychologists tell us that we need attribute blame correctly in only a few instances to get the reputation that we can do so on a regular basis.[21] We may even get help from the terrorists themselves. After all, terrorist groups thrive on publicity, as witnessed by bin Laden's boasts after the September 11 attacks. Such boasts may be a terrorist's recruiting tool, but they also help us attribute blame. Whether the same behavior would hold true in the aftermath of a WMD attack is unknown.

Overall then, significant difficulties must be overcome for a successful deterrence-by-punishment strategy aimed at religiously oriented terrorist groups. It is by no means self-evident that such groups can be swayed by threats of punishment. Yet to be successful, we must minimize the consequences of our retaliatory actions. We must demonstrate that we can attribute blame for an attack to the proper group and then carry out our threatened punishment. And we must possess intelligence on how specific groups are organized, what is valued by each part of a terrorist organization, and what the group's center of gravity is for specific types of attacks.[22] Each of these requirements is daunting in and of itself. Combined, they support the conclusion that deterrence by punishment is not a viable stand-alone option when it comes to religiously motivated terrorist groups.

---

[21] Jonathan Mercer, *Reputation and International Politics* (Ithaca, NY: Cornell University Press, 1996).

[22] Davis and Jenkins, *Deterrence and Influence*, 43.

Deterrence by Denial

Terrorist motivations. A denial strategy relies on demonstrating the ability to deny terrorists the achievement of their goals. Yet, as with deterrence by punishment, this is not a straightforward task. Al Qaeda differs from some of its affiliated groups when we consider its overall goals. Al Qaeda desires a Muslim caliphate free from Western interference and influence. While some regional or local terrorist groups may share that desire (Islamic Jihad or Jemaah Islamiyah, for example), many have separatist (for example, the Liberation Tigers of Tamil Eelam in Sri Lanka or the Chechens in Russia) or political agendas (Hamas, for example). Three specific goals stand out as worthy of consideration if we limit our discussion to groups motivated by radical religious ideologies. First and most immediately, groups such as al Qaeda need operational successes to keep their movements strong. Second, they want the West out of the Islamic holy lands. Third and finally, they want to overthrow those governments friendly to the West and replace them with Islamic republics that follow Shari'a law. A WMD attack in the United States would achieve the first goal and could arguably advance the second goal. A WMD attack against Middle Eastern regimes would also achieve their first goal and could advance the second and third goals, depending on international reactions.

Assuming that this is a valid portrayal, how could we demonstrate our ability to prevent those goals from being realized? Most immediately, we could take steps to thwart terrorist attacks by enhancing the active defense of U.S. and friendly territory. Demonstrating our success would weaken the international appeal of the terrorist group because local groups are drawn to the al Qaeda brand name for its global cachet; or to put it another way, the affiliated individuals and groups join up to be part of a larger successful cause. Group psychology—being part of a successful al Qaeda movement—becomes more important than the individual judgment (and possibly more cautious behavior) of any one individual or local group.[23] Or to use a different analogy, the al Qaeda leadership acts like venture capitalists in the broader terrorist movement.[24] An equally apt metaphor is of a large corporation (for example, McDonalds, Starbucks, etc.) that is willing to lend its brand name to local "franchises" on the condition that the local groups abide by certain standards of behavior, share profits with the parent organization, and periodically report back to the corporate office for direction. Senior al Qaeda leaders do not direct or control all operations but instead solicit ideas from affiliated groups or entrepreneurial individuals. As these operations develop, al Qaeda leaders provide inspiration and occasional oversight and correction of those

---

[23] Gerald Post, "Psychological and Motivational Factors," 273.

[24] Bruce Hoffman, "Rethinking Terrorism and Counterterrorism since 9/11," *Studies in Conflict and Terrorism* 25 (September–October 2002): 303–316.

groups.[25] Failure of individual franchises or the corporate headquarters degrades the franchise name.

Operational difficulties. Successful attacks help maintain the movement's allure and its ability to recruit and inspire martyrdom in its recruits. Thwarting terrorist attacks decreases that allure. The key problem with effective defenses, of course, is that they are tremendously expensive and are rarely perfect. Increased port and rail security, for example, is widely seen as a necessary defensive measure, but the United States has yet to implement the required procedures, due to their cost. Another long-term, deterrence-by-denial initiative could involve threatening a terrorist group's standing in its religious community as a way of ensuring that existing regimes are not overthrown in favor of fundamentalist rule. Unfortunately for opponents of terrorism, there is no accepted cannon of religious law or church hierarchy in the Muslim world that could be turned against proponents of mass-casualty terrorism. Individual Muslims are free to make religious decrees, or *fatwas*, regardless of their formal training or standing as an Islamic scholar. Western states have made little headway in convincing the majority of Muslim clerics to discredit these terrorists.

Unintended consequences. Deterrence by denial can produce unintended consequences. Increasing defenses in one area may divert attacks to softer targets rather than deterring the attacks altogether.[26] This would seem to be especially true of a terrorist WMD attack. Or consider that maintaining a Western presence in the Islamic world would serve to deny terrorists another of their goals. Yet a long-term presence can actually backfire. In the three-and-a-half years since the beginning of the Iraq war, a large military presence in Iraq arguably has galvanized the jihadists against the United States rather than deterring terrorist attacks.[27]

Deterrence by denial thus suffers from many of the same problems as deterrence by punishment, if to a different degree. Deterrence by punishment challenges our moral code; it requires better intelligence to find terrorists and near-perfect homeland defenses so that we could dare to withhold going after terrorists absent attacks. None of this is likely in the near term. Deterrence by denial is only slightly more attractive.[28] Denial does not require us to make the difficult choice between deterrence and degrading the terrorists' capabilities. Indeed, attrition of terrorist capabilities complements a deterrence-by-denial

---

[25] David Jones, Michael Smith, and Mark Weeding, "Looking for the Pattern: Al Qaeda in Southeast Asia—The Genealogy of a Terror Network," *Studies in Conflict and Terrorism* 26 (November–December 2003): 443–457.

[26] Bonner and Van Natta, "Regional Terrorist Groups"; Hoffman, "Leadership Secrets."

[27] Dana Priest, "Iraq New Terror Breeding Ground: War Created Haven, CIA Advisers Report," *The Washington Post*, 14 January 2005.

[28] Lepgold, "Hypotheses on Vulnerability," 144.

strategy. Both weaken a terrorist group's ability to achieve its goals and, by extension, weaken its appeal in the Muslim world and ultimately, threaten the group's continued existence. Yet at the same time, denial strategies suffer from operational problems (that is, there is no such thing as a perfect defense) and can lead to undesired consequences, such as attracting more adversaries through a greater presence in the Middle East. In sum, additional actions are needed to decrease the likelihood of WMD attacks against the United States or U.S. interests.

DETERRING ORGANIZED CRIME

Preventing WMD from falling into the hands of terrorists is a crucial—perhaps *the* crucial—step in preventing a terrorist WMD attack absent perfect defenses.[29] Even if there is little chance of deterring those terrorists who would actually launch WMD attacks, we may still be able to cut off the supply of WMD material by threatening those who fund or supply WMD or technical expertise to terrorist groups. Indeed, if most terrorist groups lack the expertise to build their own WMD, our focus should be on how a terrorist group could acquire such weapons.

I concentrate on transnational criminal groups because they are arguably the crucial and most likely intermediaries between suppliers of WMD material and terrorist end-users.[30] According to Lyudmila Zaitseva and Kevin Hand, the vast majority of WMD suppliers are not governments or government-sanctioned entities. Instead, they are individual civilians, rogue military personnel and security officials who operate WMD production and storage facilities. So-called rogue states are unlikely to transfer WMD materials to nonstate actors, because such states will not want to part with the few weapons or weapons components they possess; they would risk international condemnation, sanctions, or worse if they were caught, and would have little if any control over how those weapons might be used, to include against their own territory. Amateur suppliers, on the other hand, tend not to have the contacts or expertise to transport and sell WMD materials to terrorist groups.

The most effective and dangerous intermediaries are organized criminals, who seek to acquire WMD from suppliers (either through bribes or coercion) and then sell them for a profit to states and terrorists.[31] The danger is that in searching for profits, a crime group could sell WMD, component parts, or delivery vehicles to a terrorist group. That is because "the most common type of relationship between criminal organizations and terrorist groups is likely to

---

[29] Charles Ferguson and William Potter, *The Four Faces of Nuclear Terrorism* (Monterey, CA: Monterey Institute of International Studies, 2004), 6–11.

[30] Gavin Cameron, "Weapons of Mass Destruction Terrorism Research, Past and Future" in Andrew Silke, ed., *Research on Terrorism* (Portland, OR: Frank Cass, 2004), 72–90.

[31] Zaitseva and Hand, "Nuclear Smuggling Chains," 832.

be simply a matter of business and involve supplier–customer dealings."[32] Deterring such behavior is the subject of the remainder of this essay.

Deterrence by Punishment

The literature on crime and deterrence suggests that there is significant promise in using threats of punishment to deter transnational criminal groups or arms traffickers from acquiring, transporting, and then distributing WMD to terrorists. Beginning with the work of Gary Becker in the late 1960s, a large number of studies suggest that domestic crime rates are "a negative function of the probability and expected severity of criminal sanctions."[33] In other words, enforceable criminal penalties have a deterrent effect on crime, at least when the criminal is capable of evaluating the risk of being caught, the severity of threatened punishment, the expected gains from the crime, and the need for those expected gains.[34] Perhaps that is why the deterrent effect of punishment is less pronounced when violent crime is compared to property crime, in that violent crimes are often crimes of passion.[35] The deterrent effect of punishment is also less pronounced in localities suffering from severe corruption, which again is consistent with the assumption that most criminals are capable of reasoned calculation as to the expected risks, costs, and benefits of crime.[36]

The above begs the question as to whether behavioral patterns—and the prospects for deterrence—are similar between transnational criminal groups and more-mundane domestic criminals engaged in nonviolent crime. For our purposes, the crucial factor is the motivation of each group. If both types of criminal groups are reasoning entities, as opposed to behaving in response to gross passions, and both groups have similar motivations, then we might expect transnational criminals and traffickers to be deterred by increases in the likelihood of being caught or the severity of expected punishment once they are caught, just as their domestic counterparts are deterred by such threats.

---

[32] Phil Williams, "Terrorism and Organized Crime" in Brad Roberts, ed., *Hype or Reality? The New Terrorism and Mass Casualty Attacks* (Alexandria, VA: Chemical and Biological Arms Control Institute, 2000), 137; Mark Phythian, "The Illicit Arms Trade: Cold War and Post-Cold War," *Crime, Law and Social Change* 33 (March 2000), 1–52.

[33] William Niskanen, "Crime, Police, and Root Causes" (Cato Policy Analysis No. 218, The Cato Institute, Washington DC, 14 November 1994). For earlier works on the subject, see: Gary Becker, "Crime and Punishment: An Economic Approach," *Journal of Political Economy* 76 (March–April 1968): 169–217; Isaac Erlich, "Participation in Illegitimate Activities," *Journal of Political Economy* (May–June 1973): 521–567; Steven Craig, "The Deterrent Impact of Police," *Journal of Urban Economics* 21 (May 1987): 298–311; William Trumbull, "Estimation of the Economic Model of Crime Using Aggregate and Individual Level Data," *Southern Economic Journal* 26 (October 1989): 423–439.

[34] Larry Siegel, *Criminology*, 4th ed. (St. Paul, MN: West Publishing, 1992): 131–133.

[35] Niskanen, "Crime, Police, and Root Causes"; Siegel, *Criminology*, 133.

[36] Maurice Kugler, Thierry Verdier, and Yves Zenou, "Organized Crime, Corruption and Punishment" (working paper, The Research Institute of Industrial Economics, Stockholm, Sweden, 2003).

The literature on transnational crime and arms trafficking suggests that this is indeed the case. There is widespread agreement that transnational criminals are motivated predominately by profit and personal power, just as are domestic perpetrators of property crimes.[37] As Mark Pythian notes, "To a significant extent the [arms] trade has been depoliticized since the end of the Cold War, with involvement now motivated more by profit than policy considerations."[38] A number of people are attracted to the arms trade "who see it as a way of getting rich quickly."[39] For instance, A.Q. Khan is said to have been motivated by personal avarice—to the tune of an alleged $40 million personal fortune—and only secondarily by a sense of loyalty to the Muslim world.[40] Another example is Victor Bout, who works out of the former Soviet Union and, by some accounts, is the world's biggest arms trafficker after only fifteen years in the business. He is said to be motivated by money, not ideology, and is willing to sell arms to anyone (he is reported to have made a $50 million profit from an arms sale to the former Taliban regime in Afghanistan).[41] In the words of a Bout associate, "He's not here to change the world."[42] Indeed, the continued viability of the Western world is crucial for organized crime's very existence, as a source of expertise, financing, and materiel. In a crude sense, these groups are parasites on the modern world.

The implication, then, is that criminal groups should be susceptible to deterrence, even if religiously oriented terrorists are not.[43] Transnational criminals look for business opportunities that provide large payoffs with minimal risks and therefore should be much more susceptible to coercion and much less likely than religious terrorists to sacrifice their own lives for their cause.[44] After all, it is

[37] Bartosz Stanislawski and Margaret Hermann, "Transnational Organized Crime, Terrorism, and WMD" (paper prepared for the Conference on Non-state Actors, Terrorism and Weapons of Mass Destruction, College Park, MD, Center for International Development and Conflict Management, University of Maryland, 15 October 2004); Zaitseva and Hand, "Nuclear Smuggling Chains," 827–833; Phil Williams and Roy Godson, "Anticipating Organized and Transnational Crime," *Crime, Law and Social Change* 37 (June 2002): 311–355; Berryman, "Russia and the Illicit Arms Trade."

[38] Phythian, "The Illicit Arms Trade," 1.

[39] Ibid., 2.

[40] "Pakistan's Nuclear Secrets Sold," 6 February 2004, accessed on the website of *The Economist* at http://www.economist.com/world/asia/displaystory.cfm?story_id=E1_NOTNJSG, 11 October 2006; William Broad, David Sanger, and Raymond Bonner, "A Tale of Proliferation: How Pakistani Built His Network," *The New York Times*, 12 February 2004; Paul Haven, "Pakistan Nuke Scientist Bought Loyalty," Associated Press, 17 February 2004.

[41] Zaitseva and Hand, "Nuclear Smuggling Chains," 831.

[42] Peter Landesman, "Arms and the Man," *New York Times Magazine*, 17 August 2003, 57.

[43] For a summary of the differences between these two types of groups, see Williams, "Terrorism and Organized Crime." For an argument that the two groups are growing increasingly similar, see Thomas Sanderson, "Transnational Terror and Organized Crime," *SAIS Review* 24 (Winter 2004): 49–62; Tamara Makarenko, "A Model of Terrorist-Criminal Relations," 1 August 2003, accessed at *Jane's Intelligence Review*, at www.janes.com, 4 October 2006; Jane Schneider and Peter Schneider, "The Mafia and Al-Qaeda: Violent and Secretive Organizations in Comparative and Historical Perspective," *American Anthropologist* 104 (September 2002): 776–783.

[44] Williams and Godson, "Anticipating," 325; Lepgold, "Hypotheses on Vulnerability," 140.

impossible to enjoy the benefits of material wealth if you are dead. Instead, the leaders of criminal organizations prioritize their needs: their own safety and wealth first, then the continued viability of their organizations, and finally, their specific merchandise and personnel.[45] So while these individuals and groups may be willing to develop, transport, or steal a WMD device and sell it to rogue states or terrorist groups, they are unlikely to risk getting caught in an overly dangerous ploy, to say nothing of risking injury or death by detonating the WMD device themselves.[46] Members of transnational crime groups, therefore, should be vulnerable to deterrence threats that threaten their livelihood, freedom, or very existence. That said, as with any deterrence initiative, basic requirements must be met to increase the chances of success.

Identifying the opponent. Knowing whom we are trying to deter is the first requirement for deterrence by punishment. In general, we would like to deter all organized crime groups from trafficking in WMD or WMD-related technologies. Yet no state can unilaterally gather the necessary intelligence to identify every known and emerging WMD trafficker. Demonstrating publicly that other states will share intelligence on WMD smuggling is thus a crucial element in any deterrence-by-punishment strategy. Norms of cooperation on that front are still in their formative stages (see below) and are hampered by the tolerance shown by much of the industrialized world to the clandestine shipment of conventional arms. A lack of transparent intelligence sharing, unless corrected, will complicate the task of making credible deterrence threats against those criminals who traffic in WMD.

Transnational criminal groups are often intertwined with legitimate governments and government officials, which complicates multilateral coordination and hinders intelligence cooperation. Remember that in the literature on domestic crime, an important finding is that judicial and police corruption can increase crime rates rather than deter crime.[47] International WMD traffickers can attempt to influence government officials through payoffs and threats. Traffickers can even be part of existing governments. In some instances, traffickers are a key revenue source for local (and even national) economies. A.Q. Khan's proliferation network used each of these techniques. Kahn was a high-ranking official in control of a large government program. The secret nature of his work made him immune from outside scrutiny. He is reported to have engaged in extensive bribes and payoffs to maintain the loyalty of government officials, subordinates, and journalists.[48] Khan had the alleged support of two high-ranking army generals, both of whom supposedly authorized his sales to rogue states.[49]

---

[45] Williams and Godson, "Anticipating," 337–338.
[46] Dolnik, "Die and Let Die," 29.
[47] Kugler, Verdier, and Zenou, "Organized Crime," 4.
[48] Haven, "Pakistan Nuke Scientist."
[49] Tohid, "Pakistan and Its Proliferator; "Pakistan's Nuclear Secrets Sold."

His subordinate, Bukhari Tahir, was a well-connected businessman in Malaysia who used his businesses as a cover for his smuggling operation. He and his immediate family insulated themselves from scrutiny by partnering with members of the ruling elite—including members of the prime minister's and foreign minister's families—on these legitimate business ventures.[50]

Tangible progress must occur in international cooperation if we are to credibly deter potential traffickers in WMD. Working in favor of deterrence is the fact that WMD are in a category different from most trafficking (that is, guns, drugs, or people), and states realize that WMD sales can come back to haunt a government that looks the other way. We also can overcome international resistance to investigations (and possible punishment) of potential WMD traffickers through the use of rewards and punishments. An initiative containing both would be for governments to pledge not to publicize information on WMD thefts or smuggling that might occur on another country's soil, so long as that country immediately notified its international partners. Keeping the information out of the public light would decrease the international stigma that might attach to a country that cannot control its own technology. In return, however, we would demand full (if private) disclosure of all relevant information associated with the smuggling. The implicit threat here would be the public disclosure of the theft—and perhaps even military reprisals—if we found out about it before being notified. Another use of rewards and punishments for improving international cooperation would be to link foreign assistance to intelligence sharing. States that cooperated fully on intelligence matters would get modest increases in foreign assistance. States that withheld information would get less assistance. Each measure would improve international cooperation and, by extension, increase the threat to punish traffickers in WMD and related materials.

How to retaliate. The second requirement of deterrence by punishment is to know what the opponent values and to hold that at risk. As noted earlier, leaders of organized crime groups are motivated by a desire for profit and personal power, and less so by the organization's future viability and specific merchandise or underlings. The key to a deterrence-by-punishment strategy is realizing that organized crime groups "as business people can presumably be induced to stop or change locations if the operating costs become too great."[51] The lives of individual leaders and their physical assets (homes and property, yachts and planes, etc.) are particularly attractive targets to threaten with retaliation, seizure, or confiscation. Secondary targets of retaliation might include the distribution facilities, warehouses, and transportation assets needed to smuggle precursor chemicals or WMD technology such as centrifuges. Other targets could include any legitimate firm owned or invested in by criminal leaders.

---

[50] Broad, Sanger, and Bonner, "A Tale of Proliferation."
[51] Lepgold, "Hypotheses on Vulnerability," 140.

Credible will and capabilities. Arguably, the most difficult task of deterrence by punishment is to demonstrate the capability and will to credibly implement threatened reprisals. There is no doubt that modern states have the military capabilities to strike individual criminal leaders and facilities used to traffic in WMD. On the financial front, the United States and its allies now have a much greater capability to freeze financial assets, compared to their capabilities before 11 September 2001. Two issues remain outstanding, however, both related to demonstrating our credible will to implement our deterrence threat. They are first, demonstrating to traffickers that they cannot escape threatened punishment through the protection of corrupt officials, justices, or police, and second, establishing the necessary international regimes to routinize international cooperation against WMD traffickers.

The key to solving these problems is to strengthen existing international norms against the trafficking in WMD with an international legal framework that requires international cooperation on WMD trafficking and legitimizes a military response, not just a judicial response, to discoveries of trafficking. Such a combination should decrease the opportunities for corruption while increasing the domestic and international impediments to corruption. Two recent initiatives establish precedents for such a normative and legal framework: the May 2003 Proliferation Security Initiative (PSI) and the passage of UN Security Council (UNSC) Resolution 1540 in April of 2004.

The PSI is an informal agreement among fifteen nations that establishes informational exchanges and cooperation on interdiction of WMD and delivery technologies.[52] Originally announced on 31 May 2003 and agreed upon by eleven founding states on 4 September 2003, the PSI focuses on three main tasks:

- Undertaking effective measures, either alone or in concert with other states, for interdicting the transfer or transport of WMD, their delivery systems, and related materials to and from states and nonstate actors of proliferation concern;
- Adopting streamlined procedures for rapid exchange of relevant information concerning suspected proliferation activity;
- Reviewing and working to strengthen their relevant national legal authorities where necessary to accomplish these objectives.[53]

---

[52] Department of State, "Proliferation Security Initiative Frequently Asked Questions," 26 May 2005, accessed at www.state.gov/t/isn/rls/fs/46839.htm, 4 October 2006. See also: Michael Byers, "Policing the High Seas: The Proliferation Security Initiative," *American Journal of International Law* 98 (July 2004): 526–540; Chaim Braun and Christopher Chyba, "Proliferation Rings: New Challenges to the Nuclear Nonproliferation Regime," *International Security* 29 (Fall 2004): 5–49; Ferguson and Potter, *Four Faces*, 323; Michael Evans, "U.S. Plans to Seize Suspects at Will," *London Times*, 11 July 2003; and "Eleven Countries Join Forces to Combat the Trade in Weapons of Mass Destruction," *London Financial Times*, 11 July 2003.

[53] Department of State, "The Proliferation Security Initiative: Statement of Interdiction Principles," 4 September 2003, accessed at www.state.gov/t/isn/rls/fs/23764.htm, 4 October 2006.

The PSI now boasts fifteen current partner states, four of which are permanent members of the UN Security Council. Sixty additional nations have agreed to more limited cooperation with PSI states on a case-by-case basis. By the end of 2004, at least twenty public multilateral interdiction exercises had been held. Liberia, Panama, and the Marshall Islands, countries that serve as flags of convenience for innumerable foreign vessels, have agreed to allow their flagged vessels and aircraft to be boarded and inspected by PSI nations if suspected of transporting WMD.[54]

The PSI is both defensive and deterrent in nature.[55] In the case of an imminent threat from a WMD shipment, PSI states can participate directly in "defensive" interdiction, ask other PSI nations to do so, or coordinate in other ways as warranted. Within its first year of existence, according to Dr. Mitchell Reiss, the former Director of the State Department's Office of Policy Planning, "cooperation among PSI partners has resulted in the seizure of shipments of sensitive materials," the most famous of which was the *BBC China,* caught transporting WMD equipment to Libya.[56] In terms of deterrence, the Bush administration argues that "over time, proliferators, and others involved in supporting proliferation activities, will learn that there are countries determined to work together to take all possible steps to stop their efforts."[57] Indeed, Reiss has argued that "it is thought that the existence of the PSI has deterred many [WMD trafficking] attempts due to fears of being caught."[58]

The PSI was soon followed by the passage of UNSC Resolution 1540, which called upon states to "adopt and enforce appropriate, effective laws which prohibit any non-state actor to manufacture, acquire, possess, develop, transport, transfer or use nuclear, chemical or biological weapons and their means of delivery." It also called upon states to "develop and maintain appropriate, effective border controls and law enforcement efforts" to prevent the illicit trafficking in these materials.[59]

---

[54] Sean Murphy, "Proliferation Security Initiative for Searching Potential WMD Vessels," *American Journal of International Law* 98 (April 2004): 355–357; Jofi Joseph, "The Proliferation Security Initiative," *Arms Control Today* (June 2004) accessed at www.armscontrol.org/act/2004_06/Joseph. asp, 4 October 2006; Andrew Winner, "The Proliferation Security Initiative: The New Face of Interdiction," *Washington Quarterly* 28 (Spring 2005): 129–143. For an example of the flag of convenience agreements, see Department of State, "Proliferation Security Initiative Ship Boarding Agreement with Panama," 12 May 2004, accessed at www.state.gov/t/isn/trty/32858.htm, 4 October 2006.

[55] Winner, "Proliferation Security Initiative," 134.

[56] Mitchell Reiss, "Steps to a Brighter Future: The Bush Administration's Non-Proliferation Policy," 21 June 2004, accessed at www.state.gov/s/p/rem/34267.htm, 4 October 2006; Winner, "Proliferation Security Initiative," 137.

[57] Department of State, "What is the Proliferation Security Initiative?" 26 May 2005, accessed at www.state.gov/t/isn/rls/other/46858.htm, 4 October 2006.

[58] Reiss, "Steps to a Brighter Future."

[59] Sean Murphy, "UN Security Council Resolution on Nonproliferation of WMD," *American Journal of International Law* 98 (July 2004): 606.

UNSC 1540 is an important development on a number of fronts. First, it requires states to enact strong national controls over WMD and related materials, as well as to "address the threat posed by non-state actor involvement in any aspect of WMD proliferation," through improved border controls, law enforcement capabilities, and related initiatives.[60] Second, the resolution provides international legal authorization for PSI-related interdiction of WMD trafficking. According to the State Department, "If an activity is authorized under a UNSC resolution, then it could be cited by a PSI participant as authority for its participation in an interdiction. … UNSC 1540 and the PSI SOP are mutually reinforcing and are legally and politically compatible."[61] Third, the resolution requires that states compile regular, comprehensive reports on their efforts at complying with UNSC 1540. A nonproliferation committee of Security Council members has been constituted to receive these reports. Security Council members can, at their discretion, enforce compliance with the resolution's reporting requirement or other terms of the resolution under Chapter VII of the UN Charter. And while the Bush administration does not envision having to enforce UNSC 1540 requirements, they have made it plain that they are willing—and have the international legal authority—to do so if necessary.[62]

Combined, these initiatives provide the practical and international legal basis for action against WMD traffickers by both the military and law enforcement community of every UN member state, with additional, self-imposed enforcement responsibilities taken on by the PSI nations. Moreover, these combined initiatives are promising signs of an emerging international norm against the trafficking in WMD and related materials. Both developments should increase the possibilities of international cooperation in opposition to WMD trafficking. Although it is impossible to know definitively as of this writing, together these and related initiatives (that is, the Cooperative Threat Reduction [CTR], Export Control and Related Border Security Assistance, the Terrorist Interdiction Program, and the G-8's Global Partnership initiative) also may very well have increased the perceived costs of trafficking in WMD.

Operational difficulties. As promising as the aforementioned initiatives are, why should we believe that deterring WMD trafficking can be any more successful than our abysmal record at deterring drug trafficking? Indeed, after decades of the war on drugs, with billions spent on eradication and interdiction, illegal drugs trafficked to the United States actually cost less on the street than they did twenty years ago, signifying a relatively unfettered market. If we cannot stop or deter tons of drugs from coming across the border each year, how

---

[60] Andrew Semmel, "UN Security Council Resolution 1540: The U.S. Perspective," 12 October 2004, accessed at http://www.state.gov/t/isn/rls/rm/37145.htm, 11 October 2006.

[61] Department of State, "Proliferation Security Initiative Frequently Asked Questions."

[62] Ibid.

are we to deter WMD trafficking? Our dilemma is summarized by the joke that asks "How do you smuggle a nuclear bomb into the country?" and answers "You stuff it inside a bag of pot!"

There are a number of differences between drug trafficking and trafficking in WMD, however, which call into question comparisons across the two issue areas. The demand for drugs is very different from the demand for WMD materials. Of the three most commonly trafficked drugs (heroin, cocaine, and marijuana) two are extremely addictive and are used by millions worldwide. The demand for the third, marijuana, is even higher, to say nothing of being extremely common across the globe. A 2003 survey found that in the United States alone, roughly 46 percent of the population aged twelve and older (over 110 million people) had used illegal drugs at least once in their lifetimes, and of those, almost 35 million people had used illegal drugs in the last year.[63] According to a 2005 Congressional Research Service (CRS) report, "more than 14 million Americans buy illicit drugs and use them at least once per month."[64] In 2003, the UN estimated that the total annual number of drug abusers worldwide aged fifteen and over was at least 200 million people.[65] Demand for WMD and related materials is much, much less, by several orders of magnitude.

There is a huge supply of illicit drugs, swamping anything related to WMD. And while WMD supplies are concentrated in relatively select parts of the world and are technologically challenging to store safely, the supply of drugs is very diffuse and requires rudimentary technology to produce and store. Drug production is technically easy, can be accomplished at low cost, and can be shifted from locale to locale with relatively little effort. As a result, worldwide production of opium, coca, and marijuana has risen dramatically over the last decade.[66] According to CRS, "World production and supply of illicit drugs vastly exceeds world demand."[67] The same is not true of WMD materials. If anything, the supply of such materials is being constricted, albeit slowly, through CTR programs.

Enforcement is extremely variable across the globe when it comes to illicit drugs, in large part because there is little consensus on the detrimental effects of drug use.[68] Consider that while the U.S. federal government has stiff penalties for drug production and use, U.S. localities have challenged those guidelines in a number of instances. International enforcement is at least as variable. Casual

---

[63] U.S. Department of Health and Human Services, "Results from the 2003 National Survey on Drug Use and Health: National Findings," September 2004, accessed at www.drugwarfacts.org/druguse.htm, 17 January 2005.

[64] Raphael Perl, *Drug Control: International Policy and Approaches, CRS Issue Brief IB88093* (Washington DC: Congressional Research Service, 13 April 2005), 1.

[65] UN Office on Drugs and Crime, "Global Illicit Drug Trends 2003" (Vienna, Austria, June 2003) accessed at www.drugwarfacts.org/druguse.htm, 17 January 2005.

[66] Perl, *Drug Control*, 1.

[67] Ibid., 8.

[68] Ibid., 5.

drug use is a relatively accepted—and even legal—behavior in many Western countries, including Spain, Italy, Portugal, Luxembourg, and Denmark. In contrast, there is a growing, perhaps near-global, consensus that trafficking in WMD harms everyone, regardless of their locality, as witnessed by UNSC Resolution 1540.

Enforcement of anti–drug-trafficking initiatives also is harmed because of the relatively low priority that drug policy has in many nations. Consider that U.S. anti-drug initiatives at the federal level are routinely countermanded when they contradict or complicate higher priority foreign policy initiatives, such as counter-terrorism or counter-proliferation policies. As an example, consider that the United States has resisted labeling North Korea as a state sponsor of drug trafficking because such a designation would "prioritize drugs vis-à-vis more pressing issues (i.e. nuclear proliferation)."[69] Indeed, "The direction of drug policy under President George W. Bush does not appear to be an immediate top foreign policy priority for the administration."[70] Enforcement of anti–WMD trafficking, on the other hand, is a very high priority for the United States and other world powers, making it less likely that participation in the PSI, for instance, will be subsumed by other priorities.

Finally, the combination of ample drug supplies at low cost, with high global demand and lax enforcement, means that there are enormous profits to be had in drug trafficking. Estimates in 1997 put traffickers' gross profits at roughly 300 percent.[71] According to the UN, the illegal drug business is extremely lucrative, totaling more than $400 billion in annual sales in 1997, or the equivalent of 8 percent of all annual worldwide trade that year.[72] In 2001, South American coca production alone yielded roughly $93 billion worth of cocaine.[73] As these huge annual figures demonstrate, there is a relatively proven market for the drug trade. The same cannot be said for trade in WMD materials. It is true that there may be substantial payoffs for the successful trafficking of WMD materials, but they do not come anywhere near the huge amounts of money available through the drug trade. Moreover, the WMD market is far less certain than is the drug market.

For all these reasons, the analogy between the drug trade and WMD trafficking is a flawed one. There are significant differences between WMD and drug trafficking, differences that make problematic a comparison of the two

---

[69] Raphael Perl, *Drug Trafficking and North Korea: Issues for U.S. Policy, CRS Report RL32167* (Washington DC: Congressional Research Service, 4 March 2005), 2.

[70] Perl, *Drug Control*, 12.

[71] Associated Press, "U.N. Estimates Drug Business Equal to Eight Percent of World Trade," 26 June 1997, accessed at www.drugwarfacts.org/druguse.htm, 17 January 2005.

[72] United Nations Office for Drug Control and Crime Prevention (UNODCCP), *Economic and Social Consequences of Drug Abuse and Illicit Trafficking* (New York: UNODCCP, 1998), 3, accessed at www.drugwarfacts.org/druguse.htm, 17 January 2005.

[73] Perl, *Drug Control*, 2.

behaviors (and by extension the low probability of deterrence success against drug traffickers as a surrogate measure for deterrence success against WMD traffickers). There is no denying that significant obstacles still remain in crafting and implementing a strategy to deter WMD trafficking, but such obstacles are not nearly as severe as those confronting anti-drug policy-makers.

Deterrence by Denial

Denying criminal goals. A deterrence-by-denial strategy rests on preventing criminal groups from profiting due to WMD smuggling. In theory, erasing profits could be achieved by increasing the supply of goods on the market (reducing prices), increasing the seller's transaction costs (reducing profit per unit sold), or reducing the demand for the goods (driving down prices). In reality, the first option is self-defeating. Flooding the WMD market runs counter to decades of nonproliferation policies, to say nothing of increasing the chances of a terrorist group acquiring WMD. The last option may be impossible in the short run. Religious extremists will continue waging war against modern secular nation-states for the foreseeable future. We are left with the middle option of reducing WMD traffickers' profits by increasing their potential or perceived costs of doing business. Interdiction holds some promise on that score, as does expanding the CTR initiative, which would increase state control of loose WMD materials. The aforementioned PSI and UNSC Resolution should facilitate efforts on both counts.

Another means of decreasing traffickers' profits is to raise doubts as to the loyalty of their members or the fidelity of other groups they do business with. As doubts increase on either score, so too should the perceived risks of trafficking in WMD, either deterring outright such potential traffickers or increasing their transaction costs to the point that they believe there is no profit in dealing in WMD. How one would go about sowing distrust would depend on the specific organization of a particular group or network of groups.

Organizationally, criminal groups can resemble multinational corporations, in that the groups often are transnational in scope, with different elements or branches of the umbrella organization working in different countries, focusing on different tasks, but all working toward the same profit goal. Different divisions of the larger corporation focus on specific tasks. Victor Bout seems to have developed such a corporate scheme based on personal loyalty.[74] Each element or division is connected to their superiors by ties of loyalty, whether based on familial or kinship ties, shared formative experiences, or shared ethnicity.[75] In such groups, trust and intragroup bonding are extremely

---

[74] Landesman, "Arms and the Man."

[75] The above reasoning is similar to social explanations of organized crime, as detailed in Williams and Godson, "Anticipating," 328–331.

important. Defections from such organizations, or even rumors of possible defections, have the potential to fundamentally challenge the functioning of such organizations, greatly decreasing profits.[76]

Criminal groups also can operate like contractors and subcontractors. Think of individual criminal firms as relatively independent actors providing expertise in a particular area. Some launder money. Some provide weapons, weapons materials, or weapons design. Some ship goods. Cooperation between firms is on a tactical or contract basis, with the goal being to maximize individual profits regardless of whether the other firms turn a profit.[77] Cooperation between these groups is enhanced, although by no means assured, if the groups share "similar criteria of selectivity, etiquette, lexicon, and ritual practice."[78] But even then, nothing prevents any single firm from profiting at the expense of former associates when an individual contract is complete.[79] Moreover, subcontractor networks have ties to legitimate business firms to hide their activities, which gives authorities another potentially vulnerable point of access to the criminal network.[80]

Many of the entities associated with A.Q. Khan fit the contractor–subcontractor model. Khan's proliferation network relied on the financial acumen of Bukhari Tahir, who ran legitimate businesses but also operated as Khan's chief financial officer, money launderer, and salesman. Engineers from Switzerland and England provided expertise. British, Dutch, French, German, Malay, and Turkish firms supplied high-tech parts. Africa was a source for raw materials. Companies in Dubai acted as the hub for transshipments of goods and money.[81] In the words of a senior American official, "First, [Khan] exploits a fragmented market and develops a quite advanced nuclear arsenal. Then he throws the switch, reverses the flow and figures out how to sell the whole kit, right down to the bomb designs, to some of the world's worst governments."[82]

With either the transnational groups or the contractor–subcontractor networks, deterrence by denial seeks to exploit concerns about loyalty as well as the competitive nature of the criminal market. We face an easier task of sowing

---

[76] Williams and Godson, "Anticipating," 334.

[77] Ibid., 327.

[78] Schneider and Schneider, "The Mafia and Al-Qaeda," 780.

[79] Williams and Godson, "Anticipating," 334; Alison Jamieson, "Transnational Organized Crime: A European Perspective," *Studies in Conflict and Terrorism* 24 (September–October 2001): 377–387.

[80] Williams and Godson, "Anticipating," 343.

[81] David Albright and Corey Hinderstein, "Unraveling the A.Q. Khan and Future Proliferation Networks," *The Washington Quarterly* 28 (Spring 2005): 111–128; Braun and Chyba, "Proliferation Rings"; Slevin, Lancaster, and Khan, "Seven Nations"; Broad, Sanger, and Bonner, "A Tale of Proliferation"; Raymond Bonner, "Salesman on Nuclear Circuit Casts Blurry Corporate Shadow," *The New York Times*, 18 February 2004.

[82] Quoted in Broad, Sanger, and Bonner, "A Tale of Proliferation"; see also Slevin, Lancaster, and Khan, "Seven Nations"; David Sanger and William Broad, "From Rogue Nuclear Programs, Web of Trails Leads to Pakistan," *The New York Times*, 4 January 2004.

distrust within a contractor–subcontractor relationship than we do with the transnational groups, but we can take advantage of the competitive criminal marketplace to change either group's perceptions of WMD profitability. For instance, publicly threatening death, incarceration, or asset seizure against all groups we believed could *potentially* engage in WMD trafficking, should we have proof of trafficking by any one group, would give rival groups and contractor–subcontractors an incentive to monitor and police each other in the hopes of forestalling our action. This could be an especially effective incentive for established conventional arms traffickers—particularly in the former Soviet Union, where there is a history of infighting among criminal groups—to police their smaller, less-well-known, and perhaps more risk-accepting competitors who might be tempted to traffic in WMD.[83]

Conclusion

A terrorist group armed with WMD is arguably the greatest threat to the United States and its allies in the current era. The idea of a terrorist movement such as al Qaeda possessing WMD is particularly terrifying, given the difficulties associated with deterring religiously oriented terrorists. Given those difficulties, this paper explored deterrence of arms traffickers and transnational organized crime as a potential means of preventing terrorist groups such as al Qaeda from acquiring WMD materials. The profit motive of criminal groups makes them susceptible to threats of punishment. In some cases, their notoriety makes their leaders relatively easy to locate. More generally, UNSC Resolution 1540 makes it a global crime to traffic in WMD materials or delivery systems, demands improvements in border controls and internal security over WMD materials, and sets the legal framework for future interdiction and punishment. Indeed, UNSC Resolution 1540 nicely complements the PSI's procedures for interdicting potential WMD traffickers. Each of these measures, together with existing procedures allowing for the seizure of financial assets and with possible future efforts to sow distrust within and between criminal groups, increases the potential penalties associated with smuggling WMD. They also have a possible spillover effect to help deny criminal groups the profits they need to stay in business. In sum, transnational criminal groups and arms traffickers are susceptible to deterrence by punishment and denial.

The strategy advocated here cannot make the world safe from terrorist movements such as al Qaeda, yet we can partially defang the movement by deterring the transfer of WMD to al Qaeda and other terrorist groups. Implementing such a strategy will require placing a larger emphasis on the nonmilitary instruments of national power than does current U.S. policy. Intelligence

---

[83] Vsevolod Sokolov, "From Guns to Briefcases: The Evolution of Russian Organized Crime," *World Policy Journal* 21 (Spring 2004): 68–75.

and law enforcement play crucial roles in finding, infiltrating, and disrupting organized crime groups that could supply WMD and WMD technology to terrorists. Covert operatives and psychological operations will be required to sow distrust among trafficking groups or even turn these groups against each other. Careful diplomacy will be required to see the implementation of UNSC 1540 to fruition, to say nothing of making the PSI a meaningful, long-term, collective effort. The continued use of economic pressure and targeted action will be crucial to undercutting the profits associated with WMD smuggling, as will the provision of foreign assistance to cooperative states. There is obviously still a role for military force, particularly when interdiction is warranted or when disrupting a specific smuggling operation is necessary, but the lion's share of effort should be done by nonmilitary agencies. And finally, more effort should be devoted to integrating and coordinating efforts across and between governments. As the Government Accountability Office noted in January of 2005, "Strategic plans for threat reduction and nonproliferation programs are not integrated and do not address U.S. programs worldwide."[84] Integration and coordination are prerequisites for success.

Implementing this strategy will also require that we broaden our security focus beyond the fight against al Qaeda or Iraqi insurgents. Make no mistake, both are crucial tasks. Yet the reason they are crucial is due to the threat they pose to U.S. regional interests, and more importantly, to U.S. territory.[85] Deterring and disrupting the potential supply of WMD materials to either group should be a high priority for the current Bush administration and for future presidents. This essay provides an initial strategy to accomplish that task.*

---

[84] Government Accountability Office, *Weapons of Mass Destruction: Non-proliferation Programs Need Better Integration, GAO-05-157* (Washington DC: Government Printing Office, 2005), 7.

[85] James Fallows, "Success without Victory," *The Atlantic Monthly* 295 (January/February 2005): 80–90.

* The views expressed here are those of the author and not of the National Defense University, the Department of Defense, or any other agency of the United States Government. The author thanks Audrey Cronin, Bill Jamieson, Frank Mora, Michael Mazarr, Bard O'Neill, Mitchell Reiss, Harvey Rishikof, Paula Thornhill, and the anonymous reviewers for comments on earlier drafts.

The Fight against Terrorist Financing

ANNE L. CLUNAN

According to a well-informed former participant, the effort to combat terrorists' access to financial resources has been "the most successful part" of the global community's counterterrorism endeavor since the al Qaeda 11 September 2001 attacks on the United States.[1] Genuine success, however, hinges on U.S. ability to successfully frame terrorist financing as a collective action problem, both internally, to overcome interagency rivalries, and internationally, to overcome the benefits of free-riding behavior. This requires reframing the nascent pre-September 11 international anti-money-laundering regime as a counter-terrorist-financing regime as well as recasting the collective good of an open financial system as requiring collective management of its negative security externalities.

The norms and practices that make up the new counter-terrorist-financing frame have rapidly spread internationally in the past five years. However, the ultimate effectiveness, measured in terms of implementation and enforcement, of the new counter-terrorist-financing regime depends on states' redefinition of their national interests to include combating terrorist finance and a new understanding of the collective responses necessary to manage nonstate transnational actors. The U.S. case suggests that successful implementation of a counter-terrorist-financing regime will be much harder to achieve and to sustain than the adoption of regime norms, because even the experience of terrorist attacks appears to yield only temporary surges in a state's willingness to bear the costs of regime compliance. It is therefore unlikely that should present practices continue, countering terrorist financing will be counted a global success.

---

[1] Personal communication from Daniel Benjamin, former National Security Council Director for Transnational Threats during the Clinton administration, 27 September 2004. See also Thomas Kean et al., "Final Report on 9/11 Commission Recommendations," 9/11 Public Discourse Project, 5 December 2005, accessed at http://www.9-11pdp.org/press/2005-12-05_report.pdf, 16 April 2006 (hereafter 9/11 Public Discourse Project Final Report).

ANNE L. CLUNAN is assistant professor of national security affairs at the Naval Postgraduate School, Monterey, California. Her research addresses how states redefine their national security interests.

The Problem of Terrorist Financing

Terrorist financing incorporates two distinct sets of financial activities. One set involves the provision of the funds required to carry out a terrorist operation. It includes funds to pay for such mundane items as food, lodging, transportation, reading materials, and audio-video equipment, as well as purchases of legal precursors for bomb making (the 2004 Madrid bombings relied on cell phones as detonation triggers, and the 2005 London bombs were homemade from legal ingredients), as well as purchase of illegal materials for operations. Such transactions, unlike money laundering, are mainly "pre-crime": they are perfectly legal until they can be linked to support for a criminal act.[2] They are also minute in terms of monetary value and therefore extremely hard to detect in the absence of other indicators regarding the identity of the persons involved. Such identity profiles raise a number of legal and civil liberties issues.[3]

The second set of terrorism-related financial activities involves the raising of funds to support terrorist operations, training, and propaganda. Funds can be raised through illicit means, such as drug and human trafficking, arms trading, smuggling, kidnapping, robbery, and arson, which are more amenable to traditional anti-money-laundering tools. Terrorists also receive funds from legitimate humanitarian and business organizations. Charities raising funds for humanitarian relief in war-torn societies may or may not know that their funds are going to terrorism. Corrupt individuals at charities or at recipient organizations may divert funds to terrorist organizations. This appears to be one of the main means through which al Qaeda raises funds. Legitimate funds are commingled with funds destined for terrorists, making it extremely difficult for governments to track terrorist finances in the formal financial system.

The difficulties inherent in tracking terrorist finance in the formal financial system are multiplied many times over as terrorists move to informal financial systems, using money remitters and *hawaladars*, who, in turn, may engage in trade-based money laundering.[4] Al Qaeda began relying on the informal financial system around 1996. Detecting terrorist finances is therefore an extremely difficult task, more difficult even than preventing money laundering.

Countering Terrorist Financing: the Need to Redefine Collective Interests

The fight against terrorist funding is tremendously complex. It requires collective action not only internationally among states but also internally among gov-

---

[2] Author's interview with senior official in the Office of Foreign Assets Control (OFAC), Department of the Treasury, Washington DC, 14 October 2004 (hereafter OFAC).

[3] John Roth, Douglas Greenburg, and Serena Wille, *Monograph on Terrorist Financing,* Staff Report to the National Commission on Terrorist Attacks Upon the United States (hereafter *9/11 Staff Monograph*), 11.

[4] U.S. Department of State Bureau for International Narcotics and Law Enforcement Affairs, *International Narcotics Control Strategy Report, Part II. Money Laundering and Financial Crimes* (March 2004, hereafter *INCSR 2004* and March 2005, hereafter *INCSR 2005*).

ernment agencies and private actors. It essentially requires re-conceptualizing the public good of open financial systems as having negative security externalities that must be collectively managed. It involves the design and interaction of national economies and security agencies, as well as the political problems of achieving and sustaining cooperation among a very diverse set of public and private actors. To be effective, the international effort to combat terrorist financing requires well-functioning, transparent, and noncorrupt economies. Successfully disrupting terrorist financial flows therefore requires an appropriate anti-money-laundering legal framework regulating the formal and informal financial services industry and trade services. It demands an ability to enforce laws and collect real-time intelligence and documentary evidence on financial flows. It also requires experts properly trained in financial intelligence collection and criminal investigation, as well as prosecutors, regulators, customs agents, and bank employees.[5] Building all this institutional capacity to combat money laundering is a prerequisite for fighting terrorist financing.

However, because terrorist finance differs from money laundering, countering terrorist financing requires additional intelligence collection and analysis capacities for detecting "needles" in the financial "haystack." The remaining criterion for successfully combating terrorist financing is sustained political will to ensure that the power granted by legislation is actually matched by the capacity to implement counter-terrorist finance measures. Governments must be willing and able to share information and expertise with relative ease and speed across a number of policy domains and with public and private actors. They must also have the capacity to act quickly to disrupt and interdict funds and track the money trail to terrorists. In most cases, this cooperation must be transnational as well. All of this requires a long-term and high-level political commitment to combating terrorist finance.

Studies of international organization suggest that such profound political cooperation and organizational change requires participants to have redefined their interests.[6] Drawing on this insight, the argument made here is that such long-term and high-level commitment is only likely if top- and mid-level decision makers have re-conceptualized national security threats to include transnational financing of terrorists and if they have redefined the paradigm of security threats from one centered on nation-states to one incorporating transnational nonstate actors. Such a redefinition includes recognizing a need for

[5] Author's interviews in Washington DC with: State Department officials in the Office of the Coordinator for Counterterrorism's Counterterrorism Finance Unit (hereafter S/CT) and Bureau of International Organizational Affairs (hereafter IO), 20 and 23 September 2004, respectively; the Bureau of Economic and Business Affairs (hereafter EB) and International Narcotics and Law Enforcement (hereafter INL), 13 October 2004; Joseph M. Myers, former Director of Counter-Terrorist Financing at the National Security Council under the Bush administration, 12 October 2004; Treasury Department Financial Crimes Enforcement Network (hereafter FinCEN) official, 12 October 2004; and OFAC official.

[6] Ernst Haas, *When Knowledge Is Power* (Berkeley: University of California Press, 1990).

transnational and national sharing of information, moving from a paradigm of "need to know" to one of "need to share," and the subsequent re-organization of subnational and international authorities and cooperative endeavors.

Such a redefinition is most likely to occur in the aftermath of domestic experience of terrorist attacks. Even then, redefinition appears episodic and short-term. It had haltingly begun to take place among top national security officials in the White House during the last years of the administration of Bill Clinton but was discarded after the change in administrations and has not taken firm hold again. This redefinition has not systematically occurred globally, even among those states most subject to threats from transnational actors. As such, the initial counter-terrorist-financing "success"—in the form of unprecedented interagency and international cooperation—has not yet translated into the redefinition of national and international interests necessary to build upon and sustain it.

The Collective Action Problem Posed by Terrorist Financing

From a theoretical perspective, countering terrorist financing is a classic collective action problem. The majority of states benefit from limiting the ability of nonstate terrorist groups to finance violent challenges to state authority and control. They also benefit from ensuring that unofficial financial flows and a nontransparent economy do not undermine investor confidence and the state's capacity to govern. More broadly, states have an interest in ensuring that the international financial system and domestic economies are not disrupted through terrorist penetration and exploitation. Yet every state has an incentive to pass the costs of constraining terrorist financing off to others, as long as the costs of doing so are less than the benefits of attracting financial clients craving secrecy and of appeasing domestic actors (including charities, casinos, banks, money services, and civil liberties advocates) who oppose government scrutiny.

Institutional Capacity

Domestically, many states, even the most developed, lack the institutional capacity for and the political interest in successful implementation and enforcement of the counter-terrorist-financing regime's norms and practices.[7] States must have the ability to ensure compliance of private-sector actors in collecting and sharing sensitive information. Well-developed and integrated interagency cooperation is required to effectively manage the sheer complexity of combating terrorist access to finances. Competing interests among those within and those outside of government make implementing international best practices politically difficult. The difficulty of intergovernmental cooperation is considerably complicated by widespread resistance among key domestic con-

---

[7] Author's interviews with S/CT, INL, and OFAC officials, 20 September and 12-13 October 2004.

stituencies to increased regulation of financial activities and therefore a rejection of framing finance in terms of national security.[8]

In many countries, the political pain brought on by an effort to comply with an international regime, rather than merely adopt its standards, is deemed avoidable. States are much more likely to adopt but not enforce institutional changes, unless their calculus of the costs of nonenforcement changes. In the area of terrorist financing, we should expect such changes when the net costs of nonenforcement are raised (through the brandishing of international "carrots" and "sticks" that increase the costs to the state's reputation of being politically uncooperative and economically nontransparent, expose it to painful issue linkage and conditionality, or deny desired material incentives).[9] We should also expect such changes when states alter their definition of the problem to one of collective, not merely foreign, concern—which is most likely to occur after the domestic experience of transnational terrorist acts.[10]

Punctuated Learning

Change is likely to take the form of punctuated learning to redefine the national interest. Such learning is unlikely to be sustained without high-level attention and persuasion to maintain the new security paradigm and definition of national interests. The collective action required to create and pay for the public goods of an open and transparent financial system and constrained transnational terrorism is likely to be overpowered by free-riders for whom it is cheaper to pass the costs of such public goods on to others. In such cases, the power and ability of a hegemon or k-group—a small group of states wielding considerable power in the issue area—to set the rules of the game and impose them on free-riders through the manipulation of transactions costs and incentives is often critical to the successful provision of public goods.

The U.S. case is illustrative. As one of the centers of the international financial system, the United States is a necessary participant in the creation of a counter-terrorist-financing regime, whether as the hegemon or a member of the k-group. The United States should have considerable will after the terrorist attacks of September 2001 and capacity, in terms of expertise and resources, to domestically and internationally tackle the problem. If the United States is unable or unwilling to do so, then there is little reason to expect other countries with less motive and capacity to do so on their own.[11]

---

[8] Robert D. Putnam, "Diplomacy and Domestic Politics: The Logic of Two-Level Games," *International Organization* 42 (Summer 1988): 427–460.

[9] Beth A. Simmons, "International Law and State Behavior: Commitment and Compliance in International Monetary Affairs," *The American Political Science Review* 94 (December 2000): 819–835.

[10] Ernst B. Haas, "Words Can Hurt You: Or Who Said What to Whom About International Regimes," *International Organization* 36 (Spring 1982): 207–244.

[11] Mancur Olson, *The Logic of Collective Action* (Cambridge, MA: Harvard University Press, 1967/1971); and Russell Hardin, *Collective Action* (Baltimore, MD: Johns Hopkins University Press for Resources for the Future, 1982).

To support this argument, both the international effort to suppress terrorist financing as well as the "best case" of U.S. efforts to do so are developed below. International regime theory suggests that the existence of a hegemon or a small group of powerful states that is both willing and able to promote and underwrite an international counter-terrorist finance regime is often essential for such a regime to form when states have an incentive to pass the costs of the regime off to others. Such costs exist in abundance in the area of counter-terrorist financing.[12]

COUNTER-TERRORIST FINANCE EFFORTS BEFORE 11 SEPTEMBER 2001

Prior to the terrorist bombings of the U.S. embassies in Tanzania and Kenya in 1998, the issue of terrorist financing was handled almost entirely either as a problem of state sponsors of terrorism, or money laundering and criminal finance by nonstate actors (primarily drug traffickers and organized crime). Efforts to curtail the flow of funds to terrorists therefore took different approaches: pressuring states to curb their support for terrorism versus ensuring that states had the domestic capacity and incentives to suppress transnational criminal networks.

The Inklings of a New, Nonstate Terrorism Paradigm

States traditionally have been seen as the sponsors of terrorism. International focus has been on pressuring states seen to be directing or supporting violent organizations. Countries have long been divided ideologically over the political motivations of such organizations, such as the Nicaraguan *contras*, the Palestine Liberation Organization, the Irish Republic Army, Hamas, and Hezbollah. As a result, states have been unwilling to define specifically what constitutes terrorism. This lack of consensus has resulted in a host of UN treaties dealing with particular terrorist acts (such as hijackings and political assassinations) rather than with terrorism in general.[13] UN Security Council (UNSC) resolutions and treaties authorizing economic sanctions (and unilateral U.S. military strikes) were used to persuade state sponsors such as Libya and Sudan to stop their support for terrorism.[14]

State sponsorship of terrorism declined after the end of the Cold War as outcasts such as Libya, Iran, Syria, and Sudan sought to reduce their international

---

[12] Robert Keohane, *After Hegemony: Cooperation and Discord in the World Political Economy* (Princeton, NJ: Princeton University Press, 1984); and Charles Kindleberger, *The World in Depression, 1929-1939* (Berkeley: University of California Press, 1973).

[13] For the full list of anti-terrorism conventions, see United Nations Treaty Collection, "Conventions on Terrorism," 5 January 2006, accessed at http://untreaty.un.org/English/Terrorism.asp, 5 January 2006.

[14] Chantal de Jonge Oudraat, "The United Nations and the Campaign against Terrorism," *Disarmament Forum* 1 (2004): 29–37.

isolation. Terrorist organizations relied increasingly on other means, licit and illicit, to fund their activities.[15] Terrorists had long been involved in drug trafficking and organized crime, but until 1999, the international community had not explicitly linked these. The inability to agree on a definition of terrorism prevented the international community from including terrorist acts in many international efforts to suppress the drug trade and other transnational crime.

This gradually began to change in the late 1990s. The UN first explicitly linked the drug trade and terrorism after the UN Office for Drug Control and Crime Prevention highlighted the Taliban's levy of $15-27 million per year from taxes on opium production.[16] This reliance reduced the Taliban's susceptibility to sanctions applied to legal economic activity.[17] The Security Council demanded in Resolution 1214 (1998) that the Taliban stop its trade in narcotics. In 1999, the UNSC strengthened the linkage between terrorism and drugs when in Resolution 1333 it declared that the drug profits increased the Taliban's ability to harbor terrorists.

After the 1998 bombings of the U.S. embassies in Kenya and Tanzania, the United States and other Western states began to push for international recognition that nonstate actors were equally as complicit in supporting terrorism as states. The United States had led in getting international action on interdicting drug traffic, organized crime, and the laundering of their proceeds. While terrorist acts had been gradually incorporated into these efforts, after the 1998 bombings, the United States steered the Security Council to focus on transnational nonstate terrorism.[18] The Council passed Resolution 1267 in 1999, requiring states to impose sanctions on and freeze the assets of the Taliban for hosting al Qaeda. While this resolution reflected the traditional emphasis on targeting state sponsors (the Taliban), this was the first time the council had recognized that a transnational terrorist group was a threat to international peace and security.[19] Also in 1999, France led the UN in adopting the UN Convention on the Suppression of Terrorist Financing. This convention recognized that states had to work not only with each other but with private financial institutions to block the flow of terrorist funds. Under this convention, states are required to establish domestic legislation criminalizing terrorist financing and regulating financial industries within their jurisdiction.[20]

[15] Ilias Bantekas, "The International Law of Terrorist Financing," *American Journal of International Law* 97 (April 2003): 315–333.

[16] United Nations, "Report of the Committee of Experts appointed pursuant to Security Council Resolution 1333 (2000), paragraph 15 (a), regarding monitoring of the arms embargo against the Taliban and the closure of terrorist training camps in the Taliban-held areas of Afghanistan," (21 May 2001) UN Doc. S/2001/511, para. 60.

[17] Oudraat, "United Nations," 31.

[18] Ibid., 30.

[19] United Nations, "First report of the Analytical Support and Sanctions Monitoring Team appointed pursuant to resolution 1526 (2004) concerning Al-Qaida and the Taliban and associated individuals and entities," (25 August 2004) UN Doc. S/2004/679 (hereafter UN August 2004), 5.

[20] Bantekas, "International Law," 323–324.

Yet, even after the 1998 embassy bombings, the UNSC first emphasized the duty of states to suppress terrorism, without reframing the problem in terms of nonstate-sponsored terrorism.[21] For example, the 1999 UN Convention for the Suppression of Terrorist Financing highlights state responsibility for the actions of private actors operating within their jurisdiction. UN Security Council Resolution 1269 (1999) was the first to use the term "terrorist financing," but here the Security Council made clear that states harboring, funding, aiding, or failing to adopt measures to suppress terrorism would be held accountable for acts committed by those terrorists it sponsored. Sudan and Libya were effectively persuaded to suppress terrorism through this sanctions approach, in conjunction with the demise of their Cold War sponsors, but Afghanistan's Taliban were not.[22]

In 2000, the Security Council passed resolution 1333 and for the first time took on the nonstate actor al Qaeda through a freeze on the financial assets of Osama bin Laden and those associated with him, as designated on a list maintained by the 1267 Committee.[23] Resolution 1333 reflects the beginnings of the transformation of the state sponsor approach to counterterrorism to a transnational criminal finance approach.

A Piecemeal Anti-Money-laundering Regime

The bulk of the pre-September 11 multilateral cooperation that would be used after September 11 to counter terrorist financing took place in the counterdrug, counter-crime domain. Here, the major Western powers took the lead in developing a soft-law regime to combat transnational criminal finance. The strategic emphasis was on ensuring that states had the domestic capacity to combat organized criminal finance, and later, its new cousin, terrorist finance. Such capacity required enacting and enforcing domestic financial, banking, law enforcement, and anticorruption legislation. The regime developed in a piecemeal fashion.

The creation of the Financial Action Task Force on money laundering in 1989 marked the first in a series of efforts to establish informal inter- and transgovernmental bodies to handle the problem of criminal finance. The Financial Action Task Force sets and promotes best practices (put forward by the United States and the United Kingdom) in combating transnational financial crimes, and monitors the status of countries' legislative and regulatory conformity with these standards.[24] It published a set of forty recommendations in 1990 (revised in 1996), that laid out the basic framework for states to establish comprehensive anti-criminal-finance systems. In 2000, the Financial Action

---

[21] Ibid., 316.
[22] Oudraat, "United Nations," 31.
[23] UN August 2004, 5.
[24] Author's interview with INL official; and Bantekas, "International Law," 328.

Task Force began a campaign of "naming and shaming" jurisdictions that did not cooperate in the global effort to combat money laundering, which prompted many of those named to alter their domestic legislation in order to be removed from the list. It further suggested a set of countermeasures that states could take against the recalcitrant countries to prod compliance.[25] A number of regional Financial Action Task Force-style organizations were established between 1999 and 2000.[26]

In 1995, the financial intelligence units of twenty states (led by the United States and Belgium) established an informal transgovernmental network for sharing information concerning money laundering. Dubbed the Egmont Group, it grew rapidly to 58 states by June of 2001 and 101 by 2006.[27] It has served as a useful informal vehicle to improve information sharing, analysis, and training to combat money laundering.[28] The 2000 UN Convention against Transnational Organized Crime required member states to enact comprehensive domestic banking laws and regulations to deter and detect money laundering. This nascent anti-money-laundering regime would form the basis of the newly anointed international counter-terrorist-financing regime after the terrorist attacks on the United States on 11 September 2001.[29]

The progress made in the 1990s in creating formal and informal international rules on terrorism resulted from heightened awareness in the aftermath of major terrorist attacks in 1993 and 1998 against the United States. No overarching transnational security frame united the problem of terrorism and the problem of funds flowing through the international economy to finance them. Slowly and haltingly, the problems of terrorism and terrorist financing were being redefined by the Western powers as falling within a new paradigm of nonstate-sponsored actors. Led by the United States, the Security Council had begun focusing the Council's powers on nonstate actors such as al Qaeda. But other states saw little incentive to engage on an issue that was not seen as their problem, so learning was episodic and of limited duration. The same pattern plays out in the post-September 11 period.

INTERNATIONAL EFFORTS AFTER THE SEPTEMBER 11TH ATTACKS

On 28 September 2001, the UN Security Council passed a U.S.-sponsored resolution that obligated all members of the UN to act to suppress terrorism

---

[25] *INCSR 2004*, 49–50, and "NCCT Initiative," Financial Action Task Force, 16 July 2005, accessed at http://www1.oecd.org/fatf/NCCT_en.htm, 16 July 2005.

[26] *INCSR 2004*, 52–57.

[27] The Egmont Group, "Financial Intelligence Units of the World," 13 June 2001, accessed at http://www.fatf-gafi.org/pdf/EGFIUlist2001_en.pdf, 5 January 2006; and "Financial Intelligence Units of the World," 29 June 2005, accessed at http://www.fincen.gov/int_egmont.html, 5 September 2006 (hereafter *Egmont FIU List 2001* and *Egmont FIU List 2005*).

[28] Author's interviews with S/CT official and FinCEN official.

[29] *INCSR 2004*, 48; and author's interview with INL official.

and terrorist financing. Resolution 1373 is in effect a "mini treaty." It requires all of the same changes to domestic legislation, denial of safe haven, and criminalization of terrorism as the 1997 Convention on the Suppression of Terrorist Bombings and the 1999 Convention on the Suppression of Terrorist Financing. But since these treaties were not yet in force on 11 September 2001, the Security Council used its Chapter VII authority in Resolution 1373 to obligate *all* members to implement their provisions. Resolution 1373 goes beyond Resolution 1267 to require states to act against all terrorist organizations and their associates, not merely al Qaeda and the Taliban. This broad language reflects the U.S. determination to take advantage of the sympathetic post-September 11 environment in passing much tougher measures than states would otherwise have accepted.[30] Resolution 1373 established the Counter-Terrorism Committee (CTC) to monitor implementation and increase the capability of UN members to fight terrorism through the promotion and targeting of technical assistance.[31] Unlike the 1267 Committee however, the CTC does not maintain a designated terrorist list (the United Kingdom would not support such a proposal) and it adopted a neutral profile to generate as much responsiveness from UN members as possible.[32]

Problems in Sustaining Collective Action

The international response appears remarkable on its surface: over 100 nations drafted and passed laws addressing money laundering or terrorist financing shortly after September 11. The indicators used to measure the success of international efforts to combat terrorist financing include those most often cited by U.S. governmental officials (such as the amount of national and global asset freezes, establishment of financial intelligence units, conventions signed, treaties ratified and domestic legislation passed, and technical assistance programs run), as well as the International Monetary Fund (IMF) and World Bank measures of compliance.[33] After the attacks of September 11, the number of states ratifying the UN terrorism conventions soared, with 154 ratifying the 1999 Convention on the Suppression of Terrorist Financing and 148 ratifying the 1997 Convention on the Suppression of Terrorist Bombings.[34] Approxi-

[30] Bantekas, "International Law," 326.

[31] UN Office on Drugs and Crime, "Terrorism," accessed at http://www.unodc.org/unodc/en/terrorism.html, 16 July 2005.

[32] Author's interview with IO official; and Oudraat, "United Nations," 33.

[33] The indicator of assets frozen is problematic, because U.S. government reports are unsystematic. The Government Accountability Office harshly criticized the State Department and especially the Treasury Department for this. See "Terrorist Financing: Better Strategic Planning Needed to Coordinate U.S. Efforts to Deliver Counter-Terrorism Financing Training and Technical Assistance Abroad," United States Government Accountability Office Report to Congressional Requesters, October 2005 (hereafter GAO 2005).

[34] "Nuclear Threat Initiative, International Convention for the Suppression of the Financing of Terrorism," accessed at http://www.nti.org/e_research/official_docs/inventory/pdfs/finterr.

mately $147 million dollars in assets were frozen after the attacks of 11 September 2001 (about $44 million of which were in the United States).[35] Since September 11, approximately 188 countries have legislated the ability to freeze assets associated with al Qaeda and the Taliban, and 170 have passed legislation against terrorist groups more generally.[36]

In October 2001, the Financial Action Task Force expanded its anti-money-laundering mission to include terrorist financing, and it issued nine special recommendations for fighting terrorist financing. The Egmont Group also took terrorist financing under its purview. The widespread acceptance of multilateral norms to prevent terrorist use of the formal financial system led states to seek membership in the Egmont Group and ensure their removal from the Financial Action Task Force Non-Cooperative Countries and Territories list. Since 2000, the Egmont Group has grown by over 40 countries and territories to a total of 102.[37] The IMF and World Bank agreed to provide technical assistance to countries to ensure compliance with the Financial Action Task Force's anti-money-laundering and counter-terrorist-financing recommendations and inclusion of anti-money-laundering considerations in their country evaluations.[38]

Yet the international effort on terrorist financing, while impressive, has largely been superficial. States have taken steps they otherwise would not have taken in passing desired domestic legislation and in ratifying various UN terrorism conventions. The shock of the September 11 terrorist attacks on the United States, combined with Western pressure to adopt the existing pieces of the anti-money-laundering/counter-terrorist-financing regime made the costs of non-adoption higher. However, the only "carrot" offered by Resolution 1373 was technical assistance in combating terrorist financing, and total U.S. spending on technical assistance on this issue since September 11 has not exceeded $30 million.

The United States is not very active in the work of the UN CTC and devotes much more attention to the narrower purview of the 1267 Committee. The United States prefers expanding the al Qaeda and Taliban list of the 1267 Committee to sanction governments, groups, and individuals and using

---

pdf#search=%22convention%20terrorism%20financing%20nti%22, 4 October 2006; and "International Convention for the Suppression of Terrorist Bombing," accessed at http://www.nti.org/e_research/official_docs/inventory/pdfs/bomb.pdf#search=%22convention%20terrorist%20bombing%20nti%22, 4 October 2006." See Table 2, United Nations, "Report of the Secretary General to the Commission on Crime Prevention and Criminal Justice, UN Economic and Social Council," (17 March 2004) UN doc. E/CN.15/2004/8, 14 (hereafter UN March 2004).

[35] *9/11 Staff Monograph*, 45; and *INCSR 2004*, Introduction.

[36] UN March 2004, 12; and *9/11 Staff Monograph*, 45.

[37] *Egmont FIU List 2001*; and *Egmont FIU List 2005*.

[38] "Twelve-Month Pilot Project of Anti-Money Laundering and Combating the Financing of Terrorism (AML/CFT) Assessments," IMF and the World Bank Joint Report on the Review of the Pilot Project, 10 March 2004 (hereafter IMF-World Bank Joint Report).

bilateral and regional organizations to monitor and encourage compliance rather than developing a global multilateral regime focusing on technical assistance to build the capacity to implement and enforce laws against terrorist financing.[39] Of the $2.2 million given to the UN to implement technical assistance in counter-terrorist financing, the United States contributed less than 10 percent, while Austria alone made up over half of the contributions.[40] Indeed, it appears that there is disagreement at the political level in the United States over whether working through multilateral fora is anything other than "a waste of time."[41]

The available international "sticks" involve designations and sanctions (under UNSC Resolutions 1373, 1333, and 1267) and international pressure (the Financial Action Task Force's list of Non-Cooperative Countries and Territories). States initially followed the U.S. lead and designated individuals and entities that the United States named under Executive Order 13224. However, because of early U.S. errors in these designations and the widespread perception that they were intended for domestic political consumption, states—including almost all European states—now prefer to follow the UN lead on designations.[42] European citizens were among some of the early designees who were subsequently "de-listed." These mistakes raised concerns in European countries about the evidence involved, while other European countries faced lawsuits from the families of those who were designated. Of the $9 million in new asset freezes in 2004, $8 million were frozen by the United States.[43] Willingness to "name and shame" through the Financial Action Task Force's list of Non-Cooperative Countries and Territories evaporated, and political lobbying meant that as of February 2006, only Myanmar and Nigeria were listed as noncooperative while notorious money-laundering havens such as Nauru were not.[44] Some U.S. officials indicated that the Abu Ghraib scandal and the war in Iraq lessened Middle Eastern countries' interest in working with the U.S.[45]

Implementation of the best practices advocated by the Financial Action Task Force and the minimum standards required by Resolution 1373 has been much less forthcoming. Of forty-one countries surveyed in 2003, the IMF and World Bank found that compliance with the Financial Action Task Force special recommendations on terrorist financing was weakest in lower- and middle-income countries (categories that feature prominently in the list of "countries of concern" for terrorism financing compiled by Western states). The IMF and World Bank also reported that compliance was much less for the

---

[39] Author's interviews with State Department officials.

[40] See Table 1 in UN March 2004, 7.

[41] Author's interview with S/CT official.

[42] Author's interview with FinCEN official.

[43] Author's interview with OFAC official; and *INCSR 2005*, Introduction.

[44] "NCCT Current List," Financial Action Task Force, 17 February 2006, accessed at http://www. fatf-gafi.org/document/4/0,2340,en_32250379_32236992_33916420_1_1_1_1,00.html, 16 April 2006.

[45] Author's interviews with State Department officials.

more domestically intrusive and costly recommendations (such as regulating alternative money remittance systems and charities and know-your-customer requirements for wire transfers).[46]

U.S. threats of financial sanctions have produced important changes in state behavior in asset freezing and in complying with the Financial Action Task Force standards in some cases (the Philippines). But in the cases of most concern to the United States, particularly Saudi Arabia, Indonesia, and the Philippines, U.S. officials have suggested that it has only been the domestic experience of terrorism—after al Qaeda "fouled its own nest"—that sparked real action in these states on counter-terrorist financing. Even then, the bulk of cooperation has not been in the area of designations or in bolstering implementation of the counter-terrorist-financing regime, but in capturing and eliminating terrorist financiers.[47]

Problem Definition among the Most Financially Powerful States

The prospects for sustaining international collaboration on counter-terrorist financing and solidifying a global counter-terrorist financing regime are uncertain. Ongoing terrorist attacks present continual reminders of the danger of permitting penetration of national and international financial systems. In the absence of such attacks, U.S. officials have repeatedly stated, foreign governments do not see the institutional structures that facilitate terrorist financing as their problem, and they correspondingly do little to enforce anti-money-laundering and anti-terrorist-financing measures.[48] The major actors who would form any k-group interested in and necessary for sustaining a counter-terrorist-financing regime have different priorities, as the European response suggests.

There is emerging recognition of the problem posed by transnational actors among the European states. However, the European approach differs from that of the United States, suggesting fundamental disagreement on how to define the problem of counterterrorism and counter-terrorist financing. At a basic level, the original EU members are vitally concerned with ensuring that new and old members improve their counterterrorism laws. For them, September 11 and the 2004 Madrid and 2005 London bombings demonstrated that Islamic radicalism was a threat not only to the United States but to Europe as well. Yet internationally, the Europeans emphasize a global multilateral approach to anti-money-laundering/counter-terrorist-financing standard setting and technical assistance to implement such standards, and downplay the utility of designations and asset freezes. In their cooperation with the United States after September 11, the Europeans all took measures to counter terrorist fi-

---

[46] IMF-World Bank Joint Report, 48.
[47] Author's interviews with S/CT and EB officials.
[48] Author's interviews with FinCEN, S/CT, and IO officials.

nancing and to improve their compliance with the Financial Action Task Force standards.[49] However, they moved away from support of the U.S. focus on high-profile designations toward an "intelligence-based" approach that emphasized European and G8 information sharing to identify and track terrorist finances as well as greater attention to UN and EU-wide multilateral standard setting and implementation.[50]

While formally supportive of the work of the UN, the United States has chosen to use UN instruments for the narrow purpose of targeting Islamist groups rather than terrorism more broadly. The United States has favored bilateral and regional information sharing and targeted technical assistance over global multilateral efforts.[51] The United States seems to prefer the current patchwork approach of utilizing the multiple international frameworks (IMF/ World Bank, the Financial Action Task Force, 1267 Committee) when it suits U.S. interests to pressure particular countries that are sources of Islamic terrorist financing and terrorist activity. The Europeans' interests are broader, seeking to create rule-of-law economies and attack the root causes of terrorism through multilateral best practices and technical assistance. While there is not the fundamental rift in the transatlantic discussion over terrorism financing that exists over U.S. willingness to unilaterally use force in waging its war on terror, the differences between the United States and the Europeans over priorities and domestic costs are significant enough to impede collective action to create a robust counter-terrorist-financing regime.

The fundamental cause of the different approaches appears to be the lack of a common definition of the problem posed by terrorist financing and terrorism more broadly and the uneven and sporadic internalization of a new security paradigm that places nonstate actors and nontraditional concerns closer to the center of the notion of national security. Collective action theory suggests that without a common U.S. and European definition of the problem and a subsequent common interest in underwriting the costs of such a regime, it is likely that these countries will fail to produce the public good of a global financial system that is less penetrable by terrorists. A detailed study of the

---

[49] Author's interview with EB official; *INCSR 2004*; United States Department of State, *Patterns of Global Terrorism 2003,* March 2004, accessed at http://www.state.gov/documents/organization/ 31912.pdf, 4 October 2006; Francis T. Miko and Christian Froehlich, "Germany's Role in Fighting Terrorism: Implications for U.S. Policy," CRS Report for Congress, 27 December 2004; and HM Treasury, "Combating the Financing of Terrorism: A Report on UK Action, 24 October 2002," accessed at http://www.hm-treasury.gov.uk/documents/international_issues/terrorist_financing/int_terrorfinance_ combatfinance.cfm, 16 July 2005.

[50] "The Fight against Terrorist Financing," Note of the Secretary General/High Representative and the Commission to the Council of the European Union (EU Doc. 16089/04), 14 December 2004, accessed at http://ue.eu.int/uedocs/cmsUpload/EUplan16090.pdf, 4 October 2006; see also "EU Plan of Action on Combating Terrorism—Update," First Review by the Presidency of the European Council, (EU Doc. 16090/04), 14 December 2004, accessed at http://ue.eu.int/uedocs/cmsUpload/16089fight_ against_terrorist_financing.pdf, 4 October 2006.

[51] Author's interviews with all State Department officials.

U.S. case suggests that lack of continuous political attention to the problem and bureaucratic infighting prevent the United States from redefining the problem of terrorist financing.

U.S. Effort to Combat Terrorist Financing before 11 September 2001

Prior to the 2001 attacks, there was no sustained, concerted effort by the United States to counter terrorist financing. *The 9/11 Commission Report* and *The 9/11 Commission Staff Monograph on Terrorist Financing* paint an authoritative picture of disaggregated data collection, mistaken understandings regarding information sharing, conflicting organizational cultures and jealousies, and interrupted attention spans that impeded the government and Congress in focusing on the issue of terrorism and how it was funded. The only governmental body focused on the issue more or less consistently was the White House, particularly the National Security Council (NSC), which since 1985 has coordinated government efforts to counter terrorism.[52]

Terrorism was one of the first national security issues the new Clinton administration had to face, with the assassination of two Central Intelligence Agency (CIA) employees outside CIA headquarters in Virginia in January 1993 and the bombing of the World Trade Center the following month. The issues of terrorism and terrorist financing occupied the NSC from the aftermath of the 1993 World Trade Center bombing onward. Detection and prevention of weapons of mass destruction terrorism were made the very highest priority for President Clinton's own staff and all agencies; a reorganization gave the Department of Justice and the FBI the lead on the domestic front, with the CIA, the State Department, and others responsible for the foreign front.[53]

Although the issues of terrorism and terrorist financing received a high level of attention from the President and his national security advisors, the NSC was incapable of systematically engaging and directing a host of subunits within various government agencies to address the problems.[54] Because of the attorney general's concerns and the legacy of the Iran-Contra affair during the Reagan administration, the NSC Counterterrorism Security Group Director Richard Clarke was authorized only to give advice regarding budgets and to coordinate interagency guidelines for action.[55] The NSC therefore could not task agencies

---

[52] *The 9/11 Commission Report. Final Report of the National Commission on Terrorist Attacks Upon the United States,* authorized ed. (New York: W.W. Norton & Company, 2004), 98–100, 122–123, 185.

[53] Ibid., 100–102.

[54] *9/11 Staff Monograph,* 4–5; and author's interviews with OFAC, FinCEN, and INL officials.

[55] *9/11 Commission Report,* 101; and Congressional Research Service, "Terrorist Financing: Current Efforts and Policy Issues for Congress," CRS Report for Congress, 20 August 2004, 9–10 (hereafter CRS August 2004), and "Terrorist Financing: U.S. Agency Efforts and Inter-Agency Coordination," CRS Report for Congress, 3 August 2005, 14 (hereafter CRS August 2005).

to take action and appropriate funds, which one senior official suggested was the fundamental problem preventing successful interagency coordination and action.[56]

Knowledge of how terrorists financed their operations was poorly sourced and slow in coming.[57] As late as 1997, the CIA was aware that Osama bin Laden had provided funds to several terrorist organizations but not that he was at the heart of a terrorist network. Because the national security advisor had expressed a personal interest in terrorist financing, the CIA had set up a unit to track terrorist financial links in 1996. It focused solely on bin Laden, however, and moved quickly away from a focus on financial links to one on operational planning.[58]

The issue of terrorist financing gained more attention after the bombings of the U.S. embassies in Nairobi and Dar es Salaam in early August of 1998. An NSC-led interagency group on terrorist financing was established, which included the NSC, the Treasury Department, the CIA, the FBI, and the State Department. While the CIA cooperated in this group, the FBI would not meaningfully participate.[59] The NSC alone maintained pressure on the issue of terrorist financing. It led in pressing the Saudis for access to a key al Qaeda financial officer.[60] The President and the State Department, again after NSC urging, began to pressure Pakistan on its support to jihadists in Kashmir and the Taliban. The President issued Executive Order 13099, freezing all financial holdings that could be associated with bin Laden.[61]

Despite the increased focus on counter-terrorist financing from the White House, there was little change in the behavior of federal agencies. The FBI was gathering intelligence against organizations suspected of raising funds for terrorists on a field office level, but with no centralized collection or sharing system in place.[62] At NSC urging, the Treasury Department was designated in March 2000 as the home for a new Foreign Terrorist Asset Tracking Center (FTATC) and congressional authorization came in October. However, due to bureaucratic tug-of-wars between Treasury and the CIA, the FTATC was only hastily staffed three days *after* September 11.[63]

Financial Industry Objections and U.S. Capacity for Collective Action

Despite the lack of coordinated effort in the executive branch, prior to September 11 there was a somewhat ad hoc system of laws, authorities, and regulations in place that directly or indirectly addressed terrorist finances.

---

[56] Author's interview with James B. Steinberg, Deputy National Security Advisor to the Clinton administration, Washington DC, 14 October 2004.

[57] *9/11 Commission Report*, 170–171; and *9/11 Staff Monograph*, 34–35.

[58] *9/11 Commission Report*, 109.

[59] *9/11 Staff Monograph*, 40–41.

[60] *9/11 Commission Report*, 122.

[61] E.O. 13099, 20 August 1999, cited in Ibid., 126.

[62] *9/11 Commission Staff Monograph*, 4–6.

[63] *CRS August 2005*, 11–12.

These rules both criminalized the provision of funds to terrorists and provided the government the means to collect information with which to detect the flow of such funds. The 1990 Anti-Terrorism Act made material support, including funding and financial services, to foreign terrorist organizations illegal. In 1995, the Clinton administration pushed for increased federal criminal laws, making it easier to deport terrorists and to act against terrorist fund-raisers. After the Aum Shinrikyo chemical weapons attack on the Tokyo subway and the Oklahoma City bombing in 1995, Clinton proposed increased wiretap and electronic surveillance authority for the FBI and new funding for the FBI, CIA, and local police.[64] The 1996 Anti-Terrorism and Effective Death Penalty Act made the provision of support to terrorists a criminal act, and allowed civil suits against a foreign state or its instruments committing a terrorist act.[65] A series of anti-money-laundering statutes made conducting financial transactions to further or conceal criminal acts—including the destruction of aircraft and hostage taking, among many others—illegal.[66]

Despite these advances in counter-terrorist-financing legislation, the financial industry blocked most other efforts in the 1990s to strengthen the anti-money-laundering regime. A critical element of the anti-money-laundering legal framework was the 1970 Bank Secrecy Act. It required banks to create audit trails of large bank transactions and to allow law enforcement access to such information or face criminal penalties. In 1985, the Federal Reserve and the Office of the Comptroller of the Currency began requiring financial institutions to submit suspicious activity reports. The Annunzio-Wylie Anti-Money Laundering Act of 1992 added Treasury to the list of executive agencies able to require this information and required for the first time that banks keep records of wire transfers.[67] The decision on what activity was "suspicious" fell to the discretion of bank employees. The Treasury Department lobbied for controls on foreign banks with U.S. accounts in 1999 and 2000. Despite bipartisan support in the House, this effort stalled in the Senate Banking Committee, where the chair rejected further regulation of banks.

In 1999, the Treasury Department and federal financial regulators proposed draft regulations requiring banks to "know your customer." These requirements would ensure that banks took reasonable steps to know who the beneficial owner of an account was and the sources of funds flowing through accounts. This sparked such a firestorm of controversy and resistance from the banking industry that these efforts failed and Congress even considered weak-

[64] *9/11 Commission Report*, 100–101.

[65] Bantekas, "International Law," 328.

[66] Mariano-Florentino Cuellar, "The Tenuous Relationship between the Fight against Money Laundering and the Disruption of Criminal Finance" (Stanford Public Law and Legal Theory Working Paper Series, research paper no. 64, September 2003): 337–338.

[67] Ibid., 358. The Federal Reserve and Office of the Comptroller of the Currency had been requiring SARs since 1985.

ening the money-laundering controls then in place.[68] The banking industry successfully defeated Treasury's initial attempts to specify exactly what information must be collected on wire transfers. This essentially prevented the creation of standardized records, significantly impairing the efficiency and speed with which law enforcement could access such information.[69]

Additional efforts to regulate the informal financial system (for example, money remitters and other money services businesses) were also thwarted. The informal system was increasingly important as money launderers and terrorists shifted their operations outside the formal financial system. Although Congress had authorized Treasury in 1994 to draw up regulations governing the informal sector, these regulations were only issued in 1999, with an implementation date of December 2001. In the summer of 2001, the Treasury Department deferred implementation to 2002.[70]

The most powerful legal tool in the counter-terrorist-financing tool kit prior to September 11 was the 1977 International Emergency Economic Powers Act (IEEPA). Under the IEEPA, if the president declares a national emergency with regard to an "unusual or extraordinary" foreign threat, he can block, through a presidential decision directive, the assets of individuals or organizations associated with that threat, and trade between the United States and those designated. The Office of Foreign Assets Control in the Department of the Treasury then identifies the designated individuals or entities and orders their bank accounts frozen. U.S. courts have given the president wide latitude in using this authority because it relates to foreign policy and national security and is therefore a political rather than legal issue.[71] The United States has long used this tool to freeze the assets of states sponsoring terrorism, such as Iran, Libya, and Sudan.

According to the 9/11 Commission staff, "In the 1990s the government began to use these powers in a different, more innovative way, to go after non-state actors."[72] In 1995, President Clinton used his authority under the IEEPA to issue an executive order freezing the U.S. assets of Colombian drug trafficking organizations and barring U.S. businesses from dealing with the traffickers or their front companies. The same year, the Clinton administration used the IEEPA to sanction terrorists seeking to disrupt the Middle East peace process. Treasury's Office of Foreign Assets Control had hoped to target bin Laden in this way, but did not have access to the intelligence required to make the case for designating him. This would wait until after the 1998 embassy bombings, when President Clinton formally designated bin Laden and al Qaeda under the IEEPA. This had little practical effect, because bin Laden had

---

[68] *9/11 Staff Monograph*, 38.
[69] Cuellar, "Tenuous Relationship," 359–360.
[70] *9/11 Staff Monograph*, 38–39.
[71] Cuellar, "Tenuous Relationship," 360–361.
[72] *9/11 Staff Monograph*, 37.

moved most of his assets out of the formal financial system after he left Sudan in 1996 and the IEEPA only gave Treasury's Office of Foreign Assets Control authority over assets in U.S. banks and over other U.S. legal persons. In 1999, the President designated the Taliban under the IEEPA for harboring bin Laden and al Qaeda, and blocked Taliban assets worth over $34 million held in private U.S. banks and $217 million in gold and deposits held at the Federal Reserve.[73]

U.S. Inability to Redefine the Collective Interest prior to September 11

The picture of U.S. efforts to suppress terrorist financing prior to the 11 September 2001 attacks is one of fractured attention spans and lack of a comprehensive approach to the multifaceted problem of terrorist finance. During the 1990s, the Clinton administration began to slowly redefine the threat of terrorism as one separate from the traditional paradigm of state sponsors against which economic and military sanctions could be applied. But the redefinition was taking place at the NSC, and its expansion to higher levels of the government and Congress waxed and waned in sequence with the terrorist attacks against the United States in 1993, 1995, 1998, and 2000. The U.S. counterterrorism effort was fragmented among many different agencies and lacked any central coordination and direction, particularly at the FBI.[74]

The U.S. Congress had not made the shift in paradigms to a new post-Cold War, nonstate actor framing of national security. The Congress, in addition to resisting the executive branch's efforts to reframe anti-money-laundering measures as national security measures, remained enamored of economic sanctions against out-of-favor states. This hindered the U.S. ability to work with critical states such as Pakistan on suppressing al Qaeda and pressuring the Taliban.[75] Domestic ideological and political battles often interfered with serious attention to the issue of transnational terrorism, and lessened the sense of threat that nonstate actors posed to the United States. Congress only focused on nonstate terrorism in a completely reactive fashion, in the wake of attacks on U.S. targets at home and abroad. Even this attention was minimal and not sustained. According to the 9/11 Commission, "Terrorism was a second- or third-order priority within the committees of Congress responsible for national security."[76]

By the end of the Clinton presidency, nonstate terrorists and their finances were recognized in the executive branch as a serious threat to U.S. national security.[77] The White House, however, was incapable of translating this recognition into a coordinated and effective domestic and international counterterrorist

---

[73] Ibid., 37–38.
[74] Ibid., 4–6.
[75] *9/11 Commission Report*, 102–107.
[76] Ibid., 107, 118–119.
[77] Ibid., 100–102; author's interviews with Steinberg and Myers.

effort. Ironically, the government's success in finding and prosecuting the 1993 World Trade Center terrorists impeded White House efforts to reframe and prioritize terrorism and terrorist financing as a major threat.[78]

THE U.S. EFFORT TO COMBAT TERRORIST FINANCING AFTER SEPTEMBER 11

The new administration of George W. Bush did not begin its term with the understanding of nonstate threats that the Clinton administration had learned, and its foreign policy priorities, such as missile defenses, were driven by the familiar paradigm of states as the most serious threats facing the United States.[79]

The shock of the 11 September 2001 attacks caused radical changes in the way the U.S. federal government framed and managed the issue of terrorist financing. Within days, federal bureaucracies came together to act collectively to understand the financial basis of the attacks. Agencies immediately established new units to work on the problem, and agreed to interagency cooperation.

The FBI, which was harshly criticized in the 9/11 Commission Staff Monograph for its failures prior to September 11, established an interagency Financial Review Group within days of the attacks. This group became the Terrorist Financing Operations Section. It focused on ensuring that the United States developed a real-time financial tracking capability for urgent financial investigations and that each terrorism investigation had a financial component. Most importantly, for the first time, it coordinated in a single office the FBI's counter-terrorist-financing efforts.[80] Other agencies followed suit. The United States Customs Service established Operation Green Quest to investigate terrorist financing. The Justice Department reallocated resources from other areas after September 11 to create a unit devoted to conducting and coordinating terrorist-financing criminal investigations nationwide.[81] Within a week of the September 11 attacks, the CIA had created a new interagency section to develop long-term intelligence on terrorist financing, track terrorists, and disrupt their operations. In 2003, the FBI-led Joint Terrorism Task Force combined the investigative efforts of the FBI, the Justice Department, Customs (now under the Department of Homeland Security), and the IRS.

The NSC set up an ad hoc structure immediately after the attacks, which was replaced by a Policy Coordinating Committee on Terrorist Financing in March 2002.[82] The Policy Coordinating Committee was chaired by the Treasury Department Office of Legal Counsel until November 2003 and, owing largely to General Counsel David Aufhauser's personality, was able to overcome interagency dif-

[78] *9/11 Commission Report*, 73.
[79] Author's interview with Steinberg.
[80] *9/11 Staff Monograph*, 41–42.
[81] This became the Terrorism Financing Unit under the Department of Justice Counterterrorism Section. Ibid., 42.
[82] Ibid., 47.

ferences.[83] The Treasury Department's lead role in counter-terrorist financing came under fire from the Independent Task Force on Terrorist Financing at the Council on Foreign Relations, which insisted that the NSC take the lead on the PCC because of the diplomatic and intelligence aspects of counter-terrorist financing.[84] The 9/11 Commission staff also reported that the PCC was not well integrated into the broader U.S. counterterrorism effort, a criticism loudly echoed by the Council on Foreign Relations Independent Task Force.[85] A Government Accountability Office study suggested that the lack of integration continued through 2005.[86]

Bureaucratic Politics and Collective Action

Even well-endowed and motivated states such as the United States that have legal authorities in place and have recently suffered terrorists attacks find it difficult to develop the capacity to implement collective action domestically. Domestically, capacity requires interagency cooperation to produce effective counterterrorism strategies and implement them. However, domestic agencies, even after attacks as profound as those on 11 September 2001, are likely to pursue their bureaucratic interests at the expense of the collective effort against terrorist financing. Initially, government officials report, interagency cooperation was unprecedented. Yet domestically, cooperation was not well-institutionalized and bureaucratic politics undermined its effectiveness.[87]

A number of bureaucratic battles developed in the aftermath of the September 11th attacks that interfered with the implementation of domestic collective action against terrorist financing. The Treasury Department was at the center of most of them, as it sought to take the lead both domestically and internationally on designations of terrorist financiers and technical assistance training. Within the Treasury Department, the Office of Foreign Assets Control was hastily made the home of the FTATC (authorized and funded in fall 2000, but only established three days after the September attacks). The FTATC never fully functioned at Treasury. The CIA essentially took over the operation, a fact made official by November 2002, when it was renamed the Foreign Terrorist Asset Tracking Group and made an independent CIA-administered entity. After its move to the CIA, neither the Treasury Department nor the Financial Crimes Enforcement Center (FinCEN) detailed any analysts to the Tracking Group. The Tracking Group functioned as a targeting arm of the Policy Coordinating Com-

---

[83] Ibid.; author's interviews with Myers and INL and FinCEN officials.

[84] "Terrorist Financing," report of an independent task force sponsored by the Council on Foreign Relations, November 2002, 23 (hereafter 2002 CFR Report), and "Update on the Global Campaign Against Terrorist Financing," report of an independent task force sponsored by the Council on Foreign Relations, 15 June 2004, 31 (hereafter 2004 CFR Report).

[85] 9/11 Staff Monograph, 47; 2002 and 2004 CFR Reports.

[86] GAO 2005, 31.

[87] Author's interviews with Myers and FinCEN, OFAC, INL, and EB officials.

mittee on Terrorist Financing. However, this committee was given a low priority within the administration; it was left leaderless for months, and funds that were to be used for it were reallocated to build a protective barrier around the Treasury Department in 2005.[88]

Another bureaucratic battle took place between the U.S. Customs Service and the FBI Terrorist Financing Operations Section over Customs Service's Operation Green Quest. Both led overlapping interagency groups to investigate terrorist financing. This dispute was resolved in 2003 with the formation of an FBI-led Joint Terrorism Task Force, but with an agreement to ensure the continued participation of experts at Customs (now the Immigration and Customs Enforcement branch of the Department of Homeland Security).[89]

A third bureaucratic battle developed over which agency should lead in the international effort to implement counter-terrorist-financing measures through technical assistance. After September 11, an interagency Terrorist Financing Working Group was established. Co-chaired by the State Department's Office of the Coordinator for Counter Terrorism and Bureau for International Narcotics and Law Enforcement Affairs, it reported to the NSC Policy Coordinating Committee on Terrorist Financing. The Terrorist Financing Working Group identified and assisted important countries in making their financial systems less vulnerable to manipulation by terrorists. It provided technical assistance and training programs to establish and implement legal and regulatory frameworks to comply with UN Resolution 1373, create financial intelligence and financial crimes units, and prosecute terrorism finance crimes. The Treasury Department's Office of Technical Assistance worked with Congress to secure $2.2 million for counterterrorism financing training independent of the Working Group and did not cooperate in it. The Treasury Department sought to take the lead in the Policy Coordinating Committee on Terrorist Financing away from the NSC. It also sought to displace the State Department lead in the Terrorist Financing Working Group on intelligence and operations, and in the production of a counter-terrorist-financing strategy report (the annual State Department *International Narcotics Control Strategy Report* covers terrorist financing). The State Department resisted this.[90] Officials at the State Department, FinCEN, and Treasury's Office of Foreign Assets Control suggested that cooperation on counter-terrorist financing was eroding in the area of international technical assistance because of interagency problems, particularly with Treasury's Office of Technical Assistance, and a number of personalities. A FinCEN official called

---

[88] CRS August 2004, 10–12; and letter from Joshua Bolten, Director of the Office of Management and Budget, to the President, 8 June 2005.

[89] *9/11 Staff Monograph*, 44; and CRS August 2004, 27, 37.

[90] Author's interviews with FinCEN, S/CT, EB, INL, and OFAC officials. This battle has subsequently become public. See GAO 2005, 14–15; and *Terrorist Financing: Agencies Can Improve Efforts to Deliver Counter-Terrorism-Financing Training and Technical Assistance Abroad*, Committee on Financial Services, Subcommittee on Oversight Investigations, U.S. House of Representatives (testimony of David M. Walker, 6 April 2006), United States Government Accountability Office, GAO-06-632T, 1–30.

the Terrorist Financing Working Group "dysfunctional." While high-level Treasury officials continue to stress the designations and freeze process as a key tool in the counter-terrorist-financing fight, working-level officials at the State Department and FinCEN emphasize that designations are largely ineffectual because the funds move into alternative financial systems. As one State Department official said, "Any objective to block funds is a fool's chase."[91] Instead, the working-level officials stress the domestic and international need to extend anti-money-laundering measures to these systems in order to use intelligence gathered from anti-money-laundering measures to track and disrupt terrorist activities.

U.S. Inability to Redefine the Collective Interest

Underlying these battles is a fundamental debate over which of two strategies is most appropriate and effective in suppressing terrorist financing. The first strategy focuses on designating and detaining terrorists and their associates, freezing their assets, and passing the necessary legislation to make such designations and freezes legal. The second "follow-the-money" or intelligence strategy, focuses on improving regulation of formal and informal financial systems, and intelligence collection, analysis, and sharing to track and disrupt terrorist operations. The debate reflects disagreement over how the United States should define its collective interest regarding terrorist financing.

One would expect from a bureaucratic politics model that different government actors would express distinct preferences regarding these strategies.[92] The agencies with financial regulatory, anti-money-laundering, and law enforcement authorities, such as the Departments of Treasury and Justice, as well as those feeling the greatest pressure to demonstrate that actions were being taken after September 11 to combat terrorism (such as the White House), would prefer the designations-and-asset-freezing strategy. Designations are highly public and visible, with those suspected of financing terrorists rounded up in sweeps as the designations are unsealed. The freezing of assets is easily quantifiable (while the number of total terrorist assets is not widely known), providing a rapid and easily communicated measure of the government's success in vigorously suppressing terrorism. Such actions demonstrate to those who hold budgetary purse strings and to the electorate that concrete efforts and results have occurred. Prosecutorial and investigative agencies and civil liberties advocates should also prefer the designations-and-asset-freezing approach, as long as proper evidentiary standards are used.

In contrast, the intelligence strategy is preferred by the intelligence community, including that within the FBI and FinCEN, because it offers greater potential for terrorists to be tracked and killed or captured, as well as providing

---

[91] Author's interview with EB official.

[92] David Welch, "The Organizational Process and Bureaucratic Politics Paradigms: Retrospect and Prospect," *International Security* (Fall 1992): 112–146.

the data necessary for building profiles of terrorists. For the foreign affairs agencies, the private or covert nature of the intelligence strategy increases the government's flexibility in cooperating with foreign countries, inasmuch as secret assistance may be more forthcoming than public. Members of the financial services industry should favor the intelligence strategy, because it reduces the likelihood of tighter government regulation of their activities or, at a minimum, provides less publicity regarding their cooperation with government authorities regarding client information. The post-September 11 experience, while remarkably cooperative by all accounts, tends to broadly support such expectations.[93]

The strategies are not mutually exclusive, but unthinking or compartmented reliance on one can seriously impede the effectiveness of the other. Resources are not infinite. The bureaucratic interests engaged in each strategy create a tendency to withhold information and guard bureaucratic prerogatives. Such tendencies were dramatically exposed in the 9/11 Commission's report on the bureaucratic compartmentalization and turf battles that existed prior to September 11 and that, in the Commission's estimation, represent massive failures to successfully detect and prevent terrorist attacks.[94]

Lack of Common Definition of the Problem of Terrorist Financing

During the first G.W. Bush administration, the designations-and-asset-freezing approach to combating terrorist financing dominated, although both strategies were pursued.[95] As the bureaucratic model would suggest, under his IEEPA authority, President Bush issued Executive Order 13224 designating bin Laden and al Qaeda and authorizing the freezing of assets of entities associated with them, calling it the "first strike in the war on terror." This order ratified Treasury's Office of Foreign Assets Control authority (which had been derived from Clinton-era executive orders) to go after bin Laden's and al Qaeda's assets. In October 2001, President Bush signed the USA Uniting and Strengthening America by Providing Appropriate Tools Required to Intercept and Obstruct Terrorism (PATRIOT) Act into law. It significantly expanded the government's regulatory authority regarding money laundering and criminal finance. It put into effect the "know-your-customer" and wire transfer requirements that had been defeated by the banking industry in 2000.[96] Most of this power goes to the Department of the Treasury to designate countries or business sectors as failing to meet minimum anti-money-laundering standards and, in consultation with other agencies, to impose sanctions and other "special measures" such as restricting countries' or financial institutions' access to the

---

[93] *9/11 Commission Report*, ch. 3; and *9/11 Staff Monograph*, 4–6.
[94] Ibid.
[95] *9/11 Staff Monograph*, 79; and author's interviews with Myers, and IO, and EB officials.
[96] Author's interview with EB official.

U.S. financial system.[97] The USA PATRIOT Act also empowered a single government official, the Director of the Office of Foreign Assets Control at the Treasury Department, to freeze assets before legally sufficient evidence had been collected.[98] Treasury's Office of Foreign Assets Control worked feverishly after the attacks to add organizations and individuals to the designations list, using names provided by the CIA, whose intelligence was very poor.[99] Very high level and public announcements of the freezing of terrorist assets occurred soon after the September 11th attacks. As the 9/11 Report put it:

> The goal set at the policy levels of the White House and Treasury was to conduct a public and aggressive series of designations to show the world community and our allies that we were serious about pursuing the financial targets. It entailed a major designation every four weeks. … Treasury officials acknowledged that the evidentiary foundations for the early designations were quite weak. … The rush to designate came primarily from the NSC.[100]

The White House, the secretary of the treasury, and the attorney general all trumpeted these actions. However, the intelligence supporting some of the highest-profile designations was found to be seriously flawed from a legal perspective and the volume of money disrupted significantly overstated. In August 2002, the United States was forced into the embarrassing position of de-listing some foreigners under pressure from allies and U.S. citizens who filed lawsuits. The United States was also unable to obtain a conviction on a terrorism charge for a leader of an Illinois charity.[101] The CIA reasoned that designations would have little effect on terrorists, who would simply move funds to nondesignated institutions. It reportedly successfully pressed for more attention to the "follow-the-money" strategy.[102] One State Department official described the initial post-September 11 designations as a political process driven by "the need for public action and the availability of a hammer."[103]

The debate over strategies in turn depends on how closely one identifies the problem of terrorist financing with that of state responsibility and control. The powers granted to regulators and the Treasury under the PATRIOT Act are anti-money-laundering tools, designed for tracking large sums of money. But the sums transferred by terrorists to fund their operations and fund-raisers for terrorist entities are tiny when placed in the context of a multi-trillion-dollar global finance system.[104] The Treasury Department under Clinton

---

[97] Cuellar, "Tenuous Relationship," 361–362; and 2002 CFR Report, 13, 26.

[98] *9/11 Staff Monograph*, 99.

[99] Author's interview with FinCEN official.

[100] *9/11 Staff Monograph*, 79.

[101] Ibid., 80–81, 85–86 and Illinois charities case study.

[102] Eric Lichtblau and James Risen, "Bank Data is Sifted by U.S. in Secret to Block Terror," *The New York Times*, 23 June 2006.

[103] Author's interview with EB official.

[104] Author's interview with FinCEN, OFAC, and INL officials.

had already learned this when it sought freeze bin Laden's assets. Unable to gain sufficient information on these assets—in large measure because the fundraising for al Qaeda was dispersed and commingled with legitimate humanitarian donations—Treasury sought but failed to get anti-money-laundering tools from Congress more appropriate to finding terrorist finances.[105]

After early missteps in pursuing the designations strategy, the Bush administration began emphasizing the intelligence strategy.[106] In June 2006, *The New York Times* reported that secret monitoring of the SWIFT financial database—the central hub for global banking transactions—led to the arrest of the alleged mastermind of the 2002 Bali nightclub bombings.[107] Designations and the number of asset freezes declined.[108]

The change in emphasis suggests that some in the Bush administration may have started to reach conclusions similar to the Clinton administration's regarding a state's capacity to control nonstate terrorists. Rather than an emphasis on state power and responsibility to shut down terrorists' access to finances, a gradual understanding of the need for comprehensive financial regulation and information sharing to manage nontraditional national security threats emerged under the Clinton administration. Such a learning process may have begun in the Bush administration, at least in the area of counter-terrorism financing. However, the continued lack of a comprehensive counter-terrorist-financing policy, the unwillingness to allocate specific funds for counter-terrorist financing, and the dominance of the state-centric paradigm among key administration officials suggest that such a redefinition has not been internalized at either the highest or working levels of the U.S. government.[109]

CONCLUSION

What does the United States effort to counter terrorist financing augur for the global effort? By all accounts, the horror of the September 11 attacks galvanized government bureaucracies and broke down interagency walls that had withstood lesser terrorist attacks.[110] Interagency cooperation and banking industry collaboration with the government was unprecedented in the immediate aftermath of the attacks. This cooperation remains a marked improvement over the pre-September 11 situation. Working-level officials repeat that "we're not going to be the reason 9/11 happens again." It is this sentiment that makes them willing to make the interagency process work. Yet there are strong indicators that the passage of time has eroded the political will to put the national

---

[105] *9/11 Staff Monograph*, 37.

[106] Ibid., 48–49.

[107] Lichtblau and Risen, "Bank Data."

[108] Author's interview with EB, INL, IO, and OFAC officials.

[109] GAO 2005, 19; and author's interview with Steinberg.

[110] *9/11 Staff Monograph*, 48–49.

interest ahead of private and bureaucratic interests. As one official handling counter-terrorist financing said, bureaucratic "rivalries have reemerged with greater fervor."[111]

Working-level officials worry that the issue of counter-terrorist financing has slipped in the hierarchy of priorities at higher levels of government.[112] This concern is echoed in high-profile criticism from outside of government.[113] The U.S. effort to counter terrorist financing is being funded largely through re-allocations from other budget lines rather than by generating a significant new budgetary commitment.[114] Banks are reportedly experiencing "blocking fatigue." The international community is willing to act only under UN designations, and U.S. actions in Iraq have made some states reluctant to follow the U.S. lead in implementing and enforcing legislative changes. U.S. willingness to under-write the technical assistance to enable states to enforce the counter-terrorist-financing regime at home has been minimal ($20-30 million since 2001) in comparison with the broader U.S. war on terrorism.[115]

The United States and its European allies have succeeded in globalizing the anti-money-laundering framework and recasting it as a regime to combat terrorist financing. However, the U.S. domestic approach to the problem of terrorist financing has changed in the short period since 2001, and its international efforts reflect this shift. As the U.S. effort shifted away from des-ignations and asset freezes, its international efforts turned more to sharing intelligence with other states to track, capture, or kill important terrorist finance figures.[116] Its efforts have focused bilateral pressure on a small number of countries rather than underwriting a global multilateral regime. While there has been substantial and important movement through informal international bodies such as the Financial Action Task Force and the Egmont Group, the United States has been unwilling to underwrite a formal global counter-terrorist-financing regime.

Fundamentally, the United States has devoted the majority of its attention internationally to the "global war on terror," which it defines to include the war in Iraq. U.S. efforts internationally on terrorist financing illustrate that this war is not really global for the United States, but focused on about twenty-five states in which al Qaeda and other Islamic terrorists operate. Despite the fact that the number of "states of concern" to the United States has grown from nineteen to twenty-six in less than a year, the United States has focused the bulk of its counter-terrorist-financing efforts on tactically targeting groups and

---

[111] Author's interviews with all State Department, OFAC, and FinCEN officials; quotations are from FinCEN official.

[112] Author's interviews with EB, INL, IO, and FinCEN officials.

[113] See 2002 and 2004 CRF Reports and 9/11 Public Discourse Project Final Report.

[114] Author's interviews with all those interviewed. See also GAO 2005, 19–20; and Walker, *Terrorist Financing*, 1–30.

[115] Author's interview with INL official.

[116] *9/11 Staff Monograph*, 46–47.

individuals, rather than on building a robust international regime.[117] The problem with such an approach is that terrorist and other criminal finances will flow to wherever the regulatory environment is loosest, so a partial approach is likely to be ineffective. A truly global counter-terrorist-financing regime could change the operating environment of terrorists, forcing them into criminal activity that is easier to trace and prosecute than is "pre-criminal" terrorist financing. The development of a global counter-terrorist-financing regime that would change the operating environment for terrorist financiers does not appear to have genuine support from one of the critical actors needed to promote and underwrite it.

The prospects for the successful global development of national institutional capacity to combat the counter-terrorist-financing framework depends on states' recognition that terrorist financing is their problem, not someone else's. The developed countries, with the most domestic capacity to combat terrorist financing, recognize this threat. Even they, however, have been inconsistent in their willingness to enforce counter-terrorist-financing laws and engage in international cooperation. Less-developed countries without this capacity often do not even see the threat. Redefining the national interest to include countering terrorist financing unfortunately appears to rise and fall with states' experience of terrorist attacks.[118] Without such attacks, and without Western pressure and incentives, it is unlikely that a permanent redefinition of national security to include the financing of terrorism will occur or that states will take the steps to build and enforce an effective global counter-terrorist-financing regime.*

---

[117] Author's interviews with S/CT official; GAO 2005, 12; and *INCSR 2005*, Introduction.

[118] Author's interviews with all State Department officials.

* The views expressed in this document do not represent the official position of the Department of Defense or the U.S. government, but are the sole responsibility of the author.

Part III:
Nuclear Proliferation

After Saddam:
Regional Insecurity, Weapons of Mass Destruction, and Proliferation Pressures in Postwar Iraq

ANDREW FLIBBERT

The U.S. government's decision to go to war with Iraq was premised on the credible claim that a brutal and unpredictable ruler like Saddam Hussein had to be prevented from developing or retaining weapons of mass destruction (WMD). While some congressional moderates hoped to constrain Iraq's military capability through muscular inspections and close UN supervision, the Bush administration contended that removing Saddam was the best and, ultimately, the only effective course of action. Accordingly, despite global opposition and the UN Security Council's refusal to sanction military intervention, the United States fought a six-week war in March and April 2003, deposing the regime with considerable ease. In the war's aftermath, security has been slow to return to the country, U.S. troops had difficulty locating Saddam and his top advisers, continued guerrilla-style resistance has plagued the American occupation, democracy has proven elusive, and no substantial stockpile of WMD or production facilities have been uncovered. The latter problem, more than any other, has led to new debates over the war's justification, as war supporters and opponents alike continue to question the imminence of the threat to American interests underpinning administration claims and U.S. actions.[1]

Aside from concern over the politicization and manipulation of intelligence, the major challenge to international security after the war is not simply

---

[1] The administration's five major public justifications for the war included 1) claims of Iraq's continued possession and development of weapons of mass destruction in violation of UN Security Council resolutions; 2) the regime's purported ties to al Qaeda; 3) Saddam's brutal rule and gross violations of human rights; 4) the promotion of democracy in the Middle East; and 5) the improvement of Arab-Israeli relations.

ANDREW FLIBBERT is assistant professor of political science at Trinity College in Hartford, Connecticut.

ascertaining the extent of Iraqi weapons or production facilities. There is little doubt that Iraq once had active nuclear, chemical, and biological programs that would have yielded usable weapons sooner or later. A greater concern is the likelihood that future Iraqi leaders will seek WMD because of the underlying regional pressures for proliferation. U.S. or international efforts to prevent a post-Saddam Iraq from seeking WMD may well prove chimeric, perhaps even impossible in the long run. Removing the Iraqi dictator may have been desirable and even necessary, but it is far from sufficient to end the prospect of a nuclear-armed Iraq. Without a fundamental transformation of the regional security environment, too many incentives will drive any future sovereign Iraqi state to seek nuclear and other WMD. Most of the underlying causes of Iraq's pursuit of WMD remain in place today, and nothing is likely to change this continuing reality. The war launched by the United States could generate the greatest proliferation pressure of all.

The proliferation problem will be only a minor concern in the short and medium term, for it is unlikely that a capacious and independent Iraqi state will re-emerge any time in the coming decade. In fact, there is no reliable guarantee against the long-term disappearance of centralized state authority or Iraq's permanent fragmentation, both of which would preclude a serious weapons program. Even if a new Iraqi government manages to consolidate power and extend its authority beyond Baghdad, it will face the enormous task of reconstructing the country and reconfiguring a viable and supportive social coalition, whether democratic or authoritarian in nature. The United States has a vital, publicly declared interest in preventing the resumption of all prohibited weapons programs. Discoveries of hidden weapons caches or dual-use facilities are possible, but a decade of UN inspections have apparently succeeded in eliminating the lion's share of Iraq's banned programs and will prevent the thousands of Iraqi scientists and engineers from restarting their work any time soon.

In the coming years, however, circumstances are sure to change. This essay examines why such change is likely to favor the eventual resumption of Iraqi proliferation efforts. First, the essay describes and critiques the decade-long overemphasis on personalistic (first-image) analytical perspectives that have dominated popular, official, and some scholarly thinking about Iraq's drive for WMD.[2] Second, it details the domestic and international incentives propelling Iraqi proliferation and discusses their historical, strategic, and geographic impetus. Third, it shows how Iraq's security dilemma underpins its pursuit of a deterrent capability and how actions by the United States have proven unhelpful and even counterproductive in this domain. Subsequently, it assesses the major counterarguments: the claim that proliferation in general is either unproblematic or can be stopped militarily, or the alternative claim that democra-

---

[2] First-image theorizing focuses analytically on decision making by state leaders and generally leaves aside the domestic and international sources of policy. See Kenneth N. Waltz, *Man, the State, and War* (New York: Columbia University Press, 1959).

tization, enlightened leadership, or a continued American military presence will eliminate Iraq's quest for weapons. Finally, it concludes that regional conflict resolution is the only viable way to reduce the proliferation pressures that otherwise are sure to affect Iraqi military policies after Saddam.

THE PLACE OF PERSONALITY

Much of the current thinking about Iraq and weapons proliferation reflects a vital legacy of the 1990–1991 Persian Gulf crisis: the personalization of U.S.-Iraqi relations that emerged at the very outset of that crisis. In August 1990, President George H. W. Bush by all accounts was deeply offended by what he saw as a betrayal by Saddam's regime—its invasion of Kuwait—especially after he had sought to fend off congressional critics of Iraq and had worked to maintain good relations with the regime.[3] This anger translated into a domestic political strategy intended to mobilize popular support for the war to "liberate Kuwait" by personalizing the conflict and invoking Saddam's existential threat to American values and interests.[4] President George H. W. Bush was among the first to compare Saddam with Hitler, beginning in Fall 1990. Political analysts, pundits, and government officials thus began to refer to the need to "disarm Saddam," emphasizing his personal idiosyncrasies and psychological attributes as if these qualities were central to regional and global security.[5] In the subsequent decade, this personalistic approach was evident in the perpetuation of the Saddam-as-Hitler analogy, which assumed that Saddam came from a dangerous but rare breed of tyrants and that ousting him in conjunction with minimal democratic reforms would eliminate the threat and start a favorable political chain reaction in the Middle East.

Certainly, analytical attention to state leaders' personalities and decision-making proclivities is essential when explaining their behavior in high-pressure international crises or their making of flagrant blunders in foreign policy. First-

---

[3] See Bob Woodward, *The Commanders* (New York: Simon & Schuster, 1991) and George Bush and Brent Scowcroft, *A World Transformed* (New York: Vintage Books, 1998).

[4] In building international coalition support, the administration's strategy was less personalistic, emphasizing both *realpolitik* (regional balancing) and Iraq's violation of international law. In President Bush's 29 January 1991 State of the Union address, he highlighted the latter when referring to "the long-held promise of a new world order, where brutality will go unrewarded and aggression will meet collective resistance."

[5] Examples of excessive analytical personalization include Daniel L. Byman and Kenneth M. Pollack, "Let Us Now Praise Great Men: Bringing the Statesman Back In," *International Security* 25 (Spring 2001): 107–146; Efraim Karsh and Inari Rautsi, "Why Saddam Hussein Invaded Kuwait," *Survival* 33 (January/February 1991): 18–30; Laurie Mylroie, "Why Saddam Hussein Invaded Kuwait," *Orbis* 36 (Winter 1993): 123–134; Elaine Sciolino, *The Outlaw State: Saddam Hussein's Quest for Power and the Gulf Crisis* (New York: Wiley, 1991); and Judith Miller and Laurie Mylroie, *Saddam Hussein and the Crisis in the Gulf* (New York: Random House, 1990). See also Andrew Parasiliti's brief response to the Byman and Pollack piece: "The First Image Revisited," *International Security* 26 (Fall 2001): 166–169.

image theories of decision making can illuminate those moments when leaders' specific choices have immediate and substantial consequences.[6] Yet, the problems of war and peace reflect more than the choices of a handful of influential personalities, just as ensuring regional security requires more than simply removing a malevolent dictator. Even the most personalistic regimes rest on broader foundations that shape and constrain state action in foreign policy, as second- and third-image theorizing have long acknowledged.[7] In the Iraqi case, U.S. officials' obsession with Saddam all but ignored the domestic pressures and geostrategic imperatives that drive Iraq's actions. They disregarded the fact that Saddam was as much a consequence as a cause of regional insecurity and failed to contend with the more fundamental questions: What were the conditions that created and sustained such an awful regime? Why was Saddam so intent on obtaining WMD? Are his successors likely to do the same thing? International security imperatives suggest that they might.

DOMESTIC AND INTERNATIONAL INCENTIVES

Iraq's incentive to acquire WMD stems from the chronic insecurity of the region and the inherent danger faced by a state that is artificially constructed, ethnically diverse, religiously divided, rich in natural resources, and nearly landlocked. Troubled regional relations affect both domestic and international politics. Domestically, such insecurity often brings out the worst in leaders by creating justifications for despotism, undermining civil society, and distorting the economy. Wartime national security concerns erode civil liberties even in democracies, shifting resources toward defense and permitting previously unthinkable state repression.[8] In international politics, the consequences are much more straightforward: nuclear bombs in a conflict-ridden area lead almost inexorably to the demand for more bombs, no matter who is in charge of any given

---

[6] For a review of psychological approaches to international relations theory, see J.M. Goldgeier and Philip Tetlock, "Psychology and International Relations Theory," *Annual Review of Political Science* 4 (2001): 67–92; and Jerel A. Rosati, "The Power of Human Cognition in the Study of World Politics," *International Studies Review* 2 (2000): 45–75. See also Stanley A. Renshon and Deborah Welch Larson, eds., *Good Judgment in Foreign Policy: Theory and Application* (New York: Rowman & Littlefield, 2002). For an older, important account of decision making and the level-of-analysis problem, see Robert Jervis, *Perception and Misperception in International Politics* (Princeton: Princeton University Press, 1976).

[7] The domestic (second image) and international (third image) influences on foreign policy apply to both democracies and authoritarian regimes and include questions of security and political economy. See Waltz, *Man, the State, and War*.

[8] While focused initially on political economy, the literature on domestic–international interaction began largely with Peter Katzenstein, ed., *Between Power and Plenty: Foreign Economic Policies of Advanced Industrial States* (Ithaca, NY: Cornell University Press, 1978); and Peter Gourevitch, "The Second Image Reversed," *International Organization* 32 (Autumn 1978): 881–911. A valuable contribution to this research agenda for the Middle East is Steven Heydemann, ed., *War, Institutions, and Social Change in the Middle East* (Berkeley and Los Angeles: University of California Press, 2000).

state.[9] Without a higher authority to regulate the behavior of sovereign states, arms races are all but inevitable, especially in tumultuous regions with poorly developed institutional mechanisms to control conflict.[10] There may be additional, domestic-level causes of nuclear proliferation, but regional insecurity can be sufficient in itself.[11]

It is no wonder that Iraq has sought nuclear, chemical, and biological weapons. Carved in a famously arbitrary manner out of the Ottoman Empire, Iraq has clashed with every single one of its six immediate neighbors since gaining independence from Great Britain in 1932.[12] It also has lost multiple confrontations with more powerful adversaries, including two recent wars with the United States in 1991 and 2003, an air strike by Israel on its nuclear facilities in 1981, and military conquest and occupation by Britain in 1919 and 1941. These conflicts were just the latest in a history brimming with both great achievement and periodic military catastrophe for local rulers. The Abbasid Caliph founded Baghdad in 762 and laid the foundations for the Golden Age of classical Islam. But the Caliphate in Baghdad eventually declined, suffered a devastating invasion, and was sacked in 1258 by Mongol forces under Hulagu, the grandson of Genghis Khan. The area between the Tigris and Euphrates rivers, where Iraq lies, is the birthplace of civilization—where writing was invented—but for Iraqis this source of pride comes with an awareness of countless political struggles and military campaigns over several millennia. Its complex society has absorbed an extraordinary range of foreign influences as Arab, Persian, Turkish, Mongol, European, and now American invaders have dominated the region.[13]

[9] This position represents a "defensive" realist view. In general, see Benjamin Frankel, "The Brooding Shadow: Systemic Incentives and Nuclear Weapons Proliferation," *Security Studies* 2 (Spring–Summer 1993): 37–65 and Bradley A. Thayer, "The Causes of Nuclear Proliferation and the Utility of the Nuclear Nonproliferation Regime," *Security Studies* 4 (Spring 1995): 463–519. For an alternative "offensive" realist conceptualization, see John J. Mearsheimer, *The Tragedy of Great Power Politics* (New York: W.W. Norton, 2001). The distinction between offensive and defensive realism is discussed in Glenn H. Snyder, "Mearsheimer's World—Offensive Realism and the Struggle for Security: A Review Essay," *International Security* 27 (Summer 2002): 149–173.

[10] Debates over the consequences of anarchy in international relations are ongoing. For more on the connection between anarchy and arms races, see Charles L. Glaser, "The Causes and Consequences of Arms Races," *Annual Review of Political Science* 3 (2000): 251–276. On the centrality of security institutions under anarchy, see David A. Lake, "Beyond Anarchy: The Importance of Security Institutions," *International Security* 26 (Summer 2001): 129–160.

[11] I do not claim that domestic-level (institutional, bureaucratic, political economy) or individual-level explanations for nuclear proliferation are untenable. To the contrary, a state's decision to go nuclear may have international or domestic sources, depending on the particular circumstances. We may not have enough cases to make solid generalizations, but the realist paradigm suggests at least one certainty about the likelihood of proliferation. Other certainties remain to be determined.

[12] Charles Tripp, *A History of Iraq*, 2nd ed. (Cambridge: Cambridge University Press, 2002); Marion Farouk-Sluglett and Peter Sluglett, *Iraq Since 1958* (London: I.B. Taurus, 1990); and Phebe Marr, *The Modern History of Iraq* (Boulder, CO: Westview, 1985).

[13] For an overview of the region's history, see Arthur Goldschmidt, *A Concise History of the Middle East*, 7th ed. (Boulder, CO: Westview, 2002).

If Iraqis today have a long historical memory for such events, this is not due to an inherent cultural inclination to dwell on the past. It is the result of decades of state policy in which the Baathist regime and its predecessors have tried to construct a uniquely Iraqi national identity by highlighting the region's epic struggles with foreign invaders. In the 1980s, for example, this strategy included frequent reference to the Iran–Iraq war as "Saddam's *Qadisiyya*," invoking the well-known Arab victory over the Persians in 637. For more than three decades, the state also used Iraq's Mesopotamian heritage to tap into the country's celebrated ancient past, cultivating a narrower, patriotic identity to complement the broader currents of Arab nationalism.[14] After 1990, the regime shifted away from secular leftist rhetoric and toward Islamic discourse, selecting bellicose passages from the *Qur'an* and *Hadith* to frame Iraq's confrontation with foreign powers.[15] This use of the past represents a typical legitimation and mobilizational strategy for building national identities, similar to any other political actor's cultivation of historical myth to further contemporary objectives. Such efforts certainly are not exclusive to authoritarian regimes; it does not take a dictator to realize their benefits in any realm requiring communal or national solidarity.[16]

This use of history, however, will leave a legacy long after Saddam is gone. Combined with the stark realities of Iraq's geopolitical position, it will affect how Iraqis understand the international dangers they are likely to face in the coming decades. National myths can be learned and unlearned over time, but they retain a certain discursive hegemony until replaced with something else.[17] This is a slow and complicated process; it is not simply a matter of informing Iraqis about the distortions in the state-propagated worldview. Most Iraqis already understand the politicized nature of the information environment they have inhabited, but many lack a trusted reference point with which to form an alternative perspective. The abrupt, war-induced termination of decades of state propaganda will not change popular or elite threat perceptions in the short term, nor will it lead to an informed citizenry that embraces the views of its

[14] For more on Baathist cultural policy with reference to ancient Mesopotamia, see Amatzia Baram, "Mesopotamian Identity in Ba'thi Iraq," *Middle Eastern Studies* 19 (October 1983): 427–449 and Baram, *Culture, History, and Ideology in the Formation of Ba'thist Iraq, 1968–1989* (New York: St. Martin's Press, 1991). For an account of Iraqi public art under Saddam, see Kanan Makiya, *The Monument: Art, Vulgarity, and Responsibility in Iraq* (Berkeley: University of California Press, 1991).

[15] The regime's appropriation of Islam is discussed in Ofra Bengio, *Saddam's Words: Political Discourse in Iraq* (New York: Oxford University Press, 1998).

[16] Debate continues on the origins and nature of nationalism as well as the role of state power in constructing and manipulating social identities. See Benedict Anderson, *Imagined Communities* (London: Verso, 1989). More state-centric views include Ernest Gellner, *Nations and Nationalism* (Ithaca, NY: Cornell University Press, 1983) and John Breuilly, *Nationalism and the State* (Chicago: University of Chicago Press, 1982).

[17] State-sanctioned identities like race have provided a basis for political mobilization long after their creation for other purposes. See Anthony W. Marx, *Making Race and Nation: A Comparison of the United States, South Africa, and Brazil* (Cambridge: Cambridge University Press, 1998).

conquerors. Given Iraq's experience with both the United States and the sanctions-supporting international community, many years will pass before most Iraqis abandon the idea that the country is vulnerable to external threats and foreign invaders. Recent reality has done nothing to dispel the notion and may even reinforce it. While future Iraqi leaders may believe that Saddam bore responsibility for incurring the wrath of the United States, they still will seek to guard Iraqi sovereignty in the face of threats from the outside world.

Outsiders may claim that none of Iraq's present-day neighbors poses a grave and immediate threat, but the view from Baghdad is quite different.[18] Iran, to the east, is a potential nuclear power with almost triple Iraq's population, geographic advantages like open access to the sea, religious ties to the Iraqi Shia majority, and nearly quadruple the land mass. And while Iraq is roughly the size of California, Iran is larger than Alaska.[19] Turkey, a major military power and NATO member to the north, is double Iraq's size and has triple its population.[20] Iraq and Turkey have had recurring disputes over everything from Kurdish militants to water rights because Iraq's freshwater lifelines—the Tigris and Euphrates rivers—flow from Turkey.[21] Israel, just over the horizon to the west, is much smaller and acutely vulnerable, but for precisely this reason, it has become the strongest military power in the region and perhaps ranks fourth in the world.[22] Israel has undeclared nuclear, chemical, and biological weapons of its own—an open secret of sorts.[23] Finally, Saudi Arabia, a wealthy power with strategic depth on Iraq's southern flank, has a rapidly growing population and a latent military potential that no future leadership in Baghdad will ignore given Saudi acquiescence to American military intervention in Iraq. Already possessing a small but modern air force and Chinese CSS-2 ballistic missiles with a range of 2800 kilometers, Saudi power may increase in response to either

[18] Stephen Walt defines threat in terms of both the distribution of power and "geographic proximity, offensive capabilities, and perceived intentions." See *The Origins of Alliances* (Ithaca, NY: Cornell University Press, 1987), 5.

[19] See R.K. Ramazani, *Revolutionary Iran: Challenge and Response in the Middle East* (Baltimore: The Johns-Hopkins University Press, 1988).

[20] American nuclear weapons reportedly remain in Turkey at Incirlik. See the National Security Archive at http://www.gwu.edu/~nsarchiv/news/19991020/, 29 May 2003.

[21] The Turkish-Iraqi water conflict is expected to get worse as a result of Turkey's ongoing Greater Anatolia Project (GAP), which includes the Ataturk Dam and dozens of hydroelectric power plants in the Kurdish southeast.

[22] Ordinal military rankings are subjective and limited in usefulness. Of the eight nuclear powers, the Israel Defense Forces have important qualitative and quantitative advantages over all but the United States, Russia, and China.

[23] On Israeli nuclear programs and policy, see Shai Feldman, *Israeli Nuclear Deterrence: A Strategy for the 1980s* (New York: Columbia University Press, 1982) and his follow-up work, *Nuclear Weapons and Arms Control in the Middle East* (Cambridge, MA: MIT Press, 1997). On Israel's chemical and biological programs, see Richard A. Falkenrath, Robert D. Newman, and Bradley A. Thayer, *America's Achilles' Heel: Nuclear, Biological, and Chemical Terrorism and Covert Attack* (Cambridge, MA: MIT Press, 1998), 64. On reported Israeli progress in completing the strategic triad, see "Israel Can Launch Nuclear Weapons from Subs–Report," *New York Times*, 11 October 2003.

troubles with its longtime ally, the United States, or the growth of Iranian power.[24]

Just as unnervingly from an Iraqi standpoint, some of its regional rivals have been allied with each other in recent years, or at least they have cooperated extensively on the political, economic, and military fronts. An important Turkish-Israeli strategic relationship began with the establishment of diplomatic relations in 1991 and has expanded to include joint military exercises, intelligence cooperation, and arms sales, with Jordan participating on a low-profile occasional basis.[25] Syria and Iran have had significant ties, most notably during the Iran–Iraq war of the 1980s, but continuing to this day in their support for Hezbollah in southern Lebanon. Nine Arab states, including Saudi Arabia, Egypt, and Syria sent tens of thousands of troops to help drive Iraq from Kuwait in 1991.[26] Three weeks before Iraq's invasion in 1990, Kuwait held its first high-level talks with Iran since the revolution in 1979, signaling a return to its traditional foreign policy of regional balancing.[27] Even Israel and Iran, closely aligned until the latter's revolution, still managed to cooperate militarily during the infamous Iran-Contra scandal in the early 1980s, with some observers noting their ongoing potential for strategic alliance.[28]

Although Iraqi aggression prompted much of its neighbors' cooperation, shifting Middle Eastern alignments in a post-Saddam era may not prove reassuring to Baghdad.[29] Some regional partnerships will persist indefinitely, such as a Turkish-Israeli relationship now devoted to countering Syria and Iran. Moreover, no Iraqi regime will be indifferent to technological changes affecting the regional military balance, such as Iran's development of the Shihab-4 missile, with a 2000-kilometer range, and its apparent rapid progress on a nuclear

[24] Saudi annual defense expenditures have risen to approximately $27 billion since 2001. They are the eighth largest in the world, greater than all the other states in the Middle East combined except Israel. SIPRI Military Expenditure Database at http://projects.sipri.se/milex/mex_database1.html. Data on ballistic missile development and proliferation is found at the website of Lancaster University's Centre for Defence and International Security Studies: http://www.cdiss.org/btablea.htm.

[25] See Wolfango Piccoli, "Turkish-Israeli Military Agreements and Regional Security in the Gulf" in Bjorn Moller, ed., *Oil and Water: Cooperative Security in the Persian Gulf* (New York: I.B. Taurus, 2001) and William Hale, *Turkish Foreign Policy: 1774–2000* (Portland, OR: Frank Cass, 2001). See also Sabri Sayari, "Turkey: The Changing European Security Environment and the Gulf Crisis," *Middle East Journal* 46 (Winter 1992): 183–198.

[26] For a Saudi perspective on the 1991 Arab coalition, see HRH General Khalid Bin Sultan, *Desert Warrior: A Personal View of the Gulf War by the Joint Forces Commander* (New York: HarperCollins, 1995). For a broader perspective written by an influential Egyptian journalist, see Mohamed Heikal, *Illusions of Triumph: An Arab View of the Gulf War* (New York: HarperCollins, 1992).

[27] On Iranian Foreign Minister Velayati's trip to Kuwait, see *Middle East Economic Digest*, 20 July 1990, 4. A preinvasion interpretation of Kuwaiti foreign policy is found in Abdul-Reda Assiri, *Kuwait's Foreign Policy: City-State in World Politics* (Boulder, CO: Westview Press, 1990).

[28] For more on the Tehran-Tel Aviv Alignment and a broader perspective on Iranian-Israeli relations, see Ramazani, *Revolutionary Iran*, 147–161.

[29] Details of earlier Middle Eastern alliance patterns are found in Walt, *The Origins of Alliances*.

deterrent of its own, favored even by reformist factions.[30] A defensive all-Arab counteralliance centered on Baghdad is highly unlikely in the short term given the fears and resentments generated by nearly thirteen years of intra-Arab conflict over Iraq. Arab states like Kuwait would find such an alliance unnecessary at best and untenable at worst, having staked their security to a close relationship with the United States. Even an implausible new arrangement combining the six Gulf Cooperation Council states with Egypt, Syria, and Iraq could not provide substantial long-term reassurance to Iraq if it becomes situated between two regional nuclear powers. Iraq is bound to feel acute existential threats no matter what relationships it forms with local or international actors, and alliances alone are unlikely to deliver the American will or the Arab capacity to counter these threats.

Few states in the world today face a comparable combination of potential military threat and geographic constraint while also having substantial human and financial resources with which to overcome such circumstances. Geography alone dictates that Iraq under any future leadership will be exceptionally vulnerable to its neighbors.[31] Very few countries are comparably surrounded and confined—none in the Western hemisphere, only one in Asia, and a mere handful in Africa and Central Europe.[32] Perhaps none has had such troubled relations with neighbors on which it must rely so heavily. With only nineteen kilometers of coastline, no deepwater port facilities, and no unimpeded access to the high seas, Iraq's economic growth will always depend on the willingness of other states to permit the passage of its commercial traffic and oil exports via pipelines, overland trucking, and shipping through the choke points of the Persian Gulf.[33] Even if this vulnerability is unlikely to be exploited under most circumstances, all Iraqis will remember the devastating effects of more than a decade of sanctions, enforceable largely because of the country's particular

[30] Missile ranges are found at the Centre for Defence and International Security Studies: http://www.cdiss.org/btablea.htm.

[31] Iraq's geographic dilemmas are discussed in Ahmad Yousef Ahmad, "The Dialectics of Domestic Environment and Role Performance: The Foreign Policy of Iraq" in Bahgat Korany and Ali E. Hillal Dessouki, eds., *The Foreign Policies of Arab States: The Challenge of Change*, 2nd ed. (Boulder, CO: Westview, 1991). See also Charles Tripp, "The Foreign Policy of Iraq" in Raymond Hinnebusch and Anoushiravan Ehteshami, eds., *The Foreign Policies of Middle East States* (Boulder, CO: Lynne Rienner, 2002). See also the extensive discussion of geostrategic imperatives of the region from a great power perspective found in Geoffrey Kemp and Robert E. Harkavy, *Strategic Geography and the Changing Middle East* (Washington, DC: Brookings Institution Press and Carnegie Endowment for International Peace, 1997).

[32] Only eight other countries have six or more adjacent neighbors and poor (or no) access to the sea: Afghanistan (6), Austria (8), Hungary (7), Burkina Faso (6), Chad (6), Mali (7), Niger (7), and Zambia (7).

[33] A dated but still useful account of Iraq's geostrategic dilemma in the Persian Gulf is found in Gerald Blake, *Maritime Aspects of Arabian Geopolitics* (London: Arab Research Center, 1982). In 1992, pursuant to UN Security Council Resolution 687, the UN Boundary Demarcation Commission further reduced Iraq's access to the sea by moving the Kuwaiti border northward by 1,870 feet, putting part of Umm Qasr Naval Base in Kuwaiti territory.

physical location. It is not excessive geographic determinism to observe that neither changing alliance patterns nor global partnerships can transform the physical constraints limiting Iraqi independence.

DETERRENCE AND THE SECURITY DILEMMA

In managing all of Iraq's relationships and vulnerabilities in a post-Saddam world, WMD represent a potent means of deterrence.[34] This remains true even if their use would constitute an egregious violation of evolving international norms. States under military duress tend to arm themselves to the teeth even if doing so undermines their security in the long run by eliciting dramatic, escalatory responses from powerful potential rivals. This security dilemma has been evident to students of international politics at least since John Herz and Robert Jervis.[35] Most importantly, the security dilemma applies to Iraq with or without Saddam in power, for its logic operates even in the absence of dictators with much-vaunted nuclear ambitions. The militarily counterproductive, politically damaging, or morally repugnant nature of such weapons does not reduce the likelihood of state efforts to obtain them even if other factors limit the success of such efforts. And with both an educated population and the second largest proven oil reserves in the world, Iraq will have the intellectual and financial capacity to do what its leaders deem necessary and appropriate. The realities of geography, economics, technology and, most importantly, a fundamental political impulse will conspire against all long-term efforts to stop Iraq.[36]

Worse yet, arguments from the international community to stop the proliferation of WMD fall on deaf ears when they seem wholly self-interested or

[34] Thomas Schelling's concept of "passive deterrence"—letting adversaries know of a nuclear arsenal without declaring what conditions would prompt their use—is relevant here. See Schelling, *The Strategy of Conflict* (New York: Oxford University Press, 1963), 207–229. Also possible is McGeorge Bundy's "existential deterrence"—the general fear-inducing capacity that counters threats to a state's survival. See Bundy, "Existential Deterrence and its Consequences" in Douglas MacLean, ed., *The Security Gamble: Deterrence Dilemmas in the Nuclear Age* (Totowa, NJ: Rowman and Allanheld, 1984), 8–9. See also Robert Jervis, *The Meaning of the Nuclear Revolution: Statecraft and the Prospect of Armageddon* (Ithaca, NY: Cornell University Press, 1989); and Bernard Brodie, *War and Politics* (New York: Macmillan, 1973).

[35] John H. Herz, "Idealist Internationalism and the Security Dilemma," *World Politics* 2 (January 1950): 157–180 and Robert Jervis, "Cooperation Under the Security Dilemma," *World Politics* 30 (January 1978): 186–214. More recently, see Charles L. Glaser, "The Security Dilemma Revisited," *World Politics* 50 (October 1997): 171–201. Others in the Realist tradition who have written on the security dilemma range from Thucydides to Herbert Butterfield, Hans Morgenthau, Arnold Wolfers, and Kenneth Waltz.

[36] For a revealing, if speculative, account of the regime-preserving function of Iraqi WMD, see the 22 February 2002 testimony of Charles A. Duelfer, United Nations Special Commission deputy director, before the U.S. Senate Armed Services Committee, Subcommittee on Emerging Threats and Capabilities. It is reprinted as "Why Saddam Wants Weapons of Mass Destruction" in Micah L. Sifry and Christopher Cerf, eds., *The Iraq War Reader: History, Documents, Opinions* (New York: Simon & Schuster, 2003): 412–413.

hypocritical. The United States only began to abandon its offensive biological arsenal in 1969 during the Nixon administration. It acceded to the Biological Weapons Convention in 1972, but it did not ratify the agreement until late 1974. The Central Intelligence Agency kept its own, unauthorized cache of biological weapons until sometime after the Church committee revelations in 1975.[37] As for chemical weapons, the United States did not relinquish its stockpile until joining the Chemical Weapons Convention in 1992, pledging to destroy the many thousands of tons of chemical agents it had accumulated since World War II.[38] For decades, the United States maintained a chemical weapons capability while working assiduously to prevent its local adversaries in the Middle East from developing their own. In the 1980s, for example, a weak regional nemesis in Libya was the object of American military threats, public denunciations, and a concerted diplomatic campaign. In this same period, however, the Reagan and Bush administrations considered Iraq a counterweight to Iran and gave it vastly more lenient treatment, even after Iraq used chemical weapons on Iranian troops and its own Kurdish population.[39]

Most dramatically, the United States has maintained a nuclear deterrent for nearly six decades and remains the only country in the world to have used nuclear weapons in wartime. While the American strategic stockpile has been reduced considerably from its Cold War peak, U.S. officials have barely paid lip service to the American obligation under the 1968 nuclear Non-Proliferation Treaty to rid the country eventually of all nuclear weapons. Even if understandable given the magnitude of the Soviet threat and the reluctance of other nuclear powers to disarm, such a position is bound to elicit a skeptical response from critics. To this day, moreover, the United States retains scientific research programs in nuclear, chemical, and biological weapons.[40] This continued research, in part, is to contend with the very real danger of their future use against American interests. But as a matter of political reality, probably all sovereign states question the U.S. arrogation to itself of the right to limit their possession of WMD while continuing to expand American capability and knowledge in

---

[37] Jonathan B. Tucker, "A Farewell to Germs: The U.S. Renunciation of Biological and Toxin Warfare, 1969–70," *International Security* 27 (Summer 2002), 144. In mid-September 2001, Pentagon planners reportedly considered poisoning the Afghan food supply—an act of biological warfare—and very nearly presented the idea to President Bush, who that same day made public comments about Osama bin Laden being "wanted dead or alive." See Woodward, *Bush at War* (New York: Simon & Schuster, 2002), 99–101.

[38] Richard M. Price, *The Chemical Weapons Taboo* (Ithaca, NY: Cornell University Press, 1997).

[39] On U.S. concerns over the Libyan chemical weapons program and facility at Rabta, see the statement before the Committee on Governmental Affairs, Hearings on the Global Spread of Chemical and Biological Weapons, by William H. Webster, Director, Central Intelligence Agency, 10 February 1989. Iraq's 1987 use of chemical weapons against the Kurds at Halabja is documented in Human Rights Watch/Middle East, *Iraq's Crime of Genocide: The Anfal Campaign against the Kurds* (New Haven, CT: Yale University Press, 1995).

[40] Some U.S. research programs today may even violate the Biological Weapons Convention. See Tucker, "A Farewell to Germs," 144–148.

this domain. Even defensive American efforts can therefore prompt seemingly offensive responses from states like Iraq, its neighbors, and all others unconvinced of the benevolence of American power.

The phrase "weapons of mass destruction" itself is an odd antieuphemism designed to sound especially threatening, distasteful, and offensive. Its use is reasonable, since nuclear, chemical, and biological weapons are horrific in immeasurable ways. But most contemporary observers in American political discourse deploy the phrase as if it were a term of art or a technical term. In fact, it is a distinctly political term and a rhetorical device used with the clear purpose of describing the kinds of weapons that American adversaries may seek and that the United States and the international community does not want them to have. Its political function is apparent in the fact that American policy makers never refer to the U.S. military's development, possession, and potential use of WMD. Their statements on America's nuclear arsenal oscillate between cold claims of *raisons d'état* and warm reassurances of likely American restraint in the event of a crisis. Nowhere outside of the United States is this phrase used with a comparably disingenuous mix of innocence and arrogance.[41]

Those who believe that the United States alone can put the genie of WMD technology and know-how back in its early twentieth-century bottle will be disappointed.[42] The proliferation pressures on states like Iraq are too intense, and they will assure the continued flow of weapons-making knowledge, materials, and hardware to the region. Persistent demand will be met by a ready combination of footloose firms competing in the global weapons marketplace, states in desperate need of revenue, and scientists with valuable but increasingly commonplace skills. Broader trends in the history of military technology and weapons diffusion show that obtaining WMD in all their endless variety can only get easier over time.[43] Close international scrutiny of any given state might suffice for a while, but this pressure just increases the incentive to abstain from the direct international procurement of complete weapons systems in favor of embedding production in domestic civilian infrastructure. The removal of Saddam will not change any of these dynamics because it was not simply Saddam or any individual state decision maker that drove Iraqi proliferation efforts.[44]

[41] The U.S. government includes ballistic missiles in its official definition of WMD. Falkenrath et al., *America's Achilles Heel*, 13.

[42] For an argument about the difficulties of stopping proliferation through arms control, see Jonathan Schell, "The Folly of Arms Control," *Foreign Affairs* 79 (September–October 2000): 22–46.

[43] Basic nuclear weapons science no longer requires someone like Einstein. An overview of the technological aspects of nuclear weapons proliferation is found in Robert F. Mozley, *The Politics and Technology of Nuclear Proliferation* (Seattle: University of Washington Press, 1998). For another perspective on proliferation problems, see Brad Roberts, ed., *Weapons Proliferation in the 1990s* (Cambridge, MA: MIT Press, 1995).

[44] This may contradict Shai Feldman's assertion that "Iraq's massive effort to build nuclear weapons could not have been undertaken and implemented without the initiation, push, guidance, and leadership of Saddam Hussein, the country's sole leader." See Feldman, *Nuclear Weapons and Arms Control in the Middle East*, 53–54. This claim is true but tautological. Saddam certainly was the linchpin to the Iraqi program, but it does not follow that a future Iraqi effort could only be made under his leadership. There is no support for the contention that weapons programs require the patronage of individual dictators.

THE PROLIFERATION PROBLEM

Some analysts say that proliferation itself is not inherently disastrous. Deterrence even worked with the likes of Stalin because it hangs on nothing more than the fear of punishment for bad behavior. This argument of the "proliferation optimists" includes the leading neorealist of our day, Kenneth Waltz.[45] With even a minimal desire to survive, nuclear powers tend to avoid provocative gambits in foreign policy when facing rivals possessing a credible deterrent. After moving to the brink of annihilation during the Cuban missile crisis in 1962, the United States and the Soviet Union settled into a reasonably stable deterrent relationship. Similarly, Iraq's decision in 1991 not to use chemical or biological warheads against Israel or the U.S.-led coalition lends credence to the claim that Saddam was rational enough to have been deterred.[46] Likewise, no sensible Iraqi leader would ever transfer WMD to small, independent-minded nonstate actors like al Qaeda for fear of retaliation from the states these groups target. Only a weak rationality is necessary for deterrence to function; it is less a product of rationally calculated certainty and more the result of simple-to-achieve uncertainty. A wounded nuclear power might strike back with utterly devastating effect.[47]

The problem with this position is that a truly stable system of deterrence requires all potential antagonists to possess reasonably secure second-strike capabilities. In other words, all parties must have weapons that probably can survive a preemptive attack and be used to strike back at their enemies. Second-strike capabilities create both technical challenges and political problems for state leaders. These capabilities are not easy to build and maintain, as evidenced by ongoing global concern over the stability of the Indian-Pakistani deterrent relationship. One consequence of accepting proliferation, moreover, is that states like Iran and Saudi Arabia—at a bare minimum—would feel the need to acquire WMD to assure their own security. A ripple effect would be inevitable throughout the entire Middle East, North Africa, and conceivably much farther. And as critics of Waltz have pointed out, the likelihood that such weapons could be used accidentally rises with each new nuclear power.[48] Military organizations pursuing their own bureaucratic interests might even pro-

[45] See Scott D. Sagan and Kenneth N. Waltz, *The Spread of Nuclear Weapons: A Debate Renewed* (New York: W.W. Norton, 2003). A review of the broader literature on deterrence is Paul K. Huth, "Deterrence and International Conflict: Empirical Findings and Theoretical Debates," *Annual Review of Political Science* 2 (1999): 25–48.

[46] Shai Feldman, "Israeli Deterrence During the Gulf War" in Joseph Alpher, ed., *War in the Gulf: Implications for Israel* (Tel Aviv: Jaffee Center for Strategic Studies, 1992), 184–209.

[47] The role of rationality in deterrence has been the subject of great debate and a voluminous literature. For a recent discussion of deterrence theory and proliferation, see Robert Powell, "Nuclear Deterrence Theory, Nuclear Proliferation, and National Missile Defense," *International Security* 27 (Spring 2003): 86–118.

[48] Bruce G. Blair, *The Logic of Accidental Nuclear War* (Washington, DC: Brookings, 1993); and Scott D. Sagan, *The Limits of Safety: Organizations, Accidents, and Nuclear Weapons* (Princeton: Princeton University Press, 1993).

voke unintended deterrence failures that lead to the deliberate use of nuclear weapons.[49] The cost of high-intensity warfare in a nuclear Middle East is unthinkable, so proliferation gives us little cause for genuine optimism.[50]

If proliferation represents a real danger, the counterproliferation posture currently in vogue at the Pentagon may be correct in recognizing the obsolescence of traditional arms control measures and the Cold War security architecture.[51] But the end of the Cold War did not herald the end of the security dilemma. An aggressively interventionist stance, therefore, is flawed in its emphasis on rogue states as the most profound threat to U.S., regional, and global security.[52] By reducing the challenge facing the world to the purported nuclear ambitions of a handful of dictators, this approach ignores the structural sources of instability and paints a Manichean picture of international politics. The world never has been divided neatly into two contending camps with authoritarian regimes led by deposable tyrants on one side and law-abiding states amenable to arms control on the other. As a practical matter, moreover, a military assault on all potential threats to American security is simply beyond U.S. capacity. In the Iraqi case, attacks on its nuclear facilities in 1981 by Israel and 1991 by the international coalition failed to end the regime's pursuit of WMD, not simply because they left the evil of Saddam in place, but because they left Iraq itself in place, an acutely vulnerable state with the wherewithal to continue taking matters into its own hands in an era when this is increasingly possible.

The Democratic Solution

The leading counterargument to this grim cautionary tale is that democracy is the solution. This claim comes in a few varieties. The most common notion, implicit in Bush administration rhetoric, is that democracies are more moder-

[49] On the possibility of accidents, the difficulty of preserving second-strike capabilities, and other direct critiques of Waltz's position, see Sagan and Waltz, *The Spread of Nuclear Weapons*, 46–87; 156–184.

[50] Left- and right-leaning accounts of deterrence and proliferation, written for wider audiences, include Jonathan Schell, "The Case Against the War," *The Nation*, 3 March 2003 and reprinted as "Pre-Emptive Defeat, or How Not to Fight Proliferation" in Sifry and Cerf, eds., *The Iraqi War Reader*, 506–526; and Kenneth Pollack, *The Threatening Storm: The Case for Invading Iraq*, excerpted as "Can We Really Deter a Nuclear-Armed Saddam?" in Sifry and Cerf, eds., 403–411.

[51] For more on U.S. counterproliferation policy, imminent threat, and rogue states, see Section V, "The National Security Strategy of the United States," September 2002, 8–10. See also the administration's "National Security Strategy to Combat Weapons of Mass Destruction," December 2002.

[52] As stated in "The National Security Strategy of the United States," "But new deadly challenges have emerged from rogue states and terrorists. . . . Rogue regimes seek nuclear, biological, and chemical weapons as well. These states' pursuit of, and global trade in, such weapons has become a looming threat to all nations. . . . It has taken almost a decade for us to comprehend the true nature of this new threat. Given the goals of rogue states and terrorists, the United States can no longer solely rely on a reactive posture as we have in the past. The inability to deter a potential attacker, the immediacy of today's threats, and the magnitude of potential harm that could be caused by our adversaries' choice of weapons, do not permit that option," 9.

ate, reasonable, and cautious than authoritarian regimes.[53] By this logic, a democratic Iraq would never waste its considerable resources on dangerous and destructive weapons programs. But even democracy does not constitute a cure for the malady of proliferation pressure, and a democratic Iraq will not be inoculated against the temptation to go nuclear someday. Why would future Iraqi voters not want a potent and compelling deterrent? Why would they be any different from the Indian, Israeli, and Pakistani publics? After all, for more than two decades, average Iraqis have suffered the brunt of the burden for the country's ill-conceived and catastrophic foreign adventures. Regime type simply does not eliminate the external threats to national security—whether real or imagined—that lead states to pursue these weapons. If the perceived threats are high, Iraq is likely to seek WMD no matter what kind of regime governs or who rules in Baghdad.

Some observers also note that democracies are less inclined to launch wars of aggression, especially against other democracies. This particular claim points to democratic West Germany and Japan as exemplary reformed aggressors because their expansionism ended decisively with their defeat in World War II.[54] Although theories of democratic peace may have some validity, even liberal democracies are compelled to defend themselves in whatever ways they see fit. Democracies may not fight, but they do arm. Few liberal democracies exist without either their own nuclear deterrent or a rock-solid security arrangement underwritten by a powerful ally. Japan currently has the world's fourth largest defense budget, but its security pact with the United States is more likely to keep it non-nuclear than any of its constitutional provisions.[55] Iraq will have little reason to believe that its ultimate security will be assured by even a close relationship with the United States unless it has the kind of nuclear umbrella extended to postwar West Germany and Japan.[56] Just as the creation of NATO

[53] The administration took this position to promote the war in February and March 2003. See, for example, President Bush's 26 February speech at the American Enterprise Institute, in which he declared, "The nation of Iraq, with its proud heritage, abundant resources and skilled and educated people is fully capable of moving toward democracy and living in freedom. The world has a clear interest in the spread of democratic values, because stable and free nations do not breed the ideologies of murder. *They encourage the peaceful pursuit of a better life.*" (Emphasis added.)

[54] The vast "democratic peace" literature is reviewed in detail in James Lee Ray, "Does Democracy Cause Peace?" *Annual Review of Political Science* 1 (June 1998): 27–46. See also Michael E. Brown, Sean M. Lynn-Jones, and Steven E. Miller, eds., *Debating the Democratic Peace* (Cambridge, MA: MIT Press, 1996) and Bruce Russett, ed., *Triangulating Peace: Democracy, Interdependence, and International Organizations* (New York: W.W. Norton, 2001).

[55] Japan actually may have the second or third largest defense budget. U.S. assurances may become inadequate in the minds of Japanese voters and political leaders if North Korean saber rattling continues. Data on defense spending can be found at the SIPRI Military Expenditure Database, http://projects.sipri.se/milex/mex_major_spenders.html.

[56] American nuclear weapons actually were kept in Japan and twenty-six other countries and territories, according to a recently declassified Pentagon study, "History of the Custody and Deployment of Nuclear Weapons: July 1945 through September 1977," accessed at http://www.gwu.edu/~nsarchiv/news/19991020/. The study was first reported in Robert S. Norris, William M. Arkin, and William Burr, "Where They Were," *Bulletin of the Atomic Scientists* 55 (November–December 1999): 26–35.

in 1949 was not sufficiently reassuring for Great Britain and France to forgo their own arsenals, a future Iraq is unlikely to abstain from seeking the deadliest weapons available.

A final, similar counterargument is that any degree of democracy in Iraq will make proliferation less likely by having a transformative effect on the regional security environment. This assertion is intuitively appealing, but probably incorrect. One cannot improve regional security without changing regional relationships. This is a structural or relational factor, not a consequence of one regime's tendencies or attributes. Since democracies in Iraq, Iran, and Israel would not necessarily have amicable relations, one cannot assume that democratization will produce better regional relations. Even if these states signed peace treaties, each would still calculate that friendship might not last forever. Fears of the future, reinforced by memories of the past, create powerful incentives to build or retain a deterrent capability. In Europe, it took two world wars, tens of millions of deaths, a common external threat, and decades of institution building for the European Union and NATO to create the political and security community that exists there today. This outcome is not likely to be replicated in the Middle East anytime soon, even under hegemonic American tutelage.

THE LIMITS OF LEADERSHIP

One further hope of the Bush administration may be that good leadership will prevent bad things from happening, easing the transition to an inherently more peaceful democratic regime. But even the most enlightened leadership is not sufficient. If George W. Bush—better yet, George Washington—were at Iraq's helm under likely future circumstances, surely he would find himself looking for ways to defend the country against its nuclear-armed rivals near and far. If someone like Nelson Mandela or Vaclav Havel governed Iraq, the country still would have acute security concerns. F.W. de Klerk's decision to scrap South Africa's nuclear program in February 1990 and accede to the nuclear Non-Proliferation Treaty in July 1991 was only possible because of the increasingly benign regional security environment.[57] The single most important variable for determining a state's defense spending, weapons profile, and its likelihood of seeking WMD is not whether the country is run by a thuggish dictator. Nor is

---

[57] It probably was desirable because of the increasingly hostile international economic environment that apartheid South Africa faced by the late 1980s. See William J. Long and Suzette R. Grillot, "Ideas, Beliefs, and Nuclear Policies: The Cases of South Africa and Ukraine," *Nonproliferation Review* 7 (Spring 2000): 24–40 and Waldo Stumpf, "South Africa's Nuclear Weapons Program: From Deterrence to Dismantlement," *Arms Control Today* 25 (December 1995–January 1996): 3–8. Stumpf was the deputy head of South Africa's Atomic Energy Corporation. For a discussion of competing theoretical explanations for South Africa's nuclear weapons policies, see Peter Liberman, "The Rise and Fall of the South African Bomb," *International Security* 26 (Fall 2001): 45–86.

it a domestic-level variable like regime type, whether democratic or authoritarian. It is the external security environment in which a given state exists.[58]

The 1968 Treaty on the Non-Proliferation of Nuclear Weapons (NPT), which now has over 180 signatories, locked in place a nuclear apartheid of haves and have-nots that succeeded in controlling proliferation for more than two decades.[59] Yet, it probably worked because much of the world had joined a Cold War alliance system that afforded most states relative security. Critics of all political stripes now question its long-term viability.[60] Those states that declined to join the NPT, including India, Pakistan, and Israel, did so because they felt genuine insecurity despite the alliance system. Cuba, not surprisingly, did not accede until 2002 because Soviet assurances proved inadequate in the aftermath of the Bay of Pigs invasion and the Cuban missile crisis. States such as Australia, South Korea, Sweden, Taiwan, Brazil, and Argentina have reversed or abandoned nuclear programs, but only because their security situations allowed or demanded such forbearance.[61] Similarly, a transformed European security environment enabled the George H. W. Bush and Bill Clinton administrations to elicit the Ukraine's 1994 agreement to relinquish the weapons it had inherited from the Soviet era. Even Switzerland stockpiled hundreds of tons of uranium ore until 1989 because it wanted to be able to develop nuclear weapons if its security environment deteriorated significantly.[62]

Ironically, an American military invasion of Iraq to disarm the regime could make Iraq's future leaders more likely to seek WMD. Even a friendly regime in Baghdad may be quietly encouraged by North Korea's open defiance of the United States, thus far unpunished because of its unmistakable capacity to retaliate with both conventional and unconventional weapons against American intervention. As the revolution in military affairs widens the conventional military gap between the United States and the rest of the world, more state leaders will conclude that a minimal nuclear deterrent is essential to their political autonomy and perhaps their personal survival. In the current climate, any leader-

[58] American defense spending since the founding of the republic has waxed and waned, not in conjunction with the quality of American democracy, but as a function of external threats. This pattern began with John Adams's decision to expand the U.S. navy in response to concerns about French and British power, and it continued through both world wars, the Cold War, and contemporary concerns about terrorism.

[59] Indian Foreign Minister Jaswant Singh used this provocative formulation in justifying his country's May 1998 nuclear tests. See Jaswant Singh, "Against Nuclear Apartheid," *Foreign Affairs* 77 (September–October 1998): 41–52.

[60] See Jonathan Schell, "The Folly of Arms Control." For critiques by William Kristol and other prominent neoconservatives, see "Rebuilding America's Defenses: Strategy, Forces and Resources For a New Century," A Report of the Project for the New American Century, September 2000. This report and related items are available at http://www.newamericancentury.org/publicationsreports.htm.

[61] American diplomatic pressure on Taiwan to forgo nuclear weapons probably would have failed if the government of Taiwan had concluded that its security would be better served with nuclear weapons. American nuclear weapons were placed in Taiwan from 1960 to 1974. See Robert S. Norris, William M. Arkin, and William Burr, "Where They Were," *Bulletin of the Atomic Scientists*, 26–35.

[62] Falkenrath et al., 65–66.

ship at odds with the Bush administration will have a greater incentive to explore all the options. The Bush administration itself has begun to undermine the normative taboo against the use of nuclear weapons by calling for a new generation of "bunker buster" weapons that kill on a supposedly more reasonable scale, only decapitating leadership. Any potential leadership targets are sure to notice this, along with the administration's pursuit of missile defense and the Bush doctrine's substitution of preventive war for deterrence as the cornerstone of American security policy.[63]

Occupation and Outpost

Under the present circumstances, the only sure way to keep Iraq from seeking WMD will be an open-ended U.S. military occupation—too costly in human, material, and political terms. In such a scenario, American soldiers would die in Iraq on a regular basis. Perhaps this would occur only in small numbers, but it would be unavoidable if they continue to occupy much of Baghdad and other cities, just as American police officers die on duty in large cities in the United States. Nor can occupation itself be done cheaply in financial terms because Iraqi oil revenues would be insufficient to pay for both the country's domestic needs and the maintenance of tens of thousands of U.S. forces. The international diplomatic costs of a long-term American presence would not be insignificant, especially if the United States goes it alone and Iraqi domestic instability continues. On a popular political level, a permanent American occupation of Iraq would be disastrous for U.S. relations with the Arab and Muslim worlds, relations that will mean success or failure in confronting the most implacable American enemies. A similar but genuinely multinational occupation force could include only those few countries with both the political will and military capacity to contribute.[64]

A seemingly more palatable alternative to full-blown occupation would be to establish a low-profile but capable U.S. military presence at a handful of relatively isolated bases, perhaps at the international airport near Baghdad, the H2 and H3 airfields in the western desert, Tallil air base near al-Nasiriyya in the south, and at Bashur in the Kurdish north.[65] With troops and aircraft at these

[63] Essential statements of the Bush doctrine include President Bush's 1 June 2002 speech at West Point, where he declared that "new threats require new thinking," and "The National Security Strategy of the United States" (Washington, DC: September 2002). On the doctrine itself, see Robert Jervis, "Understanding the Bush Doctrine," *Political Science Quarterly* 118 (Fall 2003): 365–388. For an analysis of missile defense, written early in the Bush administration, see Charles L. Glaser and Steve Fetter, "National Missile Defense and the Future of U.S. Nuclear Weapons Policy," *International Security* 26 (Summer 2001): 40–92.

[64] Other contributors may step forward, but allied troop commitments in Afghanistan—an effort with wider international support—may combine with instability in Iraq to leave American forces with most of the burden of occupation.

[65] Bush administration officials reportedly first disclosed this possibility in April 2003. See Thom Shanker and Eric Schmitt, "Pentagon Expects Long-Term Access to Key Iraqi Bases," *New York Times*, 20 April 2003.

locales alone, the threat of direct American military intervention could underpin subtler means of economic and political control, ranging from economic aid and trade relations to security assurances and eventual arms sales. All this might induce the new regime—whether democratic or not—to make the desired choices in both domestic and foreign policy. Such an alternative promises to accommodate Iraq's security needs by delegating substantial decision-making authority to the United States, and it provides a guaranteed source of leverage against the over-development of Iraqi military power. Since the United States will have an interest in maintaining regional stability and supporting at least some aspects of Iraqi national development, this arrangement appears to cut the Gordian knot of Iraq's complex political and strategic dilemmas.

Nonetheless, Iraq's distribution of social and political forces does not predict a favorable national consensus on any form of permanent U.S. military presence.[66] Such a consensus is the only contingency that would allow domestic opponents of this arrangement to be reined in. Unlike their relative acquiescence to a temporary occupation today, many ordinary Iraqis will be leery of their country becoming an enduring American military outpost. This scenario is too reminiscent of Britain's military intervention during World War II after which most Iraqis rejected decisively a continued British presence. Even though the outpost was reduced to two Royal Air Force detachments in 1947, an Iraqi-British treaty providing for the retention of troops could not be ratified the next year because of intense popular opposition that culminated in bloody rioting in January 1948 and November 1952.[67] The present-day context may not be so different, but even if it is, the political interests of many Iraqis will differ from an Iraqi national interest that is ostensibly well-served by American protectors. This divergence will assure their resistance. Some political elites, moreover, will take advantage of nationalist sentiment to excoriate an American neocolonial role in the region. A majority of Iraqis will view it at best as an unwarranted constraint on Iraqi sovereignty and at worst as a Praetorian Guard for an illegitimate regime. The larger the U.S. force, the more likely it will provoke a political response; the smaller the force, the less capacity it will have to monitor and control Iraqi military development.

Even virtual invisibility will not prevent the issue from becoming a rallying cry of nationalist discontent, just as Britain's lingering military presence in Egypt's Suez Canal Zone energized the Muslim Brothers in 1950s Egypt.[68] A host of domestic, regional, and even global political actors will reject any long-term U.S. role that is sufficiently large to change the course of Iraqi politics, perhaps

---

[66] For historical perspective on Iraqi social cleavages, see Hanna Batatu, *The Old Social Classes and the Revolutionary Movements of Iraq* (Princeton: Princeton University Press, 1979).

[67] The demonstrations of 1948 and 1952, known respectively as *al-wathba* (the Leap) and *al-intifada* (the Upheaval) became part of the mythology of the 1958 Iraqi revolution. Tripp, *A History of Iraq*, 118–131.

[68] For an insider account of Nasser and the Anglo-Egyptian treaty ending Britain's Canal Zone garrisons, see Anthony Nutting, *Nasser* (New York: E.P. Dutton, 1972), 68–73.

delighting quietly in the political traction it will give them with their constituents. Legal Iraqi opposition groups, antisystem parties, underground terrorist
organizations, and American foes worldwide will resent and resist such a presence. There will be plenty of opponents in a country of nearly twenty-five million people: hundreds of thousands of Iraqis have lost family members to
American military power, and not all of them blame Saddam for their losses.
Iraq's particular geography and porous borders will make it difficult to interdict
foreign activists and agitators from all over, some of whom will arrive quite
openly via Baghdad international airport. American attempts to use subtler
diplomatic and economic means of control will meet international resistance
from states resentful of U.S. domination. Some Iraqis will welcome an American force, maybe in large numbers if the presence facilitates other aspects of the
country's political, economic, and social life. But a permanent foreign military
outpost has never been sustained in the heart of the region, least of all one designed expressly to limit Iraqi sovereignty and hold the country in check.

REGIONAL SOLUTIONS

Only regional conflict resolution, or at least its mitigation, can reduce to a man-
ageable level one of the most certain sources of proliferation pressure: intense
regional insecurity. Even if the security dilemma cannot be eliminated in a
world of sovereign states, recognition of its continued dynamics may help to
reduce its worst consequences. Ultimately, states seek the deadliest weapons
whenever they are caught up in intractable conflict, whether of their own making or as a legacy of past political failures. To put it more optimistically, no
state has ever sought and obtained nuclear weapons in the absence of a serious
external threat.[69] The very invention of nuclear weapons in the United States
was driven by war and insecurity: the fear that Nazi Germany would get the
bomb first.[70] No doubt, other political factors were at play in the American case,
but regional and global insecurity are among the few sure-fire causes of arms
proliferation, all but guaranteeing determined and even imprudent state efforts
to counter seeming threats to national existence.

Saddam may have passed from the scene, but peace, security, and stability
will elude the Middle East until its most serious disputes are resolved. A resolution to the Palestinian-Israeli conflict is a sensible starting point because it remains the linchpin to Arab-Israeli antagonism and its elimination would give
new momentum to regional arms control initiatives that are otherwise untena-

[69] The South African experience contradicts this claim only if entirely domestic political and economic factors gave birth to its nuclear program. This scenario is plausible but unlikely. See Peter Liberman, "The Rise and Fall of the South African Bomb."

[70] The Soviets followed suit, not necessarily because Stalin had nuclear ambitions or was bent on
world domination. To do otherwise would have permitted a vulnerability that few state leaders will
accept.

ble.[71] This alone would be insufficient, however, because Iraqi insecurity is not a result of Palestinian-Israeli enmity. A durable regional order cannot be built and maintained while states like Iraq, Iran, and Israel fear for their existence, even if such fears are unfounded and elicit self-destructive behavior. Under these circumstances, proliferation pressures are sure to undo any momentary stability achieved by a dominant party, leading to new cycles of confrontation and crisis. Iraq's future leaders will respond predictably to the regional security environment they face, regardless of their political loyalties and the hopes and wishes of the international community. While the evolution and diffusion of weapons technology creates dangerous vulnerabilities for all states, it also provides a constructive political opportunity for those seeking to change an unstable and risk-filled status quo. Conflict resolution may not eliminate all the dangers and uncertainties of international life, but it is a clear and necessary first step toward regional transformation.

A lasting regional order, like its domestic counterpart, cannot be imposed on the Middle East from the outside, especially if local political actors see it as unjust and self-interested. Even the United States lacks the capacity to remake the Middle East entirely as it wishes. These limitations notwithstanding, a durable order would benefit from both the committed leadership of the most powerful international actors and the development of strong and resilient international institutions.[72] Having taken possession of Iraq by force, America now has a responsibility and an interest in expanding the number of parties involved in determining the country's future and creating a transparent process for restoring Iraqi sovereignty without abandoning it in the face of inevitable difficulties. This process might start with the Iraqis themselves, rather than with American interlopers assuming to know best the interests and aspirations of one of the oldest settled communities in the world. It might also benefit from closer cooperation with an international community that Washington seems to have shunned since the debacle at the UN Security Council before the war. Either way, the United States needs to move beyond simple-minded notions of a post-Saddam paradise and the false promise of a hegemonic peace.

---

[71] For details on the Arms Control and Regional Security talks in the Middle East, see Feldman, *Nuclear Weapons and Arms Control in the Middle East*.

[72] For more on the construction of postwar order, focusing on great-power conflict but relevant here also, see G. John Ikenberry, *After Victory: Institutions, Strategic Restraint, and the Rebuilding of Order after Major Wars* (Princeton: Princeton University Press, 2001).

The Debate over Nuclear North Korea

VICTOR D. CHA
DAVID C. KANG

Much as political scientists would like to believe otherwise, the strength of any new U.S. foreign policy doctrine historically stands not on its principles and logic, but on its material results. In this regard, there is no denying that U.S. military victories in Iraq and Afghanistan, the capture of Saddam Hussein, the start of nuclear talks with Iran, and the agreement by Libya's Muammar el-Qaddafi to submit to international nuclear inspections are impressive even to critics of the Bush administration. Although each of these developments is far from conclusive, they offer arguable evidence of the Bush doctrine's effectiveness. Yet, one member of the "axis of evil" remains recalcitrant — the Democratic Peoples' Republic of Korea (DPRK or North Korea). In social science terms, the DPRK remains a "hard test" of the Bush doctrine's effectiveness at rolling back nuclear capabilities in rogue regimes. Unlike the suspected or potential nuclear weapons programs of Iraq or Libya, North Korea's program is real, developing, and already most likely churning out nuclear weapons. North Korean officials reportedly are fond of telling their American interlocutors that the United States should stop trying to roll back North Korea's nuclear weapons programs and should start thinking about how to live with a nuclear North Korea.

Indeed, the DPRK has emerged in the past decade as the subject of the most divisive foreign policy issues for the United States and its allies in Asia. Interested parties have disagreed vehemently over the regime's intentions and goals and over the appropriate strategy that the United States should employ in dealing with this country.

VICTOR D. CHA is associate professor of government and D.S. Song-Korea Foundation Chair in Asian Studies at Georgetown University. He is the award-winning author of *Alignment Despite Antagonism: The US-Korea-Japan Security Triangle* and coauthor, with David Kang, of *Nuclear North Korea.* Cha serves as an independent consultant of the U.S. government and financial private sector and has testified before Congress on Asian security issues. DAVID C. KANG is associate professor of government and adjunct associate professor at the Tuck School of Business, Dartmouth College. He is the author of *Crony Capitalism: Corruption and Development in South Korea and the Philippines* and coauthor of *Nuclear North Korea.*

The debates over North Korea's bombshell admission in October 2002 of a second secret nuclear weapons program, over their withdrawal from the Nuclear Non-Proliferation Treaty (NPT), and over the ensuing crisis in 2003 are only the most proximate illustrations of the perennial division of views on the opaque regime. Many "hawks" or hardliners assert that Pyongyang's conduct not only amounted to a violation of a series of nonproliferation agreements (that is, the NPT, the 1994 U.S.–DPRK Agreed Framework, and the 1992 Korean Denuclearization Declaration) but also revealed the fundamentally unchanged and "evil" intentions of the Kim Jong Il regime. Hence, to hardliners, the only policy worth pursuing is isolation and containment, abandoning the "sunshine" policy of unconditional engagement made famous by former president Kim Dae Jung of the Republic of Korea (ROK, or South Korea).[1] Others argue, by contrast, that North Korea's need for such a secret program, albeit in violation of standing agreements, derives from basic insecurity and fears of U.S. preemption. In this vein, Vice Foreign Minister Kang Sok Ju's admission of the secret nuclear program, this view purports, was a "cry for help" to draw a reluctant Bush administration into direct talks.[2] The former denigrate the latter as weak-kneed appeasers. The latter dismiss the former as irresponsible hawkish ideologues.

The North Korean problem, moreover, has become intricately tied to partisan politics: rivalries between the executive branch and Congress, controversies over intelligence assessments, the viability of the nonproliferation regime, the efficacy of homeland defense, and differing assessments of the utility of deterrence versus preemption in U.S. security doctrine. That is a pretty impressive record of troublemaking for the small, closed, and arguably most backward country in the post–Cold War world!

Obviously, the crux of the concern over North Korea stems from the threats it poses to its neighbors with its conventional military forces, ballistic missiles, and weapons of mass destruction capabilities. North Korea boasts a 1.1 million-man army in forward positions bearing down on the border separating the two Koreas (the Demilitarized Zone or DMZ). It is infamously known as an aggressive exporter of ballistic missile technology to regimes such as Iran and Pakistan. Its drive for nuclear weapons in earnest dates back to the 1980s, and its interest in them to even before then. Many experts believe the DPRK holds one of the largest stockpiles of biological and chemical agents in the world. And at the same time that the regime militarily empowers itself, it starves its citizens at home. This combination of policies elicits a plethora of colorful epithets and

---

[1] Victor Gilinsky, "North Korea as the Ninth Nuclear Power?" Nautilus Institute Policy Forum Online, PFO 02-10A, accessed at http://nautilus.org/fora/security/0210A_Victor.html, 22 October 2002; "Answering North Korea," *Washington Post*, 18 October 2002; and "North Korea and the End of the Agreed Framework," *Heritage Foundation Backgrounder* No. 1605, 18 October 2002.

[2] Jimmy Carter, "Engaging North Korea," *New York Times*, 27 October 2002; Leon Sigal, "A Bombshell that's Actually an Olive Branch," *Los Angeles Times*, 18 October 2002; and Jekuk Chang, "Pyongyang's New Strategy of 'Frank Admission,'" Nautilus Institute Policy Forum Online PFO02-11A, accessed at http://nautilus.org/fora/security/0211A_Chang.html, 24 October 2002.

hyperbole concerning the regime and its leader, Kim Jong Il. A major U.S.-based news magazine covered the unexpected death of the first leader of North Korea, Kim Il Sung, in July 1994, with the cover story, "The Headless Beast."[3] A *Washington Post* (29 December 2002) op-ed contribution referred to North Korean leader Kim Jong Il as a "radioactive lunatic."[4] The cover story of *Newsweek* (13 January 2003) carried a picture of the North Korean leader, clad in chic black, with the caption "Dr. Evil." Greta Van Susteren introduced a *Fox News* story on Kim Jong Il with the opening question, "Is he insane or simply diabolical?"[5]

Policy on North Korea has become a political football. In South Korea, the conservatives bash the liberal incumbent government over what they term an appeasement of North Korea. Kim Dae Jung's sunshine policy has become so politicized that one can no longer distinguish between criticisms of the policy and character assassinations of the president. In the United States as well, engagement of North Korea and the "Agreed Framework" have become such a partisan issue that one cannot tell whether detractors object to the merits of the policy or the policy's association with the Clinton administration. Congressmen Benjamin Gilman and Christopher Cox claimed a U.S. policy of engagement with North Korea was the equivalent of entering "a cycle of extortion with North Korea" and nothing more than a "one-sided love affair."[6] While some saw engagement during the Clinton administration as one of the "unsung success stories" of American foreign policy,[7] it was elsewhere condemned as "the screwiest policy . . . ever seen."[8] While some saw incentives as a responsible way to try to transform the regime, outspoken figures such as Senator John McCain accused the Clinton administration of being "intimidated" by a puny country and charged that the American president had become a "co-conspirator" with DPRK leader Kim Jong Il.[9] Some even argued, moreover, that the United States was encouraging North Korean aggression with a policy of appeasement that rewarded bad behavior and "encouraged all these crazy people over in North Korea to believe we are weaklings because we are giving them everything they want."[10] Pat Buchanan criticized both the Clinton and Bush administrations for giving Kim Jong Il a "fruit basket" and "sweet reason," rather than a "tomahawk missile."[11]

---

[3] *Newsweek*, July 1994, cited in Bruce Cumings, "The Structural Basis of Anti-Americanism in the Republic of Korea," (unpublished paper presented at Georgetown University, 30 January 2003): 26.

[4] Mary McGrory, "Bush's Moonshine Policy," op-ed, *Washington Post*, 29 December 2002.

[5] *Fox News*, 15 January 2003, 10:08 pm, cited in Cumings, "The Structural Basis of Anti-Americanism," 25.

[6] Press release by Benjamin Gilman, 17 September 1999; and statement by Christopher Cox, Hearing of the House International Relations Committee, 13 October 1999.

[7] Lee Hamilton, "Our Stake in Asia's Nuclear Future," *Washington Times*, 13 May 1998.

[8] Statement by Dana Rohrbacher, Hearings of the House International Relations Committee, 24 March 1999.

[9] Statement by John McCain on the Senate floor, Congressional Record, 23 June 1994.

[10] Statement by Dana Rohrbacher, Hearings of the House International Relations Committee, 24 March 1999 and 13 October 1999.

[11] Patrick J. Buchanan, "The Great Equalizer," *The American Conservative* (10 February 2003): 7.

A Debate, Not Hyperbole

These statements are a small sample of the degree to which discussion on North Korea has become emotionally charged and ideological. Rarely does good policy that serves American and allied interests emerge from such emotional and one-sided debates. Our purpose in this essay is to step back from the histrionics and offer a reasoned, rational, and logical debate on the nature of the North Korean regime and the policy that should be followed by the United States, Japan, and South Korea. Each of us has our own orientation toward the problem, ranging from more pessimistic to optimistic assessment. Nevertheless, the debate is a genuine one, apolitical and scholarly in nature, but with real implications for the basic foundations of different schools of thought on North Korea policy.

David Kang believes that the threat posed by North Korea has been unduly inflated and that despite the forward deployments on the DMZ, Pyongyang has been rationally deterred from aggression for fifty-plus years and there is no reason to believe that they would change their minds today. He believes that if one looks at the North's economic and political behavior in a broader, historical context, rather than fixating only on military deployments, there is a story of slow, plodding reform to be told. As a result, he argues that engagement works with the North. It sends the right signals to the insecure regime that the United States, South Korea, and Japan are interested in trading the North's proliferation threat for a path of economic reform and integration. Kang argues that this has already been validated by the record of DPRK responses thus far. Kang finds the October 2002 nuclear revelations a disappointing setback in DPRK efforts at reform and openness, but nevertheless sees a consistency in Pyongyang's behavior as well as an opportunity for the United States to negotiate an end to the proliferation threat on the peninsula.

Victor Cha believes that the threat posed by North Korea still remains and that although Pyongyang has been rationally deterred from attempting a second invasion, there still exists a coercive bargaining rationale for violence. In his view, the North undertakes limited but serious crisis-inducing acts of violence with the hope of leveraging crises more to its advantage, an extremely risky but also extremely rational policy for a country that has nothing to lose and nothing to negotiate with. Moreover, Cha is skeptical as to how much Pyongyang's intentions have really changed. Cha sees the October 2002 nuclear revelations as strong evidence validating hawkish skepticism of North Korean intentions. In light of these activities, his support of engagement is highly conditional (that is, only if the North Koreans return to the status quo ante); otherwise, the United States and its allies would be forced to pursue some form of isolation and containment of the regime.

The Makings of a Crisis

On 3 October 2002, Assistant Secretary of State for East Asian and Pacific Affairs James Kelly, accompanied by a delegation of administration officials, set off for two days of talks in Pyongyang with their North Korean counterparts.[12] The first of their kind in well over one-and-a-half years of nondialogue between the United States and the DPRK, the talks were preceded by protracted speculation about what policy the Bush administration would pursue with the regime. Following from the 2002 State of the Union Address in which President George W. Bush included North Korea in the "axis of evil" and later offered other choice negative personal opinions about Kim Jong Il (referring to Kim as a "pygmy" and to how he "loathed" him), many speculated a dark future for U.S.–DPRK relations.[13] Other pundits, however, cited various statements by administration officials and a June 2001 internal policy review that indicated that the administration would eventually pick up where the Clinton administration had left off, negotiating some form of engagement with the North Koreans.[14]

The meeting between Kelly and his counterpart, Vice Minister of Foreign Affairs Kim Kye Gwan, took place against a backdrop of recently thawed relations between North Korea and U.S. regional allies. Following a deadly naval provocation by the DPRK against ROK vessels in June 2002, North–South relations appeared to cycle back to a more positive path, with high-level meetings throughout the summer that resulted in ministerial talks, family reunions, resumption of infrastructure projects (road and railway corridors), and North Korean participation in the Asian Games in Pusan.[15] On 31 July, Secretary of State Colin Powell met briefly with DPRK Foreign Minister Paik Nam Sun on the sidelines of Asian multilateral meetings in Brunei. One week later, Charles Pritchard, the U.S. State Department's chief representative to the Korean Peninsula Energy Development Organization (KEDO) went to Kumho, North Korea, for the first ceremonial pouring of concrete for construction of the light-water reactor. Contemporaneous with these events, the North announced a series of new economic reforms and projects, including a special economic zone on the Sino-Korean border and, most significantly, the lifting of price controls.[16]

---

[12] Unless otherwise cited, the following description of events is based on several not-for-attribution interviews with U.S. government officials and press reports.

[13] State of the Union Address, accessed at http://www.whitehouse.gov/news/releases/2002/01/20020129-11.html, 1 June 2001. For Bush's March 2001 remarks, see "Remarks by President Bush and President Kim Dae-Jung of South Korea," 7 March 2001, accessed at http://www.whitehouse.gov/news/releases/2001/03/20010307-6.html, 1 June 2001. Also see Bob Woodward, *Bush At War* (New York: Simon & Schuster, 2002), 339–340.

[14] For the June 2001 policy review, see "Statement by the President," 13 June 2001, accessed at http://www.whitehouse.gov/news/releases/2001/06/20010611-4.html and http://www.whitehouse.gov/news/releases/2001/03/20010307-6.html, 3 July 2001. For Secretary of State Powell's remarks about picking up the threads of the Clinton administration's engagement policy, see "Press Availability with Her Excellency Anna Lindh, Minister of Foreign Affairs of Sweden," 6 March 2001, accessed at http://www.state.gov/secretary/rm/2001/1116.htm, 3 July 2001.

[15] Aidan Foster-Carter, "No Turning Back?" *Comparative Connections* (July 2002), accessed at http://www.csis.org/pacfor/cc/0203Qnk_sk.html, 1 August 2002.

[16] Marcus Noland, "West-Bound Train Leaving the Station: Pyongyang on the Reform Track," unpublished paper prepared for the Council on U.S.–Korea Security Studies, Seoul, Korea, 14–15 October 2002, accessed at http://www.iie.com/papers/noland1002.htm, 2 December 2002.

North Korean–Japanese relations also appeared to take a major step forward with the breakthrough meeting between Kim Jong Il and Japanese Premier Koizumi in Pyongyang in September 2002.[17] The summit produced a North Korean admission of and apology for the past abduction of Japanese nationals for the purpose of espionage training and held out hope for diplomatic normalization. This course of positive events led many to conjecture that the stage had finally been set for a U.S. re-engagement with North Korea.

On the contrary, Assistant Secretary Kelly's mission produced North Korea's bombshell assertion that it was secretly pursuing a second nuclear arms program through uranium enrichment technology. Kelly's initial demarche acknowledged that the United States was interested in pursuing a new relationship with North Korea in the political, economic, and security arenas, but specified that before any such path could be taken, the North Koreans needed to come clean on their past and future proliferation activities. Kelly then informed the North Koreans that the United States was aware of the North's pursuit of a secret nuclear weapons program. This program was undertaken using a different method of production—highly enriched uranium (HEU) technology—and on a scale comparable to that of the plutonium-based bomb program that had been frozen in 1994.[18] Suspicions of such a program's existence dated back to 1997 or even earlier, but intelligence was spotty. Confirming evidence took the form of intelligence tracing of North Korean purchases of high-strength aluminum (a critical secondary material associated with an HEU program) and Pakistani sales of centrifuge technology to the North Koreans in exchange for DPRK missiles.[19]

The North Koreans initially denied this accusation, claiming that it was an American fabrication, and continued on with regularly scheduled meetings (a total of four over the two days). Kim reported Kelly's statements to his superiors during the first break, and this set off all-night consultations within the North Korean leadership (presumably including Kim Jong Il). The three-hour meeting on 3 October was followed by a dinner that evening and a two-and-a-half-hour meeting with Kim Kye Gwan the next morning. The North Koreans did not respond to Kelly's initial demarche at either of these meetings. A short ceremonial meeting (of about thirty-five minutes) with Supreme People's Assembly Chairman Kim Yong Nam at 3:00 pm on 4 October followed, again with no apparent North Korean response. It was at the fourth scheduled meeting of the trip, between 4:15 and 5:10 pm on 4 October, that the North Koreans re-

[17] Victor Cha, "Mr. Koizumi Goes to Pyongyang," *Comparative Connections* (October 2002), accessed at http://www.csis.org/pacfor/cc/0203Qjapan_skorea.html, 3 November 2002.

[18] Comments by Assistant Secretary of State James Kelly at "Defining the Future of US–Korean Relations," roundtable hosted by the *Washington Post*, 6 February 2003, 3–5:30 pm.

[19] "US Followed the Aluminum," *Washington Post*, 18 October 2002; and Seymour Hersh, "The Cold Test: What the Administration Knew about Pakistan and the North Korean Nuclear Program," *The New Yorker*, 27 January 2002, accessed at http://www.newyorker.com/fact/content/?030127fa_fact., 28 February 2002.

turned with higher-level representation, Vice Foreign Minister Kang Sok Ju. In an extensive and scripted fashion that left little time for an exchange of views, Kang said that he spoke on behalf of the Party and the government of the DPRK in asserting that North Korea was justified in pursuing such capabilities and that it considered the Agreed Framework to be nullified. Kang blamed Bush for including North Korea in the "axis of evil" and declared that the DPRK had even "stronger weapons" to wield against the United States if threatened. (Kelly noted that the program in question had indeed begun before the "axis of evil" statement.)

A news blackout of sorts ensued as administration officials revealed very little of the deliberations over the following ten days (press conferences in Seoul and Tokyo during Kelly's return from Pyongyang were either shortened to official statements without time for questions or canceled; Bush did not mention North Korea publicly for five days after Kelly's return), raising speculation ranging from the very optimistic (a "grand bargain") to the pessimistic.[20] The news became public on 16 October 2002 when the administration, in order to preempt press leaks, released a statement.[21]

The United States demanded that North Korea return to the existing nonproliferation agreements before any further talks could take place and, in conjunction with the European Union, Japanese, and South Korean representatives of the KEDO board, suspended further shipments of heavy fuel oil to North Korea under the original terms of the 1994 Agreed Framework. By December 2002, the makings of a crisis (despite Bush administration assertions to the contrary) were evident as U.S. officials intercepted and boarded for inspection a North Korean ship in the Arabian Sea (carrying missiles to Yemen).

The North Koreans responded to these events in late December 2002 with a series of steps at the Yongbyon nuclear facilities that had been frozen under the 1994 agreement. Over a period of little more than one week, they removed the seals at all frozen facilities (the experimental reactor, the storage building, and the reprocessing laboratory), dismantled International Atomic Energy Agency (IAEA) monitoring cameras, and expelled the three IAEA international inspectors. In defiance of IAEA resolutions demanding that the North Koreans come back into compliance, Pyongyang announced on 10 January 2003 their withdrawal from the NPT. Evidence of subsequent North Korean

---

[20] Ralph Cossa, "Trials, Tribulations, Threats and Tirades," *Comparative Connections* (January 2003), accessed at http://www.csis.org/pacfor/cc/0204Qus_skorea.html, 28 February 2002.

[21] Inquiries by Chris Nelson of the *Nelson Report* and Barbara Slavin of *USA Today* prompted the administration to go public with the news. Some argue that the Bush administration deliberately withheld information about the program until after Congress authorized the use of military force against Iraq. Others argued that intelligence reports on the HEU program were delivered to the White House as early as November 2001, but that the September 11th attacks and war against terrorism took all high-level focus away from the assessment. See Walter Pincus, "N. Korea's Nuclear Plans Were No Secret," *Washington Post*, 1 February 2003; and Ryan Lizza, "Nuclear Test," *The New Republic*, 4 November 2002, 10–11.

actions, including tampering with stored fuel rods (a source of weapons-grade plutonium), restarting the experimental reactor, resuming missile tests, and probable plutonium reprocessing, suggested deliberate and purposeful moves in the direction of producing nuclear weapons.[22]

After seven months of nondialogue, trilateral talks involving the United States, the DPRK, and China took place in Beijing in April 2003, but these meetings only served to heighten the crisis. On the eve of the talks, North Korea released statements about its intention to follow through on reprocessing if the United States did not yield in the upcoming meetings. Then, on the first day of three days of scheduled talks, the North stated its interest in pressing forward with a resolution to the nuclear crisis if the United States was so inclined. However, in virtually the same breath, the DPRK delegate, Ri Gun, pulled Assistant Secretary James Kelly aside at dinner on the first evening of talks (in an apparent attempt to have a "bilateral" discussion with the United States). Ri allegedly told Kelly that the North possessed nuclear weapons, that it had no intention of dismantling them, and that it would consider testing them or exporting them, depending on what the United States proposed in terms of tension-reducing measures. The North then did not show up for the remainder of the trilateral talks, except for a brief formal gathering to end the meetings. Another set of talks, this time involving six countries (the United States, Japan, South Korea, China, Russia, and North Korea), took place again in Beijing in August 2003. The United States refused to engage in bilateral negotiations with the North Koreans, preferring to include all countries in the talks. The North declared that they possessed nuclear weapons and threatened to test these weapons if the United States did not offer security assurances. A third set of six-party talks tentatively scheduled for December 2003 was postponed, with no visible sign of progress toward a resolution of the problem at the start of 2004.

Our (Differing) Assessments of the Crisis

Debates raged inside the U.S. government and among outside experts as to how to respond to the 2003 nuclear revelations. Yet again, the public policy debates became quickly shaped by needlessly inflammatory invectives levied against all parties concerned. Mary McGrory's column in the *Washington Post* (9 February 2003) named Kim "the little madman with the passion for plutonium."[23] Others blasted the Bush administration's North Korea policy as the source of the crisis, labeling it "amateur hour," and an example of what happens when "[i]t talks before it thinks."[24] Still others resorted to blaming the Clinton administration as the root cause of the crisis, referring to President Clinton's negotiation of the 1994 Agreed Framework as a "queer amalgamation of Clement

---

[22] Walter Pincus, "Hints of North Korean Plutonium Output," *Washington Post*, 31 January 2003; and Doug Struck, "Reactor Restarted, North Korea Says," *Washington Post*, 6 February 2003.

[23] Mary McGrory, "Fuzzy-Headed on North Korea," op-ed, *Washington Post*, 9 February 2003.

[24] Richard Cohen, "Amateur Hour at the White House," *Washington Post*, 16 January 2003.

Atlee and Alfred E. Neuman."[25] As in the past, what was at issue substantively vis-a-vis North Korea got lost in partisan politics, bureaucratic rivalries, sensationalist arguments, and a hint of racism.[26]

DAVID KANG: GETTING BACK TO "START"

In David Kang's view, the nuclear revelations of October 2002 and the ensuing crisis intensified an already acute dilemma for both the United States and North Korea. For the United States, the focus on Iraq was now potentially diverted by an unwanted crisis over an "axis of evil" country in Northeast Asia. For North Korea, the slowly intensifying economic and diplomatic moves of the past few years were also potentially thwarted. For both sides, their worst suspicions were confirmed in the worst of ways. North Korea concluded that the United States had never had any intention of normalizing ties or concluding a peace treaty. The United States concluded that North Korea had never had any intention of abandoning its nuclear weapons program.

The North Korean regime is a brutal and morally reprehensible regime. It has enriched itself while allowing hundreds of thousands of its own citizens to die of starvation. That this regime is odious is not in question. Rather, the issue is: what tactics will best ameliorate the problems on the peninsula?

Many Western policy makers and analysts viewed the nuclear revelations with alarm and surprise. However, much of the Western hand-wringing has elements of Kabuki theater to it, and the accusations ring hollow. "Outrage and shock! at North Korean nuclear programs" is not so convincing in view of the fact that the Bush administration has been openly derisive of Kim Jong Il, has been contemptuous of the Agreed Framework, and has known about North Korea's nuclear program since June 2001.[27] An American intelligence official who attended White House meetings in 2002 said that "Bush and Cheney want this guy's head on a platter. Don't be distracted by all this talk about negotiations.... They have a plan, and they are going to get this guy after Iraq."[28] A North Korea that feels threatened and perceives the U.S. administration to be actively attempting to increase pressure on it is unlikely to trust the United States.

Does North Korea have legitimate security concerns? If not, then their nuclear program is designed for blackmail or leverage. If the North does have legitimate security concerns, then it is not that surprising that such a program

---

[25] Ben Johnson, "Appeasing North Korea: the Clinton Legacy," *FrontPageMagazine.com*, 3 January 2003, accessed at http://www.frontpagemag.com/Articles/Printable.asp?ID'5368. Also see Frank J. Gaffney, "North Korean Revisionism," *National Review Online*, 10 January 2003, accessed at http://www.nationalreview.com/gaffney/gaffney011003.asp.

[26] On the last point, see Cumings, "The Structural Basis of Anti-Americanism," 3, 4.

[27] Walter Pincus, "North Korea's Nuclear Plans Were No Secret: U.S. Stayed Quiet as It Built Support on Iraq," *Washington Post*, 1 February 2003.

[28] Hersh, "The Cold Test," 47.

exists, given the open hostility toward the regime that the Bush administration has evidenced. However, despite the furor over the revelation, not much has changed on the peninsula. Deterrence is still robust. North Korea's basic strategy remains the same: simultaneously deter the United States and also find a way to fix the economy. The United States, for its part, faces the same choices it did a decade ago: negotiate, or hope that the North collapses without doing too much damage to the region.

Without movement toward resolving the security fears of the North, progress in resolving the nuclear weapons issue will be limited. It is unsurprising that the 1994 Agreed Framework fell apart, because it was a process by which both sides set out to slowly build a sense of trust and both sides began hedging their bets very early on in that process. Because neither the United States nor North Korea fulfilled many of the agreed-upon steps, even during the Clinton administration, the Framework was essentially dead long before the nuclear revelation of October 2002. Neither side acts in a vacuum; the United States and North Korea each react to the other's positions, and this interaction has led to a spiral of mistrust and misunderstanding. Threats and rhetoric from each side impact the other's perceptions and actions, and this interaction can be either a mutually reinforcing positive or a negative spiral.[29]

The accepted wisdom in the United States is that North Korea abrogated the Framework by restarting its nuclear weapons program. The reality is more complicated, however. Both the Clinton and Bush administrations violated the letter and the spirit of the agreement. Admitting that the United States is hostile toward North Korea does not make one an apologist—the United States *is* hostile, and it is unconvincing to pretend that we are not. The Bush administration made clear from the beginning that it had serious doubts about the Agreed Framework and engagement with the North. This began with the inception of the Bush administration—South Korean President Kim Dae Jung's visit to Washington DC in March 2001 was widely viewed as a rebuke to his sunshine policy that engaged the North, with Bush voicing "skepticism" in regard to the policy.[30] By the time of President Bush's now famous "axis of evil" speech, it had long been clear that the Bush administration did not trust the North. For the Framework to have had any hope of being even modestly successful, each side needed to have worked more genuinely toward building confidence in the other.

The 1994 Agreed Framework

The Agreed Framework of 1994 was not a formal treaty; rather, it was a set of guidelines designed to help two countries that were deeply mistrustful of each

---

[29] The most well known of these situations is the "security dilemma," where one side's attempts to make itself safer provoke fears in the other side. The other side thus adjusts to counter, and both sides end up worse off. See Robert Jervis, "Cooperation under the Security Dilemma," *World Politics* Vol. 30, No. 2 (1978): 105.

[30] See, for example, Rose Brady, "The Road to Détente gets Steeper," *Businessweek*, 9 April 2001.

TABLE 1

Key Conditions of the Agreed Framework

Agreed Framework Condition	Implementation and Discussion
The United States agrees to provide two light-water reactor (LWR) power plants by the year 2003 (article 1.2).	Four years behind schedule. There has been no delay in South Korean or Japanese provision of funds. The delay has been U.S. implementation and construction.
The United States agrees to provide formal assurances to the DPRK against the threat or use of nuclear weapons by the United States (article 2.3.1).	No. The United States maintains that military force is an option on the peninsula. The United States continues to target North Korea with nuclear weapons via the "Nuclear Posture Review."
The DPRK agrees to freeze its nuclear reactors and to dismantle them when the LWR project is completed (article 1.3).	Until December 2002.
The DPRK agrees to allow the International Atomic Energy Agency to monitor the freeze with full cooperation (article 1.3).	Until December 2002.
The United States and the DPRK agree to work toward full normalization of political and economic relations, reducing barriers of trade and investment, etc. (article 2.1).	Limited lowering of U.S. restrictions on trade, no other progress toward normalization or peace treaty. The United States continues to list North Korea as a terrorist state.
The United States and the DPRK will each open a liaison office in the each other's capital, aiming at upgrading bilateral relations to the ambassadorial level (articles 2.2, 2.3).	No.

Source: Compiled from KEDO, "Agreed Framework Between the United States of America and the Democratic People's Republic of Korea," Geneva, Switzerland, 21 October 1994.

other find a way to cooperate. But both sides began backing out of the Agreed Framework well before the autumn of 2002. From its inception, the Bush administration made very clear how much it disdained the Framework, and the North had begun its nuclear program as far back as 1998. The core of the Framework was a series of steps that both sides would take that would ultimately lead to North Korea proving it had no nuclear weapons or nuclear weapons program and to the United States normalizing ties with the North and providing it with light-water nuclear reactors that could make energy but not weapons. Table 1 shows the key elements of the Framework.

Neither side fulfilled its obligations under the Framework.[31] The key elements on the U.S. side were a formal statement of nonaggression (article 2.3.1), provision of the light-water reactor (article 1.2), and progress toward normalization of ties (article 2.1). The reactor is now four years behind schedule.[32] The United States also has not opened a liaison office in Pyongyang and has

[31] For further discussion, see Moon J. Pak, "The Nuclear Security Crisis in the Korean Peninsula: Revisit the 1994 Agreed Framework," 28 December 2002, accessed at http://www.vuw.ac.nz/~caplabtb/dprk/Paknuclearcrisis.doc.

[32] See Jay Solomon, Alix Freedman, and Gordon Fairclough, "Troubled Power Project Plays Role in North Korea Showdown," *Wall Street Journal*, 30 January 2002.

not provided formal written assurances against the use of nuclear weapons. The U.S. "Nuclear Posture Review" still targets North Korea with nuclear weapons. The North did freeze its reactors and allow IAEA monitoring, but in December 2002, it backed out of the agreement and expelled inspectors from North Korea.

It is possible to argue that the uranium enrichment plant is a more serious breach of the Framework than not providing a formal nonaggression pact or not providing a reactor. But this argument will be compelling only to domestic constituencies. Given U.S. reluctance to fulfill its side of the Framework, it was unlikely that the North would continue to honor its side of the agreement in the hope that at some point the Bush administration would begin to fulfill its side. The implicit U.S. policy has demanded that the North abandon its military programs, and only after it does so would the United States decide whether to be benevolent. As Wade Huntley and Timothy Savage write:

> The implicit signal sent to Pyongyang was that the Agreed Framework ... was at its heart an effort to script the abdication of the DPRK regime. Immediate reticence by the United States to implement certain specific steps toward normalization called for in the agreement, such as lifting economic sanctions, reinforced this perception.... [S]uch an underlying attitude could never be the basis for real improvement in relations.[33]

The United States and North Korea are still technically at war—the 1953 armistice was never replaced with a peace treaty. The United States has been unwilling to discuss even a nonaggression pact, much less a peace treaty or normalization of ties. While the United States calls North Korea a terrorist nation and Donald Rumsfeld discusses the possibility of war, it is not surprising that North Korea feels threatened. For the past two years, U.S. policy toward the North has been consistently derisive and confrontational. Table 2 shows a selection of statements by U.S. and North Korean officials.

The Bush administration began adding new conditions to the Agreed Framework early on in its tenure. On 6 June 2001, the White House included reduction of conventional forces in the requirements it wanted North Korea to fulfill, saying that "The U.S. seeks improved implementation [of the Agreed Framework], prompt inspections of past reprocessing ... [and] a less threatening conventional military posture." On 11 June 2001, North Korea replied that "Washington should implement the provisions of the D.P.R.K.–U.S. Agreed Framework and the D.P.R.K.–U.S. Joint Communique as agreed upon." The Bush administration continued its stance. On 3 July 2001, a senior administration official said that "We need to see some progress in all areas ... we don't feel any urgency to provide goodies to them."[34]

---

[33] Wade Huntley and Timothy Savage, "The Agreed Framework at the Crossroads," *Policy Forum Online* #99-05A, Natuilus Research Institute, 11 March 1999.

[34] All three citations are from Michael Gordon, "U.S. Toughens Terms for North Korea Talks," *New York Times*, 3 July 2001.

In 2002, Secretary of State Powell added a reduction in the North's missile program to the list of conditions necessary for progress on the Framework. Missiles had originally been excluded from the Agreed Framework, and the Clinton administration had begun working out a separate agreement with the North about them. On 10 June 2002, Colin Powell said that "First, the North must get out of the proliferation business and eliminate long-range missiles that threaten other countries.... [T]he North needs to move toward a less threatening conventional military posture ... and [toward] living up to its past pledges to implement basic confidence-building measures."[35]

The North consistently maintained that it wanted the United States to lower the pressure. On 20 October 2002, Kim Yong Nam, Chair of the Supreme People's Assembly, said that "If the United States is willing to drop its hostile policy towards us, we are prepared to deal with various security concerns through dialogue."[36] On 3 November 2002, Han Song Ryol, DPRK Ambassador to the UN, reiterated that "Everything will be negotiable, including inspections of the enrichment program.... [O]ur government will resolve all U.S. security concerns through the talks if your government has a will to end its hostile policy."[37] As the crisis intensified, Colin Powell refused to consider dialogue with the North, remarking that "We cannot suddenly say 'Gee, we're so scared. Let's have a negotiation because we want to appease your misbehavior.' This kind of action cannot be rewarded."[38]

As one North Korean diplomat noted: "The Agreed Framework made American generals confident that the DPRK had become defenseless; the only way to correct this misperception is to develop a credible deterrent against the United States."[39] As of winter 2003, the situation was one of standoff. North Korean statements made clear their fear that the Bush administration would focus on pressuring North Korea once the situation in Iraq was stabilized. The 28 January 2003 statement of the Korean Anti-Nuke Peace Committee in Pyongyang concluded by saying that

> If the U.S. legally commits itself to non-aggression including the non-use of nuclear weapons against the DPRK through the non-aggression pact, the DPRK will be able to rid the U.S. of its security concerns.... Although the DPRK has left the NPT, its nuclear activity at present is limited to the peaceful purpose of power generation.... If the U.S. gives up its hostile policy toward the DPRK and refrains from posing a nuclear threat to it, it may prove that it does not manufacture nuclear weapons through a special verification between the DPRK and the U.S..... It is

[35] Colin Powell, remarks at the Asia Society annual dinner, 10 June 2002, quoted in Leon Sigal, "North Korea is No Iraq: Pyongyang's Negotiating Strategy," Nautilus Institute Special Report, accessed at http://nautilus.org/for a/security/0227A_Siga.html, 23 December 2002.

[36] Sigal, "North Korea is No Iraq."

[37] Philip Shenon, "North Korea Says Nuclear Program Can be Negotiated," *New York Times*, 3 November 2002.

[38] Jonathan Salant, "Secretary of State Powell says U.S. is willing to talk with North Korea," *Associated Press*, 29 December 2002.

[39] *DPRK Report* No. 19, Nautilus Institute, July–August 1999.

TABLE 2

Selected U.S.–North Korean Rhetoric over the Agreed Framework

Date	U.S. Statements	DPRK Statements
9 October 2000	"Neither government will have hostile intent towards the other." (Joint Communique)	
6 June 2001	"The U.S. seeks improved implementation [of the Agreed Framework], prompt inspections of past reprocessing ... [and] a less threatening conventional military posture." (White House press release)	
11 June 2001		"Washington should implement the provisions of the D.P.R.K.–U.S. Agreed Framework and the D.P.R.K.–U.S. Joint Communique as agreed upon." (DPRK Foreign Ministry spokesman)
3 July 2001	"We need to see some progress in all areas ... we don't feel any urgency to provide goodies to them ..." (senior administration official, on the broadened demands to North Korea)	
29 January 2002	"States like these ... constitute an axis of evil, arming to threaten the peace of the world." (George W. Bush, State of the Union speech)	
2 February 2002		"His [Bush's] remarks clearly show that the U.S.-proposed 'resumption of dialogue' with the DPRK is intended not for the improvement of the bilateral relations but for the realization of the U.S. aggressive military strategy. It is the steadfast stand and transparent will of the DPRK to counter force with force and confrontation with confrontation." (Korean Central News Agency)
1 June 2002	"We must take the battle to the enemy ... and confront the worst threats before they emerge." (George W. Bush)	
10 June 2002	"First, the North must get out of the proliferation business and eliminate long-range missiles that threaten other countries.... [T]he North needs to move toward a less threatening conventional military posture ... and liv[e] up to its past pledges to implement basic confidence-building measures." (Secretary of State Colin Powell)	
29 August 2002	North Korea is "in stark violation of the Biological weapons convention.... [M]any doubt that North Korea ever intends to comply fully with its NPT obligations." (Undersecretary of State John Bolton)	
31 August 2002		"The D.P.R.K. clarified more than once that if the U.S. has a willingness to drop its hostile policy toward the D.P.R.K., it will have dialogue with the U.S. to clear the U.S. of its worries over its security." (North Korean Foreign Ministry spokesman)
20 October 2002		"If the United States is willing to drop its hostile policy towards us, we are prepared to deal with various security concerns through dialogue." (Kim Young Nam, Chair of the Supreme People's Assembly)

(Continued)

TABLE 2

Continued

Date	U.S. Statements	DPRK Statements
5 November 2002		"Everything will be negotiable, including inspections of the enrichment program.... [O]ur government will resolve all U.S. security concerns through the talks if your government has a will to end its hostile policy." (Han Song Ryol, DPRK ambassador to the UN)
29 December 2002	"We cannot suddenly say 'Gee, we're so scared. Let's have a negotiation because we want to appease your misbehavior.' This kind of action cannot be rewarded." (Secretary of State Colin Powell)	
5 January 2003	"We have no intention of sitting down and bargaining again." (State Department Spokesman Richard Boucher)	
9 January 2003	"We think that they [Russia] could be putting the screws to the North Koreans a little more firmly and at least beginning to raise the specter of economic sanctions." (senior U.S. official)	"[W]e have no intention to produce nuclear weapons.... After the appearance of the Bush Administration, the United States listed the DPRK as part of an 'axis of evil,' adopting it as a national policy to oppose its system, and singled it out as a target of pre-emptive nuclear attack. ... [I]t also answered the DPRK's sincere proposal for conclusion of the DPRK–US non-aggression treaty with such threats as 'blockade' and 'military punishment' ...." (DPRK official announcement of withdrawal from the NPT)
23 January 2003	"First is regime change. It need not necessarily be military, but it could lead to that." (senior U.S. official)	

Sources: Jay Solomon, Peter Wonacott, and Chris Cooper, "North Asian Leaders Criticize Bush on North Korea," *Wall Street Journal*, 6 January 2003; Jay Solomon, Peter Wonacott, and Chris Cooper, "South Korea is Optimistic About End to Nuclear Crisis," *Wall Street Journal*, 4 January 2003; Michael Gordon, "Powell Says U.S. is Willing to Talk with North Korea," *New York Times*, 29 December 2002; "N. Korea pulls out of nuclear pact," MSNBC News Services, 10 January 2003; Leon Sigal, "North Korea is No Iraq: Pyongyang's Negotiating Strategy," Special Report, Nautilus Organization, 23 December 2002; Susan V. Lawrence, Murray Hiebert, Jay Solomon, and Kim Jung Min, "Time to Talk," *Far Eastern Economic Review*, 23 January 2003: 12–16.

the consistent stand of the DPRK government to settle the nuclear issue on the Korean peninsula peacefully through fair negotiations for removing the concerns of both sides on an equal footing between the DPRK and the U.S.[40]

Causes and Consequences of the October Revelation

Thus, the Agreed Framework of 1994 is dead. Both North Korea and the United States are now in essentially the same position they were in in 1994 — threatening war, moving toward confrontation. Given the levels of mistrust on both sides, this comes as no surprise. If North Korea feels threatened, threaten-

[40] Ri Kang Jin, "Statement of the Korean Anti-Nuke Peace Committee," 28 January 2003, accessed at www.kcna.co.jp/item/2003/200305/news05/13.htm, 12 June 2003.

ing them is unlikely to make them feel less threatened. Gregory Clark pointed out that "Washington's excuse for ignoring the nonaggression treaty proposal has to be the ultimate in irrationality. It said it would not negotiate under duress. So duress consists of being asked to be nonaggressive?"[41]

An intense security dilemma on the Korean peninsula is exacerbated by an almost complete lack of direct interaction between the two sides. Levels of mistrust are so high that both sides hedge their bets. The United States refused to provide formal written assurances of nonaggression to the North. The North thus retains its military and nuclear forces in order to deter the United States from acting too precipitously.

The consequences are fairly clear: the United States can continue a policy of pressure in the hope that the North will buckle and give in to U.S. pressure or collapse from internal weakness, or it can negotiate a bargain of normalization for nuclear weapons. Without resolving North Korea's security fears, the opportunity for any quick resolution of the confrontation on the peninsula will be limited. This is disappointing because North Korea, unlike Iraq, is actively seeking accommodation with the international community. Even while the Bush administration was increasing its pressure on the North, the North continued its voluntary moratorium on missile testing until 2003. The North's tentative moves toward economic openness have also been stymied for the time being. In July 2002, North Korea introduced a free-market system, allowing prices to determine supply and demand for goods and services. In September 2002, it announced a special economic zone in Shinuiju. In the last six months of 2002, work was begun to clear a section of the demilitarized zone to allow the reconnection of the railway between North and South Korea. To cap all of these developments, Kim Jong Il finally admitted in September 2002, after three decades of denials, that the North kidnapped Japanese citizens in the 1970s.

If North Korea really wanted to develop nuclear weapons, it would have done so long ago. Even today, North Korea has still not tested a nuclear device, tested an intercontinental ballistic missile, or deployed a nuclear missile force.[42] Even if North Korea develops and deploys nuclear weapons, it will not use them, because the U.S. deterrent is clear and overwhelming. The North wants a guarantee of security from the United States, and a policy of isolating it will not work. Isolation is better than pressure because pressure would only make it even more insecure. But even isolation is at best a holding measure. And the imposition of economic sanctions or economic engagement is equally unlikely to get North Korea to abandon its weapons program.

Above all, the North Korean regime wants better ties with the United States. The policy that follows from this is clear: the United States should begin negotiating a nonaggression pact with the North. It should let other countries, such as South Korea and Japan, pursue economic diplomacy if they wish. If the

---

[41] Gregory Clark, "Pyongyang is the Real Victim," *Japan Times*, 10 January 2003.

[42] Indeed, as of this writing, North Korea has still maintained the voluntary moratorium on ICBM missile testing that it began in 1999.

North allows UN nuclear inspectors back and dismantles its reactors, the United States could then move forward to actual engagement. But to dismiss the country's security fears is to miss the cause of its actions.

The Bush administration's reluctance to consider dialogue with the North is counterproductive. Even at the height of the Cold War, Ronald Reagan, despite calling the Soviet Union "the Evil Empire," met with Soviet leaders and held dialogue with them. The United States had ambassadorial relations with the Soviets, engaged in trade with the Soviets, and interacted regularly—precisely in order to moderate the situation and keep information moving between the two adversaries and to keep the situation from inadvertently escalating out of control. The United States was in far greater contact with the Soviet Union during the Cold War than it is with North Korea in 2004. By refusing to talk, the United States allows the situation to spiral out of control and harms its own ability to deal with the reality of the situation.

Does the October nuclear revelation provide any insight as to North Korea's foreign policy strategy? Essentially, no: North Korea has always sought to deter the United States and has viewed the United States as belligerent. Thus, the nuclear program is consistent with North Korea's attempts to provide for its own security. It is also important to remember that a nuclear weapons program does not mean that North Korea is any more likely to engage in unprovoked military acts now than it was before. North Korea was deterred before the revelations, and it remains deterred after the revelations. The way to resolve the crisis is by addressing the security concerns of North Korea. If the United States genuinely has no intention of attacking North Korea or pressuring it for regime change, the administration should conclude a nonaggression pact. It is not that surprising that North Korea does not believe the Bush administration's occasional assurances about having no intention of using force when the administration refuses to formalize those assurances.

In terms of U.S. policy toward the North, the revelations are actually an opening. It is impossible to negotiate with a country over an issue whose existence they deny. In the case of the nuclear program, the United States has the opportunity to actually reach a conclusion to this problem. If the Bush administration were to handle negotiations adroitly, it could possibly finally resolve an issue that has plagued Northeast Asia for far too long.

VICTOR CHA: PAST THE POINT OF NO RETURN?

Many moderates argued, as David Kang has done, that this new nuclear confession reveals Pyongyang's true intentions. Although of concern, they argue, these actions represent North Korean leader Kim Jong Il's perverse but typical way of creating a crisis to pull a reluctant Bush administration into serious dialogue. By "confessing" to the crime, in other words, Pyongyang is putting its chips on the table, ready to bargain away this clandestine program in exchange for aid and a U.S. pledge of nonaggression.[43] Moderates would, therefore, advocate continued negotiations by the United States and its allies, providing incen-

---

[43] Sigal, "North Korea is No Iraq."

tives for the North to come clean on its uranium enrichment activities as well as to extend a more comprehensive nonproliferation arrangement to replace the Agreed Framework. In exchange for this, the allies would put forward a package of incentives including economic aid and normalization of political relations.

Before the world accepts this "cry for help" thesis, however, the North's confession must be seen for what it is—admission of a serious violation of a standing agreement that could, in effect, be North Korea's last gambit for peaceful engagement with the United States and its allies. North Korea's actions constitute a blatant breakout from the 1994 U.S.–DPRK Agreed Framework designed to ensure denuclearization of the North. Those who try to make a technical, legalistic argument to the contrary are patently wrong. Although the Agreed Framework dealt specifically with the plutonium-reprocessing facilities at Yongbyon, this document was cross-referenced with the 1991–1992 North–South Korea denuclearization declaration, which banned both North and South Korea from the uranium enrichment facilities now found to be covertly held in the North. Moreover, any legal gymnastics over this issue were rendered moot by North Korea's subsequent withdrawal from the nonproliferation treaty, the first in the NPT's history.

Moreover, the implications of this act extend beyond a mere violation of legal conventions. Arguably, all of the improvements in North–South relations, including the June 2000 summit, breakthroughs in Japan–North Korea relations in 2001, and the wave of engagement with the reclusive regime that spread across Europe, Australia, and Canada in 2000–2001, were made possible by what was perceived to be the North's good-faith intentions to comply with a major nonproliferation commitment with the United States in 1994. The subtext of this commitment was that the North was willing to trade in its rogue proliferation threat for a path of reform and peaceful integration into the world community. The subsequent diplomatic achievements by Pyongyang, therefore, would not have been possible without the Agreed Framework. And now the North has shown it all to be a lie.

Alternative Explanations for North Korean Misbehavior

Many of the justifications offered by either Pyongyang or mediating parties in Seoul (an irony in itself) for the HEU program and the restarting of the plutonium program at Yongbyon are, at best, suspect. North Korea claimed its actions were warranted as responses to American failure to keep to the timetable of the Agreed Framework as well as to Washington's reneging on promises to normalize relations with the North. Moreover, they argued, the aggressive language of the United States and President Bush's "axis of evil" statements made these actions necessary. North Korean pursuit of the HEU program, however, as assistant secretary Kelly noted in the October 2002 meeting with Kang Sok Ju, predated the Bush administration's accession to office in 2001, and indeed, was well under way as Pyongyang was enjoying the benefits of Kim Dae Jung's sunshine policy from 1999 to 2002. There is no denying that the United States and the KEDO fell behind in the implementation of the Agreed Framework, in large part because the signing of the accord in October 1994 was followed by congressional elections that put in control Republicans with strong antipathy to Clinton (and by definition then, the Agreed Framework). The North Koreans were aware of this possibility and, therefore, sought during the negotiations a personal guarantee from President Clinton that the United States would do what it could to keep implementation on schedule. In other words, as far back as October 1994, Pyongyang was cognizant of such potential problems in implementation. To argue otherwise as justification for their illicit nuclear activities is a stretch. Moreover, although the Agreed Framework was not a legally binding document, arguably there is a distinction between negligence in implementing a contract and completely breaking out of one. Washington could certainly be guilty of the former, but that does not warrant the other party's actions to do the latter.

Kim Jong Il's justification that he needs to wield the nuclear threat as a backstop for regime survival and deterrence against U.S. preemption also does not hold water. This is not because anyone should expect Kim to believe Bush's public assurances that he has no intention of attacking North Korea but because any logical reasoning shows that the North already possesses these deterrent capabilities. Its 11,000 artillery tubes along the DMZ hold Seoul hostage, and its Nodong ballistic missile deployments effectively hold Japan hostage. The warning time for a North Korean artillery shell landing in Seoul is measured in seconds (fifty-seven) and for a ballistic missile fired on the Japanese archipelago in minutes (ten). There is no conceivable defense against these threats, which would result in hundreds of thousands, if not millions, of casualties. As long as the United States values the welfare of these two key allies in Northeast Asia (as well as the 100,000-plus American service personnel and expatriate community), the North holds a credible deterrent against any hypothetical contemplation of American preemption.

Finally, the argument that with the latest crisis, North Korea is seeking direct negotiations with the United States rather than a bonafide nuclear weapons capability is both disturbing and logically inconsistent. North Korea seeks a nonaggression pact, these advocates argue, and a new relationship, by using the only leverage it can muster—its military threat. There are three glaring problems with this argument. First, the notion that North Korean proliferation is solely for bargaining purposes runs contrary to the history of why states proliferate. Crossing the nuclear threshold is a national decision of immense consequence and, as numerous studies have shown, is a step rarely taken deliberately for the purpose of negotiating away these capabilities.[44] Second, even if one

---

[44] Avery Goldstein, *Deterrence and Security in the 21st Century: China, Britain, France and the Enduring Legacy of the Nuclear Revolution* (Stanford, CA: Stanford University Press, 2000); and Scott Sagan, "Why Do States Build Nuclear Weapons?" *International Security* 21.3 (Winter 1996–1997): 54–86.

were to accept these as the true North Korean intentions, the moral hazard issues become obvious. Rather than moving Pyongyang in the direction of more-compliant behavior, indulging the North's brinkmanship is likely only to validate their perceived success of the strategy. Such coercive bargaining strategies in the past by the North might have been met with engagement by the United States, but in the aftermath of the October 2002 nuclear revelations, such behavior is more difficult to countenance. The difference, as I will explain below, largely stems from the gravity of North Korean misbehavior in 2002 and violation of the Agreed Framework.

Third, the "negotiation" thesis for North Korean proliferation, upon closer analysis, actually leads one to the *opposite* logical conclusion—in other words, a North Korean "breakout" strategy of amassing a midsized nuclear weapons arsenal. South Korean advocates of the negotiation thesis maintain that Pyongyang is aware of the antipathy felt by the Bush administration toward the Clinton-era agreements made with it. Therefore, Pyongyang seeks to leverage the proliferation threat to draw the Bush administration into bilateral negotiations, ostensibly to obtain a nonaggression pact, but in practice to obtain *any* agreement with this government. Ideally, this agreement would offer more benefits than the 1994 agreement, but even if this were not the case, the key point, according to these officials, is that the agreement would have the Bush administration's imprimateur rather than that of Clinton and therefore would be more credible in North Korean eyes.[45]

Though plausible, such an argument, however, leads to a compelling counterintuitive conclusion. If North Korea wants a new and improved agreement and knows that this current administration is more "hard-line" than the previous one, then the logical plan of action would not be to negotiate away its potential nuclear capabilities (the modus operandi in 1994) but to *acquire* nuclear weapons and *then* confront the United States from a stronger position than they had in 1994. Indeed, North Korean actions in December 2002 appear to have been more than a bargaining ploy. If coercive bargaining had been the primary objective, then the North Koreans arguably would have needed to undertake only one of several steps to denude the 1994 agreement. On the contrary, their unsealing of buildings, disabling of monitoring cameras, expelling international inspectors, withdrawal from the NPT, restarting the reactor, and reprocessing represented a purposeful drive to develop weapons. As one U.S. government official observed, "[W]e made a list of all the things the North Koreans might do to ratchet up a crisis for the purpose of negotiation. They went through that list pretty quickly."[46]

What Follows Hawk Engagement?

There is no denying that Bush's "axis of evil" statements exacerbated a downward trend in U.S.–DPRK relations. But actions matter more than semantics.

---

[45] South Korean government officials, phone interviews by Victor Cha, 9 January 2003.

[46] U.S. government official, conversation with Victor Cha, 14 January 2003.

The problem is not what the United States, South Korea, or Japan may have done to irk the North. The problem is North Korea. What is most revealing about the North's actions is that hawkish skepticism vis-a-vis a real change in Kim Jong Il's underlying intentions, despite behavior and rhetoric to the contrary, remains justified.

This skepticism, as I have argued in *Foreign Affairs* (May/June 2002), is what informs the "hawk engagement" approach toward North Korea. Unlike South Korea's "sunshine policy" of unconditional engagement, this version of the strategy is laced with a great deal more pessimism, less trust, and a pragmatic calculation of the steps to follow in case the policy fails. In short, hawks might pursue engagement with North Korea for very different tactical reasons than might doves. Engagement is useful with rogues like North Korea because: first, "carrots" today can serve as "sticks" tomorrow (particularly with a target state that has very few); second, economic and food aid can start a slow process of separating the people of North Korea from its despotic regime; and third, engagement is the best practical way to build a coalition for punishment, demonstrating good-faith efforts at negotiating and thereby putting the ball in the North's court to maintain cooperation.

The 2002–2003 nuclear revelations confirm much of the skepticism that informs the hawk engagement approach. The premise of hawk engagement is that engagement should be pursued for the purpose of testing the North's intentions and genuine capacity to cooperate. If this diplomacy succeeds, then the sunshine policy advocates are correct about North Korea, and honest hawks (as opposed to ideological ones) would be compelled to continue on this path. But if engagement fails, then one has uncovered the North's true intentions and built the consensus for an alternate course of action. The nuclear violations, in this context, have created more transparency about the extent to which the North's reform efforts represent mere tactical changes or a true shift in strategy and preferences. As hawk engagement believers had always expected, Kim Jong Il has now dropped the cooperation ball. What comes next? The first step is to rally a multilateral coalition for diplomatic pressure among the allies. The fall 2002 Asia Pacific Economic Cooperation (APEC) meetings in Mexico and the U.S.–Japan–Korea trilateral statement at these meetings were important first steps in this direction. Both Seoul and Tokyo decreed that any hopes Pyongyang might have for inter-Korean economic cooperation or a large normalization package of Japanese aid hinge on satisfactory resolution of the North's current violation. (People also have wrongfully discounted the significance of a similar statement made by APEC as a whole—the first of its kind from the multilateral institution to explicitly address a security problem.) A second important step was taken in November 2002, when the three allies, through KEDO, agreed to suspend further shipments of heavy fuel oil to North Korea that had been promised under the 1994 agreement until Pyongyang came back into compliance. A third step effectively "multilateralizing" the problem occurred in August 2003, when China hosted talks involving the

United States, the DPRK, South Korea, Japan, China, and Russia. Although unsuccessful in resolving the crisis, these talks were critical to enlisting China and the region in a more proactive role in helping to solve the problem.

Pundits and critics have blasted the United States for its "no-talk, no-negotiation" position until North Korea rolls back its HEU program. Hawk engagement, in contrast, would posit that the Bush administration's relatively low-key response to North Korea's violation (especially when compared with its response to Iraq's), coupled with its withholding negotiations with Pyongyang until it first makes gestures to come back into compliance, is effectively an offer to the North of one last chance to get out of its own mess. In this sense, as Harry Rowen at Stanford University has observed, this *is* the negotiating position. Kim Jong Il needs to unilaterally and verifiably address international concerns by dismantling the HEU program and returning to the status quo ante. If he were to do this, then the possibility of new U.S.–DPRK negotiations involving quid pro quos of economic aid for nonproliferation would lie ahead.

Why Not Hawk Engagement Again?

Prominent figures in the United States, such as former President Carter, Ambassador Robert Gallucci, and others have argued for turning back the engagement clock and entering into new negotiations to gain access to the HEU program and to roll back the 1994 Agreement violations.[47] In a related vein, other commentators and journalists have argued implicitly that the United States should pursue some form of hawk engagement in the aftermath of the HEU revelations to at least "test" whether North Korea is interested in giving up the program.[48] Others have explicitly invoked the hawk engagement argument to criticize the Bush administration's nonengagement with North Korea.[49]

I do not find engagement a feasible option after the HEU revelations for one very critical reason: the initial rationale for hawk engagement was based on some degree of uncertainty with regard to the target regime's intentions. As long as such uncertainty existed, as it did in 1994, and Pyongyang remained somewhat compliant thereafter with the standing agreements that were the fruits of engagement, it would have been difficult for hawks to advocate otherwise. Hence, even when the North Koreans test-fired a ballistic missile over

---

[47] Anthony Lake and Robert Gallucci, "Negotiating with Nuclear North Korea," *Washington Post*, 6 November 2002; Carter, "Engaging North Korea"; Sigal, "A Bombshell that's Actually an Olive Branch."

[48] Comments by Joel Wit, "N. Korea Nuclear Threat," transcript of *Lehrer NewsHour* (Ray Suarez, Joel Wit, Henry Sokolski), 10 January 2003, accessed on the website of PBS Online NewsHour at http://www.pbs.org/newshour/bb/asia/jan-june03/korea_1-10.html; and comments by Wendy Sherman, "Defining the Future of US–Korean Relations," *JoongAng Ilbo–Washington Post* seminar, Washington DC, 6 February 2003.

[49] Jonathan Power, "A Hawk on North Korea Wants Bush to be a Dove," 5 February 2003, accessed at http://www.transnational.org/forum/power/2003/02.03_NorthKorea.html, 1 March 2003.

Japan in 1998, conducted submarine incursions into the South, attacked South Korean naval vessels, and undertook other acts of malfeasance, I still believed that engagement, even for hawks, was the appropriate path. However, the current violations by the North are on a scale that removes any uncertainty in regard to its intentions. Its behavior does not represent minor deviations from the landmark agreement, but rather a wholesale and secretive breakout from it. Negotiating under these conditions, for hawks, would be tantamount to appeasement.

If the current impasse is resolved diplomatically, however, and the DPRK takes unilateral steps toward dismantlement of the facilities, then regional diplomatic pressures, allied entreaties, and public opinion would again compel hawks to pursue some form of engagement. Such engagement would not be informed by any newfound trust in North Korea or its intentions. Indeed, hawk engagement in such a scenario would be informed by infinitely more palpable skepticism and distrust than existed prior to the HEU revelations and would perhaps be characterized by an even shorter tolerance for additional misbehavior by the North before switching to an alternate, more coercive path.

Isolation and Containment

If the North Koreans do not take a cooperative path out of the current crisis, then from a hawk engagement perspective, there is no choice but isolation and containment. The strategy's general contours would be to rally interested regional powers to isolate and neglect the regime until it gave up its proliferation threat. Although this would be akin to a policy of benign neglect, it would not be benign. The United States and its allies would maintain vigilant containment of the regime's military threat and would intercept any vessels suspected of carrying nuclear- or missile-related materials in and out of the North. Secondary sanctions would also be levied against firms in Japan and other Asian countries involved in illicit North Korean drug trafficking in an effort to restrict the flow of remittances to the DPRK leadership. The United States and the ROK might also undertake a reorientation of their military posture on the peninsula, focusing more on long-range, deep-strike capabilities, and betting that the DPRK will respond by scaling back forward deployments in defense of Pyongyang.[50]

This strategy of "malign neglect" would also entail more proactive humanitarian measures, including the continuation of food aid, designed to help and engage the North Korean people. The United States would urge China and other countries to allow the United Nations High Commissioner for Refugees to establish North Korean refugee processing camps in neighboring countries around the Peninsula, enabling a regularized procedure for dealing with popu-

---

[50] This is risky because the DPRK's response might also be to forward deploy even more aggressively in a "best-defense is strong-offense" strategy. For further discussion, see Henry Sokolski, ed., *Planning for a Peaceful Korea* (Carlisle, PA: Strategic Studies Institute, 2001), 3–4.

lation outflows from the decaying country. Potentially a more significant watershed in this regard would be passage of a bill clearing the way for the United States to accept any North Korean who meets the definition of "refugee" and desires safe haven in the United States. In this regard, the United States would lead by example in preparing to facilitate passage out of the darkness that is North Korea to those people who have the courage to vote with their feet.

Two critical actors in pursuing such an unattractive course of action will be China and South Korea. China's stake in propping up its old ally on the peninsula is geostrategic and keyed to a competitive U.S.–China relationship. It has no desire to see a collapse of the regime and the specter of a U.S. military presence remaining on the peninsula. Chinese equities are undeniably shifting, however, as the North Koreans pursue a nuclear weapons capability. It is official Chinese policy to oppose nuclear weapons on the peninsula, in large part because of the ripple effects that such weapons might have on Japanese and Taiwanese plans for such capabilities. Combining this worst-case contingency with frustration at continuing to pour food, fuel, and aid in large amounts (estimated around 70–90 percent of all North Korean external reliance) into a country that has shown virtually no progress toward reform might cause Chinese leaders to think differently. A more pragmatic, less-ideological Chinese leadership—in conjunction with the United States capitalizing on its more-constructive post-September 11th relationship with Beijing and helping China defray the negative externalities that might come from an isolation strategy toward North Korea—might be the key variables in the strategy's feasibility and success.[51] If Beijing were to cooperate in diplomatically pressuring the North, moreover, this decision would not be seen as kowtowing to the United States but rather as China stepping up to a leadership role in the region. China's aspirations to great power status in the region will be dependent not only on its economic capabilities but also on the type of political leadership it will be seen as providing. A proactive role in reducing the North Korean nuclear threat would provide a security good to the region that would be appreciated by all.

Where South Korea stands in a U.S. isolation policy undeniably will be a test of the alliance. Reduced perceptions of a North Korean threat since the June 2000 summit, particularly among the younger generation of South Koreans (despite little material change in the security situation on the ground), coupled with the upsurge of anti-Americanism during the December 2002 presidential elections (following the accidental USFK vehicular death of two South Korean teenage girls), resulted in an incredible phenomenon in 2003: in the face of increasing DPRK nuclear threats, South Koreans demonstrated against the alliance with the United States, blaming the United States for provoking the crisis with North Korea. If these two trends continue (that is, anti-Americanism and no fear of North Korea), then an American isolation and containment policy toward North Korea would be unacceptable to South Koreans. If

---

[51] Thanks to Tom Christensen for raising the point about the Party Congress.

South Koreans, moreover, oppose such a U.S. policy, at the price of allowing a nuclear North Korea, then the alliance might be damaged beyond repair. Two critical variables in this mix will be the leadership of the Roh Moo Hyun government and the South Korean "silent majority." In spite of Roh's past political activities and his left-leaning ideology, many argue that pragmatism and some badly needed foreign policy experience will cause him to moderate his views to be more supportive of the alliance (as was the case with Kim Dae Jung).[52] Even more important, if North Korean malfeasance grows more pronounced, the future of the alliance and a coordinated isolation strategy toward North Korea may rest in the hands of the South Korean electorate. Despite the media hype of a younger Korean generation that purportedly fears George Bush more than a nuclear-armed Kim Jong Il, polls show that a significant percentage (almost 50 percent) of the electorate hold a more somber view of North Korea's nuclear weapons obsession, and this silent majority presumably would grow as the North moves closer to such capabilities unchecked.[53] What deters many South Koreans are the costs that would come from a precipitous collapse of the DPRK regime resulting from an isolation strategy. This is understandable. South Koreans must also realize, however, that the costs of letting North Korea grow unfettered into a nuclear power would also be high. These costs might be measured in terms of not only lost alliance support from the United States but also huge potential losses in investor confidence. Already, Moody Investors downgraded South Korea's sovereign credit outlook in 2003, U.S. foreign direct investment in Korea plummeted 72 percent (in the first quarter of 2003), and the stock market dropped nearly 20 percent because of the DPRK threat.[54] A nuclear North Korea places undeniable costs on South Korea that not even the younger generation should underestimate.

No doubt there are dangers associated with an isolation strategy, not least of which is North Korean retaliation. Pyongyang states clearly that they would consider isolation and sanctions by the United States an act of war. To support isolation, however, is not to crave war on the peninsula. Indeed after engagement has been proven to fail (as it has for hawk engagers after the HEU revelations), then isolation is the *least* likely strategy to provoke war, inasmuch as the remaining options (including preemptive military strikes) are all much more coercive.[55]

There is no denying the gravity of the crisis in 2003–2004. For hawk engagement, the offer to Kim Jong Il to resolve concerns about his dangerous uranium enrichment and plutonium nuclear weapons programs if he wants to get back on the engagement path is, in effect, the last round of diplomacy. Not taking up this offer would mean a path of isolation and containment of the regime and

[52] Victor Cha, "Stay Calm on Korea," *Washington Post*, 20 December 2002.

[53] *Choson Ilbo–Gallup Korea* polls, 1 January 2003, accessed at http://www.gallup.co.kr/news/2003/release004.html.

[54] Hyun-Chul Kim, "Reality Check Takes Seoul Stocks Lower," *JoongAng Ilbo*, 17 March 2003.

[55] Victor Cha, "Tighten the Noose," *The Financial Times*, 29 July 2003.

an end to many positive gains Pyongyang has accumulated since the June 2000 inter-Korean summit. Given the high stakes involved, one hopes that Kim Jong Il makes the correct calculation.

The Last Word on the Crisis

David Kang embraces the argument that the North's blatant HEU confession is a cleverly disguised attempt to "retail" its new threat and thus draw a reluctant Bush administration into negotiations. He advocates negotiation by the United States and its allies to bring *both* the United States and the North Koreans back into compliance in exchange for a package of incentives including economic aid and normalization of political relations. As long as the United States threatens the North, Kang sees little hope that pressure will make the North disarm. But Kang sees great potential for reduced tensions and increased economic opening in North Korea if the United States makes a credible commitment to nonaggression.

The overall contours of such a package are not the point of disagreement for Cha. There are still good reasons for engaging such a dangerous regime. The primary point of departure for Cha would be the withholding of such a negotiation until the North Koreans first resolve international concerns about the HEU program and restore the status quo ante at Yongbyon. To engage with Pyongyang in the face of such a blatant breakout from the Agreed Framework would be tantamount to appeasement. However, maintaining a coalition of allies to impress upon Kim Jong Il in the strongest terms the need to first come clean in order to return to a path of engagement with the outside world appears to be the most prudent course of action. From a hawk engagement perspective, such a strategy also puts the cooperation ball clearly in the North's court, and in this sense, also contributes to a coalition for isolation and containment should Kim Jong Il drop this ball.

Despite the authors' disagreements, they agree on a number of important issues. Most significantly, both authors agree on the goals of U.S. policy and the nature of the North Korean regime. Both authors wish to see a nuclear-free Korean peninsula and a North Korean regime that either modifies its behavior or disappears. Their disagreement is not over these goals but over the tactics toward that end. Both authors also agree that the North Korean regime is a brutal and reprehensible regime that has perpetrated massive crimes against its own citizens. Finally, both authors agree that one major element of a successful policy toward North Korea is a consistently engaged United States that develops a coherent strategy toward the region.

POSTSCRIPT BY DAVID C. KANG

Two years on, North Korea has tested a nuclear weapon and the UN Security Council has approved limited sanctions against the regime. However, the basic arguments of both authors have remained roughly the same, because the fundamental issues regarding North Korea have remained roughly the same. Both authors agree that the goal remains a much reformed North Korean regime, or even its eventual demise, and that a consistently attentive United States is an important element of resolving any nuclear problem on the peninsula. The overall contours of the problem also remain much the same, as well. North Korea and the United States remain in stark disagreement over how to proceed: North Korea wants security guarantees and an end to "hostile policies" by the United States before it disarms its nuclear program; the United States wants progress on North Korean nuclear and missile disarmament before it provides a basket of incentives such as normalization to the North. For example, the six countries participating in the "six-party talks" signed an agreement in principle in September of 2005. However, almost immediately, that agreement foundered due to disagreements over implementation—the United States wants the North to make tangible progress in reducing its nuclear weapons program before it proceeds with incentives, while North Korea wants the United States to provide security guarantees first, before it proceeds with denuclearization. Finally, the authors' disagreement about North Korea's interests remains the same: Does North Korea seek nuclear weapons because of a threatening United States? Or does it seek them because of internal regime dynamics?

Yet in other ways, the situation has changed: North Korea's missile test and nuclear test of 2006 have further isolated the regime. On the economic front, Pyongyang's halting economic reform efforts have continued to slowly develop. South Korea and China have been actively pursuing economic engagement in the North, and 2006 will most likely see record levels of trade between North Korea and its two main trading partners. The U.S.–ROK alliance has come under increasing strain because of differences about how to deal with North Korea, despite both countries' attempts to find areas of common agreement. Japan has moved firmly into accord with U.S. policies, being the country in the region most actively limiting North Korean trade. All these changes, although creating an altered context for the nuclear issue, have not changed the basic contours of the problem.

For those who favor engagement, the fundamental problem has remained the same: U.S. policies that consistently threaten the North Korean regime. For the author of this postscript, coercive U.S. policies have proven to be counterproductive. When the United States pursued an engagement policy under the Clinton administration, the North's nuclear program was frozen, IAEA inspectors were at the Yongbyon nuclear site in North Korea, and Pyongyang entered into a voluntary moratorium on missile testing and development. However, the switch to a more coercive strategy under the Bush administration prompted a similar response from North Korea, and six years of coercion has resulted in the ejection of international inspectors, the restarting of the nuclear program at Yongbyon, North Korean missile testing, and a nuclear test. Kim Jong-il appears to be firmly in control of the regime in Pyongyang, and the likelihood of sudden collapse appears dim.

Alternatively, others draw the opposite conclusion: that engagement has failed, and only coercion can solve the problem. For these observers, the problem is the North Korean regime itself. Pyongyang's intransigence in the face of sincere efforts by the United States and the world community to address North Korean interests is proof for them that North Korea intends to keep their nuclear weapons no matter what the United States does. This perspective also finds South Korean and Chinese engagement of the regime as working at cross-purposes with an attempt to create a unified front with which to deal with North Korea. They believe that if all countries in the region were unified in a more hard-line policy toward the North, it would have to adjust its ways.

Despite the disagreement of these two perspectives, what is clear is that relations between North Korea and the United States have grown worse over the past six years, not better. The two countries are farther away from a resolution now than at any time since the first nuclear crisis of 1993–1994. China has increased its diplomatic profile in the region by skillfully managing its relations with both the United States and North Korea, using its limited leverage to host the six-party talks and to prod both sides to continue diplomacy. Ultimately, resolution of the nuclear issue faces more obstacles now than ever before, and whether this is possible in the short or even medium term is anyone's guess.

Iran's Nuclear Program: Motivations, Options, Consequences

JIM WALSH

The issue of Iran's nuclear program[1] could hardly be more important.[2] Iranian development of a nuclear weapon would adversely affect U.S., regional, and global security, and further, would add to the risk that nations might one day use nuclear weapons.

An Iranian nuclear weapon should not be considered a foregone conclusion, however. Indeed, the Islamic Republic is not unlike many countries that have wrestled with the question of the bomb. Inside the government, some want nuclear weapons, others oppose them, and many remain undecided. Iran's

[1] The phrase *nuclear program*, like the phrase *weapons of mass destruction*, is sufficiently vague that it is often more misleading than illuminating. In principle, a nuclear program can include anything from a civilian power reactor to paper studies of weapons-relevant technologies to full weaponization and testing. It is often used to imply a full-blown weapons program when none is in fact confirmed. In this chapter, *nuclear program* is intended as a neutral term that characterizes government-directed activities involving nuclear technology that may be of a purely civilian nature as well as those that may be directed toward weapons development.

[2] Helpful introductions to Iran and to the Iranian nuclear issue include Shireen T. Hunter, *Iran and the World* (Bloomington: Indiana University Press, 1990); Dilip Hiro, *The Iranian Labyrinth: Journeys Through Theocratic Iran and Its Furies* (New York: Nation Books, 2005); Geoffrey Kemp, ed., *Iran's Bomb: American and Iranian Perspectives* (Washington DC: Nixon Center, 2004); William H. Luers, testimony before the Committee on Foreign Relations, U.S. Senate, 28 October 2003 (Washington DC: U.S. Government Printing Office, 2003), 1–11; George Perkovich, *Dealing With Iran's Nuclear Challenge* (Washington DC: Carnegie Endowment for Peace, 2003), 1–16; Sharam Chubin, *Iran's Nuclear Ambitions* (Washington DC: Carnegie Endowment for International Peace, 2006); Ray Takeyh, *Hidden Iran: Paradox and Power in the Islamic Republic* (New York: Times Books, 2006); Kenneth Pollack, *The Persian Puzzle: The Conflict Between Iran and America* (New York: Random House, 2005).

JIM WALSH is a research associate at the Massachusetts Institute of Technology's Security Studies Program. Dr. Walsh's research and writings focus on international security and, in particular, on topics involving weapons of mass destruction and terrorism. Among his current projects are two sets of dialogues, one with representatives from North Korea and one with leading figures in Iran. He has traveled to both countries and has testified before the United States Senate on Iran's nuclear program.

nuclear future will be determined by a number of factors, not least of which is internal political struggle between different domestic factions.

American policy may also influence Iranian nuclear outcomes. A smart U.S. nonproliferation strategy can help reduce the probability of Iran acquiring nuclear weapons. Perhaps more importantly, an ill-conceived or poorly executed American response may have the counterproductive effect of making an Iranian bomb even more likely.

This chapter seeks to examine each of these issues: the nature of Tehran's nuclear ambitions and nuclear decision making, U.S. policy options and their likely effects, and the consequences of an Iranian nuclear weapon. It begins with a brief overview of the current state of Iranian national politics.[3]

IRANIAN POLITICS: PLAYERS AND DYNAMICS

The Changing Political Fortunes of President Ahmadinejad

The most important development in Iranian politics in recent years was the 2005 election of President Mahmoud Ahmadinejad. In the West, he is known for his deeply troubling remarks regarding the Holocaust and for his aggressive rhetoric on the nuclear issue. Within Iran, however, his political identity is rooted primarily in domestic, not foreign, policy. His core issue during the election campaign was economic populism—redistribution of wealth, eradicating corruption, and anti-elitism. Contrary to expectations, Ahmadinejad improved his political position during his first year in office, winning points for being the first president to travel to the provinces and meet with local people. His willingness to replace elements of the bureaucracy helped consolidate his image as a politician willing to shake things up and challenge the old elite.

Ahmadinejad's post-election honeymoon with the Iranian electorate strengthened his position and may have encouraged him to expand his political reach. In particular, he devoted increasing attention to foreign policy issues, especially the nuclear issue and the Israeli–Palestinian dispute. Several

---

[3] On Iranian policy making and politics, see Bahman Baktiari, "The Governing Institutions of the Islamic Republic of Iran: The Supreme Leader, the Presidency, and the Majlis" in Jamal S. Al-Suwaidi, ed., *Iran and the Gulf: A Search for Stability* (Dubai: Emirates Center for Strategic Studies and Research, 1996), 47–69; Wilfried Buchta, *Who Rules Iran? The Structure of Power in the Islamic Republic* (Washington DC: Washington Institute for Near East Policy, 2001). On decision making in foreign and security policy in particular, see Abbas Maleki, *Decision Making in Iran's Foreign Policy: A Heuristic Approach* (Tehran: International Institute of Caspian Studies, 2002), 1–12; Jalil Roshandel, *Evolution of the Decision-Making Process in Iranian Foreign Policy (1979-1999)* in Eric Hoogland, ed., *Twenty Years of Islamic Revolution, Political and Social Transition in Iran since 1979* (Syracuse University Press, 2002), 123–142; Heidar Ali Balouji, "The Process of National Security Decision Making in Iran" in Shannon N. Kile, ed., *Europe and Iran: Perspectives on Non-proliferation*, SIPRI Research Report No. 21 (Stockholm: Oxford University Press, 2005), 72–96; Shahram Chubin, "Whither Iran Reform, Domestic Politics and National Security," Adelphi Paper 342, International Institute for Strategic Studies (London: Oxford University Press, 2002).

commentators have suggested that Ahmadinejad was appealing to the Arab (not necessarily the Persian) on the street, that is, attempting to build his status as a regional figure. If that is the case, it appears to have backfired. The results of the 2006 local and Assembly of Experts elections suggest that Ahmadinejad may have alienated some Iranian voters. The President's failure to deliver on his economic platform, middle-class concerns about increasing tensions with the West, and a re-energized electoral opposition resulted in a significant setback at the polls.

This decline in popular support may leave Ahmadinejad especially vulnerable. For while the President had enjoyed a certain mass appeal, his relations with traditional centers of power in Iran have been less successful. Take, for example, his interactions with the national legislature, or *Majlis*. Despite the election of a harder-line parliament, relations between the President and the Iranian legislature have not been strong. Early in his term, the *Majlis* took the unprecedented step of rejecting some of Ahmadinejad's ministerial appointments.

Ahmadinejad also appears to have alienated elements of the religious center of Qom. Several grand ayatollahs have expressed unhappiness with the President. The discontent stems from a variety of factors, including his lack of respect for religious protocol, an erosion of the political access that grand ayatollahs have traditionally enjoyed, and the President's unorthodox religious views regarding the 12th Imam. Of course, attitudes toward Ahmadinejad are not uniform. He has support among senior clerics (most famously, Ayatollah Mohammad Taghi Mesbah-Yazdi Yazdi), but his supporters did relatively poorly in the Assembly of Experts election. So far, Ahmadinejad's lack of support among the grand ayatollahs has not constituted a major political vulnerability, however. This is true in large measure because clerics unhappy with the President have been reluctant to voice their displeasure as long as he enjoys the support of the Supreme Leader.

Relations between President Ahmadinejad and the Supreme Leader

The most powerful policy actor in theocratic Iran is Supreme Leader Ayatollah Sayyid Ali Khamenei. It is likely, therefore, that the most important variable in Iranian politics is the relationship between the Supreme Leader and President Ahmadinejad. Theirs is a complex and evolving relationship, one in which both parties bring something to the table but in which the Supreme Leader is clearly the dominant player. It is worth remembering that President Ahmadinejad, unlike his predecessors, is not a cleric. This is noteworthy in a theocracy, where the most important political actor is a religious figure. Khamenei is more important to Ahmadinejad than Ahmadinejad is to the Leader, but that said, Ahmadinejad's lesser position has not prevented him from indirectly challenging the Leader on occasion or from seizing issues not delegated to him for his own political interests.

The Supreme Leader has tolerated and even welcomed Ahmadinejad's antics, because both have very conservative views, and because Ahmadinejad has been popular with important segments of the populace not normally associated with the revolution in recent years (for example, the poor, some elements of the youth vote). The Supreme Leader may have also concluded that Ahmadinejad's hardball tactics have produced results that his predecessors were unable to achieve.

Factors Shaping the Future of Iranian Politics

Two features of Iranian politics may influence the course of future events. The first is that the political situation is fluid and fractured. There are multiple centers of political power in Iran, including the Supreme Leader, the President, the grand ayatollahs, the Iranian Revolutionary Guard (IRG) and intelligence apparatus, the *Majlis*, Ayatollah Akbar Hashemi Rafsanjani, the bazaar, and public opinion.

Perhaps the most overlooked of these by Western analysts is public opinion. Because commentators consider Iran's government to be authoritarian and an abuser of human rights, they often fail to grasp the central importance of public opinion. Even the Supreme Leader must not stray too far from the people. What public opinion gives (for example, support for a recalcitrant nuclear policy), public opinion can take away. Given Ahmadinejad's flair for the dramatic and Tehran's tendency to overplay its hand, swift and significant shifts in public opinion and policy cannot be discounted.

In addition, the 2006 elections may have introduced a new dynamic to Iranian politics. Some observers believe that Ahmadinejad's comparatively weak showing at the polls will further consolidate the Leader's position and will reduce the extent to which the President can challenge him. Others have suggested that the real winner was Rafsanjani, a longtime rival to the Supreme Leader. Rafsanjani is now well positioned to replace Khamenei should he have to resign for health or other reasons.

The Islamic Republic's indirect electoral system and shifting alliances make it difficult to reach firm conclusions about the impact of the 2006 elections. In any case, its domestic politics are far from set. Changes in the internal political balance of power or even in the leadership itself may produce alterations in policy and opportunities for rapid progress (or deterioration) in U.S.–Iranian relations.

A second important aspect of Iranian politics is that Ahmadinejad has adopted what amounts to a short-term strategy. As a populist challenging the elites and the old guard, he begins from a tenuous position. In other countries, populists who suddenly came to power have had to find a way to co-opt at least part of the bureaucracy and traditional leadership in order to build a basis for governing. So far, Ahmadinejad has not reached out to these groups. He has more friends among the people than he does among the elite.

Another and perhaps more important challenge for Ahmadinejad can be seen in the 2006 elections. He is an economic populist who has made expensive promises, but his statist economic inclinations and provocative foreign policy will likely scare off badly needed foreign investment. In the near term, high oil prices have brought new cash to Iranian coffers, but absent investments in infrastructure and improvements in productivity, it will be very difficult for Ahmadinejad to deliver on his core issue.[4]

Still, Ahmadinejad's apparent loss does not necessarily mean that Iran will get a chastened, kinder, gentler President. While Ahmadinejad has proven himself to be more politically adept than his critics expected, he also appears to be a person who has deep ideological convictions, and he may pursue those convictions regardless of his political standing.[5] One possibility is that Ahmadinejad's popularity will continue to decline, and that he will leave the scene as a one-term wonder. Another is that in the absence of being able to deliver on his economic promises, Ahmadinejad will seek to provoke a crisis with the United States. Indeed, some have suggested that an American air strike against Iranian nuclear facilities is precisely the sort of event that Ahmadinejad would welcome, as it would help him stay in office and perhaps even reshape Iranian domestic politics.

IRAN'S NUCLEAR AMBITIONS: WHO WANTS WHAT

Like other countries in the nuclear age, Iran's domestic constituency for nuclear technology consists of multiple players with varying ambitions. Some actors want a complete fuel cycle for purely civilian use; others want a complete fuel cycle as a hedge, that is, for the development of nuclear weapons somewhere down the road if events warrant. A third group simply wants nuclear weapons.

Westerners have had few opportunities to study Iran's nuclear decision-making process in situ, and as a consequence, analysts can offer very few high-confidence findings about Iranian nuclear decision making. Much of what is known about the program comes from International Atomic Energy Agency (IAEA) reports on safeguards compliance,[6] but that information is more about dates and outcomes than players and motivations. Still a brief, if conjectural, survey is possible.[7]

---

[4] Roger Stern, "The Iranian Petroleum Crisis and United States National Security," *Proceedings of the National Academy of Sciences of the United States of America* 104 (January 2007): 377–382.

[5] This conclusion is based on a single, two-hour meeting in September of 2006 with President Ahamadinejad and his response to a question on the importance of values versus interests in the conduct of Iranian foreign policy.

[6] "Implementation of the NPT Safeguards Agreement in the Islamic Republic of Iran," (report by the Director General, GOV/2003/40, 6 June 2003, Vienna: International Atomic Energy Agency, 2003). Numerous reports in this series have been published and continue to be issued periodically.

[7] On Iranian nuclear decision making and politics, see Fatemeh Haghighatjoo, "Factional Positions on the Nuclear Issue in the Context of Iranian Domestic Politics," *Iran Analysis Quarterly* 3 (January–March 2006): 1–10; Jalil Roshendel, "The Nuclear Controversy in the Context of Iran's Evolving Defense Strategy" in Shannon N. Kile, ed., *Europe and Iran*: 47–71; Chen Kane, "Nuclear Decision-Making in Iran: A Rare Glimpse," *Middle East Brief* 5 (May 2006): 1–8; Parisa Zangeneh, "Nuclear Politics, Mahmoud Ahmadinejad, and the Iranian People," *Iran Analysis Quarterly* 3 (January–March 2006): 11–26.

As noted above, the Supreme Leader is far and away the most important policy actor in Iran. Khamenei is said to have a genuine interest in nuclear energy and may harbor views not unlike those heard during the heady days of the 1970s, for example, that nuclear energy is the key to economic progress, and that nuclear energy is tantamount to technological development and independence. These views are not simply the Supreme Leader's but appear to be widespread and are reflected in media coverage and elite (but not expert) circles. This unadulterated view of the benefits of nuclear technology may be reinforced by a suspicion of U.S. motives, that is, the U.S. government supported nuclear development under the Shah (including enrichment), but now opposes it, ergo nuclear technology must be worth having.[8]

The Supreme Leader's views concerning nuclear technology probably represent a mix of ideas. On the one hand, there is evidence that suggests an opposition to nuclear weapons. It is said, for example, that the Supreme Leader issued a secret fatwa some years ago in response to a military inquiry regarding nuclear weapons.[9] The fatwa has not been published, but Khamenei and other clerics and officials repeatedly make reference to it in public speeches.[10] The fatwa is said to be a religious fatwa, not a political fatwa, and it allegedly cites Koranic principles that constrain the potential use and possibly the development of nuclear weapons.[11] Such a fatwa would be consistent with previous Iranian fatwas on weapons of mass destruction and would reflect a fairly strong set of Islamic principles that appear to rule out the use of nuclear weapons in all but the most extreme situations.[12] On the other hand, the fatwa

---

[8] On U.S. support of the Shah's nuclear program, see Mustafa Kibaroglu, "Good for the Shah, Banned for the Mullahs: The West and Iran's Quest for Nuclear Power," *The Middle East Journal* 60 (Spring 2006): 207–232; Dafna Linzer, "Past Arguments Don't Square With Current Iran Policy," *The Washington Post*, 27 March 2005, 15.

[9] Interview with former Iranian official "A."

[10] "Iran Warns Over Nuclear Impasse," CNN, 11 August 2005, accessed on the website of *CNN. com* at http://www.cnn.com/2005/WORLD/europe/08/10/iran.iaea/index.html, 8 January 2007. See also Eric Arnett, "Iran Is Not Iraq," *Bulletin of Atomic Scientists* 54 (January/February 1998): 12–14; Karl Vick, "In Iran, Gray Area on Nuclear Weapons: Religious View Is Not Absolute," *The Washington Post*, 21 June 2006, A15. During the Iran–Iraq War, Iranian religious officials were reported to have resisted the development of chemical weapons on religious grounds, despite their use by Iraq. See, for example, Javed Ali, "Chemical Weapons and the Iran-Iraq War: A Case Study in Noncompliance," *Nonproliferation Review* 8 (Spring 2001): 43–58; Gregory F. Giles, "Iranian Approaches to Chemical Warfare" (paper prepared for the U.S. Naval Postgraduate School Conference "WMD Employment Concepts and Command and Control," Monterey, CA, 6–8 August 1997); Joost R. Hiltermann, "Outsiders as Enablers: Consequences and Lessons from International Silence on Iraq's Use of Chemical Weapons during the Iran-Iraq War" in Lawrence G. Potter and Gary Sick, eds., *Iran, Iraq, and the Legacies of War* (New York: Palgrave Macmillan, 2004), 151–166.

[11] Interview with former Iranian official "A."

[12] A scholarly treatment of these ideas can be found in Sohail H. Hashmi, "Islamic Ethics and Weapons of Mass Destruction: An Argument for Nonproliferation" in Sohail H. Hashmi and Steven P. Lee, eds., *Ethics and Weapons of Mass Destruction: Religious and Secular Perspectives*

itself has been described as sufficiently vague that the restraint may not prove very onerous.[13]

Many analysts cite security concerns as a chief cause of Iran's interest in nuclear technology.[14] It is likely that pro–nuclear weapons advocates invoke security threats when making their case, but the empirical record does not show an especially strong correlation between a presence of or increase in security threats and a corresponding increase in pro-nuclear decisions or outcomes.[15] If anything, given its threat environment, the puzzle may be that Iran has not done more work in the nuclear area. Put another way, security threats are not unrelated to Iran's nuclear ambitions, but this program has more in common with the nuclear programs in France, India, and Latin America (programs driven by pride and bureaucratic politics) than those of China or North Korea (programs driven by security and other interests).[16]

President Ahmadinejad's private views regarding nuclear weapons are not known. In public, Ahmadinejad has been unequivocal in his opposition

---

(Cambridge, UK: Cambridge University Press, 2006), 321–352; and John Kelsay, "'Do Not Violate the Limit': Three Issues in Islamic Thinking on WMD" in Hashmi and Lee, eds., *Ethics and Weapons of Mass Destruction*, 353–363. See also a recent joint statement by Muslim and Christian clerics and religious scholars on the moral status of nuclear weapons, Muslim-Christian Initiative on the Nuclear Weapons Danger, "Statement of the Initiative," 2005, accessed on the website of the Muslim-Christian Initiative on the Nuclear Weapons Danger at http://www.mci-nwd.org/statement.asp, 8 January 2007.

[13] Interview with former Iranian official "B."

[14] Ali Larijani is said to be particularly interested in obtaining a security assurance from the United States as part of a negotiated settlement to the nuclear dispute.

[15] Jim Walsh, "Testing Theories of Proliferation: The Case of Iran" (talk given before the International Security Program, Harvard University, 30 September 2004). This conclusion is based on a comparison of the effort devoted to and progress in the nuclear program with nuclear-relevant threats faced by the regime over five decades. A copy of the presentation can be obtained from the author.

[16] For a concise statement on the importance of pride, history, and the psychological dimensions to the Iranian policy, see Abbas Amanat, "The Persian Complex," *The New York Times*, 25 May 2006. On Brazil, Argentina, and the desire for technological achievement and autonomy, see Michael Barletta, "Ambiguity, Autonomy, and the Atom: Emergence of the Argentine-Brazilian Nuclear Regime," (PhD diss., University of Wisconsin, 2000). On France, see Philip H. Gordon, "Charles de Gaulle and the Nuclear Revolution" in John Lewis Gaddis et al., eds., *Cold War Statesmen Confront the Bomb* (Oxford, UK: Oxford University Press, 1999), 216–235. On India, see George Perkovich, *India's Nuclear Bomb* (Berkeley: University of California Press, 1999). On China, see John W. Lewis and Xue Litai, *China Builds the Bomb* (Stanford, CA: Stanford University Press, 1988). On North Korea, see Leon V. Sigal, *Disarming Strangers: Nuclear Diplomacy with North Korea* (Princeton, NJ: Princeton University Press, 1998); Leon V. Sigal, "The Lessons of North Korea's Test," *Current History* 105 (November 2006): 363–364; Don Oberdorfer, *The Two Koreas* (New York: Basic Books, 2001); Victor D. Cha and David C. Kang, *Nuclear North Korea: A Debate on Engagement Strategies* (New York: Columbia University Press, 2003); James Clay Moltz and Alexandre Y. Mansourov, eds., *The North Korean Nuclear Program: Security, Strategy, and New Perspectives from Russia* (New York: Routledge, 2000); Joel S. Wit, Daniel B. Poneman, and Robert L. Gallucci, *Going Critical: The First North Korean Nuclear Crisis* (Washington DC: Brookings Institution Press, 2004).

to nuclear weapons.[17] It is also clear that Ahmadinejad has seen value in the nuclear issue as a card he can play with the public. In this context, nuclear development is meant to encourage or tap into a sense of nationalism and a feeling of injustice, for example, U.S. double standards (nuclear technology for Israel and India but not for Iran), the West versus the technological have-nots.

Ahmadinejad has close ties to the IRG and the intelligence services, both of which are generally viewed in the West as supporting the acquisition of nuclear weapons. Paradoxically, of all the elements in Iranian society, the IRG is the one group that is said to be the most loyal to the Supreme Leader. Thus, it is possible that a genuine fatwa from a Supreme Leader might actually prove to be a very important obstacle to nuclear weapons development.

Within the nuclear bureaucracy, most notably in the Atomic Energy Organization of Iran (AEOI), there are vocal advocates for a complete fuel cycle, but it is unclear how widely those views are held. Historically, the role of nuclear bureaucracies in nuclear decision making has been important, either in contributing to or in restraining nuclear weapons development.[18] Nuclear bureaucracies enjoy a monopoly of information, particularly in developing countries where the pool of nuclear and nonproliferation expertise is extremely limited. Nuclear bureaucracies also have their own self-interests. If the nuclear bureaucracy or key leaders in the bureaucracy view a nuclear weapons project as a boon to their budget or other core interests, it can be a powerful partner with other pro-weapons constituencies. Some analysts have suggested that bureaucratic politics may be playing a role in Iran's nuclear ambitions, but information is sparse.

Finally, there are the Iranian people.[19] The public has mixed and fluid views that essentially—and perhaps temporarily—assert that they want civilian nu-

---

[17] When I asked President Ahmadinejad whether there was any wiggle room in the fatwa that might permit a justifiable nuclear weapons program, he responded that "religiously speaking," the production, stockpiling, or usage of nuclear weapons was forbidden. He went on to say that as a matter of policy, Iran did not need a nuclear weapon, that in the Iran–Iraq War, Iraq used chemical weapons and was supported by the nuclear powers, and that this experience taught them they did not need nuclear weapons to defend themselves. Iranian defense, he maintained, is based on their people and their culture. Personal communication, September 2006.

[18] Studies examining bureaucratic politics and proliferation decision making include Lawrence Scheinman, *Atomic Energy Policy in France Under the Fourth Republic* (Princeton, NJ: Princeton University Press, 1965); Scott Sagan, "Why Do States Build Nuclear Weapons? Three Models in Search of a Bomb," *International Security* 21 (Winter 1996–1997): 54–86. The historical sociology of technology offers a similar perspective, often blending organizational and constructivist elements. On the historical sociology of technology and nuclear decision making, see Steven Flank, "Exploding the Black Box: The Historical Sociology of Nuclear Proliferation," *Security Studies* 3 (Winter 1993/94): 259–294; and Tanya Ogilvie-White, "Is There A Theory of Nuclear Proliferation? An Analysis of the Contemporary Debate," *The Nonproliferation Review* 4 (Fall 1996): 43–60.

[19] Some scholars have considered the domestic politics variable in nuclear decision making. They point to the influence of competition for electoral advantage, what Solingen calls "coalition politics" and what Reiss refers to as "domestic pressures." See Mitchell Reiss, *Without the Bomb: The Politics*

clear technology but are tentative about nuclear weapons, especially if the price of acquisition is high. Five years ago, the Iranian public had no views concerning nuclear technology. Once the nuclear program became public and the international dispute intensified, however, what was once a vaguely anti-nuclear mood has been transformed into salient opinion favoring civilian nuclear development. Indeed, until recently, the government's nuclear policy has been the one issue on which there seems to have been broad agreement and support in an otherwise highly fractured polity.

Still, Iranians are not prepared to defend their newly discovered "right to nuclear technology" to the death. They are concerned about sanctions and economic isolation, and they fear a U.S. military strike, both of which reduce the attractiveness of the nuclear program. Perhaps the most important characteristic of the Iranian public's view of nuclear technology is that they have been unable to grasp the link between enrichment (qua civilian nuclear technology) and nuclear weapons. They do not understand and, therefore, discount the West's proliferation concerns.

One segment of the Iranian population does support the overt development of nuclear weapons. This group tends to be younger, rather than older, and somewhat less well off economically. This pro–nuclear weapons constituency may be getting larger as the political conflict escalates. Indeed, a recent Zogby poll of Iranian public opinion appears to show higher-than-expected support for an Iranian bomb.[20]

For Iranian policymakers and the public alike, the one policy that wins the greatest support across the spectrum of actors and ideology, irrespective of support for or opposition to nuclear weapons, is the acquisition of a complete fuel cycle, including a functioning enrichment capacity. A complete fuel cycle is consistent with the agendas of both the bomb advocates and those who seek a purely civilian program.

Nuclear technology is now viewed as a priority in Iran, but it is not the most important priority, and is not important enough that it would be allowed to jeopardize other economic and security goals. What Iranians seek most is recognition and economic development. As it stands, nuclear technology is seen as a way to achieve those goals. Any attempt to steer Iran away from this course will have to redefine nuclear technology as well as provide an alternative that will allow Iranians to achieve the status and development they feel they deserve as a regional power and as the proud stewards of a great and ancient civilization.

---

of Nuclear Nonproliferation (New York: Columbia University Press, 1988), 117–119, 249–251; Sagan, "Why Do States Build Nuclear Weapons?" 63–73; and Etel Solingen, "The Domestic Sources of Regional Regimes: The Evolution of Nuclear Ambiguity in the Middle East," *International Studies Quarterly* 38 (June 1994): 305–337.

[20] See Zogby poll of Iranians conducted May–June 2006 for *Reader's Digest*, accessed on the website of *RD.com* at http://www.rd.com/images/content/071306/iranpollresults.pdf, 8 January 2007.

THE IRANIAN NUCLEAR DECISION-MAKING PROCESS

Nuclear decision making in Iran revolves around three central actors. The first is Supreme Leader Khamenei. There is a consensus among analysts that the Supreme Leader is the ultimate and most important decision maker on nuclear policy. In terms of day-to-day work, however, the principal policy actor is Ali Larijani and the Supreme National Security Council (SNSC). This former presidential candidate and current chair of the SNSC is said to enjoy the confidence of the Supreme Leader and has been characterized as conservative but pragmatic. Finally, President Ahmadinejad has, by his self-initiative, created a role for himself and may even have successfully appropriated the issue as his own—at least publicly. He frequently comments on the issue, but so far, his role appears to be more as spokesperson than policy decider.

Beyond these key players, there are many questions. What is the role or influence of Rafsanjani—former Iranian president, defeated 2005 presidential candidate, top vote getter in the 2006 Assembly of Expert elections, and reputedly the wealthiest person in Iran, with a vast network of social connections? Rafsanjani was said to be the key actor on nuclear policy in previous years, and is considered a conservative pragmatist.

And there are other question marks as well. Are there differing opinions or even divisions within the AEOI? Is there an Iranian equivalent of Pakistan's A. Q. Khan or India's Hommi Bhabha, that is, a nuclear advocate and bureaucratic champion extraordinaire?[21]

What about the financial ministries and the bazaar? Do they have a voice? Do they raise objections about the cost of the nuclear program or the possible economic consequences of a "go it alone" policy? Does the foreign minister have a say? In developing countries, foreign ministries typically represent or implement policy, not decide it, but the Iranian foreign minister's counsel may carry some weight with the President and the Supreme Leader. Finally, what is the position of the regular military versus the IRG when it comes to the issue of nuclear weapons?[22] Historically, interservice politics and rivalries have had significant impact on nuclear policy outcomes.[23] In sum, although there is a general sense about the position and influence of the major players, there may be key secondary actors about whom little is known.

---

[21] On the role of nuclear advocates like Bhabha, see Peter Lavoy, "Nuclear Myths and the Causes of Nuclear Proliferation" in Zachary S. Davis and Benjamin Frankel, eds., *The Proliferation Puzzle: Why Nuclear Weapons Spread (and What Results)* (London: Frank Cass, 1993), 193–199.

[22] On the Iranian military, see Sepehr Zabih, *The Iranian Military in Revolution and War* (New York: Routledge, 1988).

[23] See, for example, "Surprise Down Under: The Secret History of Australia's Nuclear Ambitions," *Nonproliferation Review* 5 (Fall 1997): 1–20.

U.S. POLICY OPTIONS AND ALTERNATIVES

A number of countries have become directly involved in the Iranian nuclear controversy, including France, Britain, Germany, and Russia, but the United States continues to be the dominant outside player in this dispute. The administration of George W. Bush has focused most of its energy on pushing for UN Security Council (UNSC) review of the Iranian portfolio and for the subsequent imposition of international sanctions. In addition, the American military has engaged in robust planning for a range of potential military strikes against Iran.

While Washington has been successful in getting both UNSC review and a sanctions resolution out of the UN, to date there is little to show for its policy. Iran continues its enrichment and related nuclear programs, and there is little prospect in the short term that this will change without a revision of the U.S. and Iranian positions. American diplomats did succeed in getting the sanctions resolution, but its immediate effect will be modest at best, and in the absence of a major provocation from Tehran (always a possibility), it will be difficult for U.S. officials to persuade Russia and China to approve a more muscular response to the Iranian program.

Given the current stalemate, what are Washington's options? The standard policy menu is well known and includes the following:

- Negotiate;
- Coerce: threats and pressure;
- Isolate and contain;
- Promote regime change;
- Use military force.

Many of these tactics are not mutually exclusive and thus could be combined. As a matter of practice, however, it is difficult to combine the more punitive options with negotiation, given the importance of national pride in Iranian behavior.

Negotiation

The near-term prospects for a negotiated settlement to the Iranian nuclear controversy appear to be poor. In principle, one can imagine a number of potentially successful agreements, but the track record of the EU3 (France, Britain, Germany) negotiations is not encouraging. According to Iranian sources, the fall 2006 round of Iranian–EU talks between Javier Solana and Ali Larijani produced a draft eleven-point agreement,[24] but both negotiators had difficulty

---

[24] "Iran Warns to Limit UN Nuke Inspection If Sanctioned," *Xinhua News Service*, 15 October 2006, accessed on the website of *Chinaview.cn* at http://news.xinhuanet.com/english/2006-10/15/content_5206282.htm, 8 January 2007.

selling the proposal to the relevant decision makers. Washington allegedly rejected the plan outright, and President Ahmadinejad is said to have criticized the Solana–Larijani draft, although it is unclear whether Ahmadinejad's opposition would have been determinative had the United States not rejected the deal.

The White House's lack of enthusiasm for the diplomatic track may have been signaled by President Bush's reaction to the Iraq Study Group. The Group's report recommended that the United States initiate direct talks with Iran, a recommendation that was quickly and publicly rejected by the White House.[25] Had Washington been looking for political cover to upgrade its diplomatic efforts, the Iraq Study Group report, whose recommendations enjoyed broad public support, would surely have provided the opportunity to do so.[26]

For its part, Iran continues what is at best an ambivalent posture toward the negotiating process. Lack of progress in the EU3 process has reflected Iranian skepticism that benefits can be guaranteed in the absence of a direct U.S. commitment. Tehran also feels that it has been taken advantage of in past negotiations. Moreover, many Iranians feel that the nuclear issue is just window dressing for what is really an anti-regime policy, and that even if the nuclear issue were resolved, the Americans and Europeans would find another issue to use against the Islamic Republic.

One irony in this position is that while Iran's leaders doubt the results of any process that does not involve the United States, neither are they sure they want to engage directly with the United States. During President Mohammad Khatami's term, both the President and the main nuclear negotiator, Hassan Rowhani, favored direct engagement with the United States. The Supreme Leader was highly skeptical and blocked most moves in this direction. Today, the Supreme Leader continues to be suspicious of U.S. motives but is more open to direct talks with the United States. This stems in part from a greater confidence in the negotiating team and a feeling that Iran is in a stronger position from which to negotiate. Still, suspicions persist.

As noted earlier, Iran's ideal outcome would be a complete fuel cycle, an end to its international isolation, recognition of its status as a regional and cultural power, and economic development by way of improved access to foreign investment. Tehran also recognizes that it cannot have it all and that a provocative nuclear program reduces its ability to meet its economic objectives.

Some Iranians, driven by a nationalist fever and a deep sense of victimization, are prepared to pay a high cost for their nuclear program. Simply put, some things are more important than money. It is a view that is reinforced by the

---

[25] The Iraq Study Group, James A. Baker III and Lee H. Hamilton, chairs, *The Iraq Study Group Report: The Way Forward—A New Approach* (New York: Vintage, 2006).

[26] Peter Baker, "Americans Say U.S. Is Losing War; Public, Politicians Split on Iraq Panel's Ideas," *The Washington Post*, 13 December 2006, A1.

conviction that no matter what Iran does, the United States will try to squeeze it anyway. Others are less sure.

The current Iranian policy consensus is probably something like the following: Iran cannot give up its existing centrifuge cascade, but some deal beyond that is possible, including some form of interim suspension of the enrichment program. It is likely that the Supreme Leader continues to be suspicious of talks with the United States but may allow Larijani to take it as far as he can.

The Iranians are shrewd and tactically proficient negotiators, but they are also prone to overplaying their hand, for example, by being too provocative and too intransigent and having a tendency to alienate sympathetic negotiating partners. The same might be said of the United States. Washington also has the additional constraints that result from problems in Iraq and Afghanistan. More often than not, Iranian missteps have bailed out a weak U.S. bargaining position, and this dynamic may very well repeat itself in the future.

In sum, there are a variety of obstacles to progress on the diplomatic front. Given the current positions of the United States and Iran and the profound and often justified suspicion each has of the other, little can be expected in the short term. A change in leadership following the 2008 U.S. elections, combined with the continuing evolution of the Iranian leadership situation and deterioration of the Iranian economy, could produce the conditions for progress at a later point, however.

Coercion, Containment, and "Soft" Regime Change

Coercion (for example, political and economic sanctions) has been the primary instrument of American policy vis-a-vis Iran since 1979.[27] Bill Clinton adopted a policy of "dual containment" against Iran and Iraq, interspersed with occasional attempts to engage Tehran.[28] Under President Bush, American policy has included a mix of increased coercion, isolation, and "soft" or indirect regime change (for example, support for exiled Iranian opposition groups and anti-regime radio stations).[29]

---

[27] For a summary of U.S. sanctions, see "Washington Tightens the Screws: An Overview of Nonproliferation Statutes and Executive Orders Related to Iran," *Iran Watch Bulletin* 2 (November 2006), accessed at the website of *IranWatch.org* at www.iranwatch.org/ourpubs/bulletin/2-2-washingtontightensscrews.htm, 8 January 2007.

[28] On dual containment, see Anthony Lake, "Confronting the Backlash States," *Foreign Affairs* 73 (March–April 1994): 45–55. On Clinton's policy, see also Hooshang Amirahmadi, ed., *US-Iran Relations in Clinton's Second Term: International Perspectives*, Proceedings of the Fourth Conference on US-Iran Relations, 25 April 1997 (Princeton, NJ: American-Iranian Council, 1998).

[29] On the Bush Iran policy, see Farah Stockman, "US Unit Works Quietly to Counter Iran's Sway, Backs Dissidents, Nearby Nations," *Boston Globe*, 2 January 2007, A1. For examples of the "soft regime change" perspective, see Ilan Berman, testimony before the Subcommittee on Federal

American attempts to punish and isolate Iran have had modest to negligible effects on Iran's nuclear program.[30] If anything, the nuclear program may enjoy more political support today than it did six years ago. (Indeed, had Ahmadinejad delivered on his economic promises, he might well have earned enough political capital to have taken an even more provocative posture on the nuclear issue.) Moreover, it is unlikely that small changes on the margin of American policy will result in near-term policy success. Many Iranians are prepared to bear costs in defense of what they perceive is an unfair attack on their dignity. They would prefer to avoid paying such costs, but if that is the only option, many Iranians will support the government's nuclear policy.

Efforts to contain Iran have also proven difficult, and success in this area has more often than not been a result of Iranian missteps and ill-advised provocations. Containment is difficult, given Iran's central position in the Middle East and Central Asia; ongoing problems in Iraq, Afghanistan, and Lebanon; and the declining but nevertheless important role of Iran's oil industry. On any number of issues, it is nearly impossible to craft a solution that is sustainable without Iranian support and participation.[31]

This is not to suggest that coercion and/or containment are instruments without any potential effect. Comprehensive sanctions by the EU3 would have a significant impact on the Iranian economy, and as Iran's oil infrastructure continues to degrade, the sanctions' "bite" increases. Indeed, coercion against a regional power such as Iran is typically a long-term process. So too, containment is a policy that requires a time horizon of decades, not months. Unfortunately for Washington, the issue of an Iranian nuclear capability does not afford the luxury of a strategy that takes decades to reach fruition. Moreover, the use of coercion and isolation can make the nuclear option even more attractive in the short term.[32]

Financial Management, Government Information and International Security, U.S. Senate Homeland Security and Governmental Affairs Committee, 109th Cong., 1st sess., 20 July 2006 (Washington DC: U.S. Government Printing Office, 2006); Michael A. Ledeen, testimony before the Subcommittee on Federal Financial Management, Government Information and International Security, U.S. Senate Homeland Security and Governmental Affairs Committee, 109th Cong., 1st sess., 20 July 2006 (Washington DC: U.S. Government Printing Office, 2006).

[30] On the utility of sanctions against Iran, more generally, see Hossein G. Askari, John Forrer, Hildy Teegen, and Jiawen Yang, *Case Studies of US Economic Sanctions: The Chinese, Cuban, and Iranian Experience* (Westport, CT: Praeger, 2003), 171–220; Anthony H. Cordesman and Khalid R. Al-Rodhan, "Iranian Nuclear Weapons? Options for Sanctions and Military Strikes," working draft, revised 30 August 2006 (Washington DC: Center for Strategic and International Studies, 2006).

[31] On the central position of Iran and thus the need for direct engagement, see Report of the Independent Task Force, Zbignew Brzezinski and Robert Gates, Co-chairs, *Iran: Time for a New Approach* (New York: Council on Foreign Relations, 2004), as well as the report of the Iraq Study Group.

[32] On isolation as a contributing cause of proliferation, see Richard Betts, "Paranoids, Pygmies, Pariahs and Nonproliferation Revisited" in Davis and Frankel, *The Proliferation Puzzle*, 100–124; Pierre Lellouche, "The Garrison States" in William Kincade and Christopher Bertram, eds.,

Much the same can be said about a policy of "soft" regime change. Despite the penchant for wishful thinking, it is highly unlikely that the Iranian regime will simply collapse anytime soon. Social scientists have a poor record at predicting regime collapse, but there is nothing obvious that would lead one to believe that domestic implosion is likely—regardless of the number of exiles funded or satellite television programs supported. More importantly, soft regime change is a long-term strategy for what is a near-term problem, that is, the nuclear issue. In short, radio broadcasts are not a substitute for a nonproliferation policy.

Internal change will be a longer-term, indigenously driven process, and ham-handed efforts by the United States to support domestic opponents only serve to discredit the reformers and give the intelligence apparatus greater leeway to crack down on dissent. As noted before, a soft regime policy only serves to undermine Iranians' interest in a diplomatic solution, since any attempt at engagement is seen as deception intended to mask the "real" aim of regime change.

Use of Military Force

The use of force against Iranian nuclear and/or strategic targets has become a subject of serious discussion in the last couple of years.[33] Given the 2006 U.S. midterm election results, the continuing deterioration in Iraq, and the complete absence of any support from American allies, military strikes do not seem probable. Still, U.S. military planners continue to "work the problem," and as the President likes to say, "all options are on the table." As such, it is worth considering the possible costs and benefits of a military strike against Iran. We begin with the costs.

The use of military force against Iran entails substantial risks. Chief among these is the likelihood that military action against Iran will require that more American troops be deployed to Iraq and that deployment times for American troops would be lengthened. This would be necessary, if only as a precautionary step, insofar as there would be a possibility of retaliation by Iran in Iraq. Indeed, military action against Iran would substantially increase the probability of failure in Iraq. As it is, the project is difficult, but given a hostile Iran on the border, success could very well be impossible.

There are other dangers as well. An attack would inflame the Muslim world and could help terrorist organizations meet or exceed their recruit-

---

Nuclear Proliferation in the 1980s: Perspectives and Proposals (New York: St. Martin's Press, 1982), 63–111.

[33] On the use of force against Iran's nuclear facilities, see Whitney Raas and Austin Long, "Osirak Redux? Assessing Israeli Capabilities to Destroy Iranian Nuclear Facilities," SSP working paper (Cambridge, MA: MIT Security Studies Program, 2006); Michael Duffy, "What Would War Look Like?" *Time*, 25 September 2006; Henry Sokolski and Patrick Clawson, eds, *Getting Ready for a Nuclear-Ready Iran* (Washington DC: Nonproliferation Policy Education Center, 2005); Cordesman and Al-Rodhan, "Iranian Nuclear Weapons?

ment goals. Iran could retaliate and attempt to cause trouble in Afghanistan, Lebanon, the Gulf States, or the oil markets. Military action would likely cause a "rally around the flag" effect within Iran that would benefit the regime's hard-liners. In addition, sustained military, peacekeeping, or nation-building operations could prove very expensive, even more expensive than the very costly war in Iraq.

Perhaps the most important consequence of a military attack against Iran is that it would increase the probability of Iran acquiring nuclear weapons—regardless of the person or type of regime in power. An attack would further stoke feelings of nationalism and victimization and would galvanize Iranians across the ideological spectrum in favor of nuclear weapons development. Under this scenario, the chances that Iran might abandon its nuclear program in the future become exceedingly small.

There are also potential benefits to the use of force. The two most frequently cited are that the use of force would delay Iran's development of a nuclear weapon, and that it might catalyze a democratic change and governmental transition. Use of force would almost certainly delay Iran's progress, but for reasons discussed above, it might have the counterproductive effect of guaranteeing that Iran becomes a nuclear weapons state in the long term. While it is possible that military force could trigger regime change, it seems just as likely or even more likely that it could also play into the hands of hard-liners and push Iran in an even more extreme direction.

Given these very different but plausible scenarios, on what basis should policymakers evaluate the military option? Three points are particularly relevant.

First, the stakes are high. Mistakes regarding the use of military force would likely have a profound impact on the future standing of the United States, on the future of the American military, and on Iran's nuclear program. Second, judgments about Iran's motivations, capabilities, and responses are based on limited data, and thus any premises or assumptions necessarily suffer low confidence levels. American intelligence on Iran is poor, the situation in Iran is complex and fluid, Washington's assumptions about the region have often proven wrong, and reform of the interagency and strategic assessment processes that have led to errors in Iraq is still a work in progress. Third, the Iranian nuclear issue, while important, is not characterized by a high degree of urgency; in other words, so-called last resorts are not called for in the near term. It will be some years before Iran can cross the nuclear weapons threshold.

Taken together, the high stakes, low confidence, and extended time line of the Iranian nuclear issue argue for caution on the part of policymakers. Now is not the time for winner-take-all or -lose-all gambles. American national interests would be best served by a flexible, opportunistic policy that keeps options open rather than narrowing them. Under these circumstances, the use of force would be a high-risk choice with very uncertain prospects for success and the potential for catastrophic failure.

POLICY CONUNDRUMS AND PARADOXES

The familiar reality facing policymakers grappling with Iran is that there is no quick fix and that all options carry risks and drawbacks. In addition, policy aimed at Iran's nuclear program produces its own particular set of policy conundrums and paradoxes.

The first paradox is that the Islamic Republic appears most forthcoming in the face of pressure but that pressure tends to politically strengthen hard-liners and pronuclear sentiment. In the absence of the threat of sanctions or military strikes, it is unclear whether Iran would have been as forthcoming about its concealed nuclear activities, and yet pressure has contributed to a situation in which the nuclear issue has become one of the few issues that unites Iranians.

Another paradox is that a successful negotiation requires a face-saving solution, so that both parties can claim victory to their domestic audiences. Doing so, however, helps the hard-liners claim that they got results when the reformers were unable to deliver. On the other hand, a confrontational crisis would also help the hard-liners. On balance, the advantage of being able to claim results may be limited as Iranians turn away from the nuclear issue and begin to focus on problems at home, so it is probably worth embracing the first scenario to avoid the second.

A third paradox or conundrum is that U.S. policy intended to isolate and weaken Iran (for example, sanctions) can actually discourage Tehran from entering negotiations. Iran does not want to negotiate from a position of weakness and has sought to avoid direct talks in the past when it perceived itself as weak.

Finally, most forms of pressure are likely to impose long-term costs but short-term benefits. Iranian businesspeople are already sensitive to the fact that political uncertainty regarding Iran's nuclear program and the international response have resulted in a freeze or, in some cases, a reduction in foreign investment. These developments are significant, but the pocketbook consequences for most Iranians will not be felt for years. In the near term, a full-blown crisis would likely drive up the price of oil, fill Iran's hard currency reserves, and enable the President to spend the "new money" on redistributive projects. The result would likely be inflation, as the supply of money increased with no corresponding increase in productivity, but again, these effects will hit home in the medium term, not the short term that typically defines a political actor's time horizon.

ALTERNATIVE POLICY APPROACHES

As with any policy issue confronting governments, there are no simple, high-certainty, low-cost options for dealing with the prospect of an Iranian bomb. Still, it is possible to identify some areas in which alternatives might be considered.

Addressing National Pride

If national pride is one of the main factors contributing to Iran's nuclear ambitions, then it must be part of the policy mix. Carrots and sticks will not be enough. To its credit, some policy pronouncements by the U.S. government appear to recognize this point. The change in tone and content in the comments of some (but not all) American officials improves the likelihood that Iran can respond positively to American initiatives.

The United States has traditionally done a poor job of recognizing and responding to the sometimes powerful influence of psychological factors such as pride, humiliation, and resentment. When tackling the challenge of unfriendly states, American conservatives tend to emphasize threats and American liberals tend to emphasize incentives, but neither is very good at addressing either the internal politics or the psychological factors that feed nuclear programs. If the Iranian program is at least partially driven by pride (and thus some are willing to pay material costs or forgo benefits, even if that is "irrational"), then American policy instruments must be fashioned to address that cause. Ignoring this dimension makes failure more likely.

Being Smart about the Internal Politics

Second, American policy vis-a-vis Iran needs a clearer strategy regarding the internal constituencies and power centers associated with the nuclear program. Proposals need to be crafted in ways that give key players, such as the nuclear bureaucracy or the regular military, more reason to support a negotiated settlement than a hedging strategy or an outright bomb program. This logic would also apply to lesser players like the economic ministries or the bazaar.

Though nuclear policy is almost always made in secret, a potentially important element is public opinion. American policy has completely failed, to the extent it has even tried, to frame the nuclear issue in a way that could be attractive to the Iranian public. This is a difficult task, given the low level of the public's (including the elite's) understanding of nuclear issues. Still, the United States would benefit as much from supporting an honest public discussion of the costs and benefits of nuclear technology (civilian and military alike) as it would from trying to promote regime opponents.

Direct Talks and the Possibility of Normalized Relations

Third, as many have suggested, the President should consider direct talks with Iran (in addition to and not as a substitute for the P5+1 process). Moreover, the possibility of normalized relations should be on the table. Direct talks and the possibility of normalized relations speak to both Iranian interests and to the often-ignored psychological dimension. Of course, direct talks are not a cure-all. They carry risks and do not guarantee results. They are a necessary but not sufficient step toward a resolution of the nuclear and other disputes in the U.S.–Iranian relationship.

Administration officials are often quoted as saying that the President intends to keep all options on the table, including military action. Curiously, "all options" does not include direct talks and normalization. It is time for "all options" to mean all options.

A Comprehensive versus "One-issue-at-a-time" Strategy

Finally, the United States should consider pursuit of its objectives within a broader strategic context. The U.S.–Iranian relationship is highly complex, plagued by domestic politics on both sides, and grounded in a history that gives each country good reason to suspect the intentions of the other. Under these conditions, pursuit of a "comprehensive strategy" may seem impossibly difficult. One does not have to revisit the age-old debate on the merits of comprehensive versus incremental approaches, and it can be stipulated up front that the comprehensive approach has more than its share of shortcomings.

Still, Iran is so geopolitically connected and so intertwined with so many issues that it is hard to imagine that a sustainable solution can be found to a single issue (such as the nuclear question) when so many other issues that could derail progress lie in wait. Certainly, Iran and the United States have many common interests, common interests that are typically forgotten or pushed aside. On issues involving energy, Afghanistan, Iraq, the drug trade, and Sunni extremist terrorism, to name a few, there are potential areas of agreement and cooperation.

The 2006 conflict between Israel and Lebanon serves as a reminder of the interconnectedness of the Iran–U.S. agenda. Some observers suspect an Iranian role in the Hezbollah kidnapping that catalyzed the conflict. Certainly, it could be argued that the timing may have helped deflect attention from Iran's nuclear program during the G8 summit. Others point to Syria or Hezbollah's own motivations as the cause.

But whether by design or by consequence, Hezbollah's actions highlight Iran's potential role for good or for ill. The Iranian–Hezbollah relationship means that an Iran under attack by sanctions or military strikes could make life very difficult for American policy in the Middle East, even if one sets aside the question of Iraq. There is also a flip side. Despite the views of many American commentators, Iran cannot dictate to Hezbollah any more than the United States can dictate to Israel—despite the fact that both patrons are a primary economic and military provider to their respective allies. Still, both have leverage. Iran has used this leverage in the past for positive ends and could do so again. A comprehensive strategy that accounts for the many issues that divide *and* unite the United States and Iran might provide a more sustainable basis for a working relationship in the future.

AN IRANIAN BOMB: TIMING, CONSEQUENCES

When and If

High-confidence knowledge regarding Iran's nuclear development is extremely limited. Complicating matters is Iran's tendency to exaggerate claims of technical achievement for its own domestic purposes. As several sources have suggested, U.S. knowledge and understanding of weapons of mass destruction (WMD) activities in Iran is poor, perhaps no better than it was for Iraq on the eve of the war.[34] And as with Iraq, the largest and best set of data on Iranian nuclear activity comes from the IAEA.

Former head of American intelligence John Negroponte has estimated that Iran might be able to acquire a nuclear weapons capability in the next five to ten years ("by the middle of the next decade"), assuming the government makes a command decision to focus on nuclear weapons development.[35] On several occasions, Israeli officials have claimed that Iran was approaching a "point of no return" in its nuclear capability. Indeed, the repeated nature of the claim calls into question its accuracy or usefulness.[36] Other worst-case scenarios suggest an Iranian nuclear weapon in as little as three years, but worst-case scenarios rarely provide accurate predictions of the future and cannot be acted on without major costs.

One problem with all of these assessments is that they ignore issues like program management and internal politics. As the Commission on the Intelligence Capabilities of the United States Regarding Weapons of Mass Destruction observed, the failure to understand the internal politics of a potential proliferator's nuclear program (while instead focusing on technical capabilities) has been a crippling flaw in American WMD intelligence estimates.[37] This was certainly true in the case of Iraq.

[34] The Commission on the Intelligence Capabilities of the United States Regarding Weapons of Mass Destruction, *Report to the President of the United States* (Washington DC: U.S. Government Printing Office, 31 March 2005); Rupert Cornwell, "Dead Wrong: The Damning Verdict of America's Official Report into the Reasons for Going to War in Iraq," *Independent* (London), 1 April 2005, accessed on the website of the *Independent* at http://news.independent.co.uk/world/americas/article8838.ece, 8 January 2007.

[35] Robert Siegel, "Interview of Ambassador John D. Negroponte, Director of National Intelligence," *National Public Radio*, 1 September 2006, accessed on the website of National Public Radio at http://www.dni.gov/interviews/20060901_interview.pdf, 8 January 2007.

[36] Editorial, "Iran's Bomb," *The Washington Post*, 22 September 2003, A22; Ewen MacAskill, "Iran Nears Nuclear 'Point of No Return,'" *Guardian* (London), 27 January 2005, 2; Steven R. Weisman and Douglas Jehl, "Estimate Revised on When Iran Could Make Nuclear Bomb," *The New York Times*, 3 August 2005; Mark MacKinnon, "Israel Raises Alarm Over Iran, *Globe and Mail* (Canada), 15 December 2005; Anton La Guardia, "Has Iran Reached Nuclear Point of No Return?" *Daily Telegraph* (London), 12 April 2006, 14; Yaakov Katz, "Sanctions on Iran—Too Little Too Late for Israel's Security Establishment," *Jerusalem Post*, 24 December 2006, 3.

[37] Commission on the Intelligence Capabilities, *Report to the President*, 13–14, 173–175.

The bottom line is that the United States has at least three and more likely five to seven years (or more) before Iran acquires a crude nuclear weapons capability. Regardless of which estimate one uses, it is clear that Iranian nuclear activity does not yet pose an imminent threat to U.S. national security.

It also has to be said that there may be no "point of no return," that is, Iran could reverse its program and do so even after a weaponization decision. Most countries in the nuclear age that have had an interest in nuclear weapons have later abandoned their efforts.[38] There are also examples of countries that have reversed course even after having built or acquired a nuclear arsenal. South Africa dismantled its nuclear weapons program.[39] Governments in Belarus, Kazakhstan, and, most notably, Ukraine gave up their inherited nuclear programs. Who can say that a decade after having built a bomb, an Iran under new leadership (a post-revolution, democratic-leaning leadership) might not dismantle in order to rejoin the international community or win normalized relations with the United States. Obviously, there are other, less-happy scenarios, but this one—often ignored by policymakers—cannot be discounted. This is especially true in the case of Iran, where the political consequences of generational change are widely expected to produce a new style of government at some point in the future.

What Will Happen If Iran Gets the Bomb?[40]

An Iran armed with nuclear weapons reduces Iranian, regional, global, and U.S. security. Preventing an Iranian nuclear weapon should, therefore, be considered to be among the highest policy priorities. Still, there is a strong and dangerous predilection for analysts to exaggerate the risks—especially the short-term risks—of Iran's entry into the nuclear club.

Modern Iran has been a status quo power. It sees itself as the most important player in the region, and the other Gulf States worry about its

---

[38] Jim Walsh, *Learning from Past Success: The NPT and the Future of Non-proliferation*, Paper no. 41 (Stockholm: Weapons of Mass Destruction Commission, 2006).

[39] On the South African program see, Mitchell Reiss, *Bridled Ambition: Why Countries Constrain Their Nuclear Capabilities* (Washington DC: Woodrow Wilson Center Press/Johns Hopkins University Press, 1995); J.W. de Villars, Roger Jargine, and Mitchell Reiss, "Why South Africa Gave Up the Bomb," *Foreign Affairs* 72 (November/December 1993): 98–109; Robert E. Kelley, "Two Substantially Different Approaches to Proliferation: The Cases of South Africa and Iraq" (paper presented for the Conference on Non-Proliferation, IGC, University of California, held at Limassol, Cyprus, 18 August 1995); Frank Pabian, "South Africa's Nuclear Weapons Program: Lessons for U.S. Nonproliferation Policy," *Nonproliferation Review* 3 (Fall 1995): 1–19; Peter Liberman, "The Rise and Fall of the South African Bomb," *International Security* 26 (Fall 2001): 45–86.

[40] On the consequences of an Iranian bomb and responses to it, see Barry Posen, "A Nuclear-Armed Iran A Difficult But Not Impossible Policy Problem," Century Foundation Report (Washington DC: Century Foundation, 2006); Sokolski and Clawson, eds, *Getting Ready*; Iran Watch Roundtable, 13 April 2005, *How Would the United States and Other Countries React to a Nuclear-armed Iran?* (Washington DC: Wisconsin Project on Nuclear Arms Control, 2005).

ambitions, but it does not have a history of initiating inter-state war. For all the talk of "exporting the revolution" in the years following the 1979 revolution, Iran has not engaged in military adventures abroad. Moreover, as many strategists have pointed out, nuclear weapons are essentially defensive in nature, good for deterrence but poor for use offensively or politically.[41] Since the end of WWII, no nation has used nuclear weapons for offensive purposes. In addition, nuclear blackmail has proven difficult, in part, because nuclear threats over comparatively small issues cannot be credibly made.

It is feared that Iran would transfer nuclear weapons to a terrorist group. This seems extremely unlikely. Despite close ties with Hamas and Hezbollah, Iran has never shared WMD with these organizations. Neither group has ever employed a chemical, biological, nuclear, or radiological device in a terrorist attack. In fact, no country has ever transferred WMD to a nonstate actor, despite the presence of nuclear weapons since 1945, chemical weapons since at least WWI, and biological weapons prior to that. Like every relevant government of the modern era, Tehran would view a nuclear weapon as a special prize best held tightly and certainly not something to be shared with an uncontrollable third party.[42]

Indeed, the "nuclear Iran is the end of the world" view is only possible if one ignores the historical record, one in which "rogue" and other states far more dangerous than Iran have acquired nuclear weapons.[43] Perhaps the most terrifying nuclear "rogue" state of all time was China under Mao Tse-tung. Mao pulled out of the UN, said he would share nuclear weapons with the developing world, suggested that nuclear weapons were paper tigers, and asserted that China could win a nuclear war because of its large population. Under Mao, China became the first and only country to attempt a live nuclear test shot over its own territory. Still, in practice, China's nuclear policy was far more benign than its rhetoric or regime type would have suggested.[44]

[41] See, for example, Robert Jervis, *The Meaning of the Nuclear Revolution: Statecraft and the Prospect for Armageddon* (Ithaca, NY: Cornell University Press, 1989).

[42] Jim Walsh, "Nuclear and Radiological Terrorism: Risk, Consequences, and Response" in Arne Howitt, ed., *Countering Terrorism: Dimensions of Preparedness* (Cambridge, MA: MIT Press, 2003); Matthew Bunn and Anthony Wier, "Will States Give Terrorists the Bomb?" (Cambridge, MA: Harvard University Press, 2003) for the Nuclear Threat Initiative, accessed on the website of the Nuclear Threat Initiative at http://www.nti.org/e_research/cnwm/overview/path2.asp, 8 January 2007.

[43] On the dubious concept of "rogue states," see Michael Klare, *Rogue States and Nuclear Outlaws* (New York: Hill and Wang, 1995); Ashok Kapur, "Rogue States and the International Nuclear Order," *International Journal* 51 (Summer 1996): 420–439; Mary Caprioli and Peter F. Trumbore, "Rhetoric Versus Reality: Rogue States in Interstate Conflict," *Journal of Conflict Resolution* 49 (October 2005): 770–791.

[44] On the perceived threat from "Red China" and American perceptions at the time, see Francis J. Gavin, "Blasts from the Past: Proliferation Lessons from the 1960s," *International Security* 29 (Winter 2004): 100–135; William Burr and Jeffrey T. Richelson, "Whether to 'Strangle the Baby in the Cradle': The United States and the Chinese Nuclear Program, 1960-64," *International Security* 25 (Winter

Is Pakistan, which has a military government, large pockets of al Qaeda operatives, and a sometimes intense rivalry with India, less of a nuclear threat than Iran? What about North Korea? Many observers in the intelligence community believe that North Korea has possessed at least one nuclear weapon since the mid-1990s. The United States has not taken military action against nuclear programs in China, Pakistan, or North Korea, and most analysts would agree that these were prudent and correct choices. Is Iran more of a nuclear threat than these cases? Probably not.

It has to be said, however, that concern about a nuclear-armed Iran is understandable. Ahmadinejad's oft-repeated phrase about "wiping Israel off the map" has a particularly emotional resonance with Western and Israeli audiences. The fact that the Leader, not the President, is in charge of Iran or that most of the Iranian foreign policy and technocratic classes reject this view provides little assurance or comfort.

While there has been some semantic dispute about what the President said, it is clear from direct questioning that Ahmadinejad does, in fact, believe that Israel should be "wiped off the map." He views Israel as an imperialistic project imposed on the Palestinians and completely lacking in legitimacy. It must also be said, however, that his position is that this should be achieved politically, not by the use of force. He advocates a complete right of return for Palestinians, followed by a referendum to determine the future of the government. He assumes, probably correctly, that in the unlikely event that such a referendum took place, it would dissolve the state of Israel and reconstitute a Palestinian nation, and thus Israel would be "wiped off the map."[45]

Ahmadinejad does not call for a war to push Israel into the sea, and in fact, the record of post-revolutionary Iran—even during Ahmadinejad's tenure—has not been one that can be characterized as militarily provocative, let alone aggressive. Some analysts argue that Ahmadinejad, and even Khamenei, see a religious duty to destroy Israel, and yet if that is the case, why has Iran not attacked in the two-and-a-half decades since the Shah was toppled? In short, despite the incendiary rhetoric, there is little or no evidence to suggest that Iran would proactively seek to use nuclear weapons against Israel. As a practical matter, however, it is unlikely that such arguments will carry much weight. This is yet another reason why progress in resolving the nuclear dispute or in U.S.–Iranian relations will probably have to wait until Ahmadinejad passes from the political scene.

To be clear, a nuclear Iran brings many dangers, including strengthening pro–nuclear weapons advocates in neighboring and other states, undermining confidence in the nonproliferation regime, introducing the possibility of a nu-

2000–2001): 54–99. On the evolution of Mao's thought on nuclear weapons, see Shu Guang Zhang, "Between 'Paper' and 'Real Tigers': Mao's View of Nuclear Weapons" in John Lewis Gaddis et al., eds, *Cold War Statesmen*, 194–215.

[45] Personal communication with President Mahmoud Ahmadinejad, September, 2006.

clear exchange with Israel, adding to the total amount of nuclear material that might be subject to theft by terrorists, and risking a breakdown in nuclear security during regime transition—to name just a few. Therefore, every effort should be made to support a smart nonproliferation policy that has the greatest chance of success with the least chance of catastrophic failure.

An Iranian nuclear weapons status would prove costly for all parties, including Iran. It is unlikely, however, to result in the dangers most often cited, such as immediate nuclear use, blackmail, or transfer to terrorists. The danger posed by an Iranian bomb should not be discounted, but neither should it be exaggerated.

IS AN IRANIAN NUCLEAR WEAPON INEVITABLE?

The historical record suggests that nuclear proliferation can be stopped. Contrary to virtually every prediction by scholars and policymakers, nuclear weapons have not spread like wildfire.[46] Indeed, the rate of proliferation has for the most part declined since the 1960s, and today, fewer countries seek nuclear weapons than during any previous decade in the nuclear age. Despite all the talk about "inevitability," proliferation has been largely stopped and in many cases reversed.[47]

Still, old habits die hard, and the tendency to assume inevitability is hard to resist.[48] In Washington today, any number of pundits and policymakers intone that Iran is determined to get the bomb and that nothing can stop them—a conclusion that seems erroneous on both counts. History suggests that most

[46] On the failure of these predictions to come true, see George H. Quester, "The Statistical 'n' of 'nth' Nuclear Weapons States," *Journal of Conflict Resolution* 27 (March 1983): 161–179; Mitchell Reiss, "The Future That Never Came," *Wilson Quarterly* 19 (Spring 1995): Examples are plentiful. The most widely cited erroneous prediction was John F. Kennedy's. See *Public Papers of the President of the United States: John F. Kennedy, 1963* (Washington DC: U.S. Government Printing Office, 1964), 280. Proliferation, wrote Gallois, was "as irreversible as ... the generalization of firearms." Pierre Gallois, *The Balance of Terror* (Boston, MA: Houghton Mifflin, 1961), 229. It was a view echoed more than a decade later: Bryan Bender, "US Saw Spread of Nuclear Arms as 'Inevitable' 1975 Outlook Bleak; Progress Has Been Made," Boston Globe, 6 August 2005, A3. For more contemporary predictions from the neorealist camp, see Benjamin Frankel, "The Brooding Shadow: Systemic Incentives and Nuclear Weapons Proliferation," in Davis and Frankel, eds., *The Proliferation Puzzle*, 37–78; John J. Mearsheimer, "Back to the Future: Instability in Europe after the Cold War," *International Security* 15 (Summer 1990): 5–56; Bradley A. Thayer, "The Causes of Nuclear Proliferation and the Nonproliferation Regime," *Security Studies* 4 (Spring 1995) 463–519; John Mearsheimer, "Here We Go Again," *The New York Times*, 17 May 1998.

[47] Walsh, *Learning from Past Success*. See also, Reiss, *Without the Bomb*; Reiss, *Bridled Ambition*; Robert J. Einhorn, Mitchell B. Reiss, and Kurt M. Campbell, eds., *The Nuclear Tipping Point: Why States Reconsider Their Nuclear Choices* (Washington DC: Brookings Institution Press, 2004).

[48] Graham Allison, for example, has offered what can only be described as a vintage 1960s prediction of a proliferation debacle. Graham Allison, "The Cascade of Proliferation," *Atlantic Monthly* 296 (October 2005).

nuclear weapons programs get derailed. A minority succeed. Iran may yet be one that crosses the nuclear threshold, but that will not be the result of inexorable forces. A smart American nonproliferation policy can reduce the chances of a nuclear-armed Iran, but unfortunately, just as likely, if not more likely, is an American policy whose effect is to strengthen the domestic position of Iranian bomb advocates, thus increasing the odds of an Iranian bomb.

Avoiding that outcome will require that American officials discard assumptions of inevitability and do the hard work of understanding the complex and changing dynamics of Iranian politics. Fixed ideas about Iranian intentions will prevent the United States from seeing and taking advantage of opportunities to redirect the Iranian course. A failure to understand the importance of national pride and a preoccupation with coercion and regime change will produce the same poor policy results that have characterized the last fifteen years of American nonproliferation efforts with Iran. Can the Iranian bomb be stopped? Most certainly. Whether U.S. policymakers will have the wisdom and deft touch required to accomplish such a feat remains to be seen.*

* This chapter is based, in part, on testimony delivered before the Senate Subcommittee on Federal Financial Management, Government Information & International Security of the Committee on Homeland Security & Governmental Affairs on 20 July 2006. I wish to express my gratitude to Senators Tom Carper and Tom Coburn for their invitation and to Mehreen Zaidi and Angelina Piatelli for research and editorial support. Many of the insights and impressions offered in this chapter are based on discussions with over 100 Iranian officials, scholars, and others whom I met or interviewed in the course of my 2006 trip to Iran and as a result of my participation in various Track II dialogues since 2002. For obvious reasons, much of the information gleaned in these discussions must remain unattributed.

Part IV:
Moral, Ethical, and Constitutional Repercussions

Killing Civilians Intentionally: Double Effect, Reprisal, and Necessity in the Middle East

MICHAEL L. GROSS

The principle of noncombatant immunity is undoubtedly the linchpin of humanitarian law during armed conflict. Recognizing that warfare takes the lives of civilians and other noncombatants, noncombatant immunity limits the harm that noncombatants will inevitably suffer by prohibiting intentional harm in all but perhaps the most extreme cases. At the same time, the rules of modern warfare permit adversaries to unintentionally take a reasonable or proportionate number of civilian lives when militarily necessary. This normative framework, however vague and undefined it may be, forms the basis for assessing the morality of killing civilians during war.

As they attack civilians, belligerents sometimes raise the claim that there are no noncombatants in modern war. It is certainly true that a number of ambiguous actors litter the field in the Mideast. These include reserve soldiers and armed settlers on the Israeli side, and ununiformed militias, "mature" minors, and civilian accessories to the fighting on the Palestinian side. Nevertheless, it is equally clear that many civilians have no role in the fighting. For the purposes of this essay, I will limit the discussion to civilians and adopt the definition fixed by the 1949 Geneva Conventions. Civilians are "people who do not bear arms." They are a subset of noncombatants, that is, "persons taking no active part in the hostilities."[1] This definition, however, says nothing about innocence, and civilian leaders may bear far more responsibility for war

---

[1] Commentary and Article 3, Convention (IV) relative to the Protection of Civilian Persons in Time of War, Geneva, 12 August 1949, accessed at http://www.icrc.org, 14 September 2005.

MICHAEL L. GROSS is senior lecturer in the Division of International Relations, The University of Haifa, Israel. He is the author of *Ethics and Activism: The Theory and Practice of Political Morality* (Cambridge, 1997) and *Bioethics and Armed Conflict: Moral Dilemmas of Medicine and War* (MIT, 2006).

than do simple soldiers in the field. Here, however, I am concerned with the status of what may be called "ordinary" civilians, and although it is true that they may provide succor and support for combatants, they do not bear arms or take an active part in the hostilities. They are, for the most part, also innocent, that is, they are not responsible for prosecuting the war or for the harm befalling enemy soldiers and civilians. Ordinary civilians remain the intended beneficiaries of the principle of noncombatant immunity.

If ordinary citizens ever enjoyed protection from intentional harm, recent events in the Middle East are rapidly eroding this norm and testing the limits of noncombatant immunity. Beginning in 2000, fighting between Israel and the Palestinian Authority (PA) has witnessed the unprecedented use of terror: massive, lethal attacks against civilians for purposes ranging from breaking Israeli morale and wresting further political concessions to destroying the State of Israel. In response, Israel reoccupied the West Bank (and, until 2005, the Gaza Strip), severely curtailed Palestinian civil liberties, and undertook military action resulting in civilian deaths. Each side invokes self-defense and national interest. As Palestinians are repeatedly called upon to renounce the use of terror in their struggle for national self-determination, Israel is censured for indiscriminate and disproportionate harm to civilians. This discourse stands to radically affect the way in which the international community views the imperative to avoid intentional harm to civilians.

INTENTIONALLY KILLING CIVILIANS

When asked about the use of terror, Mohammed Dahlan, commander of Palestinian security forces in Gaza in 2002, warned Israel that "whoever harms civilians must expect similar responses."[2] Unpacked, Dahlan's argument reveals a multipronged, controversial claim:

1. *Intentionality and its corollary argument, the doctrine of double effect (the DDE), do not matter.* The standard Israeli and, indeed, Western response to Dahlan's argument draws on the DDE and asserts that civilian casualties resulting from Israeli attacks on the PA are foreseen but unintended side effects of a legitimate military operation that is both necessary and proportionate. As a result, civilian casualties do not merit moral condemnation. A reasonable counterargument of the type that might underlie Dahlan's assertion may move in one of two directions. First, it may push intentionality to the sidelines, suggesting that the consequences of an intended act, that is, the death of innocent civilians resulting from an intentional military operation, make Israel morally responsible for the deaths of Palestinian civilians. Alternatively, one may embrace intentionality but argue instead that Israel violates its conditions. In neither

[2] Serge Schmemann, "US Peace Envoy Arrives in Israel as Fighting Rages," *Ha'aretz*, 15 March 2002.

case are the arguments trivial, for they suggest that Israeli actions are morally blameworthy and may invite legitimate reprisals.

2. *Israeli citizens are the legitimate targets of reprisal.* Once established that there is no moral justification for Israeli attacks on Palestinian civilians, either because intentionality does not matter or because Israel has violated its conditions, Dahlan implies that Palestinian attacks are justified reprisals for morally unjustified Israeli actions. What could this justification be? Dahlan does not say, but if reprisal lies at the core of the argument, then it turns on punishment and deterrence. Although international law increasingly frowns on reprisals against civilians, there is a history of Israeli reprisal raids in response to Arab attacks on Israeli civilians. Why, the Palestinians seem to be asking, can they not undertake similar actions? Alternatively, Dahlan's position might suggest that asymmetry of arms or the prospect of imminent defeat justifies intentional attacks on civilians.

3. *Supreme emergencies justify attacks on civilians as a measure of last resort.* By attacking civilians, Palestinians may not only hope to deter future attacks by Israel but may also hope to break local morale and exert pressure on the Israeli government to acquiesce to Palestinian political demands. This is not a novel argument, but emerged conspicuously during WWII as military planners and civilian observers debated the relative virtues of area bombing. In this debate, any attempt to justify intentional civilian deaths was linked to dire necessity or supreme emergency. In the present context, terror is also tied to asymmetry of arms. Because the Palestinians lack a military capability similar to Israel's, terror bombings are a justified weapon of last resort. The argument complements those characterizing supreme emergency that allow self-defense to override entrenched moral principles and the laws of armed conflict.

The following discussion considers the DDE as it plays out in the Israeli–Palestinian conflict. The doctrine presents difficulties for Palestinians and Israelis alike. Palestinian terrorists intentionally target civilians, whereas Israelis push unintentional harm to its outer limits when they regularly acknowledge, and regret, killing civilians in the course of military operations. If *unintentional* harm drives the DDE, *intentional* harm remains the explicit and often acceptable goal of reprisals and actions taken during supreme emergencies. The extent to which reprisals and necessity justify the deaths of civilians in the current conflict is the subject of the final two sections.

Intentionality and the DDE

"Perhaps the most basic rule of the law of armed conflict is that civilians and civilian objects must not be made the object of direct attack, although incidental injuries caused to such persons or objects in the course of a legitimate attack must be proportionate to the purpose of the attack."[3]

The moral intuition underlying this basic rule is enshrined in the DDE. If its original task was theological, the DDE quickly evolved into a secular principle of just war, allowing combatants to kill civilians as long as their cause is just and noncombatant deaths are an unintended, although foreseen, side effect of a necessary and proportionate military operation that produces less harm than one reasonably hopes to forestall. Armed with these provisions, belligerents feel morally insulated when they kill civilians in the name of military necessity and a just cause.

Although adversaries in a conventional war generally have no particular interest in killing civilians, the DDE allows them to do so under what appear to be carefully controlled circumstances. In reality, the DDE may be excessively lax, allowing the killing of civilians whenever their deaths accompany military action. Perhaps because it has been so lax, or perhaps because it has allowed each side to pursue roughly equivalent levels of civilian deaths with minimal moral consternation, conventional combatants have rarely questioned the DDE in the same way that terrorist and insurgent organizations are now doing.[4] For a long time, combatants on each side have used the DDE to justify the inevitable killing of civilians during wartime. The argument packs a powerful moral and practical punch. On one hand, a compelling moral principle linking intentionality with responsibility and liability stands behind the DDE. Lack of intention retains, as the early Christian theologians noted, a "pure heart" and attenuates moral responsibility, liability, and guilt because one's motives are good.[5] Practically speaking, the DDE offers a convenient argument for harming civilians when their welfare conflicts with military necessity and, at the same time, it sets the conditions for protecting noncombatants from indiscriminate harm.

The force of the DDE is often demonstrated by comparing the actions of two agents, a strategic bomber (SB) and a terror bomber (TB). SBs destroy military targets in order to hasten the end of the war. In doing so, they often kill

---

[3] Leslie C. Green, *The Contemporary Law of Armed Conflict*, 2nd ed. (Manchester, UK: Manchester University Press, 2000), 124.

[4] I use the word "insurgents" to describe Palestinian forces engaged in armed combat against Israel. Defined by the Oxford English Dictionary as one who "rises in active revolt," "insurgent" also captures the meaning of the word "*Intifada*" (uprising) that the Palestinians use to describe their conflict. Insurgent forces include terrorists and members of the various Palestinian security forces and militias. The latter are lawful combatants, insofar as their military organizations maintain an "internal disciplinary system," enforce "compliance with the rules of international law applicable in armed conflict," and commit their soldiers to carrying their arms openly during military engagements, although not necessarily to wearing identifying uniforms or insignia (Protocol I, 1977, Articles 43, 44). Terrorists are those insurgents who indiscriminately and intentionally target civilians and wantonly violate the laws of armed combat.

[5] Robert L. Holmes, *On War and Morality* (Princeton, NJ: Princeton University Press, 1989), 193–200.

civilians, whose deaths are unintended but foreseen. TBs aim at population centers. Their purpose is to kill civilians, destroy their infrastructures, and weaken enemy morale in order to hasten the end of the war. They aim intentionally at civilians. The British bombing of Germany during WWII is the example commonly cited. The DDE explains why the unintentional harm that strategic bombing causes is permitted, whereas the intentional harm that terror bombing causes is not.

In the present Mideast context, however, strategic and terror bombing assume a different character. Strategic bombing represents any Israeli action to destroy a Palestinian military target. These targets are not large military installations but often include single individuals or groups of individuals, bomb-manufacturing plants, or police and military installations. In nearly all cases, these targets are nested in built-up, civilian areas. Terror bombing, by contrast, aims specifically at civilian targets and is carried out by suicide bombers, by cells planting explosive devices or car bombs, or by squads that attack civilians with small arms. Unlike the area bombers of WWII, they make no claim to destroy infrastructures of any kind.

By the simple logic of the DDE, TBs kill their victims intentionally and are therefore morally responsible and criminally liable for their deaths, whereas SBs do not and are therefore absolved of responsibility and liability. The DDE only holds sway, however, when each side accepts its logic and is more or less equally equipped to wage war with minimal involvement of noncombatants. Terrorists and insurgents, however, attack the logic of the principle. Intentionality does not matter or, perhaps more realistically, no one unintentionally kills civilians.

The DDE and Intentionality: Does Intentionality Matter?

In its original formulation, the DDE confronted a rather simple difficulty that adversaries faced during war: how could one justify killing civilians who were innocent but inevitably harmed during armed conflict? The answer turned on intentionality. It was permissible only insofar as one did not *intend* to harm them. Early Christian theologians believed that without intent, it was possible to allay responsibility. It was never entirely clear, however, what intentional harm meant or how one could determine whether one harmed another intentionally, particularly during war. If intentionality only meant *rens mea*, an evil mind, then the DDE would be particularly difficult to apply in practice. One could easily ask how anyone can know whether SBs act with good intentions or whether TBs, for that matter, act with evil ones.

Modern legal and moral theorists wrestle with similar difficulties and often limit the exculpatory power of good intentions. Good intentions may, at best, mitigate punishment; they do not necessarily redeem the badness of the act itself. "We may judge the [bomber] pilots differently," writes Robert Holmes, "if we believe that one acted with good intentions and the other with bad intentions. But the fact of their different intentions would not affect the moral assessment of *what* they did."[6] If intentions are particularly difficult to ferret out in wartime and, at best, only mitigate punishment, it is not entirely clear what intentionality adds to the DDE and the general prohibition against killing civilians.

H. L. A. Hart, for example, describes the case of an Irish Nationalist (IN) who inadvertently kills civilian bystanders while blowing out a wall to free his friends from prison.[7] IN did not intend to kill anyone; the deaths he caused were not a means to his end but only an "undesirable byproduct" of his actions. Nevertheless, he was, in Hart's opinion, rightfully convicted of murder. Hart's view is intuitively appealing, for clearly, an agent should be liable for the harmful effects of an intended action, however unintended the effects may be. It is difficult to see, then, why SB should not be convicted of killing civilians and how he could turn to the DDE to not only mitigate his punishment but to erase the badness of the act itself. The only difference between SB and IN is, if anything, the good end that SB invokes; their intentions are equally pure. Because neither intends to kill civilians, we are left judging the act not by intention but by the goodness of goal. The DDE masks, in this case, an enlightened principle of "the ends justify the means," insofar as the ends are good, a condition usually augmented by two others: the good end must not be attained by evil means, and the accompanying harm, if any, must be proportionate to the good one seeks and minimized where possible.

Although all three conditions are commonly associated with the DDE, only the second, the obligation to avoid evil means, may distinguish between TB and SB. Just cause (that is, a good end) is reasonably claimed by most adversaries. This is certainly true in the Mideast conflict, inasmuch as Palestinians claim the right to national self-determination and Israelis claim the right to self-defense in response to terror. Each adversary also appropriates proportionality with equal zeal. Moreover, proportionality is most often a subjective determination, nothing more than "I know it when I see it," whereas the imperative to minimize harm is only uncontroversial when choosing between two equally effective actions.

Steering clear of evil means to attain one's end, on the other hand, is often identified—some scholars say confused—with intentionality. Supporters allow an agent to invoke the DDE if, among other things, he or she does not use evil means to attain a good end. Consider Hart's example. Why was IN convicted of murder? Hart does not say, but one reason might be that IN violated the DDE by pursuing a bad end, at least in the eyes of those who judged him. Another reason may be IN's failure to minimize harm. Each of these is a subjective

---

[6] Ibid., 199.

[7] H. L. A. Hart, *Punishment and Responsibility, Essays in the Philosophy of Law* (Oxford: Oxford University Press, 1968), 119–120.

determination. IN's peers, for example, would most likely have exonerated him on the same counts. The same peers, however, might not have looked as kindly upon their fellow nationalist had he murdered the same civilians who were unintentionally killed in order to gain the release of their comrades. Murder would push IN across the line, even in the eyes of those who sympathized with his cause. Similarly, although TB might claim proportionality and a good end, he remains morally culpable, because he cannot claim that his means—killing civilians—are good.

Here we must ask whether intentionality plays any role at all. Consider again TB's dilemma. Although he thinks his ends are good and the harm he causes is proportionate, "he cannot claim that his means—killing civilians—are good." At this juncture, critics would argue that it simply makes no sense to talk of "*intentionally* killing civilians" in this context or, at least, that it adds nothing of moral significance to the conditions necessary to prohibit TB's or IN's actions. Their actions stand or fall on the goodness (or badness) of the end they adopt, the means they pursue, and the degree of harm they cause. The moral repugnance of TB's action, in this view, lies not in the agent's intention or malevolent state of mind but in the fact that he uses inherently evil means to realize his end. Intentionality, for all intents and purposes, does not matter and, for this reason, some observers regard the DDE as incoherent, superfluous, or otiose.[8]

The argument focusing on the actual means an agent employs is important, for it sidesteps the problem of subjectivity or determining the agent's state of mind before one can invoke the DDE, and directs one's attention to the act, as opposed to the agent. Rather than dispensing with the DDE entirely, however, it may be more fruitful to adopt a principle that condemns TB because he uses evil means to obtain his ostensibly good end. This, and not the agent's state of mind, offers a richer and more easily operationalized formulation of intentionality that allows observers to identify violations of the DDE.

The DDE and Intentionality: An Operational Definition

Whether we dispense with intentionality altogether or define it in terms of using evil means to obtain a good end, one is still left to determine criteria for identifying both "evil means" and "use." What means, in other words, are evil, and how do we know when SB or anyone else is using them?

Harming civilians constitutes the evil means addressed by the DDE. This includes not only death and injury directly caused by military action but also indirect effects of war: destitution, disease, lawlessness, and insecurity. Neither

---

[8] Alison MacIntyre, "Doing Away with Double Effect," *Ethics* 111 (January 2001): 219–255; Holmes, *On War*, 199.

type of harm can be a legitimate means to an end, however good. Although extreme harm—killing—remains the focus of the DDE, the evil is not in the killing itself but in using the death of civilians for another purpose. Observers frequently express their abhorrence of this type of exploitation. Hart, for example, suggests that actions similar to TB's elicit a "feeling that to use a man's death as a means to some further end is a defilement of the agent: his [a murderer's] will is thus identified with an evil aim that is somehow morally worse than the will of one who, in the pursuit of the same further end, does something which, the agent realizes, renders the man's death inevitable as a second effect."[9] Here is the underlying intuition of the "double" effect. The moral consequences of the "second effect" are cushioned, not so much because it is unintended but because it serves no purpose in the agent's plans.

Warren Quinn fleshes out the argument further. The critical question is whether "the victims are made to play a role in the service of the agent's goal that is not (or may not be) morally required of them and this aspect of direct agency adds its own negative moral force—a force over and above that provided by the fact of harming or failing to prevent harm."[10] Commenting on Quinn's view, Jeff McMahon suggests that "intention simply magnifies the wrongness of violating a pre-existing right."[11] This moral fact is decisive for Quinn, who readily points out that an SB "perhaps . . . cannot honestly say that this [harmful] effect will be 'unintentional' in any standard sense, or that he 'does not mean' to kill them. But he can honestly deny that their involvement . . . is anything to his purpose."[12]

These lines of thinking form the basis for a richer interpretation of intentionality that forms a firm criterion for distinguishing the actions of SB and TB. Intentionally killing civilians means using them without their consent or against their will to procure one's ends. Defining intentionality in this way allows one to search for violations of the DDE not in the agent's subjective intentions or motives but in his plans and the means he uses to achieve them. The "acid" test of intentionality is whether agents profit from the evil effect in any way.[13] Susan Uniacke calls this the test of failure: would the mission fail if the harmful effects were avoided? In the case of SB, the answer is no, but in the case of TB, the answer is yes: TB cannot succeed unless he kills innocent civilians.[14] As a result, TB intentionally causes harm and violates the DDE. TB is morally responsible for killing civilians, and his act is reprehensible.

---

[9] Hart, *Punishment and Responsibility*, 127.

[10] Warren S. Quinn, "Actions, Intentions and Consequences: The Doctrine of the Double Effect," *Philosophy and Public Affairs* 18 (Fall 1989): 334–351.

[11] Jeff, McMahon, "Revising the Doctrine of Double Effect," *Journal of Applied Philosophy* 11 (1994): 207.

[12] Quinn, "Actions," 342.

[13] A. J. Coates, *The Ethics of War* (Manchester, UK: Manchester University Press, 1997), 244.

[14] Susan Uniacke, "Double Effect, Principle of" in Edward Craig, ed., Routledge Encyclopedia of Philosophy (London: Routledge, 1989), 202. Some philosophers also have suggested that TB, like SB,

Understanding the DDE in this way also repudiates Mideast terror: if TBs force their victims to play a role that they have not consented to and which is not required of them and benefit directly from their victims' deaths, then their acts violate the DDE and are morally objectionable. Regardless of the justice of their cause, terrorists have used evil means to achieve their end. Although this easily condemns Palestinian TBs, it is doubtful that most terrorists sincerely claim that their means are good. Instead, their argument is more nuanced, asserting that the injunction against using an evil means—killing civilians—is not absolute and may be overridden when one is faced with supreme emergency or the need to reprise against similar actions. These claims are considered shortly. To make these claims, however, particularly the latter, Palestinian TBs must argue that Israeli SBs similarly violate the DDE. To do this, they must argue that SBs also benefit from civilian deaths.

Intentionality and Side Benefits

Establishing intentionality according to the benefits gained from unintentional civilian deaths raises serious and sometimes fatal difficulties for SBs. While versions of the DDE espoused by Quinn or Uniacke may serve to distinguish between a simple case of SB or TB, the situation on the ground in the Mideast is more complex. Rarely is it the case, particularly in limited wars in built-up areas, that civilian deaths do not carry benefits independent of those obtained when the target that civilians are unlucky enough to live near is destroyed. Counter-insurgency measures, including unintended but foreseen civilian deaths, are sometimes expected to unbalance the civilian population and drive a wedge between terrorists and their local base of support. Although one may not set out to harm civilians for this purpose, one may clearly benefit when civilians are killed as part of a military operation.

Moreover, Israelis readily acknowledge the benefits of collateral damage. Consider the following two cases of side benefits that result from the bad effect of an intended action.

1. "The deaths of women and children during IDF operations against wanted men has become routine ... but this week a senior officer was

---

does not actually need to cause civilian deaths in order to demoralize the enemy and hasten the end of the war. All TB requires is the *appearance* of their death. McMahon, "Revising the Doctrine," 202. "If, unbeknownst to the government, the civilians were to escape harm by hiding in deep shelters until after the surrender, this would not frustrate the terror bomber's plan." (The *Hezbollah*, for example, will often leave the impression of having killed their victims without ever confirming that this is so. They have created the appearance of death necessary to undermine enemy morale without necessarily having actually killed anyone. Something like this occurred when they kidnapped three Israeli soldiers in 2000. A year later, the Israeli army declared the soldiers dead but only recovered their bodies in 2004. While the *Hezbollah* sought to trade information about the soldiers for captives held by Israel, the action undoubtedly affected the morale of soldiers serving on the Lebanese border. Their morale was equally undermined regardless of the state of health of the those kidnapped earlier.

even quoted, in response to the civilian deaths in Al Bureij (fighting in the Al Bureij refugee camp killed 10 Palestinians and wounded 20), as saying that a 'large number of casualties has deterrent value.'"[15]

2. Following a period (9 November to 31 December 2000), during which Israeli forces assassinated nine Palestinian militants while killing six civilian bystanders and injuring two, one Israeli official remarked: "The liquidation of wanted persons is proving itself useful.... This activity paralyzes and frightens entire villages and as a result, there are areas where people are afraid to carry out hostile action."[16]

In each instance, there is a direct or indirect reference to deterrent benefits that civilian deaths bring. Do these admissions lend credence to the claim that Israeli actions are morally on a par with terror attacks? If benefit is the sole test of the DDE and the principle fails when there are side benefits to collateral damage, then the answer appears to be yes.

The question remains, however, whether intentionality is any richer than the criterion of side benefits implies. What if the side benefit is unintended or one takes steps to avoid collateral damage that nonetheless benefits SB? Can an unintended ex post benefit impugn the moral standing of SB? The DDE allows unintended harm; after all, that is its purpose, but does it allow unintended side benefits? One might be inclined to argue that it does not, for unintended side benefits are the very test of intentional harm and ferret out intentionality when it is not obvious or is disclaimed by the agent. When side benefits are present, SB cannot deny that civilian deaths were anything to his purpose.

Some readings seem to support this contention:

1. "The good effect must be produced directly by the action, not by the bad effect. Otherwise, the agent would be using a bad means to a good end, which is never allowed."

2. "The bad cannot be a means to the good."

3. "To arrive at a sound moral estimate ... it is often useful to consider whether the evil effect *de facto* contributes to the ultimate good desired, even if not explicitly willed as a means."[17]

Each of these readings suggests that unintended side benefits violate the DDE. Quinn's analysis is also ex post: SB satisfies the DDE because he can honestly deny that civilian deaths are anything to his purpose. But what if he cannot deny this? What if civilian deaths contributed to his purpose? If so, he is then using a bad means, however unintended, to a good end.

---

[15] Ruevan Pedazur, "The Wrong Way to Fight Terrorism," *Ha'aretz*, 11 December 2002.

[16] Eldar Akiva, "Liquidation Sale for the Peace Process," *Ha'aretz*, 4 January 2001.

[17] McIntyre, "Doing Away," 229, citing the traditional DDE; Holmes, *On War*, 199; John C. Ford, "The Morality of Obliteration Bombing" in Richard A. Wasserstrom, ed., *War and Morality* (Belmont, CA: Wadsworth Publishing, 1970 [1944]), 27.

Unintended side benefits, therefore, violate the prohibition of intentionally harming civilians.

Yet, the issue is not so easy to resolve. Israeli soldiers who shelled Arab villages in 1948 were witness to a mass exodus that later brought clear political and strategic advantages. Yet their purpose was to capture a strategic position and win the war, not to expel local residents. Later, Israeli forces intentionally undertook and/or condoned isolated acts to encourage evacuation when it was understood that population displacement had clear strategic benefits.[18] Corresponding roughly to SB with unintended side benefits and TB, these seem to be distinct moral categories, yet both, according to the reading above, violate the DDE in the same way. One practical solution might be to sidestep the problem with the observation that unintended side benefits do not remain unintended for long. Once acknowledged, any action resulting in civilian deaths with known side benefits violates the DDE. Thus, if the observations noted above underlie a trend among Israeli policy makers, then they have violated the DDE despite the fact that civilian deaths do not contribute to the primary mission. One cannot acknowledge side benefits the first time and then claim the second time that they are unintended. By itself, this realization can go a long way toward limiting collateral damage.

But can we push further and argue, as the citations above suggest, that unintended benefits also violate the DDE? This certainly invokes the spirit of the DDE, which, it must be remembered, is a principle designed to protect civilians from harm. At its core, the DDE assumes that any harm to innocents is morally bad, and it therefore sets strict conditions where their welfare is concerned. To condemn unintended harm that brings unintended benefits limits permissible harm to "pure" cases of military necessity in which civilian casualties play absolutely no part. But these pure types, SB or TB, are illusory. Arthur Harris's bombing campaign during World War II was never called "terror" bombing but "area" or "saturation" bombing. Critics called it "obliteration" bombing: "*strategic* bombing of industrial centers of population, in which the target to be wiped out is not a definite factory, bridge or similar object, but a large section of a whole city, comprising one-third to two-thirds of its built-up area, and including by design the residential districts of workingmen and their families."[19] Area bombing was, in other words, SB with intended side benefits that included the destruction of civilian population centers and, was, therefore, prohibited by the DDE and contemporary international humanitarian law. "Precision bombing," on the other hand, characterized Allied attempts to destroy German military targets but, owing to the imprecision of their instruments or the difficulties posed by night-time bombing, it often brought significant civilian causalities.

---

[18] Benny Morris, *Righteous Victims: A History of the Zionist–Arab Conflict, 1881–1999* (New York: Knopf, 1999), 161–258.

[19] Ford, "The Morality of Obliteration Bombing," 24, emphasis added.

Just as area bombing has strategic value, precision bombing also has terror value. The situation is exacerbated in insurgency warfare, in which any attack on a strategic target may cause civilian casualties together with side benefits measured in broken morale, population displacement, and internal dissent. To rule out unintended harms that bring unintended side benefits would severely limit the scope of counterinsurgency warfare and conventional aerial bombardment. The DDE would effectively become a pacifist doctrine.

In one more sense, the idea of unintended side benefits is unworkable. In fact, the entire idea of side benefits deriving from harm to civilians is problematic. Throughout the entire discussion, we have assumed that harm to civilians has beneficial effects relative to the war aims of the bomber. Terror bombing makes this assumption, as did the Israeli officials cited above. However, as many observers repeatedly point out, this is usually not the case. Area bombing failed to affect, and may have even strengthened, German morale.[20] Thus, to invoke side benefits to test the DDE demands a test for efficacy, which is usually unavailable and, if history is any example, nearly always negative. Under these circumstances, there is no reason to assume that collateral harm to civilians has any long-term benefits whatsoever. If it has no benefit, then unintentional harm to civilians *cannot* violate the DDE. We now have no reasonable test of intentionality and the DDE collapses.

If it is impossible to evaluate the side benefits of strategic bombing, or if empirical data are so contradictory that the DDE is either so eviscerated or so fortified as to be rendered useless, then the test for the DDE can only be found in *intended* benefits or *expected* utility, that is, those benefits that the SB or his planners think or hope will accrue when civilians are unintentionally harmed during a mission to destroy a strategic target. In this regard, then, Quinn's caveat stands: one looks to the extent to which one *tries* to involve civilians in one's cause when they are not morally required to participate. Whether they ultimately help or hinder the cause is not a relevant test of the DDE.

Defining intention in this way may suggest that we have not come very far. Intended side benefits are as subjective and as difficult to determine as is intentional harm. In both cases, observers are dependent upon the admissions of the perpetrators. The fact remains, however, that the admissions are qualitatively different. Few officials or soldiers could admit to intentionally harming civilians without risking the acknowledgement of a grievous breach of humanitarian law and the violation of their own moral sensibilities. They are less reticent, however, about recognizing the deterrent benefits that come from the harm civilians suffer during legitimate military operations. Indeed, military

[20] Ibid.; Geoffrey Best, *Humanity in Warfare* (London: Methuen, 1980), 242–285; Biddle Tami Davis, "Air Power" in Michael Howard, George J. Andreopoulos, and Mark R. Shulman, eds., *The Laws of War: Constraints on Warfare in the Western World* (New Haven, CT: Yale University Press, 1994), 140–159; Frits Kalshoven, *Belligerent Reprisals* (Leyden: A. W. Sijthoff, 1971); George H. Quester, "The Psychological Effects of Bombing Civilian Populations: Wars of the Past" in Betty Glad, ed., *The Psychological Dimensions of War* (Newbury Park, CA: Sage Publications, 1990), 201–235.

planners may find it useful to quietly acknowledge side benefits by suggesting that civilian deaths are neither futile nor entirely unfortunate, both to allay guilt among the bombers and to enhance pacification of the enemy. Here the DDE is particularly important, for it prohibits this line of argument. Side benefits do not mitigate the harm unintentionally befalling civilians. Quite the opposite; when policy makers believe or expect that their strategic bombing has side benefits that come from harm to civilians, they can no longer say that they do not intend to harm civilians. It is then, time to invoke the DDE and prohibit strategic bombing of this sort.

At this juncture, then, there are grounds to argue that Israeli SBs violate the DDE. Israeli actions against Palestinian military targets kill civilians, and this may be inevitable, but once these attacks take notice of the benefits they produce, they violate the DDE and are subject to censure. Are they also subject to reprisal?

Intentionally Targeting Civilians: The Doctrine of Reprisal

As the Israeli case shows, it is often difficult to justify collateral harm to civilians that accompanies counterinsurgency warfare, particularly when this harm is beneficial to the counterinsurgent's cause. In this respect, terror bombing and strategic bombing with intended side effects are equally bad acts. Equally bad acts, in turn, open the door to retaliation and reprisals against civilians. By this argument, civilians retain their protected status but the unique logic of reprisals allows one side to override noncombatant immunity and deliberately target civilians. Reprisals are one of the rare instances in which belligerents are allowed to intentionally harm civilians. Supreme emergency, considered below, is another.

The Logic of Reprisal

Arguments that Palestinian terror attacks are reprisals for Israeli actions or that Israeli attacks on Palestinian terrorists are reprisals for terror are not easily disentangled. The Palestinians, for their part, make the explicit argument that terrorist attacks are reprisals for Israeli attacks on civilians. A nation would not have the right to reprise against attacks on civilians that are sanctioned by the DDE, but if the DDE fails to justify civilian deaths, as in some of the cases noted above, then belligerents may be vulnerable to reprisal.

The principle of "self-help" anchors reprisal and the right of a belligerent to violate the laws of war as a last-resort response to a prior violation by the other side.[21] Reprisals are not acts of ordinary self-defense, for they are an inherently

---

[21] Kalshoven, *Belligerent Reprisals*; Michael Walzer, *Just and Unjust Wars* (New York: Basic Books, 1977), 207–222; Burton M. Leiser, "The Morality of Reprisals," *Ethics* 85 (January 1975): 159–163; Andrew D. Mitchell, "Does One Illegality Merit Another? The Law of Belligerent Reprisals in International Law," *Military Law Review* 170 (December 2001): 155–177.

unlawful response to past, discrete, and unlawful acts. Nor is retribution or vengeance the primary purpose of reprisal. Rather, reprisals are forward looking; they aim to prevent similar, unlawful acts in the future and to restore compliance to international norms of behavior. The underlying logic is utilitarian: reprisals are a legitimate form of international law enforcement because they force violating states to comply with international law. Reprisals, therefore, form a carefully circumscribed form of warfare restrained by strict proportionality. They are guided by the magnitude of the initial infraction, not the goal of deterrence, which, admittedly, might demand far harsher measures than a proportionate response to an adversary's breach of law. This reinforces the one-shot nature of reprisals. Justified by an unlawful act of war, but unlawful acts themselves, reprisals cannot exceed the illegality of the initial infraction. To do otherwise only creates grounds for counterreprisals.

Reprisals against Civilians

Civilians have not always enjoyed protection from the strong urge to reprise against noncombatants. Although the 1949 Geneva Conventions safeguard the lives of civilians in occupied territories, only the 1977 Protocols to the Geneva Conventions, Articles 51–58, protect enemy civilians and civilian objects (property, cultural sites, and places of worship) in unoccupied territory from reprisal. With Protocol I, the international community prohibits reprisals absolutely. Yet some nations, particularly the powerful industrial nations of the West, have been slow to relinquish the right of reprisal. The United States, for example, refused to ratify Protocol I because, among other things, "the total elimination of the right of reprisal ... would hamper the ability of the United States to respond to an enemy's intentional disregard of the limitations established in the Geneva Conventions of 1949 or Protocol I."[22] Although Britain, Italy, France, and Germany ratified Protocol I, each, to varying degrees, reserved the right take measures otherwise prohibited by Protocol I and retaliate against the civilian population of any nation egregiously violating noncombatant immunity.[23] Commenting upon these reservations, Frits Kalshoven cautions that they may set aside a nation's obligation to refrain from reprisals "when the situation turns really serious: a 'worse case reservation' so to speak." The same developments lead Christopher Greenwood to conclude that the "trend in international law against belligerent reprisals has now been taken further than the development of international society can really justify." Ultimately, he warns, the provisions regulating reprisals are "too restrictive

---

[22] Abraham Sofaer, "Agora: The US Decision not to Ratify Protocol 1 to the Geneva Conventions on the Protection of War Victims (contd): The Rationale of the United States Decision," *American Journal of International Law* 4 (October 1988): 784–787.

[23] See "States, Parties and Signatories," accessed at http://www.icrc.org/ihl.nsf/WebNORM?OpenView& Start=1&Count=150&Expand=52.1#52, 14 September 2005.

and likely to be ignored in a conflict marked by large-scale violations of the law by one or more parties."[24]

Reprisals remain attractive for several reasons. One is efficacy: military planners often assume that reprisals against civilians are an effective tool for forcing nations to observe international law. Another is the oft-repeated reference to *lex talonis*, retaliating with evil for evil. This is the simplest reading of Dahlan's warning cited earlier: you kill our civilians and we will kill yours. Although modern treatises on reprisal gloss over *lex talonis* on the assumption that it is but a remnant of primitive law, there is no doubt that targeting civilians in reprisal for unlawful acts of war, particularly those aimed at civilians to begin with, retain a certain appeal based not on vengeance but on simple justice. Civilian lives are precious assets and, if targeted, certainly invite reprisals in kind. Nevertheless, sound moral reasons remain to limit the scope of reprisals while nonetheless permitting recourse to certain forms of reprisal beyond those envisioned by Protocol I.

Limiting Reprisals against Civilians

Utilitarian and deontological arguments go a long way toward discrediting reprisals against civilians. Reprisals are subject to two basic principles of just war: the limited nature of war and the principle of noncombatant immunity. If modern wars are fought to disable rather than annihilate an enemy, they are, in principle, limited. Any practice, therefore, that unnecessarily extends a war or prevents its conclusion is morally objectionable. To meet the condition of limited warfare, reprisals must be effective and must not spiral into a bloody cycle of vengeance and retaliation that only serves to perpetuate hostilities. Unfortunately, reprisals often do just that. The psychological urge to pay back in kind, or worse, is difficult to overcome, and it is doubtful that reprisers would or could respect the rule of proportionality: "You don't understand the logic of vengeance," Claudio Monteverdi admonishes, in *The Coronation of Poppea*: "on every slight pay back in blood and slaughter."[25] Moreover, one cannot seize upon legal lacunae that fail to fully protect civilians from certain acts of war to make a moral argument. If civilian immunity is to have any meaning whatsoever, then ordinary civilians cannot be made to pay for the crimes of others, regardless of the actions of one's state (or quasi-state). Similarly, one

---

[24] Frits Kalshoven, "Belligerent Reprisals Revisited," *Netherlands Yearbook of International Law* 21 (1990): 67; C. Greenwood, "The Twilight of the Law of Belligerent Reprisals," *Netherlands Yearbook of International Law* 20 (1989): 61, 65.

[25] Less poetically: "The psychological reality prompting [reprisals] was often merely thirst for revenge, lust to hurt and punish, or simply self-indulgent desire to save trouble [that] unless carefully regulated tended to escalate into horrid spirals of cruelty and counter-cruelty"; see Best, *Humanity of War*, 167. See also Bryan Brophy-Baermann and John A. Conybeare. "Retaliating against Terrorism: Rational Expectations and the Optimality of Rules vs. Discretion," *American Journal of Political Science* 38 (February 1994): 196–210; and Kalshoven, *Belligerent Reprisals*, 214.

cannot look forward and justify killing one group of civilians to prevent the killing of another group in the future. In neither case has the targeted group lost its right to life. This is the single strongest argument against civilian reprisals and should thoroughly repudiate any attempt by Palestinians to target Israeli citizens in reprisal for Israel's violation of the DDE.

These considerations leave reprisers to target other assets of the offending state. Inasmuch as the military assets of the state are generally vulnerable during wartime and are subject to destruction without moral compunction, the only remaining targets are assets that belong to civilians: their property and their civil rights. Although Protocol I outlaws these targets, together with attacks on civilian lives, the destruction of civilian property and other forms of nonlethal harm remain the last refuge of legitimate reprisal if we take human rights seriously.

Legitimate Reprisal

Israel's policy in response to terror attacks in the Occupied Territories exemplifies some of the limits of legitimate reprisal. These encompass the destruction of property and periodic destruction of physical infrastructures of a nonmilitary nature, measures aimed against civilians short of killing and assassination. Although Israel has argued—unconvincingly, to many observers—that assassinations or targeted killings are legitimate acts of self-defense during wartime, it may be more fruitful to view them as a form of reprisal. Perfidious and treacherous, there are good reasons to conclude that assassination is unlawful.[26] Yet in response to attacks on Israeli civilians, it makes for a legitimate reprisal, even within the narrow parameters of Protocol I, which permits reprisals against military targets: assassination is an "in kind" response to an unlawful act, its aim is to deter future unlawful acts, and it is a proportionate act that aims, unlike most reprisals, at responsible parties operating within an adversary's armed forces. At the same time, there are reasonable efforts to minimize collateral damage.[27]

Acts against civilians that deny civil rather than human rights or aim at civilian property may also form the basis for legitimate reprisals. Human rights protect dignity, innocent life, and bodily integrity and are generally inviolable. Civil liberties, however, remain the purview of the state and include the right of assembly, movement, speech, and political participation. These are not inviolable but, rather, derogable rights and may be set aside or modified, particularly when human rights are at risk. Such is often the case during war.[28]

[26] Michael L. Gross, "Fighting by Other Means in the Mideast: A Critical Analysis of Israel's Assassination Policy," *Political Studies* 51 (June 2003): 350–369.

[27] These efforts are not always successful. According to B'tselem, forty-two civilians were killed and eighty-six Palestinians were assassinated. "Fatalities in the al-Aqsa Intifada, 29 September 2000– 15 February 2003," accessed at http://www.btselem.org/, 18 February 2003.

[28] See also John Rawls, *The Law of Peoples* (Cambridge, MA: Harvard University Press, 1999), 79–80 for a similar distinction. A liberal society upholds human and civil rights, whereas a decent society need only respect human rights. For Rawls, human rights roughly encompass articles 1–18 of the Universal

Unlawful acts by a state, as reprisals are, cannot deprive civilians of their human rights, but they can deprive them of their civil liberties and restrict their freedom of movement. In many ways, Israeli policies of expelling terrorists and their supporters (and families), destroying their homes, and, in general, restricting civilian movement to thwart and apprehend terrorists are reprisals against the citizens of a state that practices terror. Note, however, that reprisals against the civil liberties of civilians do not have the "one-shot" character of expulsions or property destruction pursued against specific individuals in response to specific acts of terror. Restricting the civil liberties of many civilians is continuous and, in this sense, may function as a measure of self-defense rather than reprisal. But this is not always easy to determine. The closure and encirclement of West Bank villages sometimes follow a specific terrorist act; in other instances, they are preventive and are undertaken in anticipation of terrorist activity. Moreover, reprisals against civil liberties are not strictly "in kind." If terrorists deprive their victims of basic human rights, that is, the right to life, reprisals deny civil and property rights, that is, the maximum harm civilians may suffer.

The Limits of Legitimate Reprisal

Reprisal theory has long been noted as a back-door justification for unlawful acts that cannot otherwise be defended. Nevertheless, it does offer legitimate recourse to unlawful action if reprisals are responses to unlawful acts, avoid targeting civilian lives, and are reasonably effective. In the context of Israeli policy, these conditions show just how far one might push reprisal theory. Although reprisals may restrict civil liberties but may not infringe upon human rights, there is no doubt that encircling Palestinian cities and restricting civilian movement creates economic hardship and distress. Reprisals, however, breach their limits when they cause avoidable civilian deaths, as they do, for example, when closures and other measures restricting free movement deny civilians access to medical care.[29] Moreover, reprisals may not directly risk the lives of

---

Declaration of Human Rights. The International Covenant on Civil and Political Rights (1976, Article 4) is less restrictive. The only nonderogable rights during war or public emergency include the right to life, freedom from torture, slavery, servitude, and retroactive legislation, freedom of conscience, the right to recognition before the law, and the right to not be imprisoned for breach of contract.

[29] Human rights organizations document avoidable deaths due to delays at roadblocks as well as increased rates of infant mortality among Palestinians. See Physicians for Human Rights, "Targeting Medical Care: Israel's Recent Incursion into the West Bank Renews Attacks on Ambulances" 4 April 2002, accessed on the website of Physicians for Human Rights, Jerusalem, at http://www.phr.org.il/phr/article.asp?articleid=198&catid=41&pcat=5, 14 September 2005; B'Tselem, The Israeli Information Center for Human Rights in the Occupied Territories, "Wounded in the Field: Impeding Medical Treatment and Firing at Ambulances by IDF Soldiers in the Occupied Territories," accessed on the website of B'Tselem at http://www.btselem.org/Download/200203_Medical_Treatment_Eng.pdf, 14 September 2005; B'Tselem, the Israeli Information Center for Human Rights in the Occupied Territories, "No Way Out: Medical Implications of Israel's Siege Policy," accessed on the website of B'Tselem at http://www.btselem.org/Download/200106_No_Way_Out_Eng.doc, 14 September 2005.

civilians, and although civilians die when assassination attempts go awry, there is increasing concern that these military actions indirectly target civilians to achieve the side benefits described in the previous section. As belligerents cross these lines, it is increasingly difficult to justify reprisal.

However, the strictest limit imposed on reprisals of any kind is effectiveness, and, as many scholars have argued, reprisals are notoriously ineffective.[30] This is no less true in the Israeli case. Assassination, whether construed as self-defense or legitimate reprisal, often brings swift retaliation by Palestinian terrorists. On at least two occasions, in November 2001 and January 2002, assassinations shattered periods of relative quiet, escalated violence, and resulted in scores of dead on both sides. Moreover, the efficacy of reprisal measures against civilians, particularly closure, curfew, expulsions, and the destruction of homes, is open to conflicting interpretations. In early 2003, the Israel Defense Forces announced a turning point in the war against terror, citing a significant decline in the number of successful terror attacks since massive military intervention in April 2002 and, in particular, since the reoccupation of the West Bank in late June 2002.[31] Nonetheless, and in spite of a policy that severely restricts Palestinian civil liberties, civilian casualties on the Israeli side *increased* during that same period.[32] Although military planners claim that they blunted an upwardly moving trend that killed sixty-seven civilians in March 2002, the fact remains that reprisals against Palestinian civilians and militants have not stemmed the tide of Israeli civilian deaths that prompted the reprisals in the first place.

Utilitarian outcomes, particularly the ineffectiveness of reprisals, make it difficult for military planners in Israel to convincingly defend assassinations or restrictive actions against civilians. Ineffectiveness, of course, is not restricted to an evaluation of reprisals and, indeed, should be a factor for assessing any military action. Whether construed as reprisals or legitimate military actions, assassination, closure, curfews, and similar abridgements of civilian civil rights often fail the test of efficacy. Granted, this picture may change, but until there are firm indications that it will, Israeli actions remain unjustifiable. Deontological moral considerations on the other hand, most strikingly those

[30] Ford, "The Morality of Obliteration Bombing," 24, emphasis added.

[31] In the first quarter of 2002, before the operation, there were 40 suicide bombings inside the 1967 borders; in the second quarter, 23, in the third, 17, and in the fourth, 12, and in the first quarter of 2003, 5; see Amos Harel, "Uneasy Quiet on the Western Front, *Ha'aretz*, 24 April 2003; and Amos Harel, "Relative Success Fighting Terror" *Ha'aretz*, 9 February 2003 (Hebrew).

[32] For the twelve-month period (March 2001 through February 2002), 99 civilians were killed by terrorists within the pre-1967 borders (8.25 per month). In March, 2002, 67 civilians were killed, prompting Israeli military action. In the twelve months since March 2002 (April 2002 through March 2003), 159 were killed (13.25 per month). Civilian deaths since 21 June 2002, the date marking the complete reoccupation of the West Bank, total 96 (through March 2003), or 10.7 deaths per month. All figures from B'Tselem, The Israeli Information Center for Human Rights in the Occupied Territories, accessed on the website of B'Tselem at http://www.btselem.org/english/statistics/Casualties.asp, 14 September 2005.

that protect civilians from grievous harm, repudiate any attempt by Palestinians to respond to Israeli injustices by targeting civilians. No degree of necessity, short of dire necessity, can justify intentionally killing civilians.

In contrast to the DDE, reprisals allow one to deliberately target civilians. Although the DDE cannot countenance using bad means to achieve good ends, reprisals do so explicitly and justify harm to civil rights in response to egregious violations of international law, insofar as reprisals are proportionate and effective. Dire necessity, often referred to as "supreme emergency," is different from both the DDE and reprisals. Like reprisals, supreme emergency allows combatants to violate the DDE and intentionally harm civilians. In contrast to reprisals, however, supreme emergency can excuse intentional killing of civilians in the face of an existential threat. In this way, supreme emergency overrides but does not entirely set aside the moral prohibition against killing civilians. As such, any agent invoking a supreme emergency must provide a vigorous defense of his actions.

INTENTIONALLY KILLING NONCOMBATANTS: THE NECESSITY DEFENSE WRIT LARGE

The argument from supreme emergency is perhaps the last that Palestinians and other insurgent groups may raise in defense of intentionally targeting civilians. It is tied to both asymmetry of arms and an imminent existential threat: lacking recourse to similarly lethal weapons, Palestinians have no option but to terrorize Israeli citizens with the hope of demoralizing the nation and forcing a change in Israeli policy, without which the Palestinian people face certain destruction.

The doctrine of supreme emergency, articulated most famously by Michael Walzer, remains exceptionally controversial and extraordinarily difficult to apply in practice.[33] In many regards, it is an extension of the "necessity defense" common to municipal law and anchored in utilitarianism. Necessity may *exempt* from criminal responsibility a person who violates the law in the face of imminent harm, if the individual acts "in order to avoid consequences which could not otherwise be avoided and which would have inflicted grievous harm or injury [and] provided that he or she did no more harm than was reasonably necessary [nor] disproportionate to the harm avoided."[34] Necessity demands five conditions: the threat of (1) grievous and (2) unavoidable harm and a (3) proportionate, (4) effective, and (5) last-resort response. The term "exempt" is subject to conflicting interpretations. Most legal scholars agree that the necessity defense "excuses" rather than "justifies" one's action so that

---

[33] Walzer, *Just and Unjust Wars*, 251–268; see also Brian Orend, "Just and Lawful Conduct in War: Reflections on Michael Walzer," *Law and Philosophy* 20 (January 2000): 1–30.

[34] Israel's Penal Law, section 22, cited in Landau Commission (3,11 "Commission of Inquiry into the Methods of Investigation of the General Security Service Regarding Hostile Terrorist Activity," *Israel Law Review* 2, 3 (Spring, Summer 1989): 146–188.

the law one overrides in the name of necessity retains some measure of force.[35] This force exerts itself in the form of either mitigated punishment or regret and restitution.

Supreme emergency carries this idea to the level of the nation-state or political community facing grievous harm in the form of an existential or genocidal threat that might only be blunted by harming innocents. However, it is important to emphasize that the necessity defense does not have the same legal basis at the international level that it has at the domestic level. International law does not recognize the necessity defense. On the contrary, many international instruments go out of their way to specifically prohibit a nation from violating human rights when facing war or the threat of war. Rather, supreme emergency is a moral argument that belligerents may invoke to convince the international community that their actions are excusable. In the context of the current conflict, the argument from supreme emergency makes three independent claims: First, belligerents may target civilians when their nation faces an existential threat; second, the Palestinians and/or the Israelis face an existential threat; and, third, killing civilians effectively forestalls that threat.

Targeting Innocent Civilians to Forestall Harm

The notion of supreme emergency turns, first and foremost, on the question of whether utility can ever allow one to intentionally kill combatants. Military necessity has always stood juxtaposed to noncombatant immunity, a debate that waged heatedly in the last half of the nineteenth century until decided largely in favor of human rights.[36] As the argument unfolded, the principle of noncombatant immunity assumed either an absolute, inviolable form, which many saw as a necessary bulwark against civilian harm, or a nonabsolutist form that allowed one to override the principle of noncombatant immunity in extreme cases.

Calculating or identifying cases of overriding necessity demands that one first assess simple utility, that is, determine whether an action will bring more good than harm. This requires two calculations that include both the magnitude of the harm one wishes to avoid and the probability that attacking a particular target will effectively forestall the unwanted outcome. If one's goal, for example, is to shorten a war and reduce overall casualties by targeting civilians, one must have an idea as to how many lives will be saved, their relative weights (for combatant and noncombatant lives are not necessarily commensurable), and an indication of the *increased* probability that killing civilians, apart from the other means one takes, will achieve this goal. If not impossible, it remains very difficult to make this calculation and even less likely that the calculation will lend any weight to the

---

[35] David Cohen, "The Development of the Modern Doctrine of Necessity: A Comparative Critique" in Albin Eser and George C. Fletcher, eds., *Justification and Excuse: Comparative Perspectives*, vol. 2 (Freiburg: Eigenverlag MPI, 1987, 1988), 973–1001.

[36] Best, *Humanity in Warfare*, 174–179.

utility of intentionally killing noncombatants. If WWII is any example, killing civilians does not significantly raise the chances that war will end any sooner or save a significant number of additional lives.[37]

Beyond this, one has to ask whether utility alone is sufficient justification for egregiously violating noncombatant immunity. Absolutists will deny, of course, that utility can ever justify intentionally killing civilians, but nonabsolutists, too, are wary of utility. Some scholars back off, arguing that the complex calculations just mentioned are impossible to make during wartime.[38] Others suggest that the test is not simple utility but overwhelming utility. Killing civilians must not only tip the scales in favor of marginally increased utility, it must decisively forestall a significantly more harmful outcome. Under these conditions, respect for innocent life may be put aside if a nation is faced with *substantial* harm, that is, genocide or the annihilation of its political community. Assuming that one can distinguish between simple and overwhelming utility, one must also contend with a workable definition of "substantial harm."

The Nature of Substantial Harm

For a nation to invoke the necessity defense, it must face a grievous and unavoidable threat, and target civilians only as a last resort and in a way that is proportionate and effectively meets the threat before it. What constitutes a threat of this magnitude? If confined to an existential threat, then the conditions of supreme emergency are not met unless a nation or ethnic group faces genocide. Yet, genocide constitutes nothing less than a massive war crime that either brings about the collapse of the entire war convention or, at the very least, allows the aggrieved party the right to retaliate in kind. This is certainly what Britain and the United States have in mind as they look askance at Protocol I's prohibition of reprisals against civilian populations. If, on the other hand, supreme emergency is interpreted to include any threat that war poses to a political community, then the prospect of defeat alone is sufficient to allow the threatened party to attack innocent civilians. This cannot be right, for it renders the war convention entirely superfluous. Yet, if one takes seriously the example many commentators use to illustrate supreme emergency, namely Britain's position vis-a-vis Germany in the early part of WWII, then it is hard to escape the impression that the mere prospect of defeat is sufficient to trigger a supreme emergency.

Imagine France prior to its surrender. Would the probability of defeat and occupation have constituted a supreme emergency? If so, it seems that losing sides everywhere might call upon supreme necessity to justify violations of noncombatant immunity. The bombing of Hiroshima is an even less-convincing

---

[37] See Quester, "The Psychological Effects," 201–235.

[38] C. Curran, *Themes in Fundamental Moral Theology* (Notre Dame, IN: University of Notre Dame Press, 1977) cited in Coates, *The Ethics of War*, 261.

example of supreme emergency. After abandoning its preference for precision bombing and cooperating with the British in the firebombing of Dresden in February 1945, the United States mounted similar raids of its own against Tokyo and other Japanese cities. Nuclear bombing—considered nothing more than a natural progression of strategic, incendiary bombing—followed in quick succession. The effects of both types of warfare, together with their underlying logic, are nearly identical. Killing tens of thousands in a single raid, military planners could only appeal to military necessity to justify these massive civilian casualties. The argument, however, remains intensely problematic. By 1945, military necessity could not mean supreme emergency, for neither the United States nor its allies faced an existential threat. Interpreting military necessity more narrowly to justify killing enemy civilians to save the lives of American soldiers entirely undermines the principle of noncombatant immunity. Assuming, for a moment, that one can ignore the controversy surrounding the last months of WWII and can suggest that area bombing breaks morale, that the course of events entirely justified Allied goals of unconditional surrender, and that destroying Tokyo, Hiroshima, and Nagasaki were necessary and proportionate means to attain this end, one is still left with the simple argument that any prospect of casualties or defeat justifies intentional harm to noncombatants. The argument may be tempting, but it leaves humanitarian law in tatters. Just as no nation may invoke supreme emergency when it faces any fate less than genocide, no army may appeal to the same principle to stave off defeat or expedite its war.

In the current Middle East conflict, neither party faces an existential threat, but each is subject instead to the relative disadvantages at which warring parties are apt to find themselves. The claim that the Palestinians went to war to wrest additional political concessions from Israel following the collapse of peace talks at Camp David is probably correct.[39] Nevertheless, the Palestinian refusal to accept Israel's offer of less than 100 percent of the West Bank and Gaza, together with the continued occupation that ensued, only serve, at best, as *casus belli*; they do not serve to legitimate attacks on Israeli civilians. Palestinians may claim that terror has brought them closer to political independence,[40] but this is not the test of supreme emergency. One invokes supreme emergency to prevent disaster, not to expedite war. The fact that Palestinians cannot formulate their gains in terms of preventing disaster points readily to the absence of any

---

[39] Yezid Sayigh, "Arafat and the Anatomy of a Revolt," *Survival* 43 (Autumn 2001): 47–60; Kirsten E. Schulze, "Camp David and the Al-Aqsa Intifada: An Assessment of the State of the Israeli-Palestinian Peace Process, July–December 2000," *Studies in Conflict and Terrorism* 24 (May–June, 2001): 215–233; Rema Hammami and Salim Tamari, "The Second Uprising: End or New Beginning?" *Journal of Palestine Studies* 30 (Winter 2001): 5–25; David Makovsky, "Taba Mischief," *The Public Interest* 151 (Spring 2003): 119–129.

[40] In a 2002 poll, 66 percent of Palestinians believed that armed confrontations have so far helped to achieve Palestinian rights in ways that negotiations could not. Palestinian Center for Policy and Survey Research, Public Opinion Poll # 6, 14–22 November 2002, accessed at http://www.pcpsr.org/survey/polls/2002/p6a.html, 11 February 2003.

existential threat. Any political arrangement, such as that outlined by Bill Clinton's peace plan, that preserves a measure of national autonomy, let alone a measure of sovereignty and independence, cannot be construed as a threat to the political community. Otherwise, any group denied political independence has grounds to claim supreme emergency and to slaughter its adversary's citizens. The fact that some groups make this claim only indicates that they misunderstand the rights of a political community. These rights cannot always entail national independence on one group's terms alone.

The Israeli case for supreme emergency is similarly confounded when sometimes raised to justify violations of humanitarian law or disregard for civilian life. Talk of supreme emergency surfaces frequently on the Israeli side, inasmuch as many observers describe terror as an existential threat to the Jewish state. But, if the conditions just described are correct, Israel no more faces an existential threat than do the Palestinians. Terror, however heinous, does not jeopardize the political integrity of Israel. As a result, there are no grounds for invoking supreme emergency to justify violating humanitarian law. As long as Israel violates the nonhumanitarian aspects of international law, that is, civil and not human rights, then their actions constitute legitimate reprisal. Embracing terror, the Palestinians do not have recourse to this claim. Once the claim of an existential threat is set aside, there is no place to evaluate the morality of the response. Because no response is warranted, any discussion of the other conditions of necessity—proportionality and last resort—is irrelevant in the context of the current Mideast conflict.

These arguments should also go a long way toward repudiating the claim that asymmetry of arms justifies terrorism as a "last-resort" form of warfare. In response to occupation, and to the counterinsurgency warfare it often entails, groups fighting for national self-determination sometimes suggest that their relative lack of arms coupled with the justice of their cause justifies deviating from the rules of war and humanitarian law. It is odd that the argument has surfaced with such regularity in recent times, when, in fact, material asymmetry is the rule rather than the exception in armed conflict. Were adversaries symmetrically armed, war would rarely begin and nearly never end. Instead, nations often go to war, justifiably or not, when they assume that they have a material edge. They demur when they sense a disadvantage. Nevertheless, a disadvantaged nation forced to defend itself is not released from its international and humanitarian obligations. "In ships we are inferior [and] in money we have a far greater deficiency," warns Archidamus as he counsels his countrymen to avoid war with Athens. Nevertheless, he continues, "if while still unprepared we are induced to lay waste have a care that we do not bring deep disgrace and deep perplexity upon Peloponnese." All this in spite of Athens's "open" aggression.[41]

---

[41] Thucydides, *The Peloponnesian War*, the Crawley translation, revised and edited with an introduction by T. E. Wick (New York: The Modern Library, 1982), I, 80–82. I admit to a rather liberal interpretation. Archidamus may simply be saying, "If you must go to war, make sure you don't lose."

Today the lesson resonates stronger still. A material disadvantage does not exempt an adversary from norms of conduct during armed conflict as long as the stronger nation respects humanitarian law and pursues a limited war rather than a total war of annihilation against the weaker nation. Should the stronger nation abuse civilians and pursue a genocidal war, then, and only then, might the weaker nation consider setting aside humanitarian law. There is nothing in the current conflict, however, to suggest that this is the case.

Conclusion: Terror, Counterterror, and Noncombatant Immunity

Arguments justifying terror fall before the principle of noncombatant immunity. But as they do, they redefine the very nature of the debate and bring to the fore a number of important theoretical and practical conclusions. First, they force a close reading of the doctrine of double effect, raising the DDE not so much to justify terror but to condemn counterinsurgency warfare that kills civilians. By prohibiting belligerents from intentionally killing civilians and by measuring intentionality by means of side benefits, the DDE casts a pall over what many think is legitimate collateral damage during battles with insurgents.

Second, a clear understanding of modern reprisals stymies any attempt to argue that terror is a legitimate form of reprisal when an adversary violates the DDE. The argument is not trivial, for enemy civilians have been, for the longest time, acceptable targets of reprisal. If this changed in 1977, it may not be of much concern to Israelis and Palestinians, who neither ratified Protocol I nor entirely removed themselves from the culture of blood feuds, vengeance, and retribution that characterizes the new-old Middle East. Nevertheless, reprisal theory has moved toward honoring the same combatant and noncombatant rights that Palestinians wish to claim for their own. This forbids reprisals against civilian lives. For Israelis, this limits counterinsurgency measures to those that effectively prevent terror, and, although these actions may abridge civil rights, they must preserve human rights. Closure, siege, expulsion, and property destruction sometimes meet these criteria. For Palestinians, their means are necessarily limited to attacks on military targets and civilian property or, should they be inclined to pursue it, nonviolent means of fighting occupation.

Third, the argument of supreme emergency points to the limits of the argument from material asymmetry. Material asymmetry is an ever-present feature of war, whether waged between state actors or between state and substate actors fighting for national self-determination. Yet neither asymmetry nor occupation offers sufficient cause for violating noncombatant immunity. On the contrary, they offer grounds for broadening the protection due combatants and noncombatants under humanitarian law. Protocol I addresses this concern directly, inasmuch as it extends combatant status to irregular, insurgent forces, ensuring that they will not be tortured or killed when captured and, at the same time, widens the range of noncombatant immunities to protect civilians from the ravages of a war of national self-determination against an adversary determined to deny them their just rights.

There is nothing in this formulation, however, to protect the citizens and armed forces of an occupying power when insurgents violate humanitarian law. On the contrary, Protocol I deliberately hamstrings occupying forces who may find themselves unable to clearly identify combatants and severely constrains the actions they can take against civilians. This may tempt insurgents to abuse combatant and noncombatant protections and pursue terror. It further forces the occupying power to make a hard choice: either develop novel tactics that may infringe on civil liberties or dispense with humanitarian law altogether. Although it is unlikely that any Western nation will argue that terrorism justifies a reciprocal breach of international law, nations fighting insurgents that embrace terror should be free to make the weaker claim that self-defense allows certain measures that infringe upon civil rights or jeopardize civilian property.

Occupation and terror test the limits of humanitarian law and, in particular, the principle of noncombatant immunity. Each side often sees itself as significantly disadvantaged. Palestinians complain of their inability to respond to modern military technology in kind and Israelis of their inability to respond to terror in kind. Yet, in the context of modern warfare and humanitarian law, there is no doubt that Israel enjoys a clear advantage. Terror and reprisals against civilian lives have no place in the international order, whereas collateral damage and reprisals against civilian civil rights do. There is, it appears, a moral as well as material asymmetry relative to the means each side employs in the current conflict.

It is ironic that an occupying power should find itself in such a position, successfully pleading self-defense and military necessity against a far weaker adversary. Two points are, however, in order. First, Israel's advantages are limited, even as it fights terror. Neither the DDE nor reprisal theory can justify all aspects of current Israeli policy. The discussions above have shown this much. Second, the moral asymmetry currently in Israel's favor will reverse once terror is abandoned. Once the Palestinians or any other insurgent group renounces terror and restores the principle of noncombatant immunity, they may find it possible to reenter the community of nations and successfully press their claims for national self-determination.

Tragic Choices in the War on Terrorism: Should We Try to Regulate and Control Torture?

JEROME SLATER

What should be done about the problem of torture in the war on terrorism? Which is better—or worse: the continuation of a principled but ineffective "ban" on torture, or an effort to seriously regulate and control torture, at the price of its partial legitimization?

Until 11 September 2001, the issue scarcely arose. Since the end of the eighteenth century, nearly every civilized society and moral system, certainly including the Judeo-Christian, or Western, moral system, in principle (although not always in practice) has regarded torture as an unmitigated evil, the moral prohibition against which was to be regarded as absolute.[1] Since September 11, however, many Americans—not just government officials, but a number of moral and legal philosophers, as well as media commentators—are far from sure that torture must be excluded from our defenses against truly catastrophic terrorism. In any case, there no longer can be any question that since September 11, agencies of the American government, particularly the armed forces and the Central Intelligence Agency (CIA), have systematically used various forms of physical and psychological coercion, beatings, or even outright torture (especially "waterboarding," or near-drowning) on suspected terrorists, both directly, as in Afghanistan, Iraq, and Guantanamo Bay, or indi-

[1] For a brief history of the use of torture in European judicial systems and practice, see James Ross, "A History of Torture" in Kenneth Roth, Minky Worden, and Amy D. Bernstein, eds., *Torture: Does it Make Us Safer? Is It Ever OK?: A Human Rights Perspective* (New York: Human Rights Watch, 2005), 3–17.

JEROME SLATER, a frequent contributor to *Political Science Quarterly*, is a university research scholar at the State University of New York at Buffalo. He is working on a history of U.S. policy in the Arab-Israeli conflict.

rectly, by turning over suspected terrorists to allied states that are known to torture.[2]

To be sure, in some cases, lower-level soldiers have apparently gone beyond what was authorized, or at least tacitly condoned. However, various reports and investigations have left no serious doubt that the overall use of methods that have long been considered to amount to torture, or something close to it, have been either authorized, defended as legal, or, at a minimum, condoned at the highest levels of the American government, apparently including Secretary of Defense Donald Rumsfeld, if not beyond him.[3]

Assuming that this assessment is accurate, what can be done about it? Even more pointedly, what *should* be done about it? I will address these issues in the framework of traditional just-war analysis, a very useful perspective that often has been neglected in the recent discussions about torture. My premise is that the war on Islamic terrorism is indeed legitimately regarded as a war, however untraditional; if so, I will argue, the issues raised by torture should be regarded as simply a special case of the issues raised by any normally unjust means that may or may not be employed in a just war.

There are essentially three positions that can be taken about the problem of torture. The first is the traditional moral position: torture is categorically (that is, absolutely) prohibited, and there are no exceptions.

[2] These practices have been revealed in reports by the International Red Cross, Human Rights Watch, and Amnesty International; by a number of investigative reporters; and even by internal American military investigations that have been leaked to the press. The most detailed and authoritative works are Amnesty International, "Guantanamo and Beyond," May 2005; Mark Bowden, "The Dark Art of Interrogation," *Atlantic Monthly*, October 2003, 51–76; Mark Danner, *Torture and Truth: America, Abu Ghraib, and the War on Torture* (New York: New York Review of Books, 2004); Seymour M. Hersh, *Chain of Command: The Road from 9/11 to Abu Ghraib* (New York: HarperCollins, 2004); Human Rights Watch, "Torture in Iraq," 25 September 2005; Joseph Lelyveld, "Interrogating Ourselves," *New York Times Magazine*, 12 June 2005, 36–69; Jane Mayer, "The Experiment," *New Yorker*, 11 and 18 July 2005; PBS *Frontline* Special Report, "The Torture Question," 19 October 2005. See also Carlotta Gall, "Rights Group Reports Deaths of Men Held by U.S. in Afghanistan," *New York Times*, 14 December 2004 and 19 December 2005; David Johnston and James Risen, "The Reach of War: The Interrogations," *New York Times*, 27 June 2004; David Johnston, "Rights Group Cites Rumsfeld and Tenet in Report on Abuse," *New York Times*, 24 April 2005; Warren Hoge, "Investigators for UN Urge U.S. to Close Guantanamo," *New York Times*, 17 February 2006; Douglas Jehl, "Report Warned on CIA's Tactics in Interrogation," *New York Times*, 9 November 2005; Anthony Lewis, "Making Torture Legal," *New York Review of Books*, 15 July 2004; Eric Schmitt and David Rohde, "About 2 Dozen GIs to Face Trial or Other Punishment in Deaths of 2 Afghan Prisoners," *New York Times*, 2 September 2004.

[3] For a summary of the evidence that torture and actions "tantamount to torture" (in the language of a report by the International Red Cross) are "a direct product of an environment of lawlessness, created by policy decisions taken at the highest levels of the Bush Administration," see Kenneth Roth, "Justifying Torture" in Roth, Worden, and Bernstein, eds., *Torture; Does It Make Us Safer?*, 191. For a similar assessment, charging that the Bush Administration had made "a deliberate policy choice" to employ abusive interrogation in the interrogation of terrorism suspects, see the 2005 Annual Report of Human Rights Watch, summarized in "Rights Group Assails the U.S. Over Abuse of Terror Suspects," *New York Times*, 19 January 2006.

The second position is that the legal and moral norm of categorical prohibition must be maintained in principle, law, and rhetoric—even as we recognize and tacitly accept that there might be certain exceptional circumstances in
which there is a strong case for overriding the norm. Thus, although we should
not provide the authorities with any institutionalized or advance authorization
for torture, in the exceptional cases we may rightfully decide not to punish
those representatives of the state who have violated the norm. "We'll do what
we have to do," as Joseph Lelyveld puts it: "Don't ask, don't tell."[4]

The third position is that terrorism—especially but not necessarily limited
to terrorism with weapons of mass destruction (WMD)—is likely to be a long-
term if not permanent threat and is so grave that "exceptional circumstances"
have become the norm. Consequently, the task today is to create some type of
legal and institutional framework for the regulation and control of torture, to
ensure that it is resorted to in the war on terrorism *only* when the consequences
of not doing so are so terrible as to outweigh the terrible nature of torture itself.

I shall defend the third position, arguing that the question of means in just
wars must be considered from two different perspectives (sometimes com-
plementary, but sometimes in conflict): that of national security, and that of
morality or justice. Proceeding from that premise, I shall argue that in the war
on terrorism, physical or psychological coercion and, in especially exceptional
circumstances, even outright torture may be defensible from both of those
perspectives, certainly from the perspective of national security, and even—as
a lesser evil—in terms of moral consequences. At the same time, however, the
risks that torture will be used—indeed, is already being used—when it is *not*
defensible from either perspective are so great that serious institutional controls over torture must be established.

Perhaps I should add this: in making this admittedly painful argument, it is
not my intention to be polemical. The torture issue is no longer considered to
be beyond—or beneath—debate. My purpose here is to join this emerging
debate, both at the analytical level and to make explicit the arguments and
policy suggestions that seem to follow from the analysis. However, inasmuch as
we are still at an early stage in this debate, those who are participating in it may
well make logical, moral, or empirical errors; if these occur, they can be corrected only by further debate.

DEBATING TORTURE: THE RECENT LITERATURE

Until quite recently, there has been considerable doubt among moral, legal,
and political philosophers about whether there ought to be any public debate
about torture. Most of these thinkers believed that torture should be regarded
as simply beyond the pale; public discussion or debate might have the perverse
consequence of legitimating it. Indeed, even the few scholars who argued that

---

[4] Lelyveld, "Interrogating Ourselves," 69.

torture could sometimes be seen as a lesser evil sometimes conceded that the risk of legitimation precluded public discussion. Whatever the validity of this concern, the issue is now moot. In the last few years, there have been a number of discussions of the torture issue in leading media, as well as in academic conferences and, especially, in the recent publication of major works by some of America's leading political, legal, and moral thinkers.[5] Thus, the meta debate (that is, should there be a debate?) is effectively over, and the substantive debate has begun.[6]

The main issues in this debate are these: What constitutes torture? Should all forms of physical or mental coercion be considered torture? If so, should all of them be unconditionally prohibited? If, on the other hand, it is legitimate to make distinctions, where is the line to be drawn? Are there real-world cases in which some kinds of coercion—or perhaps, in extreme cases, *any* kind of coercion, including torture by any definition—are morally justifiable, if only by a lesser-evil argument? If so—and in the context of the existing realities, this may be the most important question of them all—how can coercion or torture be limited to only those cases in which it is indeed a lesser evil?

What Is Torture?

Surprisingly, the very definition of torture has become more controversial in the last few years, and efforts to clarify it for both legal and moral purposes have created a dilemma: if it is defined too broadly, it fails to make morally relevant distinctions, but if it is defined too narrowly, it opens the door to various euphemisms that may seem to condone many forms of severe prisoner abuse that fall outside the definition.

According to all the major dictionaries, torture means more than the infliction of physical duress, stress, or even mere pain; it consists of the infliction of "intense," "excruciating," "great," or "severe" pain.[7] Similarly, the UN

---

[5] The major works that will be examined here are Karen J. Greenberg, ed., *The Torture Debate in America* (New York: Cambridge University Press, 2006); Philip B. Heymann and Juliette N. Kayyem, *Protecting Liberty in an Age of Terror* (Cambridge, MA: MIT Press, 2005); Michael Ignatieff, *The Lesser Evil: Political Ethics in an Age of Terror* (Princeton, NJ: Princeton University Press, 2004); Sanford Levinson, ed., *Torture: A Collection* (New York: Oxford University Press, 2004); Roth, Worden, and Bernstein, eds., *Torture: Does It Make Us Safer?*; Michael Walzer, *Arguing About War* (New Haven, CT: Yale University Press, 2004).

[6] A useful discussion of the meta debate can be found in Oren Gross, "The Prohibition on Torture and the Limits of the Law" in Levinson, ed., *Torture: A Collection*, 249–250. Gross concludes that public debate on torture is critical: "The alternative to no debate ... (or, indeed, to discussion that merely consists of repeating the mantra that torture must be absolutely prohibited) is not the disappearance of the practice of torture. ... By not discussing [torture] ... we do not make it go away; we drive it underground. ... We may as well make ... choices in as informed a manner as possible, taking into account the widest panoply of relevant moral and legal considerations."

[7] See Webster's Third New International Dictionary, the Oxford English Dictionary, and Cambridge International Dictionary.

Convention Against Torture (to which the United States is a party) distinguishes between torture ("any act by which severe pain or suffering, whether physical or mental, is inflicted") and "other acts of cruel, inhuman, or degrading treatment or punishment which do not amount to torture." Although both are legally prohibited, only "torture" is done so in absolute terms: "No exceptional circumstances whatsoever, whether a state of war...or any other public emergency, may be invoked as a justification of torture."

Pentagon officials and legal advisers to the administration of George W. Bush have relied on these dictionary and UN definitions to deny that recently revealed U.S. interrogation measures—such as hooding prisoners, keeping them naked, binding them in painful "stress" positions, threatening them with dogs, subjecting them to sustained loud noises as well as heat and cold, or depriving of them sleep—constitute torture. In their initial position (the Bybee memorandum), Bush legal advisers sought to narrow the definition even further, taking advantage of the UN language in order to distinguish interrogation methods that were "merely" cruel, inhuman, or degrading from outright torture, defined as actions that "produce pain and suffering...equivalent in intensity to the pain accompanying serious physical injury, such as organ failure, impairment of bodily function, or even death."[8] However, after severe criticism, the Justice Department formally retreated from the Bybee memorandum in late 2004; the Bush administration now officially accepts that any "severe" physical and mental pain and suffering constitutes torture and is therefore prohibited by U.S. as well as international law.[9]

In some recent discussions of the torture issue, the varying administration distinctions have been regarded as meaningless or hypocritical, mere euphemisms that are designed to conceal the harsh reality that "at the highest levels of the Pentagon there was an interest in using torture as well as a desire to evade the criminal consequences of doing so."[10] Yet, although lawyers for the Bush administration are hardly disinterested parties in the debate over torture, it is undeniable that most of the other major participants in the ongoing debate are agreed on the need to distinguish torture from lesser abuses, suggesting

---

[8] Memorandum from Assistant Attorney General Jay Bybee, 1 August 2002, reprinted in Danner, *Torture and Truth*, 115, 141.

[9] On the revised administration position, see a statement of Secretary of State Condoleeza Rice, in Joel Brinkley, "U.S. Interrogations Are Saving Lives, Rice Says," *New York Times*, 6 December 2005, and Neil A. Lewis, "U.S. Spells Out New Definition Curbing Torture," *New York Times*, 1 January 2005. However, a number of investigations have established that the administration has used "waterboarding" in its interrogations of captured high-level al Qaeda officials. Waterboarding—forcing a person's head under water until he almost drowns, or at least fears drowning—is torture by any reasonable definition; nonetheless, Porter Goss, the head of the CIA, has defended it as "a professional interrogation technique." Roth, "Justifying Torture" in Roth, Worden, and Bernstein, eds., *Torture: Does It Make Us Safer?*, 194.

[10] James Fellner, director of U.S. programs for Human Rights Watch, quoted in "The Reach of War: Legal Opinions," *New York Times*, 8 June 2004.

names like "coercion," "physical or mental abuse," "torture lite,"[11] or "highly coercive interrogation."[12]

The case for drawing distinctions is a strong one. If we were to insist that torture must be understood as comprising all forms of interrogation that go beyond the noncoercive, we would then have to invent other words to capture the morally relevant distinctions between, say, sleep deprivation and other kinds of nonfatal physical and mental pressures and the more truly fiendish, nearly unimaginable forms of torture or murder that fanatics, sadists, or psychotic autocrats have inflicted on their victims throughout history.

That said, the rather odd distinctions in the UN Convention Against Torture will not do; the distinction between torture and "cruel, inhuman, or degrading" treatment does not seem morally compelling. Similarly, it is not clear that the distinction between "highly coercive interrogation" and "torture" is meaningful—at least not sufficiently meaningful that the former may sometimes be acceptable but the latter must always be categorically prohibited. Perhaps the best solution is to distinguish between "torture," which should continue to be defined as the infliction of severe physical or mental pain, and "coercion," defined as significantly less-severe measures than torture (as already mentioned, stress binding, sleep deprivation, exposure to heat and cold, and the like)—although such measures, if sufficiently intense and sustained, might well become indistinguishable from outright torture. In short, in order to maintain the dictionary and everyday usages as well as to facilitate the making of morally relevant distinctions, it is important to distinguish between torture and coercion, even though sometimes the line between them may be thin.

IS TORTURE OR COERCION EVER MORALLY ALLOWABLE?

At least among lawyers and legal scholars who are not working for the Bush administration, there is no serious doubt that not merely outright torture but all forms of "cruel, inhuman, or degrading practices" or physical coercion are illegal under American law, whether derived from the Constitution, from congressional legislation (such as the recent McCain amendment), or from international treaties to which the United States is legally bound. Thus, the central issue in the current debate is—or should be—whether the terrorist threat has made current law outmoded, considered from the perspectives of both national security and morally acceptable consequences.

As is widely understood, the most extreme case that would test the existing categorical prohibitions on torture—so far hypothetical, but one that may not be remote in the foreseeable future—would be an apparently imminent terrorist attack against cities, using biological or nuclear weapons that could kill hundreds of thousands of innocents. Less extreme are the already-existing

---

[11] Bowden, "The Dark Art of Interrogation," 4.
[12] Heymann and Kayyem, *Protecting Liberty*, 12.

cases, which are highly likely to reoccur—non-WMD terrorist attacks that do not destroy entire cities but do kill large numbers of innocents, as in the terrorist attacks on the World Trade Center and on the passenger trains in Madrid.

Just-war Theory and the Torture Issue

The most useful, systematic, and sophisticated framework in which to examine the moral issue of torture in the war on terrorism is just-war theory. A good place to begin is with a reexamination of the writing of Michael Walzer, the most authoritative contemporary just-war thinker,[13] following with an assessment of two recent major philosophical books that analyze, either explicitly or inferentially, the torture issue in just-war terms: Michael Ignatieff, *The Lesser Evil: Political Ethics in an Age of Terror* (Princeton University Press, 2004), and Sanford Levinson, ed., *Torture: A Collection* (New York: Oxford University Press, 2004).

Both Walzer and Ignatieff consider the age-old but still perplexing issue of whether "the end justifies the means": is it morally allowable to use unjust means if the use of them is necessary to reach a just end or realize a just cause? In broad terms, there are two different philosophical or ethical systems or traditions that consider this issue: consequentialism (or utilitarianism) and categorical morality. Consequentialist moral reasoning holds that we may morally judge actions only in terms of their practical consequences; categorical morality holds that there are certain rules or principles that must never be violated, regardless of the circumstances—or, as the Catholic moral tradition holds, evil may never be done so that good can come of it.

In general, Walzer is a categorical moralist, for he insists that we must make separate moral evaluations of the causes for which wars are fought (*jus ad bellum*) and the means by which wars are fought (*jus in bello*). Even just wars, then, are absolutely prohibited from employing unjust means, which principally means that innocent civilians or noncombatants may never be deliberately attacked. The same reasoning, it would appear, would preclude the use of torture—surely an unjust means.

There is, however, one critically important exception to Walzer's application of categorical morality to warfare: "supreme emergency," which "exists when our deepest values and our collective survival are in imminent danger."[14] Walzer examines the British bombing of German cities early in World War II, when Britain's defeat seemed imminent, no other means of defense was working, and the bombing of cities seemed to have some chance of dissuading Hitler

---

[13] Michael Walzer, *Just and Unjust Wars* (New York: Basic Books, 1977); Michael Walzer, *Arguing About War* (New Haven, CT: Yale University Press, 2004). Although Walzer does not directly address the issue of torture, it seems reasonable to infer his position, both from his overall moral philosophy as well as his decision to allow the reprinting of his famous essay, "Political Action: The Problem of Dirty Hands" in Levinson, ed., *Torture: A Collection*, 61–75.

[14] Walzer, *Arguing About War*, 33.

from attacking. In these circumstances of "supreme emergency," Walzer becomes a consequentialist:[15] there are no longer any prohibitions on methods that are genuinely necessary to win a just war, not even indiscriminate bombing of cities. In his recent work, Walzer puts it this way: "When our deepest values are radically at risk, the constraints lose their grip, and a certain kind of utilitarianism reimposes itself. I call this the utilitarianism of extremity, and I set it against a rights normality. ... No government can put the life of the community itself and of all its members at risk, so long as there are actions available to it, even immoral actions, that would avoid or reduce the risk."[16]

To be sure, not everyone accepts Walzer's supreme emergency argument, but for those who do (like this author), the same logic must hold true for torture. That is, if it is not categorically prohibited to deliberately attack many thousands of innocent civilians if and when no other means in a just war are available to ensure the literal survival of entire societies, then it is hard to see why it should be absolutely forbidden to torture terrorist combatants if it is necessary to do so to save cities—or even, perhaps, when the stakes in terms of innocent lives are very high but short of constituting a supreme emergency. I shall return to this argument below.

It is an observable and unsurprising fact that in this debate, there is a direct relationship between how seriously one takes the threat of mass-casualty terrorism and the position one takes on the torture issue. Some of those who are participating in the recent debate seem to implicitly or even explicitly minimize the threat.[17] That is not the view, however, of the National Commission on Terrorist Attacks Upon the United States (hereinafter, 9/11 Commission), which cited the evidence that Osama bin Laden and al Qaeda have been actively seeking to acquire WMD, nor of most academic specialists in international security—particularly those who have some governmental experience in either defense or intelligence agencies.[18]

---

[15] But *only* in these circumstances, as opposed to the later British and American city bombings of Germany and Japan, when the allied victory was already assured.

[16] Walzer, *Arguing About War*, 40, 42.

[17] For example, the journalist and commentator William Pfaff writes that to most of the democratic world, the American claims about the threat of terrorism seem grossly exaggerated, and therefore U.S. behavior is disproportionate. William Pfaff, "What We've Lost: George W. Bush and the Price of Torture," *Harper's Magazine*, November 2005, 50–56. Similarly, the General Counsel for Human Rights Watch clearly minimizes the dangers of WMD terrorism when she denies that "we live in an entirely different world than has ever existed at any time or place." (Dinah Pokempner, "Command Responsibility for Torture" in Roth, Worden, and Bernstein, eds., *Torture: Does It Ever Make Us Safer?*, 171. The lawyer Joshua Dratel, the law professor Stephen Holmes, and the legal philosopher David Luban also tend to dismiss the WMD threat as exaggerated, not "realistic," or not "representative." Greenberg, ed., *The Torture Debate*; see especially 114, 127.

[18] On the September 11th Commission's finding, see its *Final Report*, 4 August 2004. See also the authoritative work by a leading academician and former high government official, Graham Allison, *Nuclear Terrorism: The Ultimate Preventable Catastrophe* (New York: New York Times Books, 2004). Stephen Van Evera of MIT, another leading national security expert, points out that Osama Bin

Thomas Kean, chairman of the 9/11 Commission, has summed up the consensus of the governmental and academic specialists: "We have no greater fear than a terrorist who is inside the United States with a nuclear weapon. The consequences of such an attack would be catastrophic for our people, for our economy, for our liberties."[19] Indeed, if anything, this formulation *understates* the threat: why just one nuclear weapon in one city? If organized terrorist groups succeed in acquiring and detonating one nuclear weapon in one city, what will prevent them from acquiring other nuclear weapons and detonating them in other cities?

In short, a review of the literature suggests that the more seriously one takes the threat of terrorism—especially, but not necessarily exclusively, the threat of WMD terrorism—the less persuasive are the arguments against coercive interrogations, "torture lite," or even, in some instances, outright torture. One of the few exceptions is Michael Ignatieff, whose credentials in national security are not in doubt. Ignatieff argues for a categorical or absolute prohibition against not only torture but also physical (although not "nonphysical") coercion. Presumably, then, he would hold to these prohibitions even in the case of a genuine supreme emergency, such as an imminent WMD attack against a city.[20] Leaving aside, for the moment, whether this is a morally persuasive position, it would seem to be quite anomalous in light of Ignatieff's overall consequentialist argument that in the war on terrorism, it will be necessary to choose lesser evils to avoid even greater ones, and that included among these necessary and justified lesser evils are various forms of violence, assassinations, and perhaps even preemptive war.

Laden has explicitly said that "to kill Americans ... civilian and military—is an individual duty for every Muslim" and that al Queda's press spokesman, Suleiman Abu Ghaith, "has claimed the right to kill four million Americans, including two million children." Van Evera further notes that the leaders of al Qaeda "seek to acquire weapons of mass destruction and may also have the opportunity: enough nuclear materials remain poorly secured in Russia to make tens of thousands of Hiroshima-sized atomic bombs. Many Soviet nuclear and biological weapons scientists also remain underpaid or unemployed, ripe for hiring by terrorists." Stephen Van Evera, "Why U.S. National Security Requires Mideast Peace," MIT Center for International Studies, May 2005, 1–2.

[19] Quoted in Philip Shenon, "Sept. 11 Report Card Assails U.S. Progress Against Terror," *New York Times*, 15 November 2005.

[20] To be sure, Ignatieff does concede that "when we have to face terrorists who control weapons of mass destruction ... most bets—and gloves—would be off." Ignatieff, "The Lesser Evil," 10. But this is not his judgment of what, morally speaking, should or at least must be done, but only his prediction of what realistically will happen. In a more recent essay, Ignatieff similarly hedges his argument a bit, conceding that most Americans will not agree with him, and that in a crisis they will "privilege security over liberty and thus reluctantly endorse torture in their name." Michael Ignatieff, "Moral Prohibition At a Price" in Roth, Worden, and Bernstein, eds., *Torture: Does It Ever Make Us Safer?*, 27. Although this concession is not inconsistent with his normative position, it does suggest that categorical prohibitions against not merely torture but all forms of coercive interrogation are wholly impractical.

In the recent literature, a number of eminent lawyers, as well as political, moral, and legal philosophers, examine in forthright fashion the arguments for and against continuing to treat torture as categorically and unconditionally prohibited. Surprisingly, only a minority seem to hold to the traditional position that torture should be both defined broadly and totally banned (among them, the playwright and novelist Ariel Dorfman; Joshua Dratel, a defense attorney; the legal philosopher David Luban; and Kenneth Roth, Executive Director of Human Rights Watch).

Several other powerful condemnations of torture nonetheless end by reluctantly seeming to accept—either directly (Henry Shue) or by implication (Elaine Scarry)—that in some extreme circumstances, torturers might be able to plausibly argue that torture was necessary to avoid catastrophe. Still others would ban torture more narrowly defined, but accept "torture lite" or "highly coercive interrogation" in extreme circumstances.[21] Several other essayists even more explicitly argue that torture should be regarded as a lesser evil in extreme cases, and still others—in particular, Jean Bethke Elshtain, John T. Parry, and Judge Richard A. Posner—suggest (either explicitly or by unavoidable implication) that even in some situations short of supreme emergency, torture might legitimately be regarded as a lesser evil.

Only a few writers, however, notably Alan Dershowitz,[22] Andrew C. McCarthy (a former Federal district attorney),[23] and Heymann and Kayyem, argue that because torture (or only great coercion, for the latter writers) is sometimes necessary, the law should be changed and torture/coercion brought within the U.S. legal system, so that they can be regulated and controlled. In particular, Dershowitz argues, the security services must be required to apply to judges for "torture warrants," in which they must present evidence that torture is required in each case in which it is contemplated. Only judges, trained to evaluate evidence and to balance competing values, such as "the needs for security against the imperatives of liberty," should decide—openly and under the law—whether torture is (literally) warranted.

The Dershowitz proposals have been widely rejected, often with anger and contempt—a "stunningly bad idea," in Elshtain's words[24]—even by those who (like Elshtain herself) accept that in some cases, torture may be the lesser evil.

---

[21] See especially Heymann and Kayyem, *Protecting Liberty*, 12–13. However, given the emphasis that these authors place on protecting national security against very real threats, including the threat of WMD attack, and their willingness to countenance "highly coercive interrogation" in extreme situations, it is not easy to understand why they draw the line at torture. The explanation is probably that they give great weight to not violating the law of the land, which indeed prohibits torture—but if the threat is great and the line between highly coercive interrogation and torture is very thin, then why not simply argue for a change in the law?

[22] Alan Dershowitz, "Tortured Reasoning" in Levinson, ed., *Torture: A Collection*, 257–280.

[23] Andrew C. McCarthy, "Torture: Thinking About the Unthinkable" in Greenberg, ed., *The Torture Debate*, 98–100.

[24] Jean Bethke Elshtain, "Reflection on the Problem of 'Dirty Hands'" in Levinson, ed., *Torture: A Collection*, 83.

Hard cases make not only bad law but also bad ethics, it is often said. Rather than normalizing, institutionalizing, or legitimizing torture, it is argued, it is far better to continue the formal and official prohibition—even if an after-the-fact necessity defense might be available to those who authorize or engage in torture. In extreme circumstances, the consensus position holds, military and security professionals must be prepared to do what must be done, while later seeking to avoid punishment by convincing the courts or public opinion that there was no other choice.

Confronting the Arguments against Torture

Let us suppose that the security services capture someone who (on the basis of substantial evidence) is almost surely a member of a terrorist cell that is on the verge of carrying out a major attack against a city. Should this situation occur, we might ask ourselves three questions: In all likelihood, what *would* the authorities do? What *should* the authorities do? And, if torture or coercion cannot or should not be ruled out in this situation, then how can they be limited to only those situations in which they are the lesser evil?

Surely there can be no doubt about what the authorities would do in those circumstances—and in practical terms alone, that suggests the need for serious consideration of how to prevent abuses. Further, because there is an increasingly widespread understanding that the stakes are so high in the war on terrorism, especially but not limited to WMD terrorism, it seems evident that most Americans—including, as we now know, many eminent moral philosophers—would also agree that the authorities should do whatever it takes to prevent catastrophe.[25]

It does not necessarily follow, of course, that the opinion of the public or of a number of philosophers is persuasive; the moral issue must be examined on the merits. My central argument is that the moral issue raised by torture in the war on terrorism should be regarded as no different in principle from the broader moral issues inherent in war, generally. We do not absolutely proscribe war if the cause is sufficiently just—indeed, as WMD spread, it is possible (at least in principle, although not necessarily in practice) that in some circumstances, even preemptive war might be justified. Moreover, no matter how accurate the weaponry and how hard we may try to avoid it, it is inevitable that there will be civilian casualties. If wars that will surely result in the killing of hundreds or thousands of innocent noncombatants cannot be morally prohibited if the stakes are high enough, then how can it be morally prohibited to inflict non-fatal and reversible pain on a few anything-but-innocent terrorists,

---

[25] See Oren Gross: "Most of us believe that most, if not all, government agents, when faced with a genuinely catastrophic case, are likely to resort to whatever means they can wield, including ... torture. ... *And most of us hope they will do so.*" Gross, "The Prohibition on Torture," 249, emphasis added.

if that is the only way to save hundreds, thousands, or even hundreds of thousands of innocent lives?

Even so, before we can conclude that torture may sometimes be justified, we must first confront several practical arguments that challenge the "lesser evil" defense. First, it is often argued that torture does not work, for people will tell the torturers anything they want to hear. Although this argument has a certain surface plausibility, on closer scrutiny it is not persuasive: the historical evidence leaves no serious doubt that torture has often produced information that otherwise would not have been revealed, especially about the organization and location of members of resistance or insurgency groups. To be sure, in the overwhelming majority of such cases, the torturers had no just cause and therefore no moral right to such information, but that is another matter altogether.

Thus, leaving aside for the moment the issue of whether torture is ever justifiable, the strictly empirical issue of whether it "works" is not difficult to ascertain. There is little doubt, for example, that in the 1950s, the French torture of Algerian captives temporarily succeeded in destroying the underground revolutionary movement; similarly, there is evidence that in Ireland, British torture or coercion succeeded in gaining useful information.[26] More recently, there is evidence that in 2002, Sri Lanka tortured three terrorists into revealing the location of a bomb set to explode later that day,[27] and it is known that in "ticking-bomb" cases, Israel tortures—or, at least, inflicts physical and mental coercion upon—captured Palestinian militants, who have sometimes apparently revealed information that has prevented terrorist attacks against civilians.

Elsewhere as well, torture appears to be producing valuable information in the current war on terrorism. Dershowitz and others have cited cases in which Jordanian and Philippine torture resulted in the breaking up of terrorist plans and networks, including a plot to bring down a number of airplanes,[28] and both the Schlesinger and 9/11 Commission reports stated that interrogation of captured al Qaeda officials—widely known to include severe coercion and probably outright torture—has provided important information about that organization's structure and plans.[29]

---

[26] Heymann and Kayyem, *Protecting Liberty*, 165.

[27] Ibid., 166.

[28] Alan M. Dershowitz, *Why Terrorism Works: Understanding the Threat, Responding to the Challenge* (New Haven, CT: Yale University Press, 2002), 136–138.

[29] See Douglas Jehl, "Captured Terrorists Hint at New Plan, Officials Say," *New York Times*, 13 July 2004; Douglas Jehl and David Johnston, "CIA Expands Its Inquiry into Interrogation Tactics," *New York Times*, 29 August 2004; Bowden, "The Dark Art of Interrogation," especially 55–56. Although the Schlesinger Report, *Final Report of the Independent Panel to Review DOD Detention Operations*, reprinted in Danner, *Torture and Truth*, 329–399, does not say that the useful information was the result of torture; in fact, it is widely known that the interrogation methods of leading suspects includes severe coercion and waterboarding. According to widespread reports, almost no one can hold out against waterboarding; for example, Joshua Dratel—a severe critic of torture—reports that a CIA station agent told him that because everyone succumbs to torture, if he were captured, he would avoid pointless suffering and simply talk immediately. Greenberg, ed., *The Torture Debate*, 21–22.

A second practical argument against torture is that in the long run, it backfires and ends by being self-defeating: it engenders implacable hatreds, hardening the terrorists in their hostility and creating new ones. The usual case cited is Algeria in the 1950s and 1960s, when despite French torture, the revolutionary movement was reconstituted and soon succeeded. "The use of torture may have won the battle of Algiers for the French, but it cost them Algeria."[30]

It is important, however, to notice the differences between the Algerian situation and the present one. First, the perpetuation of French colonialism in the face of the nationalist demand for liberation and independence was not a just cause, so of course, the French use of torture was not justified; there is no moral or practical dilemma if an unjust method is used to pursue an unjust cause. Secondly, it may be rhetorically effective to say that it was torture that caused the French to ultimately lose in Algeria, but it is not accurate; they resorted to torture precisely because they feared defeat if they did not—and it is hardly implausible that they indeed would have been defeated even sooner had it not been for the temporary success of torture in destroying the revolutionary movement. In other words, the French may well have lost in Algeria despite their use of torture, not because of it.

Even so, it cannot be denied that the use of torture has already had a variety of costs, including international costs. It is only too plausible that the American torture in Afghanistan and Iraq will engender new acts of terrorism—and not only in those countries, but elsewhere, including against the United States itself. Moreover, it is certainly possible that the international backlash against torture in the war on terrorism—especially torture that is clearly illegitimate by *any* defensible criteria, as in Afghanistan and Iraq—will lead some otherwise friendly countries to refuse to cooperate or to minimize their cooperation with American intelligence efforts.

Still, in the final analysis, if torture and coercion are confined—as they should be—to protecting large numbers of innocent human lives, then it is not necessarily convincing to argue that in the long run, the political costs will be too high. To begin with, long-run political costs are inherently difficult to predict, and might well be minimized if torture was seriously controlled and plausibly necessary to save many innocent lives. Beyond that, the immediate stakes may be so high that they preclude guesswork about long-run consequences. And in the limiting case of WMD terrorism, the classic rejoinder to the long-run consequences argument—in the long run we'll all be dead—is redundant: if we fail to prevent WMD terrorism, by whatever action it takes, in the *short* run we'll all be dead.

Perhaps the most troubling of the arguments against torture in extreme circumstances is the innocence problem. Undoubtedly, there cannot be complete certainty that the person being tortured really has useful knowledge of an impending terrorist attack, but we do know that almost inevitably, errors will be

---

[30] Donald P. Gregg, "Fight Fire With Compassion," *New York Times*, 10 June 2004.

made—indeed have already been made in Afghanistan, Guantanamo, and Iraq, where a number of investigative reports have concluded that many innocent civilians have been abused by American forces.[31]

Given the stakes, however, in this writer's reluctant judgment, the innocence problem, tragic though it is, cannot be regarded as a decisive argument for a categorical prohibition of torture—after all, the criminal justice system also suffers from less than 100 percent reliability, but we do not abolish prisons on that account, even though we know that many innocents inevitably will pay a very high cost. Moreover, painful as it is to contemplate, it is hard to avoid the conclusion suggested by Alan Dershowitz and Richard Posner: "The dogma that it is better for ten guilty people to go free than for one innocent person to be convicted may not hold when the guilty ten are international terrorists who, moreover, are seeking and may succeed in obtaining weapons of mass destruction."[32]

What does follow, however, is that we must take the innocence problem very seriously, and take whatever steps we can to minimize it. Indeed, it is the very possibility of error that strengthens the argument for serious institutional controls over torture, to ensure that the evidence requiring it is very strong, or that it is stopped if it becomes increasingly likely that the victim either is innocent or has no further information that we are entitled to have.

SHOULD TORTURE BE REGULATED AND CONTROLLED?

I have argued that torture (or coercion) in the war on terrorism is both inevitable, and in some circumstances, justifiable as a lesser evil than unchecked terrorism. If that is persuasive, it would seem to follow that torture should be minimized, regulated, and controlled by subjecting it to the rule of law. On the other hand, there are powerful arguments against seeking to do so, so we must first address these arguments.

The Price for Ending Hypocrisy Is Too High

Some skeptics about the need for or desirability of institutionalizing controls over torture concede that torture in the war on terrorism is inevitable—and perhaps even in some circumstances, a lesser evil than otherwise-unsuccessful efforts to prevent the mass murder of innocents—and that therefore it is true that our professed absolute rejection of torture is hypocritical. Even so, their argument is that total consistency is not truly necessary; occasional hypocrisy

---

[31] For brief discussions of the innocence problem, see Elaine Scarry, "Five Errors in the Reasoning of Alan Dershowitz" in Levinson, ed., *Torture: A Collection*, 281–290; and Ross, "A History of Torture," 9–10.

[32] Richard A. Posner, "Torture, Terrorism, and Interrogation" in Levinson, ed., *Torture: A Collection*, 295.

may be a tolerable price for a political order to pay, especially if the alternative price—abandoning long-held norms prohibiting torture—is too high.

On the other hand, hypocrisy also may have serious costs. As McCarthy has argued, "By imposing an absolute ban on something we know is occurring, we promote disrespect for the law in general."[33] In any case, the ending of hypocrisy is not the main argument for institutionalizing controls over torture as well as less-intense kinds of coercion. Rather, it is that the price we pay for the current situation—uncontrolled, unregulated, unaccountable, and typically unpunished torture that cannot be justified by a lesser-evil argument—is higher than the undoubted price we would pay by abandoning the fiction that torture can *never* be justified by a lesser-evil argument.

The Legitimization Problem

A second argument against seeking to control torture is that the effort to do so will "legitimize" torture and thus, presumably, make it even more prevalent. Some writers have drawn an analogy between torture and the development of the absolute prohibitions against slavery or genocide. Not so long ago, they argue, slavery was also thought to be "inevitable," and it would appear that genocide is still inevitable, yet we do not say that because slavery and genocide are inevitable, we should try to minimize and regulate them.

This argument is surely right about slavery and genocide, but it ignores the crucial distinction between those unconditional evils and the evil of torture: slavery and genocide are *never* a necessary (but evil) means to a desirable end. Thus, there can be no consequentialist argument to be made on behalf of slavery or genocide. Put differently, because there is no conceivable end that would justify slavery or genocide, these cannot be "lesser evils" to anything. Tragically, in the world in which we now live, we cannot say that about torture.

In any case, to say that a formerly banned practice has become "legitimized" can be understood in two senses. First, it may be understood as an empirical statement: as a matter of fact, like it or not, the practice has become widely accepted. Second, it may be understood normatively, meaning that what was previously thought to be categorically wrong in a moral sense is no longer so regarded.

If this deconstruction of the term "legitimize" is correct, then, the argument against controls may be becoming moot. Understood in its empirical sense, torture is well on its way to be becoming "legitimized" in the United States, for scarcely a week goes by without new revelations of American torture—directly, by American soldiers or CIA personnel and indirectly, through "rendering" suspects to foreign collaborators. To be sure, recently, there has been growing congressional concern over the torture issue, but there is reason to be skeptical about whether this concern will be sustained and result

---

[33] Greenberg, ed., *The Torture Debate*, 108.

in real controls over torture. Beyond a handful of courts martial prosecutions of soldiers near the bottom of the chain of command, as of early 2006, very little had been done by the armed forces, the administration, or Congress to seriously investigate, let alone punish, those guilty of ordering, condoning, or acquiescing in the American torture or outright killing of alleged terrorist suspects in Afghanistan, Iraq, or Guantanamo.[34]

Moreover, it is evident that most of the cases of torture are not in response to "ticking-bomb" situations—even of conventional bombs, let alone WMD; nor has the practice been limited to torture of high-level officials of terrorist organizations, who presumably know of plans for mass-murder terrorism. Indeed, according to newspaper reports and several international non-governmental organization investigations, some 70–90 percent of Iraqis rounded up by American soldiers were neither terrorists nor insurgents.[35] Consequently, it appears that most of the actual cases of torture or coercion cannot be defended as necessary in the war on terrorism; they remain greater evils, not lesser ones. Under these circumstances, the argument here is that on balance, the need for effective controls over torture outweighs the not-unreasonable concern that controls will succeed only in legitimizing and perhaps even increasing torture.

Judicial Controls Are Often Ineffective

A similar set of arguments point to the well-known problems of judicial control of state authorities. For example, a number of critics of Dershowitz's call for advance judicial authorization—"torture warrants"—point out that the existing criminal warrant system is frequently abused by the police, who may either gather evidence illegally or plant evidence even after getting warrants.

Indeed, for that matter, we cannot assume that the judges themselves are immune from politics, ideology, or simple error—Luban argues that "politicians pick judges, and if the politicians accept torture, the judges will as well," and tellingly observes that Jay S. Bybee (of the infamous Bybee memorandum) is now a federal judge.[36] In the same vein, other critics have noted that judges are not the voice of pure law or reason, but rather actual people operating within a particular (and fallible) institutional structure. Moreover, where will they come from? Will they be elected, or chosen—and if so, by whom? For these and other reasons, it cannot be simply assumed that judges will be either independent or wise.

These are all legitimate and cogent observations and criticisms, but in my judgment, they are not decisive. Of course, the judicial system is flawed in a

---

[34] For an impressive marshalling of the evidence, see Roth, "Justifying Torture," 184–201.

[35] Even the semi-official Schlesinger Report conceded that American soldiers had rounded up "any and all suspicious-looking persons—all too often including women and children," and that "some individuals seized the opportunity provided by this environment to give vent to latent sadistic urges." Reprinted in Danner, *Torture and Truth*, 344.

[36] Greenberg, ed., *The Torture Debate*, 51.

variety of ways, and undoubtedly any efforts to control and regulate the use of torture by means of that system would be difficult and would sometimes fail. But compared to what? Compared to the current system, in which torture is largely uncontrolled, especially when ordered or tolerated by officials at the top of the system, who are not held accountable for their behavior? Is justice more likely to emerge from a system of no accountability, or one that demands accountability and the adherence to the rule of law, however short of perfection that system falls?

In any event, it should not be beyond our capacity to improve the existing system, and to devise effective principles, procedures, and institutions to control torture, in order to ensure that it is resorted to only when an overwhelming emergency leaves no other rational or, indeed, morally defensible choice. A good place to begin is by ending the current practice of "rendition"—turning over suspects to allied governments that have no compunction about torture. In this case, for several reasons, categorical prohibition is appropriate. First, on its face, rendition is particularly sleazy, designed as it is to evade U.S. legal prohibitions against torture. Moreover, it is widely *seen* to be sleazy, and it has been so widely exposed that it has defeated the purpose of giving the U.S. government "plausible deniability" that it uses torture in the war on terrorism; indeed, in the eyes of much of the world, including the West, hardly any accusations against the American government—probably even those that are false—are any longer plausibly deniable.

Further, although torture in general entails the risk that false confessions will result, rendition is especially likely to do so, for governments who are anxious to demonstrate their value to the United States have much less incentive to be skeptical and to verify all such "intelligence."[37] Finally, rendition is obviously inconsistent with the need to develop a system of executive, legislative, and judicial controls over torture and coercion.

An institutionalized process for controlling torture would begin with some kind of system of advance authorization—something like Dershowitz's "torture warrants," perhaps, but one that would be less likely to suffer from the problems (police evasions, dishonesty in gathering evidence, and other abuses) that sometimes occur in the existing judicial warrant system. In any case, judicial control of coercion and torture should not be limited to an authorization

---

[37] For example, there have been a number of reports that the Bush administration based its claim that the Saddam Hussein government in Iraq was linked to al Qaeda on a "confession" made by a high-level operative captured by American forces and turned over to Egypt for interrogation under torture, a statement later recanted when the al Qaeda leader was no longer in Egyptian custody. Douglas Jehl, "Qaeda-Iraq Link U.S. Cited is Tied to Coercion Claim," *New York Times*, 9 December 2005. See also a television interview of Craig Murray, the former British Ambassador to Uzbekistan, another U.S. ally that cooperates with American rendition policy. Murray states that many "confessions" obtained under particularly horrible forms of torture by the Uzbekistan government have been demonstrably false, producing dangerous misinformation in the war on terrorism. (Murray's testimony is in *Torture*, a British documentary televised on the Sundance channel, 12 December 2005.)

process, but must also encompass post-facto judicial review, sanctions when appropriate, and judicial remedies for those wrongly tortured.

How, precisely, would a system of judicial control operate? Andrew C. McCarthy, a former Assistant U.S. District Attorney and currently a law professor, has suggested the creation of a single federal "national security court." Such a court—perhaps similar to the existing special federal court that decides whether U.S. intelligence agencies can engage in domestic spying—would allow the judges to develop expertise in matters of national security.[38] Any violations of the legal norms, rules, and procedures—at any level, in principle up to and including the Commander in Chief—must be treated as impeachable offenses or outright crimes, and if serious enough, punishable by jail terms.

Moreover, controlling coercion and torture in the war on terrorism should be the responsibility not only of the judiciary, for Congress could and should also play a much greater role, not only through legislation, but also by more vigorous use of its investigative and oversight powers, to ensure that the executive branch is complying with the law.

Other than these general suggestions, it is beyond the scope of this paper—and certainly beyond this author's competence—to provide a detailed prescription for how the current system can be improved.[39] My premise is that a recognition of the problem, together with a serious will to deal with the torture issue in a manner that both protects national security and is morally defensible, could find institutional expression.

Even so, in the final analysis, it cannot be denied that any system of institutionalized controls over torture must rely to a certain extent on trust that the authorities—especially at the top of the political system—will not seek to evade and bypass them. In this context, it is instructive to consider the McCain Amendment, now the law of the land, and President Bush's reaction to it. In signing McCain—which purports to categorically prohibit not merely torture but also the "cruel, inhuman, or degrading treatment" of any terrorists captured by the United States—Bush issued a statement in which he reserved the right to interpret it according to his own judgment of the constitutional authority of the president, especially in his capacity as Commander in Chief of the armed forces.

In view of the administration's overall record, then, there is every reason to suspect that in some circumstances, it will seek to avoid the McCain prohibi-

[38] Greenberg, ed., *The Torture Debate*, 109–110. To be sure, it is ominous that the Bush administration chose to bypass this court in certain circumstances, but its actions have generated a number of lawsuits and a considerable uproar in public opinion and in Congress. Perhaps, then, the existence of the special court may yet prove to be an effective constraint on executive overreaching. Once again, though: whatever the outcome, it would hardly follow that a system of no judicial authorization and review would be better.

[39] However, for a number of detailed suggestions on how all three branches of the government can improve the institutions and procedures for controlling "highly coercive interrogation," see Heymann and Kayyem, *Protecting Liberty*, especially 35–39.

tions. Moreover, even McCain himself has conceded that his legislation would not (should not?) apply to a "million to one" extreme ticking-bomb situation, in which the "the president will authorize whatever techniques he thinks will work," but should take responsibility for doing so.[40]

In short, it is not yet knowable whether the McCain amendment, the first serious effort to assert legislative control over the executive branch on how the war on terrorism may be fought, will be effective or indeed *should* be effective in extreme circumstances—even, apparently, in the eyes of its architect. But it does not follow that this early effort to institutionalize controls over torture demonstrates the futility of trying to do so. For one thing, the McCain amendment could well prove to be a significant constraint when it should be, if not on Bush, then perhaps on future presidents, as well as on the professionals in the CIA, the Pentagon, and the armed forces.

Beyond that, once again we must ask: compared to what? If a genuine, total, and unconditional ban on coercion or torture in the war on terrorism is neither practical nor wise, serves neither the requirements of national security nor of morally acceptable consequences, then it is hard to see why the present, largely uncontrolled system should be regarded as more trustworthy.

THE CRITERIA GOVERNING TORTURE

What moral criteria or principles should guide a system of judicial controls? Just-war theory provides the appropriate guidelines: just cause, last resort, and proportionality.

Just Cause

As in decisions to go to war, an unambiguously just cause is a necessary precondition of resorting to either severe coercion or outright torture—otherwise, of course, torture could never meet the lesser-evil criterion. Because of the terrible nature of this method, just cause should be interpreted particularly narrowly to exclude any purpose other than clear self-defense against terrorist attacks on civilian populations.

To be sure, as already noted, a common objection to making just cause a criterion for justifying torture is that it may be abused by untrustworthy governments. For example, Levinson asks: "Why in the world would we necessarily trust a highly politicized state elite, with its own potential political interests in creating a perception of danger," to decide when a genuine catastrophe exists?[41] A legitimate concern, certainly—but no different from allowing states to go to war on the basis of "self-defense," or, for that matter, on humanitarian

---

[40] Associated Press, "McCain Makes Exception on Torture," *Buffalo News*, 20 December 2005; David E. Sanger and Eric Schmitt, "Bush Says He's Confident that He and McCain Will Reach Agreement on Interrogation Policy," *New York Times*, 13 December 2005.

[41] Sanford Levinson, "Contemplating Torture" in Levinson, ed., *Torture: A Collection*, 33.

grounds. Both self-defense and humanitarian intervention can be abused (as some observers would argue was the case in Iraq), providing pretexts rather than convincing justifications for the use of force. Nonetheless, we do not throw out the principles. In short, as in the broader principle of self-defense, an argument justifying torture in catastrophic circumstances is just that—an argument, and one that may or may not be persuasive, or even honest. There is no way around the problem, but the alternative—no limiting criteria—is worse.

That said, it is important to make a number of distinctions, even within the framework of self-defense. There are at least three possible scenarios, unfortunately all, to one degree or another, realistic ones, in which the issue of torture is certain to be—and must be—considered: the capture of terrorists at the field level who are about to engage in WMD attacks on cities, the capture of terrorists about to engage in non-WMD attacks on cities, and the capture of terrorist leaders who are planning or who know about the plans for future major terrorist attacks.

Let us begin with consideration of the easiest case: preventing the destruction of entire cities. Assume, in the usual fashion, that the authorities have captured a member of a terrorist cell and that the evidence is very strong that he has information that could prevent an imminent WMD attack. As discussed earlier, preventing such an attack constitutes a supreme emergency (in Walzer's terms) or "an ultimate catastrophe," in the terminology of several contributors to the Levinson book. To repeat an earlier point: if early in World War II, a genuine supreme emergency (avoiding defeat at the hands of Nazi Germany) allowed Britain to legitimately override the principle of noncombatant immunity by deliberately killing (through bombing of cities) tens of thousands of German civilians—some of them, undoubtedly, strongly opposed to Hitler—then it is hard to see why torture of a few non-innocent terrorists in a different but genuine supreme emergency should be regarded as beyond the pale.

The case for torture to prevent more-limited attacks is obviously less overwhelming. Even so, non-WMD attacks can also kill thousands of innocents, as on September 11, or perhaps "merely" hundreds, as in the Madrid railroad bombing. Although short of constituting supreme emergencies, such conventional attacks may well be sufficiently catastrophic to justify torture if there is no other way to avert them. Suppose, for example, that on 10 September 2001, the authorities, learning of an impending massive attack in the United States but not knowing where or by what means, had captured Mohammed Atta or one of the other leaders of the attack on the World Trade Center, and all other efforts to gain the necessary information had failed? Who would have wished to argue that torture would have been illegitimate even if it had succeeded in preventing the attack?

To be sure, it is certainly the case that this is a troubling line of thought. As one internal critic of U.S. government torture asked: "How many lives [have] to be saved to justify torture? Thousands? Hundreds? Where do you draw the line?"[42] A cogent and disturbing question indeed, and one that is impossible to answer in the abstract. Yet, in actual and specific cases, such as September 11, the answer may be reasonably apparent.

The ticking-bomb cases aside, the third scenario in which torture or at least "highly coercive interrogation" must be considered is the capture of high-level al Qaeda leaders (already a reality, as we now know)—or, perhaps eventually, Iraqi terrorist leaders, like Abu Masab al-Zarqawi—who, after some period of regular interrogation, are refusing to talk about their organization or plans for future attacks. Because large numbers of innocent lives are genuinely at stake in such cases, as well as in obvious ticking-bomb situations, it is hard to see why torture (when both normal interrogation and coercion short of torture had failed) should be ruled out. Indeed, such cases might also constitute ticking-bomb situations—for all we know, major attacks might well be imminent.

Put differently, because the key to winning the war on terror is accurate intelligence, it is not evident that there is a compelling national security *or* moral distinction between using methods genuinely necessary to extract tactical intelligence to prevent imminent attacks and using those necessary to extract strategic intelligence (information about the organization, finances, membership, and location of terrorist groups) in order to prevent future attacks.

Last Resort

As has been already suggested, it is morally obvious that torture can be legitimately resorted to only in order to extract information that is crucial to save innocent lives, and then only when other methods of gaining the necessary information have been tried and failed: that is, normal methods of interrogation or even various forms of physical or psychological coercion, short of outright torture.

Moreover, neither coercion nor torture can ever be resorted to—and this *is* a categorical prohibition, one for which it is impossible to imagine any exceptions—for any purpose other than an urgent need to avert a catastrophe: not to humiliate, not to punish, not to take revenge. It is now evident that the U.S. armed forces violated this prohibition in Afghanistan and, especially, Iraq. Under a system of serious controls, any torture that was not a last resort and was for illegitimate purposes would be severely punished. And that would include anyone in the chain of command—right to the top—who ordered, authorized, or merely acquiesced in torture for such purposes.

Proportionality, or the Sliding Scale

As discussed earlier, it is a well-established principle in Western morality—or, more accurately, one to which we give lip service—that "the end doesn't justify

---

[42] Jane Mayer, "Annals of the Pentagon: The Memo," *New Yorker*, 27 February 2006, quoting Alberto Mora, the former general counsel of the U.S. Navy.

the means." Given the current realities, however, it would appear that we can no longer afford to insist that the moral judgments we make about means (*jus in bello*) be entirely separate from the judgments we make about ends (*jus ad bellum*).

Philosophers generally agree that moral constraints on behavior cannot be impossible of realization—that is, so demanding that they are antithetical to human nature itself. In that sense, then, it would appear that it is beyond human nature to truly live by an unconditional principle that a just end never justifies unjust means, even if the end is overwhelmingly just (the prevention of mass murder) and the means (torture) are genuinely imperative to achieve it. That is, in certain circumstances the end *does* justify the means.

The argument can be put even more strongly. It is not only beyond human nature but morally unpersuasive on the merits to have an absolute ban on torture that is necessary to prevent human catastrophes. It would be both irrational, in terms of national security, and morally incoherent to place a higher value on not inflicting temporary pain on one or several terrorists than on doing what is necessary to protect both national security and innocent human lives—in the most extreme case, perhaps hundreds of thousands of innocent lives.

The guiding principle concerning torture, then, must be proportionality, or the sliding scale, in which all actions are judged by their consequences for both justice and national security. The greater the evil to be averted, the fewer the restrictions on the means that are required to do so. And if the fate of an entire city, or indeed *many* cities, hangs in the balance—and some day that may well be the case—then there can be no limits at all. When what is at stake is, for all practical purposes, an infinite evil, the guiding principle of the authorities seeking to prevent it will be, must be, and should be: whatever it takes.[43]

CONCLUSION

If we are to succeed in the war against terrorism, we surely must do much more than defend ourselves against terrorist attacks. The broader task is to do whatever can be reasonably and legitimately done to address the causes of terrorism, as well as the motivations of terrorists to target the United States. In my view, such measures must include great changes in American foreign policy—a far more balanced policy in the Israeli–Palestinian conflict, for example, as well as a general policy of military noninterventionism, except in those few cases in which truly vital national interests are at stake. Meanwhile, though, we need to prevent attacks on American cities.

In attempting to do so, we confront a terrible dilemma. On the one hand, of course torture violates a central moral command of any civilized society;

---

[43] For a similar argument, see Posner, "Torture, Terrorism, and Interrogation," 293.

as a number of recent writers have emphasized—as if there were contrary views that needed refuting—torture is evil, antithetical to the values for which America stands, and destructive of the souls of the torturer as well as the tortured. Similarly, it has often been said that the war on terrorism is a war to preserve American values, so that if we resort to torture "the terrorists will have won," and the like.

On the other hand, the rhetoric does not do justice to the complexity of the problem and it will not do to simply dwell on the undoubted horrors of torture without consideration of the even greater horrors entailed in the mass murder of innocents. The crisis is unprecedented, the stakes are catastrophically high, and values are in conflict. Self-defense and the protection of innocent lives are also important values, and the terrorists will have "won" even more decisively if they succeed in destroying cities, the national economy, and possibly, the entire fabric of liberal democracy. Indeed, it should be regarded as instructive that it is not merely the United States but also some of the most civilized European liberal democracies that have evidently found it necessary to sometimes effectively condone or at least acquiesce in the torture of terrorist suspects.[44]

Put differently, so long as the threat of large-scale terrorist attacks against innocents is taken seriously, as it must be, it is neither practicable nor morally persuasive to absolutely prohibit the physical coercion or even outright torture of captured terrorist plotters—undoubtedly evils, but lesser evils than preventable mass murder. In any case, although the torture issue is still debatable today, assuredly the next major attack on the United States—or perhaps Europe—will make it moot. At that point, the only room for practical choice will be between controlled and uncontrolled torture—if we are lucky. Far better, then, to avoid easy rhetoric and think through the issue while we still have the luxury of doing so.

As I have argued, there are three general positions on the problem of torture in the war on terrorism. The first we can call "absolute prohibition": even in the present circumstances, we must retain and enforce a categorical prohibition against torture. The second we can label (perhaps not too unfairly) "absolute prohibition, except when absolutely necessary": retain the norm and the laws that torture is categorically prohibited, but expect that the authorities will disregard the law—and *rightfully* disregard the law—if torture is the only means to prevent catastrophic terrorist attacks. The third is "legalize in order to control," in which the fiction that torture is categorically prohibited is abandoned so that we may create laws, procedures, and institutions to ensure

---

[44] Kenneth Roth of Human Rights Watch points out that a number of European governments, including those of Sweden, Germany, Austria, the Netherlands, and the United Kingdom "seem to be toying with emulation" of the United States by becoming "complicit in torture"—for example, by sending terrorist suspects to countries known to torture or, in the case of Britain, refusing "to rule out information extracted from torture in court proceedings." Roth, "Justifying Torture," 199–200.

that torture is resorted to only when the evidence—presented *before* the fact—strongly indicates that coercion, and perhaps even torture, is indeed the necessary last resort to prevent mass-murder terrorism.

All of the choices have substantial defects. As I have argued, a categorical prohibition of torture today fails all the important tests: that of national security, that of moral consequences, and (because it has no chance of being observed under certain circumstances) that of practicality, a necessity in any meaningful system of moral constraint. For these reasons, many moral and legal philosophers, as well as political leaders (like John McCain), explicitly or in effect choose the second option: ban coercion but allow for exceptions, after the fact. In essence, this position concedes that in extreme circumstances, torture may be unavoidable, but nonetheless argues that our society would be better off if we continued to act *as if* torture were categorically prohibited. However, this choice also has major defects. First of all, of course, it is clearly hypocritical. As argued earlier, although one can concede that civilized and stable societies must often live with useful hypocrisies, in this case, the price may be too high. Aside from encouraging general cynicism about the rule of law, more particularly we are likely to forfeit our ability to control torture if we do not explicitly recognize it and treat it as a necessary evil under some circumstances.

Put differently, the second option, a compromise between absolute prohibition and control through partial legalization, reflects an empirical judgment as much as or more than a moral norm, for it is premised on the assumption that the fiction of categorical prohibition will lead to less torture, especially less clearly illegitimate torture, than if torture (even in extreme circumstances) were to become "legitimized." However, the historical record demonstrates that when torture is formally banned in principle but unregulated in practice, it almost always becomes an instrument of governmental police thugs or outright sadists, not only when the end does not justify the means but also when the end itself—such as punishment, intimidation, revenge against political dissidents, or even the amusement of sadists—is unjust.

That the United States is not immune from that danger is already all too clear. Indeed, we could end up with the worst of all worlds: uncontrolled torture that violates every morally necessary constraint, undermines national security by turning the world against us, produces little or no useful information, and precipitates rather than diminishes terrorism. In Iraq, Afghanistan, and probably Guantanamo, the use of torture by American soldiers and intelligence personnel is, from all the evidence now available (and who can doubt that more will be forthcoming), widespread and, indeed, not confined to stopping terrorism. Yet, it appears unlikely that in the end much is going to be done about it, at least at the top of the chain of command. Nor is this new. A convenient amnesia about the Vietnam War has triumphed in the United States; American soldiers engaged in coercion, torture, murder, and other war crimes in Vietnam, and in most cases, little or nothing was done about that either.

This history, past and present, demonstrates that we should not continue to leave the decision on whether to order, condone, or acquiesce in the torture of captured terrorists to unregulated and unaccountable political and military leaders who have already abundantly demonstrated that they are not to be trusted with this terrible power. For these reasons, there is a strong argument for developing laws, institutions, and procedures to authorize, monitor, and control torture, as well as, when necessary, to severely punish unauthorized and illegitimate torture.

To be sure (as I have already discussed), this course also has significant defects: judicial and institutional controls will not always work, imperial presidents may simply disregard the law, and an explicit acknowledgment of torture is likely to harm the image of the United States throughout the world. On the other hand, we have already suffered enormous damage as a consequence of our resort to uncontrolled and unaccountable torture, so it is not unreasonable to expect that an acknowledgment of the problem, accompanied by an honest and sustained effort to fix it as best we can, would make things better. Anyway, the operative question remains: compared to what? Because torture cannot, will not, and, in some catastrophically bad circumstances, should not be banned, on balance a system of controls would seem to best serve this country's national interests as well as have acceptable—or, perhaps better said, least evil—moral consequences.

If this conclusion is accepted, the task becomes to institute controls that are as powerful as we can devise, in order to ensure that torture is resorted to only when there is no other rational or morally defensible choice. We must devise a judicial system that meets three criteria: it must be independent of the government, the armed forces, and the intelligence services; it must be capable of continuous and sustained authorization, observation, and control of torture; and it must have the authority to impose severe criminal sanctions against anyone—no matter at what level of government—who authorizes, engages in, or acquiesces in illegitimate torture. As indicated above, several measures that could meet these criteria have already been proposed, and assuredly more would be forthcoming once a decision in principle was made to move in this direction.

I have argued that there are no good choices in the war on terrorism, only tragic ones. It cannot be denied that any legitimization of torture is a morally painful and historically dangerous step. In some circumstances, though, our only real choice, in terms of both national security and moral consequences, will be between controlled and uncontrolled torture. We gain nothing by pretending differently. In the struggle against deadly terrorism, some of world's most civilized democracies are themselves unwilling to shrink from doing what they think is necessary. Such are the times in which we live.

The Detention and Trial of Enemy Combatants: A Drama in Three Branches

MICHAEL C. DORF

Within a week of the attacks of 11 September 2001, the United States Congress authorized the President to "use all necessary and appropriate force against those nations, organizations, or persons he determines planned, authorized, committed, or aided the terrorist attacks...."[1] Although this Authorization for Use of Military Force (AUMF) was not literally a declaration of war, President George W. Bush interpreted it as activating his full wartime powers as Commander in Chief, including the power to detain enemy combatants. Then, claiming that Taliban, al Qaeda, and other irregular fighters in Afghanistan and elsewhere were entitled neither to the procedural protections of the criminal justice system, nor to the humanitarian protections of the Geneva Conventions, the Bush administration asserted an entitlement to hold detainees indefinitely, subject them to harsh methods of interrogation, and try them, if it chose not to simply hold them, before specially constituted military commissions. Moreover, the administration eventually claimed, the civilian courts were powerless to rule on the legality of such measures.

Inevitably, and almost immediately, these policies were challenged in the federal courts. However, the cases did not make their way to the point of a Supreme Court decision until June of 2004, and during the intervening period, Congress was almost entirely silent. Indeed, Congress would not legislate on the subject of detainee treatment until it enacted the Detainee Treatment Act (DTA) at the end of 2005,[2] and even then, it spoke with less than complete

---

[1] *Authorization for Use of Military Force*, U.S. Public Law 107-40, 115 Stat. 224 107th Cong., 1st sess. (18 September 2001), note following 50 U.S.C.A. §1541 (2000 ed., Supp. III).

[2] *Detainee Treatment Act of 2005*, U.S. Public Law 109-148, div. A, tit. X, 119 Stat. 2739 109th Cong., 1st sess. (30 December 2005) (to be codified at 42 U.S.C. §§2000dd to 2000dd-1 and other provisions of the U.S. Code).

MICHAEL C. DORF is the Isidor & Seville Sulzbacher Professor of Law at Columbia University and an expert in U.S. constitutional law and federal court jurisdiction. His most recent book is *No Litmus Test: Law Versus Politics in the Twenty-First Century*.

clarity. Accordingly, in assessing the legality of the administration's treatment of detainees, the Supreme Court has had to address the delicate question of constitutional limits on the political branches' respective war powers, while attempting to squeeze meaning from highly ambiguous statutory text. Thus far, the Court's approach has been to avoid sweeping decisions about the scope of individual rights. Instead, in each of its three leading rulings—*Hamdi v. Rumsfeld*,[3] *Rasul v. Bush*,[4] and *Hamdan v. Rumsfeld*[5]—the Court has rejected the proposition that the initial 2001 AUMF conferred on the President the sweeping powers he has claimed.

The Court's decisions have thus been "democracy-forcing," in the sense that they have required the President to seek authorization for his approach from Congress, and in the fall of 2006, Congress largely obliged. Its enactment of the Military Commissions Act (MCA)[6] authorized indefinite detention based on findings of a military panel, trial by special military commission, and only limited access to domestic courts to challenge these determinations. Notably, although the DTA and MCA maintain criminal penalties for U.S. military and civilian personnel who commit future acts of torture or other "grave breaches" of the Geneva Conventions' Common Article 3, they provide immunity for some past such acts, and they prevent detained aliens from objecting to such practices in a civilian court. This essay explains how the interactions among a largely passive Congress, an extraordinarily assertive President, and a divided but determined Supreme Court led to the MCA.

Unlawful Enemy Combatants

The lynchpin of the Bush administration's claimed authority over detainees is the category of "unlawful enemy combatants." Persons engaging in ordinary crime within the United States are entitled to be tried in civilian courts, thereby triggering the well-known protections of the Bill of Rights: right to counsel, right to present evidence, right to confront adverse witnesses, and so forth. Persons engaging in warfare, however, need not be treated as criminal defendants. In a conventional war, captured enemy soldiers must be treated humanely and cannot be tried for their acts on the battlefield, unless those acts violated the law of war. The law of war, in turn, originally derived its authority from the customary practices of nations, but in the twentieth century became codified in a series of treaties to which the United States is a signatory: the Geneva Conventions.

There is, in addition, an intermediate category between common criminals and prisoners of war: persons who engage in warfare but because of

---

[3] *Hamdi v. Rumsfeld*, 542 U.S. 507 (2004).

[4] *Rasul v. Bush*, 542 U.S. 466 (2004).

[5] *Hamdan v. Rumsfeld*, 126 S. Ct. 2749 (2006).

[6] *Military Commissions Act of 2006*, U.S. Public Law 109-366, 120 Stat. 2600 109th Cong., 2nd sess. (17 October 2006).

the methods and organization of their forces, sacrifice the protections of the Geneva Conventions. "Unlawful enemy combatants" sacrifice much of the protection afforded by the international law of war—just how much has been one of the most hotly contested questions—either because they target civilians or blend into the civilian population so as to render the enemy unable to distinguish between civilians and combatants. The 1977 Additional Protocols protect even such guerilla fighters,[7] but the United States never ratified these provisions. Accordingly, the Bush administration has consistently argued that Taliban, al Qaeda, and other irregular fighters can be detained, questioned, and tried without regard to the niceties of the Geneva Conventions.

DETENTION VERSUS TRIAL AND ALIENS VERSUS CITIZENS

The leading cases have thus far addressed two principal questions. First, what limits, if any, apply to the president's power to detain persons deemed unlawful enemy combatants? And second, if the administration opts to try a detainee for war crimes, what kind of tribunal must it use? No Supreme Court case has yet challenged the conditions of confinement at the U.S. naval base at Guantanamo Bay or elsewhere, although the Court's rulings in the detention and trial cases have implications for conditions of confinement.

Although the vast majority of detainees held by the government are aliens, a few citizens have also been captured, detained, and charged. John Walker Lindh, an American convert to Islam, was captured in Afghanistan and, for reasons that were never made clear by the administration, charged in a civilian court, in which he pleaded guilty to fighting for the Taliban and carrying a weapon. He was sentenced to twenty years' imprisonment.[8] Another American convert to Islam, Jose Padilla, by contrast, was held in military custody. A federal appeals court ruled that form of detention unlawful,[9] but the Supreme Court vacated the ruling because it found that Padilla had filed his habeas corpus petition in the wrong federal court.[10] After further proceedings, the government announced, again without explanation, that it would charge Padilla in civilian court after all.[11] Meanwhile, the government chose to prosecute one alien detainee—Zacarais Moussaoui—in civilian court, yet again without

---

[7] Protocol Additional to the Geneva Conventions of 12 August 1949, and Relating to the Protection of Victims of International Armed Conflicts (Protocol I), 8 June 1977, 1125 U.N.T.S. 3; Protocol Additional to the Geneva Conventions of 12 August 1949, and Relating to the Protection of Victims of Non-International Armed Conflicts (Protocol II), 8 June 1977, 1125 U.N.T.S. 609.

[8] See Katherine Q. Seelye, "Threats and Responses: The American in the Taliban; Regretful Lindh Gets 20 Years in Taliban Case," *The New York Times*, 5 October 2002.

[9] *Padilla v. Rumsfeld*, 352 F.3d 695 (2d Cir. 2003).

[10] *Rumsfeld v. Padilla*, 542 U.S. 426 (2004).

[11] See *Padilla v. Hanft*, 126 S. Ct. 1649, 1650 (2006) (Kennedy, J., concurring in the denial of certiorari).

explanation for the choice of forum. Moussaoui pled guilty to conspiring with al Qaeda operatives,[12] and was sentenced to life imprisonment.[13]

THE *HAMDI* CASE

The Supreme Court has thus far addressed the merits of exactly one case in which the government sought to hold a U.S. citizen in military custody without civilian judicial oversight. That case concerned Yaser Esam Hamdi, who was born in Louisiana. Under Section I of the Fourteenth Amendment, he is therefore a citizen of the United States, even though he spent most of his life outside this country. After being captured during the Afghanistan conflict, Hamdi was initially held at the naval base in Guantanamo Bay, Cuba. But when his American citizenship came to light, the government transported him from there to the brig at the Norfolk naval station. Habeas corpus petitions were filed on his behalf, and after a number of contentious proceedings in the lower federal courts, Hamdi's case reached the Supreme Court. Throughout the course of litigation, the government took the position that a wartime determination by the President or his deputies that an individual was an unlawful enemy combatant should be conclusive on the courts.

According to the government, Hamdi's citizenship was no bar to military custody. The government placed principal reliance on the so-called Nazi Saboteur Case, *Ex Parte Quirin*.[14] There, the Supreme Court rejected statutory and constitutional challenges to the trial by military commission of German agents who, during World War II, landed submarines in the United States, discarded their uniforms, and proceeded to attempt to destroy civilian infrastructure. The Court found that neither the international law of war nor the Articles of War that Congress had adopted extended procedural protections of the sort sought by the petitioners to "unlawful enemy belligerents." Crucially, one of the petitioners, Herbert Hans Haupt, was a U.S. citizen; yet the Court did not find this fact significant.

Understandably, much of the technical legal argument in *Hamdi* centered around how to read the *Quirin* decision. A pair of odd bedfellows, Justice Antonin Scalia, arguably the Court's most conservative member, and Justice John Paul Stevens, arguably its most liberal member, would have utterly rejected the government's position. In their view, the Supreme Court's decision in *Quirin* "was not [its] finest hour."[15] Further, even if respected, *Quirin* itself suggested a crucial distinction: there, the petitioners conceded that they were

---

[12] See Neil A. Lewis, "Moussaoui Tells Court He's Guilty of a Terror Plot," *The New York Times*, 23 April 2005.

[13] See Neil A. Lewis, "Moussaoui Given Life Term by Jury Over Link to 9/11," *The New York Times*, 4 May 2006.

[14] *Ex Parte Quirin*, 317 U.S. 1 (1942).

[15] *Hamdi v. Rumsfeld*, 542 U.S. 507, 569 (2004) (Scalia, J., joined by Stevens, J., dissenting).

part of the German force; Hamdi, by contrast, claimed that he had been mistakenly swept up in Afghanistan. As a U.S. citizen, Justices Scalia and Stevens would have ruled, Hamdi was entitled to be tried, if at all, for treason by a civilian court with its full procedural protections.

At the other extreme, Justice Clarence Thomas would have accepted the government's argument. Allowing for the possibility that Congress might have the power to limit the president's ability to employ military commissions, Justice Thomas nonetheless noted that Congress had taken no such limiting action. On the contrary, he read the AUMF as adding congressionally sanctioned authority to the president's already considerable powers as Commander in Chief. The power to detain unlawful enemy combatants, Justice Thomas concluded, "includes making virtually conclusive factual findings."[16]

The lead opinion in the *Hamdi* case was written by Justice Sandra Day O'Connor, and it staked out a middle course between the two aforementioned positions.[17] Justice O'Connor conceded two crucial points to the administration. First, on the strength of *Quirin*, she acknowledged that the Constitution poses no bar to military detention of a U.S. citizen, even if he contests the grounds for his detention. Second, she read the general language of the September 2001 AUMF to include the usual incidents of war, including detention of persons deemed enemy combatants.

Despite these substantial concessions to the Bush administration, the most quotable line from the lead opinion in *Hamdi* was a rebuke: "A state of war is not a blank check for the President when it comes to the rights of the Nation's citizens."[18] In substance, this meant that while the government could hold U.S. citizens in military custody, the Court would scrutinize the procedures used to determine whether someone is in fact an unlawful combatant. The president's say-so is not sufficient.

Just what procedures were required? The *Hamdi* lead opinion invoked a 1976 precedent that set forth a general test for due process that balances the individual interest against that of the government.[19] Weighing these factors, the plurality found that at a minimum, a person the government seeks to designate as an unlawful enemy combatant must "receive notice of the factual basis for his classification, and a fair opportunity to rebut the Government's factual assertions before a neutral decisionmaker."[20] He would also be entitled to assistance of counsel. At the same time, the Court gave considerable leeway to

---

[16] *Hamdi*, 542 U.S. at 589 (Thomas, J., dissenting).

[17] Justice O'Connor spoke for a plurality of herself, Chief Justice Rehnquist, Justice Kennedy, and Justice Breyer. Yet a fourth view was taken by Justices Souter and Ginsburg, who would have ruled that the AUMF did not authorize Hamdi's detention, which was therefore unlawful under another federal statute, the *Non-Detention Act*, 18 U.S.C. § 4001(a). The latter prohibits imprisonment or detention of a citizen "except pursuant to an Act of Congress."

[18] *Hamdi*, 542 U.S. at 536.

[19] See *Mathews v. Eldridge*, 424 U.S. 319, 335 (1976).

[20] *Hamdi*, 542 U.S. at 533.

the government to depart from procedures associated with civilian courts in criminal cases. The government could place the burden of disproving its evidence on the defendant, could introduce hearsay, and could utilize military as opposed to civilian tribunals to make the combatant status determination.

Thus, while *Hamdi* sent a powerful rhetorical message about the limits of presidential power even in wartime, it was hardly an unqualified triumph for civil liberties.

THE *RASUL* CASE

The same day that it decided *Hamdi*, the Supreme Court decided another case, *Rasul v. Bush*, that was of far greater practical significance. For while the *Hamdi* case addressed the standards applicable to the classification and detention of Hamdi and a tiny handful of other U.S. citizens held by the government, *Rasul* concerned the detention of aliens, who comprised the overwhelming majority of detainees.

The issue in *Rasul* was whether aliens held at the U.S. naval base in Guantanamo Bay, Cuba, could file habeas corpus petitions in federal court. The government took the position that they could not. Even if their detention violated federal statutes, the U.S. Constitution, and international law, according to the government, the federal courts had no jurisdiction to entertain the alien detainees' challenges.

Just as the government had relied in *Hamdi* on the World War II case of *Ex Parte Quirin*, so in *Rasul* the government invoked another World War II precedent, *Johnson v. Eisentrager*.[21] The United States had tried German nationals captured in China for the crime of continuing to engage in warfare after their government had surrendered. The Germans challenged the lawfulness of the military commissions that tried and convicted them, but the Court rejected their claims on jurisdictional grounds.

The *Eisentrager* Court found that the habeas corpus statute did not authorize suit, and that this result was fully consistent with the Constitution. The Constitution confers on nonresident aliens no right of access to U.S. courts, the Court reasoned.

Nonetheless, in *Rasul*, a divided Supreme Court ruled that there was jurisdiction over habeas corpus petitions filed by Guantanamo Bay detainees. The justices suggested that some of the factors that had led the *Eisentrager* Court to find no constitutional entitlement to habeas were absent in *Rasul*. Ultimately, however, the Court found no need to resolve the constitutional question. The majority concluded that because the naval base was, for all practical purposes, U.S. territory, the habeas corpus statute applied to persons held there. The statutory aspect of *Eisentrager*, the *Rasul* Court said, had been superseded by subsequent decisions.

---

[21] *Johnson v. Eisentrager*, 339 U.S. 763 (1950).

Accordingly, the *Rasul* majority paved the way for the lower courts to entertain habeas petitions from all Guantanamo Bay detainees. The Supreme Court said nothing, however, about the substantive merits of the claims pressed by the detainees.

The *Hamdan* Case, the Detainee Treatment Act, and the Military Commissions Act

There matters stood until the Supreme Court granted review in *Hamdan*. After the Court accepted the case for review, but before the case was argued, Congress enacted the DTA. Among other things, it stripped the federal courts of the authority to hear habeas corpus petitions by detainees facing the possibility of trial by military commission, although it did provide for statutory and constitutional (but not international-law-based) challenges to be brought after conviction by such a commission. Yet it was not entirely clear whether the DTA's jurisdiction-stripping provisions even applied to pending cases such as Salim Ahmed Hamdan's, rather than applying only to future cases. Nor was it clear whether the application of the DTA to pending cases would satisfy the Constitution, absent a valid suspension of the privilege of the writ of habeas corpus.

Although once again avoiding a constitutional ruling on the permissible limits that can be placed on habeas corpus, the Supreme Court's decision in *Hamdan* was, in nearly all of its particulars, a major setback for the Bush administration's executive unilateralism.

As for the facts, Hamdan himself appeared to be closer to the events of 11 September 2001 than either Hamdi or Shafiq Rasul. Hamdan was delivered to U.S. military forces in Afghanistan in late 2001, detained at the U.S. naval base at Guantanamo Bay, Cuba, and eventually charged with conspiracy to attack civilians in his alleged capacity as driver and bodyguard for Osama bin Laden. Hamdan argued that trial by military commission was illegal, but lost in the court of appeals, where John Roberts, then a circuit judge, joined a decision finding, among other things, that Hamdan's claims were premature.[22] Because of his earlier participation, now-Chief Justice Roberts took no part in the case at the Supreme Court.

Justice Stevens wrote the lead opinion in *Hamdan*, which Justices David Souter, Ruth Bader Ginsburg, and Stephen Breyer joined in full, and which Justice Anthony Kennedy—true to form as the crucial swing vote on the post-O'Connor Court—joined in part. Justices Scalia, Thomas, and Samuel Alito dissented from nearly every important aspect of the Court's ruling. Justice Stevens garnered a full, five-justice majority for the following propositions:

- The DTA did not apply to pending cases and thus did not strip the Supreme Court of jurisdiction to hear Hamdan's case, nor would it deprive lower courts of jurisdiction over petitions filed before the DTA was enacted in late 2005.

---

[22] See *Hamdan v. Rumsfeld*, 415 F.3d 33 (D.C. Cir. 2005).

- Military commissions other than ordinary courts-martial of the sort authorized by the Uniform Code of Military Justice (UCMJ) are constitutionally permissible only if warranted by military exigency or Act of Congress.
- Given Hamdan's detention for years, far away from an active battlefield, no exigency warranted the use of military commissions in his case.
- No Act of Congress authorized the military commissions.
- Indeed, the UCMJ, by incorporating the international law of war, made the so-called Common Article 3 of the Geneva Conventions, governing treatment of prisoners and noncombatants, applicable to any effort to try combatants for war crimes.
- Common Article 3 applied notwithstanding the guerilla tactics of al Qaeda, because the conflict occurred in Afghanistan, a territory covered by the Conventions, making resort to the 1977 Protocols (to which the United States is not a signatory) unnecessary.
- Accordingly, detainees could only be tried before a tribunal that afforded the same protections as a court martial, absent impracticability.
- The commissions manifestly failed to afford the same procedural protections as courts martial.
- The administration had offered no persuasive evidence of the impracticability of using courts martial or their equivalent.

In portions of the lead opinion that Justice Kennedy did not join—because he thought them unnecessary to the resolution of the case—and that therefore represented the views of only four justices, Justice Stevens also made two further determinations:

- The indictment was invalid on the grounds that conspiracy, standing alone and without any charge of overt acts by the person charged during the wartime period, is not a recognized war crime.
- The military commissions were defective because they would have permitted important portions of the trial to occur outside the presence of the accused. (Although Justice Kennedy shared the majority's disapproval of other procedural differences between the military commissions and courts martial—especially the dependence of the former on persons within the chain of command—he did not reach the plurality's conclusion that they were defective for this further reason.)

IMPLICATIONS

We can identify at least six important implications of the foregoing determinations.

Narrowing the World War II Precedents

As discussed above in connection with the *Hamdi* and *Rasul* decisions, ever since the Bush administration decided that military detention and military commissions would feature in its response to the attacks of 11 September 2001, the administration has invoked World War II–era cases as support for its approach. In both *Quirin* and *Eisentrager*, as well as a third case, *In Re Yamashita*,[23] the Court had in one way or another rejected a challenge to the outcome of a military tribunal.

Critics of administration policies had urged the Supreme Court to repudiate its World War II–era jurisprudence and return to the principles announced in a Civil War–Era case, *Ex Parte Milligan*.[24] In *Milligan*, the Court stated, in sweeping terms, that where no military emergency prevents the civilian courts from operating, military courts are unconstitutional.

Justice Stevens did not exactly oblige these critics in *Hamdan*, but he may have given them something better: Without overruling any of the World War II cases, he said that in important respects, they had been rendered inapplicable by changes in federal law and the international law of war. Further, he actually invoked these cases to bolster his arguments in light of those changes.

Affirming the Role of Congress

Hamdan was also a blow to the administration's broad assertion of presidential power. In presidential signing statements and other contexts, the Bush administration has repeatedly claimed that as Commander in Chief of the armed forces, the president has broad discretion to act in military matters.

That claim is partly right but mostly misleading. There is an important difference between, on the one hand, the president's power to act to defend the country where Congress has remained silent or authorized his action, and, on the other hand, the president's attempts to act in a manner contrary to congressional mandate. In the latter case, Supreme Court case law has repeatedly made clear, the president cannot act contrary to a valid enactment of Congress.[25]

In both the lead opinion of Justice Stevens and the concurring opinion of Justice Kennedy, the *Hamdan* Court reaffirmed this bedrock principle. The Constitution expressly grants to Congress numerous powers over the conduct of war and the armed forces. Accordingly, the Court ruled, the president's status as Commander in Chief gives him no authority to contravene the UCMJ or the international law of war that it incorporates.

Thus, *Hamdan* must be understood as having not all that much to do with individual rights, and everything to do with separation of powers. As both Justice Kennedy and Justice Breyer emphasized in their respective concurring opinions, if the President truly needed the powers he asserted in *Hamdan*,

---

[23] *In Re Yamashita*, 327 U.S. 1 (1946).

[24] *Ex Parte Milligan*, 71 U.S. 2 (1866).

[25] The leading precedent is *Youngstown Co. v. Sawyer*, 343 U.S. 579 (1952), commonly called "the Steel Seizure Case."

Congress could give them to him. And indeed, Congress did just that a few months later when it enacted the MCA.

The Applicability of the Geneva Conventions

The *Hamdan* Court (including Justice Kennedy on this point) found the Geneva Conventions' requirement that enemy detainees be tried, if at all, by tribunals equivalent to civilian courts or regular courts martial applicable to alleged al Qaeda members. Although not directly relevant to the *Hamdan* case itself, that determination might have had grave collateral consequences for military and Central Intelligence Agency (CIA) personnel who have used extreme methods of interrogation on captives, were it not for the fact that the MCA, enacted several months after *Hamdan*, provides partial immunity to U.S. personnel for past breaches. The precise scope of that immunity remains uncertain, however, and so *Hamdan* retains importance on this point, insofar as it provides a window into the thinking of a majority of the Supreme Court.

Common Article 3 also requires that detainees "shall in all cases be treated humanely." This provision certainly bans torture and equally certainly bans some forms of interrogation—such as "waterboarding," which simulates the experience of drowning—that the administration is widely believed to have authorized under the assumption that the Geneva Conventions do not apply. As Justice Kennedy stated straightforwardly, yet potentially ominously for the administration: "By Act of Congress . . . violations of Common Article 3 are considered 'war crimes,' punishable as federal offenses, when committed by or against United States nationals and military personnel," and "there should be no doubt . . . that Common Article 3 is part of the law of war as that term is used in" the UCMJ.[26]

Indefinite Detention Remains an Option

In the wake of *Hamdan*, some human rights organizations and countries whose nationals were being held (and, as of this writing, continue to be held) at Guantanamo Bay seized upon the ruling as grounds for the administration to close the prison there, an option that even President Bush has on occasion stated he would like to pursue.[27]

Yet the *Hamdan* ruling in no way casts doubt on the ability of the government to detain alleged enemy combatants at Guantanamo. The majority conceded that persons who have fairly been determined to be enemy combatants can be held as long as hostilities last. Given the continuing conflict in Afghanistan, not to mention the broader "war on terror," that means the Guantanamo Bay prison can remain open for business.

[26] *Hamdan*, 126 S. Ct. at 2802 (Kennedy, J., concurring in part).
[27] See Linda Greenhouse, "The Ruling on Tribunals: The Overview; Justices, 5-3, Broadly Reject Bush Plan to Try Detainees," *The New York Times*, 30 June 2006.

Thus, for civil libertarians *Hamdan* may seem worse than a pyrrhic victory. It says that the government cannot put detainees on trial because the military commissions as originally established were defective, but the ruling allows detainees to be held without trial indefinitely. Such a "victory" takes detainees out of the frying pan and throws them into the fire. Perhaps the most that can be said in this regard is that the *Hamdan* ruling adds to the moral authority of those who want to see the Guantanamo Bay prison closed.

The Secret Prison Alternative

Even before enactment of the MCA, the administration may have had at its disposal a ready means to circumvent the *Hamdan* ruling. It could simply have moved the Guantanamo Bay prisoners to another, perhaps secret, site. After all, the *Rasul* Court's determination that federal courts had jurisdiction over habeas corpus petitions filed by aliens held at Guantanamo Bay was based in part on the justices' refusal to apply the presumption that statutes lack extraterritorial effect: because the United States exercised sovereignty in all but name over Guantanamo Bay, they said, application of the habeas statute to petitions originating there did not count as extraterritorial.

Suppose, then, that the administration moved the Guantanamo Bay detainees to a prison in a friendly eastern European or central Asian country. Might the presumption against extraterritoriality *then* bar the filing of a habeas petition? The *Rasul* case leaves this possibility open.

Accordingly, and again, even without the congressional assistance it received in the MCA, the administration could find a way to try captives by military commission abroad in manifest violation of the *Hamdan* ruling, because the courts, having no jurisdiction, would be powerless to stop such trials. In fact, however, two events have made this option unlikely, at least in the short run. First, the passage of the MCA probably renders the use of other sites unnecessary. Second, rather than moving Guantanamo Bay detainees to other sites, in early September, the Bush administration announced that it was doing just the opposite, moving fourteen detainees from secret CIA prisons to Guantanamo Bay for trial by military commission.[28]

The Precariousness of the Hamdan Majority

The *Hamdan* case was decided by a 5-3 margin, but it is quite clear that if Chief Justice Roberts had not been recused, he would have voted with the dissenters. After all, he voted against Hamdan's claims as an appellate court judge. Thus, going forward, the case should be regarded as resting on a single vote.

---

[28] See Sheryl Gay Stolberg, "Threats and Responses: The Overview; President Moves 14 Held in Secret to Guantanamo," *The New York Times*, 7 September 2006.

Justice Stevens, the author of *Hamdan*, is eighty-six, and though he appears to be in remarkably good shape, rumors of his imminent retirement inevitably circulate. To be sure, even if one of the justices in the *Hamdan* majority should retire in the near future, one or more of the dissenters might choose to leave the result in place out of respect for precedent, at least to the extent that the MCA does not supersede it. But on the broader question of how to understand the Constitution's allocation of power between the president and Congress, there is no reason to think that any of the *Hamdan* dissenters would soften his pro-president view.

We may rightly regard *Hamdan* as a victory for the principle of checks and balances, even if, as an immediate practical matter, it will have little impact in light of the MCA. If the Supreme Court's point in *Hamdan* was that the president cannot establish military commissions without congressional approval, subsequent congressional approval does not show that the Court was wrong; it shows instead that Congress, finally, took some responsibility for the treatment of detainees.

Yet even conceived as a victory for the principle of checks and balances, *Hamdan* will not necessarily prove a lasting victory. Whether it does will depend very much on how seriously the Senate takes that very principle if and when it next confronts a Supreme Court nominee with a commitment to broad presidential power.

Part V:
Conclusions

Do Counterproliferation and Counterterrorism Go Together?

DANIEL BYMAN

Americans heard a rare note of harmony during the otherwise acrimonious 2004 debate between President George W. Bush and Senator John Kerry. When moderator Jim Lehrer asked the candidates to identify "the single most serious threat to the national security of the United States," both stressed the danger of nuclear weapons falling into the hands of terrorists.[1]

Given this sentiment, it is not surprising that the President's foreign policy is designed around the nexus of counterterrorism and counterproliferation. The result is the "Bush doctrine," a foreign policy that stresses countering this nexus by transforming hostile tyrannies into friendly democracies through coercion and even regime change. This transformation can be done in a variety of ways, but the Bush doctrine stresses that the United States should act alone if an international consensus cannot be achieved.[2] Democrats have noisily criticized the President for embracing unilateralism too easily, but that is a critique of modalities rather than objectives. They, too, regularly beat the drum of alarm with regard to nuclear weapons and terrorism.

Nuclear proliferation and terrorism, however, are not twin horrors and do not result in a single set of policy guidelines. The problems of when nation states proliferate and when terrorist groups attack are often quite distinct from the

---

[1] For a transcript, see "The First Bush–Kerry Presidential Debate." Commission on Presidential Debates, 30 September 2004, accessed at http://www.debates.org/pages/trans2004a.html, 15 January 2007. This essay will focus on the question of terrorist use of nuclear weapons. While terrorist use of chemical or radiological weapons would have a tremendous psychological impact, it would be unlikely to inflict mass casualties. Terrorist use of biological weapons could potentially pose a deadly threat and deserves additional attention.

[2] For a review, see Robert Jervis, "Understanding the Bush Doctrine," *Political Science Quarterly* 118 (Fall 2003): 365–388. For a defense of the Bush Doctrine as the toll of the Iraq war became clear, see Norman Podhoretz, "Is the Bush Doctrine Dead?" *Commentary* 122 (September 2006): 17–31.

DANIEL BYMAN is the Director of the Center for Peace and Security Studies at Georgetown University School of Foreign Service and a non-resident senior fellow at the Saban Center for Middle East Policy at the Brookings Institution.

problem of when terrorist groups might gain access to nuclear weapons. In general, proliferators and sponsors of terrorist groups have distinct motivations, and the solution sets for both problems are even more different. When this generic problem is scrutinized with today's terrorist groups and potential nuclear suppliers in mind, the disjuncture becomes far greater. Not only do efforts that join counterterrorism with counterproliferation fail to solve the problems of proliferation and terrorism as they relate to groups like al Qaeda and countries like Pakistan, but aspects of them make the problem worse.[3] Moreover, U.S. policy is often focused on the wrong aspects of this nexus.

Notionally, the proliferation problem with regard to terrorism can be divided into three categories: the deliberate transfer of nuclear weapons or fissile material from a state to a terrorist group; a decision to sell weapons or materials on the black market to terrorists or intermediaries who might provide them to terrorists; or an unwilling diversion in which the weapons or fissile material is stolen or provided by sympathizers without the knowledge or support of the regime.[4] The leakage problem, as I argue below, is the most dangerous with regard to the nuclear terrorism issue and is quite distinct in characteristics and solutions from the broader problems of nuclear proliferation and the spread of terrorism. Similarly, the terrorism problem can be thought of in two ways: as hostile regimes actively backing terrorists (Iran and Hezbollah) and as regimes that allow terrorists to operate on their soil due either to indifference (the United States and the Provisional Irish Republican Army during the 1970s) or incapacity (Afghanistan today and the remnants of the Taliban).

At a general level, going it alone to solve these problems is a mistake, because allies are central to both counterterrorism and counterproliferation. Even beyond the question of unilateralism, coercion attempts can often make the problem of support for terrorism and proliferation worse, strengthening a regime's determination to acquire nuclear weapons or gain friends who can act as a form of deterrence against a militarily superior superpower. Though difficult and costly, regime change can indeed help with proliferation, but the transition to a new government is often exceptionally dangerous for counterterrorism, weakening regime capacity and thus allowing terrorists to flourish.

---

[3] Valuable works on nuclear proliferation include Ariel Levite, "Never Say Never Again: Nuclear Reversal Revisited," *International Security* 27 (Winter 2002/2003): 59–88; Robert Litwak, "Nonproliferation and the Dilemmas of Regime Change," *Survival* 45 (Winter 2003–2004): 7–32; Robert S. Litwak, *Regime Change: U.S. Strategy through the Prism of 9/11* (Baltimore, MD: Johns Hopkins University Press and Wilson Center Press, 2007); Peter Lavoy, "The Strategic Consequences of Nuclear Proliferation: A Review Essay," *Security Studies* 4 (Summer 1995): 695–753; Richard A. Falkenrath, Robert D. Newman, and Bradley A. Thayer, *America's Achilles' Heel: Nuclear, Biological, and Chemical Terrorism and Covert Attack* (Cambridge, MA: MIT Press, 1998); Scott D. Sagan, "Why Do States Build Nuclear Weapons? Three Models in Search of a Bomb," *International Security* 21 (Winter 1996/97): 54–86.

[4] Other analysts further break this down, distinguishing between theft and deliberate transfers by low-level sympathizers without regime permission. See Charles Ferguson and William Potter, *The Four Faces of Nuclear Terrorism* (New York: Routledge, 2005), 54–61.

The problems become even more pronounced when the particular threats most prevalent today are examined. Most of the discussion focuses on deliberate transfers to terrorist groups with close ties to supportive governments. Even hostile regimes like Iran and North Korea, however, have shown no intention of transferring nuclear weapons to terrorists, let alone countries like Israel, Russia, China, and India, which, like the United States, are engaged in conflicts with radicals who often resort to terrorism. The bigger danger is that Russia or Pakistan might fail to prevent the sale or diversion of a weapon or fissile material, a problem that regime change or unilateralism would do little to prevent and could worsen.

On terrorism, the greatest threat of nuclear use does not come from Hezbollah, Palestine Islamic Jihad, or other groups that have historically enjoyed close relations with supportive and potentially nuclear-capable states. Indeed, state support often acts to discourage rather than accelerate group demands for nuclear weapons. Rather, the threat of nuclear terrorism comes from al Qaeda and the loose network of Sunni jihadists who look to Osama bin Laden for inspiration, if not always direct support. Since the fall of the Taliban regime in Afghanistan, these jihadists have not had a state sponsor. Indeed, almost every government in the West and in the Muslim world is at war with them. This lack of a haven and worldwide pressure have made it far more difficult for them to develop their own weapons programs or to conduct a sophisticated acquisition and smuggling operation. Nevertheless, they have flourished in countries that tolerate their activities, such as Pakistan, or in states like Yemen, Afghanistan, and Iraq where the government's writ is weak. Here the key is building up government strength rather than weakening governments through coercion and regime change. Moreover, the jihadist phenomenon is so widespread that alienating local regimes through coercive counterproliferation efforts is counterproductive: counterproliferation requires constant police and intelligence cooperation in dozens of countries.

Policymakers concerned about the problem of nuclear terrorism should focus on several areas where there is policy overlap between counterproliferation and counterterrorism and focus on the specific manifestations of this threat. The most important shift would be to recognize that the problem is states that lack the capacity to control their populations and borders rather than hostile aggressors bent on challenging U.S. primacy. Attention should focus on building up countries that might proliferate or allow terrorists to take root despite the wishes of the regime. Ideological states, which emphasize advancement of a set of anti–status quo ideas as opposed to material or power concerns, deserve particular attention. The return of a highly ideological Iran, or the emergence of a regime that cared little for international norms, economic prosperity, strategic risk, or the other basic shapers of the behavior of most regimes could change the equation dramatically with regard to the deliberate transfer of nuclear weapons.

The country that deserves the greatest attention today is Pakistan. Pakistan hosts a large domestic jihadist presence and significant numbers of foreign jihadists while possessing a nuclear weapons program that it has demonstrated it does not, or will not, control. The possibility of leakage is more than plausible, and the results could be catastrophic for the region and for the United States. Unfortunately, the United States will have to make trade-offs between working with Pakistan to fight terrorism and its efforts to stop proliferation.

This essay first reviews the various challenges inherent in both counterproliferation and counterterrorism, dissecting both in order determine which particular aspects of each problem are the most dangerous. Both the "supply" side of potential proliferators and the "demand" side of potential terrorism customers are considered. With this in mind, it then argues for a set of alternative policies that can better reconcile two worthy foreign policy objectives that at times conflict.

COUNTERPROLIFERATION VERSUS COUNTERTERRORISM

Counterproliferation and counterterrorism differ with regard to the focus on policy and the instruments involved.[5] Three aspects deserve particular attention: the number and identity of the states of concern; the states' motivations; and the relevant policy instruments.

Target States

For counterproliferation, the number of states of concern is finite. The nuclear club has nine members (the United States, Russia, China, France, Britain, India, Pakistan, Israel, and now North Korea), and the number of aspirants is for now, at least, rather limited, with Iran being the most eager to join. Several of these countries are extremely close U.S. allies. Moreover, by the standards of recent history, the number of aspirants is low, and for now, at least, does not appear close to be rising dramatically. Many countries have given up their nuclear programs, including Algeria, Australia, Brazil, Egypt, Germany, Japan, Kazakhstan, Libya, South Africa, South Korea, Sweden, Switzerland, Taiwan, and the Ukraine.[6] India's and Pakistan's transformation from covert to overt nuclear powers in 1998 did not spark a new round of acquisition in South Asia. It is possible that the 2006 North Korean nuclear test or Iran's future acquisition of a nuclear bomb could prompt other states to proliferate, but so far, there are few signs of this, despite the progress and open existence of both programs for decades.[7]

---

[5] For my views on the diplomatic demands of counterterrorism, see Daniel Byman, "Remaking Alliances for the War on Terrorism," *The Journal of Strategic Studies* 29 (October 2006): 767–812.

[6] Scott D. Sagan, "How to Keep the Bomb from Iran," *Foreign Affairs* 85 (September/October 2006): 45–61.

[7] Stephen Peter Rosen posits a plausible postproliferation world and argues that in such a world, many standard assumptions about the use and deterrence of nuclear weapons are at best strained and at worst dangerously naïve. See Stephen Rosen, "After Proliferation," *Foreign Affairs* 85 (September/October 2006): 9–15.

In counterterrorism, in contrast, the number of states relevant to Sunni jihadist–linked terrorism is vast and goes beyond the narrow U.S. list of state sponsors of terrorism, which includes only two—Iran and Syria—that are highly active. A commonly cited estimate is that al Qaeda has a presence in perhaps fifty countries. These include not only countries in the Arab world, but also Muslim-majority states in Asia and Africa. They also include many states in Europe and elsewhere (notably India) that have large Muslim minority communities. Since September 11, countries that have experienced serious problems with jihadist terrorism include Afghanistan, Algeria, Egypt, France, India, Indonesia, Iraq, Israel, Jordan, Kenya, Kuwait, Libya, Morocco, Pakistan, Russia, Saudi Arabia, Singapore, Spain, Tajikistan, Thailand, Tunisia, the United Kingdom, the United States, Uzbekistan, and Yemen.

Motivations

Motivations for acquiring nuclear weapons or for using terrorism also differ considerably. States seek nuclear weapons to deter other states, to enable conventional military options, to placate a status-hungry and weapons-focused military (or nuclear bureaucracy à la India), for domestic politics, and to assert their place among the top rank of nations, among other reasons.[8] Support for terrorism, however, often stems from a state's weakness. Ties to terrorists can compensate for otherwise weak power projection capabilities and can give a regime a way to influence neighbors when its military and economic capacity is low. In some instances, ideology plays a critical role. Regimes may often back terrorist groups to spread a revolution or otherwise advance a set of ideas, even when the costs are considerable.[9]

In contrast to seeking nuclear weapons, state inaction can be as risky as an active state program when it comes to terrorism.[10] States can passively back terrorists, allowing them access to their territory or to the resources of their population with little interference, even when they do not actively support their goals and activities. The United States, for example, allowed members of the Provisional Irish Republican Army to raise money, acquire weapons, and find

---

[8] Sagan argues that no single explanation adequately explains the various cases of nuclear acquisition. See Sagan, "Why Do States Build Nuclear Weapons," 54–86. See also Litwak, "Nonproliferation and the Dilemmas of Regime Change," 9; and Sagan, "How to Keep the Bomb from Iran," 47. See also Lavoy, "Strategic Consequences," 739–745.

[9] Daniel Byman, *Deadly Connections: States that Sponsor Terrorism* (New York: Cambridge University Press, 2005). See also Paul R. Pillar, *Terrorism and U.S. Foreign Policy* (Washington DC: The Brookings Institution, 2001), 157–196.

[10] More rarely, but importantly, passive support for nuclear proliferation is also a problem. The United Arab Emirates, for example, allowed the A.Q. Khan network to enjoy a hub for logistics and finance. See "United Arab Emirates/Dubai." Wisconsin Project on Nuclear Arms Control, accessed at http://www.wisconsinproject.org/countryinfo.html#dubai, 15 January 2007 for a number of articles on this subject.

safe haven on its territory even though the U.S. government did not approve of the terrorist campaign against the United Kingdom.[11]

Motivations for abandoning proliferation or support for terrorism differ even more. Robert Litwak points out that a state's allies' preferences, and norms (such as those embodied in the Nuclear Non-Proliferation Treaty [NPT]), a fear of isolation, a changing security environment, and changes to civil–military relations have led governments to abandon nascent nuclear programs.[12] With regard to terrorism, states often change their level of support for it but are less likely to abandon it altogether. The regularization of ideology often plays a role, with regimes decreasing their support as realpolitik and economic concerns crowd out ideology. The passive support problem, however, involves a different set of concerns. Here, allied pressure, a growing threat from the group that before was seen as focused elsewhere, changes in domestic support for the terrorists' cause, and capacity changes play a major role in turning states against terrorist groups that operate from their soil.[13]

Policy Instruments

The day-to-day of policy is also quite different. Counterterrorism requires an alliance of security services around the globe. Each may have a piece of intelligence that forms part of the entire picture. The U.S. role is to direct and integrate this effort as well as to collect its own information.[14] In addition to collection, each state must actively monitor and disrupt militants on their territory. Such efforts occur daily, and often with little public notice. Where the local government is strong, U.S. policy largely involves managing the relationships of the country's security services. The rub comes when the local government is weak. Here, outside powers must build up security services and, at times, act on their own; both courses are fraught with problems.

Counterproliferation, however, is less of a day-to-day activity. Outside powers may intercept a shipment of parts or even conduct a bombing raid, but this is done perhaps once a month rather than daily.[15] Much of the effort involves forging an effective coalition to influence would-be proliferators, using

---

[11] Jack Holland, *The American Connection: U.S. Guns, Money, and Influence in Northern Ireland* (Boulder, CO: Robert Reinhart Publishers, 1999), xvii, 28–29; Ed Moloney, *A Secret History of the IRA* (New York: W.W. Norton and Company, 2002), 16, 421.

[12] Litwak, "Non-proliferation and the Dilemmas of Regime Change," 10.

[13] Daniel Byman, "Passive Sponsors of Terrorism," *Survival* 47 (Winter 2005): 117–144.

[14] Paul Pillar, "Intelligence" in Audrey Kurth Cronin and James Ludes, eds., *Attacking Terrorism* (Washington DC: Georgetown University Press, 2003), 128.

[15] The United States claimed two dozen interdictions of WMD and missile-related items under the Proliferation Security Initiative between April 2005 and April 2006. See Robert G. Joseph, U.S. Undersecretary for Arms Control and International Security (2006), "Broadening and Deepening Our Proliferation Security Initiative Cooperation," Warsaw, Poland, 23 June 2006, accessed at http://www.state.gov/t/us/rm/68269.htm, 15 January 2007.

a mix of diplomatic, military, and economic power. Although having a global alliance is desirable, it is more important to gain the cooperation of key economic and political players—those that have the most coercive leverage.

The military can play a role in both counterproliferation and counterterrorism, but this role is often quite limited. In both cases, the military acts as a deterrent, threatening massive damage if nuclear weapons are used or terrorist acts are committed. Yet the dynamics of credibility are different for each. An adversary's possession of nuclear weapons is (or should be) a sobering fact as military strikes are planned. Indeed, in such cases, the military is most useful either as a deterrent or to strike and change a regime *before* proliferation occurs. For counterterrorism, however, the political will to use military force is often a challenge, as terrorism inflicts few casualties and many states use terrorists as proxies because this gives them some deniability. Military strikes in these cases are often limited, trying to be proportionate. Rarely is there a case like the U.S. removal of the Taliban, where terrorism alone provokes a military drive toward regime change.

Intelligence also comes from different sources. Imagery plays a vital role in counterproliferation, identifying potential research and manufacturing areas as well as determining whether a state is openly weaponizing its programs. For counterterrorism, imagery can play a minor role, but signals and human intelligence are far more important.

As this brief comparison suggests, counterproliferation and counterterrorism have different foci and compete heavily for resources. Should senior policymakers be wooing Indonesia's President Susilo Bambang Yudhoyono in an attempt to encourage a crackdown on a cell in Sulawesi or pressing Japanese Prime Minister Shinzo Abe to cut investment if Iran continues its nuclear program? Ideally, both—but senior officials only have so much time. Should the intelligence community spend more on satellites to monitor North Korea's nuclear program or hire and train more speakers of Pashtu and Dari? Ideally, both—but the U.S. intelligence budget is only so big. The biggest issues come with regard to policy trade-offs in particular countries. Iran and Pakistan both have nuclear programs and are problematic with regard to terrorism: which issue should take priority? (So far, it is the nuclear program with Iran and terrorism with Pakistan.)

WHERE COUNTERPROLIFERATION MEETS COUNTERTERRORISM

To understand the overlap between counterproliferation and counterterrorism, it is vital to distinguish the different challenges of counterproliferation. The proliferation problem can be roughly divided into three related but distinct types: providers, sellers, and leakers.

Providers are countries whose government transfers nuclear capabilities to other countries or actors for strategic or other nonfinancial reasons. The Soviet Union, for example, was instrumental in building the Chinese program, while

France played a major role in building Israel's nuclear effort. In both cases, the providers believed they could assist an ally and discomfit an enemy, and thus improve their own security.[16] Sellers, like providers, deliberately transfer nuclear capabilities, but they do so for financial rather than strategic reasons. Leakers, however, pose a distinct problem. In this case, the regime does not intend to transfer nuclear capabilities, but rather the transfer occurs because it cannot control the nuclear materials or knowledge.

In theory, terrorist groups could be aided by all three types of proliferators. It is easy to spin up a scenario in which Iran would pass on its newfound nuclear capability to Hezbollah or in which a cash-starved North Korea would sell a bomb on the black market to a jihadist group backed by a Saudi billionaire. Leakage, as argued below, is a particular problem, as jihadists, in particular, have many sympathizers and could infiltrate a facility or otherwise gain an opportunity to acquire a weapon with a government's deliberate support.

The Bush administration has largely conceived of the state–terrorism nexus as one of the deliberate transfer of weapons to a terrorist group, but this is probably the least likely danger. In the lead-up to the Iraq war, President Bush declared "Iraq could decide on any given day to provide a biological or chemical weapon to a terrorist group or individual terrorists"—a theme administration officials repeated endlessly as they sought to build public support for the war. Despite the Iraq debacle, this view has not gone away. Norman Podhoretz, defending the Bush administration's policies, describes them as treating terrorists "as the irregular troops of the nation states that harbored and supported them."[17] The Bush administration is not alone: Harvard professor and former Clinton administration official Graham Allison warns that Iran might transfer nuclear weapons to Hezbollah to deter an Israeli attack or that Hezbollah might act on its own against the United States.[18]

The deliberate transfer of nuclear weapons to terrorist groups is unlikely for several reasons. First, many states acquire nuclear weapons to gain a deterrence capability and thus employ them carefully. Because these weapons can be devastating, they would be far more likely to provoke escalation than would support for conventional attacks. State sponsors usually count on it being difficult for low-casualty terrorist attacks to generate enough political will for a military response, but that issue goes away when the nuclear card is played.

---

[16] Gregory Koblentz, "The Politics of Nuclear Cooperation: Why States Share Nuclear Weapons Technology" (paper presented at the 2005 annual meeting of the American Political Science Association, Washington DC, 1–4 September, 2005); Matthew Kroenig, "The Enemy of My Enemy Is My Customer: Why States Provide Sensitive Nuclear Assistance" (PhD diss., submitted, University of California, Berkeley, 2007).

[17] "Remarks by the President on Iraq" at the Cincinnati Museum Center, 7 October 2002, accessed at http://www.whitehouse.gov/news/releases/2002/10/20021007-8.html, 15 January 2007; Podhoretz, "Is the Bush Doctrine Dead," electronic version, 2.

[18] Graham Allison, *Nuclear Terrorism: The Ultimate Preventable Catastrophe* (New York: Times Books/Henry Holt, 2004), 36.

Second, states in general fear terrorists acting outside their control. This is a problem with regard to limited conventional attacks, let alone a nuclear one.[19] Few states trust their proxies, and indeed they often gravely weaken movements they support in order to control them. Syria, for example, in theory backed the Palestinian movement but in practice supported myriad Palestinian groups against one another in order to try to maintain control of the movement and threaten leaders who would not kowtow to Damascus.

In addition, nuclear weapons are widely seen as heinous, potentially delegitimating both a group and its state sponsor. Perhaps not surprisingly, no country has ever transferred chemical or biological weapons or agents to its nonstate proxies, despite many having the capability to do so. Nuclear weapons, which are far rarer and far more dangerous, are particularly unlikely to be transferred.

Looking at Iran's relationship with the Lebanese Hezbollah is instructive. Iran and Hezbollah represent perhaps the closest current partnership between a state and a terrorist group—if any state is likely to trust its proxy, it is Iran with Hezbollah.[20] Nevertheless, Iran has been cautious with regard to unconventional weapons systems and has not transferred chemical weapons to even close proxies such as the Lebanese Hezbollah.

Tehran has also sought at least a degree of deniability in its use of terrorism—a reason it often works through the Lebanese Hezbollah to this day when backing terrorists. As Iran expert Kenneth Pollack notes, a chemical or biological attack (to say nothing of a nuclear strike) would lead the victim to respond with full force almost immediately.[21] The use of Hezbollah as a proxy for a nuclear attack would not shield Iran from retaliation.

Trust and plausible deniability are inversely related when it comes to state backing of terrorists. Iran trusts Hezbollah and works openly with it, but this close relationship is far from secret. Iran also has ties to a range of Palestinian and Iraqi groups, but while these relationships are more covert, and thus more deniable, they are not built on trust. Thus, Iran lacks deniability for the groups to which it might transfer more-advanced systems, but lacks the trust that would make it more likely to transfer advanced systems.

Tehran is not likely to change its behavior on this score except in the most extreme circumstances. Traditional terrorist tactics such as assassinations and truck bombs have proven effective for Tehran. Only in the event of a truly grave threat such as an invasion of Iran would many of Tehran's traditional cautions go out the window.

Sellers are a less likely problem. The few cases of the transfer of nuclear capacity have often involved an attempt to undermine a mutual adversary when the transferring state itself saw little danger from the recipient. Money

---

[19] Pillar, *Terrorism and U.S. Foreign Policy*, 164.
[20] Byman, *Deadly Connections*, 79–116.
[21] Kenneth Pollack, *The Persian Puzzle* (New York: Random House, 2004), 420–421.

has played a role in only a few instances.[22] North Korea may have threatened to transfer nuclear weapons in April 2003, but the threat was ambiguous and North Korea has mostly backed away from it.[23]

With this model in mind, terrorists represent at best a limited market for states. First, as noted above, the risks in terms of isolation and even attack are considerable. Second, the state cannot be sure that the group to which it transfers nuclear weapons will not turn against it. The history of terrorism is replete with cases of states turning on groups and groups turning on their former masters. Third, most terrorist groups, even al Qaeda, are poor by the standards of states and thus weak markets for nuclear weapons.[24]

Leakage: The Supply Problem

Inadvertent leakage of a nuclear weapon, whether due to infiltration or low-level bribery, is a far greater danger than is a deliberate transfer for financial or strategic reasons.[25] A state may have a policy that strongly opposes the transfer of nuclear weapons to terrorists, but an individual soldier or technician with access to a nuclear weapon may sympathize with the terrorists' cause or simply want the money they offer him.[26]

The leakage problem has several components: capacity of security officials, overall levels of corruption, and the level of penetration by terrorists

[22] Greg Koblentz finds a financial role in France–Pakistan, France–Iraq, and West Germany–Brazil (as well as the murkier case of Pakistan–Libya). Koblentz, "The Politics of Nuclear Cooperation."

[23] Andrew J. Coe, "North Korea's New Cash Crop," *The Washington Quarterly* 28 (Summer 2005): 73–84. Daniel Pinkston and Philip Saunders contend that Li Gun's reference to the possible sale of nuclear material "should be interpreted as an attempt to pressure the United States into reaching a negotiated settlement of the nuclear crisis rather than a serious statement of North Korean intentions." Daniel A. Pinkston and Philip C. Saunders, "Seeing North Korea Clearly," *Survival* 45 (Autumn 2003): 79–102. Furthermore, since that time, James Kelly has testified that "I would note that after a remark of April of 2003 by a North Korean interlocutory that it might be possible for them to transfer nuclear material or weapons but that they have gone quite the other direction and, in fact, in response to specific questions have repeatedly stated that they would not transfer nuclear weapons or fissionable material to any other destination outside of their country. But that assurance, like all the assurances from North Korea, has, unfortunately, not an unlimited value." Senate Foreign Relations Committee, 108th Cong., 2d sess., 15 July 2004. I would like to thank Greg Koblentz for bringing this to my attention.

[24] John Roth, Douglas Greenberg, and Serene Wille, "Monograph on Terrorism Financing," staff report to the National Commission on Terrorist Attacks Upon the United States (2004), 3. Accessed at http://www.911commission.gov/staff_statements/911_TerrFin_Monograph.pdf, 15 January 2007. Earlier reports that Aum Shimrikyo had close to $1 billion are probably exaggerated. See Gavin Cameron, "Multi-track Microproliferation: Lessons from Aum Shinrikyo and Al Qaida," *Studies in Conflict and Terrorism* 22 (October–December 1999): 277–310.

[25] Litwak, *Regime Change*, 293.

[26] Scott D. Sagan notes that the Nuclear Regulatory Commission, which screens foreign-born individuals who work at nuclear power plants, often does not have complete information on individuals' criminal records or activities overseas. This is an opening for criminals or foreign agents to gain access to nuclear materials. Scott D. Sagan, "The Problem of Redundancy Problem: Why More Nuclear Security Forces May Produce Less Nuclear Security," *Risk Analysis* 24 (August 2004): 935–946.

or their sympathizers. Skilled security officials can foil plots and put in place sophisticated defenses to prevent the unwanted transfer of nuclear weapons. Corruption, however, can offset defenses, as individuals charged with guarding the nuclear facility may aid the jihadists. Similarly, terrorists (particularly jihadists) are trying to penetrate the military establishments of many countries, and in several countries have had members rise to senior levels. In both Egypt and Saudi Arabia, which are engaged in violent conflicts with domestic jihadists, the security services have had problems with penetration.[27] In Pakistan, several assassination attempts on Pervez Musharraf appear to have involved military officials linked to jihadists. Each component, by itself, is important, but together they present an exceptionally dangerous combination.

Data are hard to find on the characteristics of those who guard nuclear facilities. For example, there are significant numbers of jihadists in France, India, and the United Kingdom. Even Israel has a significant number of hostile Arabs who live within its pre-1967 borders. In all of these cases, however, the governments are extremely careful to limit who guards nuclear facilities. Israel openly discriminates against Arabs in its military and security forces, as does France. Although, in general, Iran has skilled security services, elements of the Iranian regime are particularly close to the Lebanese Hezbollah, with long-standing personal ties that could be used to circumvent formal regime controls.[28]

Table 1 provides a brief description of the supply side problem of leakage. In this Table, Pakistan stands out as an exceptionally dangerous combination of high levels of corruption and a high risk of terrorist penetration, with at best a medium-level security force. Other countries that are corrupt and do not have highly competent security forces do not have a grave risk of terrorist penetration.

The Mixed Rewards of Regime Change

The chance of leakage, ironically, can result from the change in regime of a country suspected of being a provider or seller of nuclear weapons. Regime change is usually thought of as a solution to the nuclear terrorism problem, but in practice, it can greatly increase the risk of leakage. As its proponents correctly argue, regime change can dramatically influence whether a state seeks

---

[27] Anonymous, *Imperial Hubris: Why the West is Losing the War on Terror* (Washington DC: Brassey's, 2004), 72. Anonymous has subsequently been identified as Michael Scheuer.

[28] Probably the best work on decision making in Iran is Wilfried Buchta's *Who Rules Iran? The Structure of Power in the Islamic Republic* (Washington DC: The Washington Institute for Near East Policy, 2000), though it is now somewhat dated. More-recent works include Hossein Seifzadeh, "The Landscape of Factional Politics and Its Future in Iran," *Middle East Journal* 57 (Winter 2003): 57–75; Abbas Maleki, "Decision Making in Iran's Foreign Policy: A Heuristic Approach," *Journal of Social Affairs* 19 (Spring 2002): 39–59; and Mehdi Moslem, *Factional Politics in Post-Khomeini Iran* (Syracuse, NY: Syracuse University Press, 2002).

TABLE 1

Leakage Characteristics of Nuclear Weapons States

Country	Security Capacity	Corruption Levels[a]	Terrorist Penetration Risk	Overall Risk
China	High	Medium	Low	Low
France	High	Low	Low	Low
India	Medium	Medium	Low	Low
Iran[b]	Medium	Medium	Medium	Medium
Israel	High	Low	Low	Low
North Korea	High	Medium	Low	Medium
Pakistan	Medium	High	High	High
Russia	Medium[c]	High	Low	Medium
United Kingdom	High	Low	Low	Low
United States	High	Low	Low	Low

Source: Based on Transparency International's "Corruption Perception Index 2006." See http://www.transparency.org/policy_research/surveys_indices/cpi/2006. North Korea is not listed on the Transparency International report.

[a] The "medium" coding is used because of the poor level of development, which usually suggests a high degree of corruption.

[b] Iran is included as a nuclear weapons state even though it is years away from a nuclear weapons capability. It is included because of the current attention to the program with regard to the terrorism–nuclear nexus and because any discussion of policies should be robust for at least the medium term.

[c] Russia's security forces are quite strong by most measures. However, they face a tremendous problem, given the dispersed nature of the program and its vast size. See Litwak, *Regime Change: U.S. Strategy through the Prism of 9/11*, 316.

nuclear weapons and how it might use those it possesses. And regime change may be necessary should a regime arise that might defy the conventional wisdom presented above that downplays the likelihood of a deliberate transfer of nuclear weapons to terrorists.

But regime change can lead to an increased chance of leakage. Corruption may increase as war and uncertainty ravage the economy. The many controls that states put on their nuclear arsenals could vanish in the case of regime change. The competent security forces may dissipate. Worse, members of the security establishment might find themselves vengeful (or broke) and transfer nuclear weapons to terrorists who oppose the intervening power, or might themselves take up arms.

Consider Saddam Hussein's Iraq, and suppose that a significant nuclear weapons program had been found in the country. Various after-action reports suggest that the United States failed to secure the suspected nuclear facilities or otherwise smoothly manage the risk of transfer after the end of Saddam's regime.[29] In particular, massive quantities of conventional explosives were not secured after the invasion. Had there been a nuclear program, it is plausible (perhaps likely) that much of the technology would have been smuggled out of

[29] Jeff Stein, "Army General Tells a Little-Known Tale of Pre-War Intelligence on Iraq," 20 October 2006, accessed on the website of *Congressional Quarterly* at http://public.cq.com/public/20061020_homeland.html, 7 January 2007.

the country or diverted to radicals within it, as happened to much of Iraq's conventional arsenal.

In addition, many of Saddam's elite security forces from the Special Republican Guard and other elite units have worked closely with anti-U.S. insurgents. The infiltration rate is high in Iraq and already poses major problems for the U.S.-backed regime.[30]

The Demand Problem

Despite their devastating effect and psychological power, few terrorist groups have sought, or actively seek, nuclear weapons or other weapons of mass destruction (WMD). There are several reasons for this.

Most important, few terrorists seek to kill in large numbers. As Brian Jenkins noted, "Terrorists want a lot of people watching and a lot of people listening but not a lot of people dead." Over thirty years later, Jenkins's assertion holds true for the majority of terrorist groups around the world. Using the low bar of twenty-five deaths per attack, analyst Chris Quillen finds seventy-six separate such attacks in the second half of the twentieth century (a figure that can be updated slightly to include several very bloody attacks in Iraq). Still, the number of terrorist acts that have killed over a hundred people is quite low—only forty-six, and many of these occurred during wars such as those in Algeria and Iraq.[31] And September 11 itself is still off the charts: no other single attack has killed over 500 people, let alone 3,000.

When assessing the risk of nuclear terrorism, much of the debate conflates chemical, biological, radiological, and nuclear weapons with WMD. For example, in an alarmist book about homeland security, the former inspector general of the Department of Homeland Security lumps radiological and nuclear trafficking.[32] Similarly, Graham Allison's *Nuclear Terrorism* reports that Chechen rebels "attempted nuclear terrorism" when they mixed cesium-137 and dynamite in a bomb that they planted but deliberately decided not to detonate.[33] But, in general, most uses of chemical or biological weapons by terrorists have not been attempts to kill large numbers of people.[34] The Liberation

---

[30] Bryan Bender, "Insurgents Infiltrating Coalition, US Says," *The Boston Globe*, 25 December 2004, A1.

[31] See Wm. Robert Johnston, "Incidents of Mass Casualty Terrorism," 24 November 2006, accessed at http://www.johnstonarchive.net/terrorism/wrjp394.html, 15 January 2007; see also Chris Quillen, "A Historical Analysis of Mass Casualty Bombers," *Studies in Conflict and Terrorism* 25 (September–October 2002): 279–292.

[32] Clark Kent Ervin, *Open Target: Where America Is Vulnerable to Attack* (New York: Palgrave Macmillan, 2006), 118.

[33] Allison, *Nuclear Terrorism*, 32.

[34] John V. Parachini, "Comparing Motives and Outcomes of Mass Casualty Terrorism Involving Conventional and Unconventional Weapons," *Studies in Conflict and Terrorism* 24 (September–October 2001): 389–406. The Aum Shinrikyo attacks are a notable exception to this generalization. See

Tigers of Tamil Eelam, for example, used an improvised chlorine gas attack to take a Sri Lankan Army post after the guerrillas had run out of ammunition, while the Revolutionary Armed Forces of Colombia has used cyanide-tipped bullets, which, while slightly more lethal than conventional ones, are hardly a WMD.

The reasons for this apparent restraint are complex, but most center around a desire to avoid offending potential constituents, a fear of provoking too harsh a state backlash, the bounds set by state sponsors, and the self-perceptions of terrorist group members, who often see themselves as "warriors" rather than "killers." In addition, terrorist groups have finite resources, and prefer to expend them on counterintelligence, operational security, or planning and executing conventional attacks.[35] Terrorists are also operationally conservative. Truck bombs, suicide attacks, kidnappings, and other tried-and-true methods work.[36]

The glaring exception to this generalization today is al Qaeda, and the jihadist cause more broadly. Ramzi Yousef, who masterminded the 1993 World Trade Center bombing, sought to kill 50,000 people, by his own admission. He wanted Americans to "share the pain" felt by the Muslim world.[37] Before September 11, bin Laden tried to acquire nuclear weapons, directing his lieutenants to acquire them in Sudan. Bin Laden has openly justified his group's possession of these weapons and has sought out scientists with knowledge on weapons programs. Bin Laden has also tried to acquire tactical nuclear weapons in the former Soviet Union.[38] The Central Intelligence Agency concludes that al Qaeda could make a crude nuclear device if it could gain access to fissile material.[39]

Troublingly, the movement is active in Pakistan and the former Soviet Union, both of which are at risk using the supply criteria identified above. The movement is also active in China, France, India, and the United Kingdom, all of which are at less risk but still of concern. Of these, the greatest concern is Pakistan, where the al Qaeda core, as well as the broader jihadist movement,

---

also Jonathan B. Tucker, ed., *Toxic Terror: Assessing Terrorist Use of Chemical and Biological Weapons* (Cambridge, MA: MIT Press, 2000).

[35] John Parachini, "Putting WMD Terrorism into Perspective," *The Washington Quarterly* 26 (August 2003): 37–52.

[36] Bruce Hoffman, "The Modern Terrorist Mindset" in Russell D. Howard and Reid L. Sawyer, eds., *Terrorism and Counterterrorism: Understanding the New Security Environment* (Guilford, CT: McGraw Hill, 2002), 89; Paul Pillar, *Terrorism and U.S. Foreign Policy* (Washington DC: The Brookings Institution, 2001), 22.

[37] Parachini, "Comparing Motives and Outcomes," 392.

[38] Michael Scheuer, *Through Our Enemies' Eyes* (Washington DC: Potomac Books, Inc., 2006), 199–203; National Commission on Terrorist Attacks upon the United States, *The 9/11 Commission Report: Final Report of the National Commission on Terrorist Attacks upon the United States* (New York: Norton, 2004), 60–61.

[39] As quoted in Litwak, *Regime Change*, 297.

has an extensive presence. (Indeed, it is arguable that Pakistan is the current center of the jihadist movement.)

Both al Qaeda and the broader movement recognize the importance of technical capabilities. Al Qaeda has tried to recruit technicians to its own cause and to work with those of the former Soviet Union and Pakistan.[40] Al Qaeda itself is bureaucratic in the positive sense of the word, able to devise broad goals and ensure long-term funding and support for implementing them. The United States has broken this organization down but has not completely destroyed it.

Outside of the narrow group of individuals tied directly to bin Laden, a larger movement flourishes and has embraced the possibility of nuclear use. In 2003, Sheikh Nasir bin Hamad issued "A Treatise on the Ruling Regarding the Use of Weapons of Mass Destruction against the Infidels" justifying a nuclear attack that would kill ten million Americans.[41] Sheikh Nasir is not a voice in the wilderness, but rather a respected and admired cleric in Saudi Arabia.[42] Jihadists more broadly have embraced an apocalyptic and bloody worldview that sees mass slaughter as both deserved and necessary.

The limit of the jihadist movement is capabilities, not intentions. The al Qaeda core has been hit hard by the U.S. counterterrorism effort since September 11. Senior leaders are either dead, in jail, or on the run. Command and control has been heavily disrupted.[43] It is now far more difficult for this group to engage in sophisticated long-term plots that require global coordination—and many of the scenarios involving nuclear weapons require just this sort of effort, given the need to locate, purchase or steal, store, transport, and perhaps weaponize whatever is diverted. The broader jihadist movement is more amateurish and less globally coordinated. It is highly decentralized, which poses an intelligence challenge but also makes it harder for the group to conduct a global plot (particularly one involving an attack on the U.S. homeland).[44]

A Different Road to Go Down

U.S. and international efforts to discourage terrorism and proliferation should continue, and when the two concerns overlap, they deserve particular atten-

---

[40] Joby Warrick, "Suspect and a Setback in Al-Qaeda Anthrax Case," *The Washington Post*, 31 October 2006, A01. The leader of al Qaeda in Iraq also recently issued a call for WMD scientists: see "New Leader of Al-Qaeda in Iraq Calls for use of Unconventional Weapons Against U.S. Forces; Possible Poisoning of Iraqi Security Forces at Central Iraq Base." WMD Insights. November 2006, accessed at http://www.wmdinsights.com/I10/I10_ME1_NewLeaderAlQaeda.htm, 15 January 2007.

[41] Daniel Benjamin and Steven Simon, *The Next Attack* (New York: Times Books, 2005), 72.

[42] After being arrested by Saudi authorities, Nasr recanted his teachings on this subject.

[43] Paul R. Pillar, "Counterterrorism after Al Qaeda," *The Washington Quarterly* 27 (Summer 2004): 101–116.

[44] Pillar, "Counterrorism after Al Qaeda," 104.

tion. The United States and the international community should consider several changes.

Choose Our Battles

Allison warns correctly that loose nuclear weapons and new nuclear programs and states can be dangerous; few observers disagree that these are dangerous, and preventing these should be priorities.[45] For nuclear terrorism, however, not all states and programs are created equal. Because the terrorist danger is so much greater from jihadists with ties to or a mindset like that of al Qaeda, the focus should be on existing nuclear states that are at risk from Islamic extremism.

A related key is preventing the emergence of additional countries like Pakistan that could be at the center of a terrorism–nuclear nexus. Recent instances of proliferation could lead to a "tipping point" in which new states seek nuclear weapons.[46] Saudi Arabia, Egypt, Indonesia, and the United Arab Emirates are four countries that could conceivably go nuclear in the years to come, and they have a large jihadist problem. To go back to the criteria presented in Table 1, all four of these countries have at least some problem with corruption (though not as high as Pakistan's) and, like Pakistan, have high levels of insurgent penetration. Even more worrisome, the security forces of these countries are, on average, *less* competent than those of Pakistan. Having Japan or South Korea go nuclear in response to the North Korean bomb or having Brazil or Argentina re-start their programs is not desirable, but the danger from nuclear terrorism is far less in these instances than if Saudi Arabia, Indonesia, or another state with a jihadist problem and sympathizers in government ranks were to go nuclear.

The United States must also be careful of pushing too hard on counterterrorism to the detriment of counterproliferation. One (but only one) of Iran's motivations for acquiring nuclear weapons is fear of a U.S. attack, a fear made worse by regular U.S. threats against the clerical regime; these threats, in turn, are motivated in part by Iran's backing of terrorists and other radical groups. For countries that are involved in both activities, the relationship between the two must be recognized as policy is formulated.

It is conceivable that, at times, the United States may have to choose between counterterrorism and counterproliferation. Pakistan, for example, has been only a lukewarm partner on counterterrorism, but has been even less helpful on

---

[45] Several current counterproliferation programs' regimes deserve to be strengthened. The Proliferation Security Initiative and the Cooperative Threat Reduction Program (often referred to as Nunn-Lugar) are two obvious ones. As few experts disagree on these, I will not explore them in detail. *9/11 Commission Report,* 381; Allison, *Nuclear Terrorism,* 141–176.

[46] Litwak, "Non-proliferation and the Dilemmas of Regime Change," 9; Kurt M. Campbell, "Nuclear Proliferation Beyond Rogues," *The Washington Quarterly* 26 (Winter 2002–03): 7–15.

counterproliferation. Similarly, in the past, the United States pushed Libya on counterterrorism, making that a priority over counterproliferation.[47] In such cases, the key criteria are the extent of the nuclear program versus the danger of terrorism from that country. Libya's nuclear program was judged to be a fledgling, while its terrorism capacity was well-proven after Pan Am 103 and other horrors. When in doubt, the emphasis should be on counterproliferation. Even such horrors as September 11 would pale before a nuclear attack, and reducing the probability of the latter is always vital.

Timing is particularly important when determining policy. When a country has not yet acquired nuclear weapons but seeks to do so, preventing the nuclear program should take precedence over conventional terrorism support. However, once a country has crossed the nuclear line, the emphasis should shift toward ensuring that its nuclear program is secure from terrorists.

Influence Global Opinion

The United States must also remember that the overall popularity of U.S. policies plays into this essay's rather narrow focus on counterproliferation and counterterrorism. In countries where public opinion matters for policy (and of the current nuclear states, only North Korea is an exception to this), defying U.S. pressure can become an important political benefit for area regimes. As Robert Jervis argues, "These views eventually will be reflected in reduced support for and cooperation with the United States."[48] Perceptions of the United States also are vital when regimes are considering the acquisition of nuclear weapons in the first place. Because of U.S. conventional military preponderance, nuclear weapons are one of the few means states can use to level (slightly) the playing field.

Popular opinion matters tremendously for counterterrorism. If anti-U.S. jihadists are seen as heroes, which they are in Pakistan and Saudi Arabia, then the population in general is less likely to provide intelligence on them and on people who might assist them. Similarly, individuals who hold security positions or work with nuclear programs might be more likely to assist the jihadists in the belief that their cause is just.

Improve Technologies for Recognizing Nuclear Attribution

The United States is already engaged in a considerable effort to identify whether the fissile material from a blast originated in Pakistan, Russia, or

---

[47] Martin Indyk, "The Iraq War Did Not Force Gadaffi's Hand," *Financial Times*, 9 March 2004; and Bruce W. Jentleson and Christopher A. Whytock, "Who 'Won' Libya? The Force-Diplomacy Debate and Its Implications for Theory and Policy," *International Security* 30 (Winter 2005/06): 47–86.

[48] Robert Jervis, "Why the Bush Doctrine Cannot Be Sustained," *Political Science Quarterly* 120 (Fall 2005): 351–378.

another state. Such efforts on the attribution of a blast give teeth to U.S. threats that it will hold states accountable for any involvement in nuclear terrorism. Effective coercion against a state requires being able to show convincingly that it is at fault, both to domestic and to international audiences. If state leaders know that they will be held responsible for a blast that occurred with nuclear material diverted from their country, they are more likely to take the necessary action to secure it. This is no guarantee against incompetence or failure, but it does increase the chances that leaders will act, as they do (or should) fear the U.S. response in the event of an attack.

Build State Capacity

Building up state capacity is essential for both counterproliferation and counterterrorism. Security services of new proliferators require extensive and continuing training. However, there is a passionate debate over such assistance, particularly to countries like India and Pakistan, which never accepted the NPT. Such aid legitimizes the program, and thus can plausibly act as a spur for other countries, as they know they would suffer only a relatively brief period of isolation before being embraced again by the nuclear community. In addition to legitimating the programs, such assistance might also allow new proliferators to deploy weapons more effectively in a crisis. But even worse is the risk that the state could lose control over them. Jessica Stern and Greg Koblentz point out that there is a tension between security and deployability.[49]

Norm-based institutions such as the NPT do have value, but they are at best a small part of most states' decisions to pursue or abandon nuclear weapons. The additional assurances of nuclear security outweigh the marginal loss with regard to undermining the NPT.

Training programs should focus on the police and domestic security services as well as the military. A strong police force can reduce the possibility of a robust criminal network that would steal a nuclear weapon.

Because of the possibility of leakage, corruption also becomes a national security issue. Countries must be sure to offer high salaries to those involved in

---

[49] "There may be a tension, however, between security and stability. Elaborate protective measures and locks enhance security, but, depending on a state's nuclear weapons doctrine and the threats it faces, such security measures could make the arsenal more vulnerable to a first strike and thereby decrease stability. In general, the more centralized the weapons, the more secure they are, but the more vulnerable they are to preventive or preemptive strikes. Conversely, the more dispersed the force (everything else equal), the more vulnerable the weapons to seizure by terrorists, theft by insiders, or unauthorized use. These tensions can be exacerbated if a state adopts a launch on warning posture or plans to limit damage through preemption. The dilemma faced by states is ensuring that their nuclear forces will *always* be able to be launched by proper authorities and *never* be used in an unauthorized manner." Jessica Stern and Gregory Koblentz, "Preventing Unauthorized Access to and Use of Nuclear Materials and Weapons: Lessons from the United States and Former Soviet Union" (paper presented by Jessica Stern at the Center for International Security and Cooperation Conference on Preventing Nuclear War in South Asia, Bangkok, Thailand, 6 August 2001).

their nuclear programs, even if they are relatively low-level officials. Yet a higher salary is often at best a scant inducement toward honesty.

Democratization should be approached with caution in states of concern. Democratization does not necessarily lead to a rejection of a nuclear program. Litwak points out that an appeal to national chauvinism when a new government came to power was one of the reasons for the 1998 Indian nuclear test.[50] More broadly, he argues that it is the intention of a regime, rather than regime type, that is the key determinant of proliferation. Democratization that does not address issues of prestige, a need for deterrence, and other reasons for proliferation will do little to change the overall regime desire for nuclear weapons.[51]

Democratization also offers risks for counterterrorism as well. Democratization often leads to the weakening of security services. In addition, the rule of law inherent in democratization limits the ability of governments to do massive roundups or otherwise engage in harsh crackdowns against radical groups. Finally, democratization may usher in a strongly anti-American regime. In Pakistan, for example, a government that reflected the will of the Pakistani people would probably be far more hostile to the United States than is the Musharraf government.

Avoid the Unilateral Temptation

The Bush administration is regularly slammed for its unilateral approach to foreign policy, a criticism stemming conceptually from its September 2002 "National Security Strategy of the United States" and the 2003 war with Iraq, which was waged without a final UN resolution authorizing it and to which only a handful of countries contributed significant military capabilities. In practice, however, the Bush administration has been multilateral in its response to both the North Korean and Iranian nuclear programs. Moreover, the day-to-day of counterterrorism is highly multilateral, involving cooperation between and among the security services of dozens of countries.

Multilateralism is also essential for effective counterproliferation, particularly when the goal is to isolate the regime in question. South Africa and Ukraine, for example, rejected their nuclear programs in order to be integrated into the world's political and economic system.[52] The most dramatic turnaround was Libya, which rejected terrorism and later its WMD programs in exchange for an end to political and economic isolation, particularly from the United States.

The good news is that allies should be especially forthcoming on the nuclear terrorism issue. This issue, of course, is the ultimate test of global citizenship. More cynically, the major powers in particular face threats of their own that put them at risk for catastrophic terrorism. Russia has its Chechens, China its Uighurs, India

---

[50] Litwak, "Non-proliferation and the Dilemmas of Regime Change," 13.
[51] Ibid., 11, 27.
[52] Ibid., 12.

its Kashmir problem, and Europe its home-grown and imported militants.[53] Not all of these groups will necessarily seek nuclear weapons, but the potential is real enough to alarm these governments.[54] Only Japan is left out of this equation, and Tokyo is usually careful to follow the U.S. lead on key security issues.

Recognize the Limits of Military Power

Military strikes short of regime change can also be exceptionally dangerous. It is difficult for such strikes to succeed tactically. After the Israeli raid on Osiraq, nuclear weapons seekers learned to disperse their facilities, put key sites underground, and shroud their programs in deception. Superb intelligence and sustained strikes are necessary for any chance of success. More-limited attacks could conceivably delay a program by hindering the production of key components. However, they also can lead to increased regime and popular determination to acquire nuclear weapons, raising the stakes in terms of threat and provoking a nationalistic backlash.

If nuclear weapons have already been acquired, a military strike makes it more plausible (but still unlikely) that states may transfer them to terrorist groups. Here the target regime may see the terrorist group as a way of ensuring a secure second strike: by giving terrorists access to the weapons, the regime has a means of striking back even if it is decapitated. That is still a remote possibility, given limits on trust and control, but there remains a real risk that a threatened regime will delegate control of the weapons to local commanders to avoid a devastating first strike on its command and control.

The Pakistan Perplex

Most of the above recommendations are general principles that can be applied (and tailored) to different situations. However, the United States and the international community must focus tremendous attention on Pakistan, the most dangerous country in the world with regard to nuclear terrorism. U.S. counterproliferation and counterterrorism goals are in tension in Pakistan. For now, the United States has emphasized counterterrorism, accepting Pakistan's rather pathetic excuses with regard to the A.Q. Khan network in order to preserve cooperation on counterterrorism and maintain decent relations in general. Unfortunately, Pakistan has a large jihadist presence, a weak government, high levels of corruption, and a nuclear program and evidence that it has difficulty controlling scientists who have aided state and nonstate actors (to say nothing of

---

[53] Robert S. Leiken, "Europe's Mujahideen," *Foreign Affairs* 84 (July/August 2005): 120–135; Javier Jordan and Nicola Horsburgh, "Mapping Jihadist Terrorism in Spain," *Studies in Conflict and Terrorism* 28 (May–June 2005): 169–191. Russia's efforts to improve nuclear security are surprisingly slow, given the gravity of its problems with the Chechens. See Matthew Bunn, "Cooperation to Secure Nuclear Stockpiles," *Innovations* 1 (Winter 2006): 115–137.

[54] Allison makes this point with regard to Russia, China, and the West. *Nuclear Terrorism*, 187.

an ongoing standoff with India and endemic civil strife and support for the Kashmiri insurgency). Al Qaeda now has a de facto haven in several remote tribal parts of Pakistan and is in the process of reconstituting itself. The A.Q. Khan network suggests that Pakistan cannot, or will not, control key nuclear scientists, an alarming development.[55] Even more worrisome are the security risks posed by Pakistani nuclear scientists sympathetic to the jihadi movement. This was demonstrated by the activities of Umma Tameer-e-Nau, a nongovernmental organization founded by Pakistani nuclear scientists that provided information to Osama bin Laden and the Taliban about nuclear weapons.[56]

There are few good choices with regard to Pakistan, and the United States has hitched its wagon to Musharraf's rather dim star as a default option. For now, this may be the only realistic choice, but correcting this paucity of options should be a priority. Washington should aggressively court various factions in Pakistan, hedging its bets should Musharraf fall. In addition, the United States should provide economic assistance and other ways of building up the Pakistani state and increasing favorable opinions of the United States.

Washington should also be willing to break with its general policy of punishing states that defy the NPT in order to help Pakistan ensure the security of its nuclear program. The U.S. principle is correct, and it usually should be followed. However, Pakistan is that rare combination of a dangerous leaker and a jihadist hotbed. It is worth weakening the norm the NPT fosters and even legitimating Pakistan's nuclear program to combat this dangerous combination.

Remember What Ain't Broken

Finally, the United States should also continue some policies that have been successes, albeit unsung ones. Most obviously, the United States must work to maintain pressure with regard to any transfer of unconventional systems. This has been a clear success for U.S. policy. Preventing any transfer of unconventional weapons was a concern that received tremendous attention during the Clinton administration and even more from the Bush administration after September 11. As a result, states today are more cautious than ever in their

---

[55] David Albright and Corey Hinderstein, "Unraveling the A.Q. Khan and Future Proliferation Networks," *The Washington Quarterly* 28 (Spring 2005): 111–128; Guarav Kampani, "Proliferation Unbound: Nuclear Tales From Pakistan," CNS Research Story, 23 February 2004, accessed at http://cns.miis.edu/pubs/week/040223.htm, 15 January 2007.

[56] The founder of UTN, Bashir-ud-Din Mahmood, was formerly the director for nuclear power at the Pakistani Atomic Energy Commission (PAEC); another active member was Abdul Majeed, a former high-ranking official at the PAEC and an expert in nuclear fuels. The best summary is David Albright and Holly Higgins, "A Bomb for the Ummah," *Bulletin of the Atomic Scientists* 59 (March/April 2003): 49–55. More details can be found at David Albright and Holly Higgins, 30 August 2002, "Pakistani Nuclear Scientists: How Much Nuclear Assistance to Al Qaeda?" ISIS, accessed at http://www.exportcontrols.org/print/pakscientists.html, 15 January 2007. I would like to thank Greg Koblentz for bringing this to my attention.

support for terrorism and recognize that providing chemical, biological, nuclear, or radiological weapons would cross a U.S. "red line."

In addition to continuing this pressure at a diplomatic level, the link between terrorists and WMD must remain a top intelligence priority. Although it would be difficult to inflict mass casualties with many chemical, nonviral biological, or radiological agents or weapons, the psychological impact of the use of these—and thus the effect on the world economy and overall confidence in government—would still be considerable. One clear indicator of the potential for the transfer of such weapons would be the transfer of mid-range technologies, such as surface-to-air missile systems, from a state to a terrorist group, suggesting that the state in question has little fear of escalation.

Another problem would be the emergence of a highly ideological regime with links to terrorist groups. Iran under Khomeini, Sudan in the early 1990s, and the Taliban, until September 11 were all highly ideological regimes that often did not share the traditional concerns about economic punishment or political isolation that have made other state sponsors of terrorism cautious. The reemergence of an ideological regime in a weapons state should be cause for grave concern and should lead to a policy of regime change, as this is a rare case where deterrence may not hold.[57]

FINAL WORDS

This essay argues that the terrorism–WMD nexus is indeed of grave concern but that U.S. policy has both flaws in its overall design and particular problems with regard to its practice. However, although there are few easy answers to the challenge of WMD terrorism, there are better ones. By changing the emphasis of U.S. policy to better address the issue of leakage and focusing more on a few key countries like Pakistan, the United States will be better able to prevent terrorists from acquiring nuclear weapons.

In guarding against high-end threats, we must not lose track of the fact that terrorists are far more likely to conduct mid- and low-level attacks. The rare instances of terrorism involving unconventional weapons have killed few people, whereas terrorists have myriad ways of killing many people with conventional weapons. Arson, sabotage at a chemical plant, and attacks on aviation security all are well within terrorist group capabilities and could kill hundreds. Such attacks, of course, do not pose a risk of catastrophic harm, but a U.S. policy that increased the already-considerable risk of such attacks at home and abroad in the name of stopping nuclear terrorism would deserve considerable scrutiny to ensure that the trade-offs are indeed sensible.[*]

---

[57] Scott Sagan points out that a major reason that Iran seeks a nuclear weapon is to resist a U.S. program of regime change and that abandoning this policy may lead Tehran to stop pursuing a nuclear weapon. Sagan, "How to Keep the Bomb from Iran," 55.

[*] Particular thanks go to Greg Koblentz, Rob Litwak, and Jeremy Shapiro, all of whom carefully reviewed an early draft of this manuscript and offered innumerable insights.